From Canaan to Israel

From Canaan to Israel:

THE MAKING OF THE JEWISH PEOPLE

Igor P. Lipovsky

American Academy Press
Washington D.C.

AMERICAN ACADEMY PRESS

Hellenistic works quotations are the author's own translation.

Printed and bound in the United States of America
FIRST EDITION.

Library of Congress Cataloging-in-Publication Data
Lipovsky, Igor P., 1950–
From Canaan to Israel: The Making of the Jewish People / Igor P. Lipovsky.
p. cm.
Includes bibliographical references and index.
1. Jews—History—To 70 A.D.—Historiography. 2. Palestine—Ethnology—History. 3. Canaanites—History.
4. Jews—Origins. I. Title.

ON THE COVER: 1. The Twelve Tribes of Israel. Mosaic from Old Jerusalem Jewish Quarter; 2. The envoys from Canaan and Amurru. A painting from the Theban tomb of Sobekhotep (c. 1400 BCE).

ISBN: 979-8-234-05941-3
Library of Congress Control Number: 2026909839
American Academy Press

To my wife, Helen Lipovsky (Muldt),
whose love, encouragement, and faith made this book possible

Contents

Acknowledgments

I WOULD LIKE TO EXPRESS my sincere gratitude to the American Academy of Arts & Sciences for its high recognition of my work, as well as for the awards and grants that made the writing and publication of this book possible.

I also consider it my duty to thank my former colleagues at Boston University for their moral and scholarly support during the preparation of this book.

Finally, I would like to express my heartfelt appreciation to my sons, Daniel and Ilya, for their care and assistance in bringing this book to publication. I am equally grateful to my daughter-in-law, Maria, who devoted considerable time to selecting the illustrations and maps included in this volume.

Introduction

Canaan – "A Land Flowing with Milk and Honey"

The land of Canaan, where the biblical patriarch Abraham settled, was relatively small – in size, it was only slightly larger than the Nile Delta. However, in terms of its diversity of natural conditions, climate, and flora, it had no equal in the entire Fertile Crescent. Its northern border was marked by the snow-capped peak of Mount Hermon, while its southern border reached the hot sands of Sinai. To the west, the land descended to the Mediterranean Sea, and to the east, it bordered the desert that separated it from Mesopotamia.

The regional contrasts were stark: while water was abundant in the northern region of Galilee, the southern Negev desert suffered from chronic drought. The only river that did not dry up during the summer was the Jordan, which flowed from north to south and divided the country into two parts: Transjordan (east) and Cisjordan (west). The eastern part was much drier and less populated, and for a long time was dominated by semi-nomadic groups. The western part was more favorable for agriculture and was home to a predominantly settled population. Originally, the name "Canaan" applied only to the areas west of the Jordan; only later did it come to encompass Transjordan as well.

Canaan has always occupied a special place in the geopolitics of the ancient Near East. It was the only land bridge between Africa and Asia – between Egypt on the one hand and Syria, Mesopotamia, and Asia Minor on the other. The most important trade routes passed through

Canaan, linking the civilizations of the Near East with Egypt. No conquering power could achieve true hegemony in the ancient Near East without gaining control of Canaan's territory.

This land was destined to become unique not only in political terms, but also in the cultural and spiritual history of the world. It was in Canaan, rather than in Mesopotamia or the Nile Valley, that the earliest Neolithic civilization and the first Neolithic cities emerged. Here, for the first time, the so-called "Neolithic Revolution" took place – the decisive transition from gathering to agriculture and from hunting to animal husbandry. The peoples of Canaan made an invaluable contribution to the treasury of world culture. It was here that the world's first alphabet was created – an invention that became the foundation for all subsequent alphabetic writing systems. The first monotheistic religion, Judaism, arose in this land, and Canaan also became the cradle of another monotheistic faith, Christianity. The most influential and widely read book in human history, the Bible, was written here.

But what was this land like in ancient times, when all the great empires and powers of the Near East fought relentlessly for its possession? What kind of country was it that, according to the Bible, God promised exclusively to the descendants of the patriarch Abraham – despite the fact that many peoples already lived on it and even more laid claim to it?

Fragmentary accounts from the works of ancient Near Eastern and Hellenistic authors have come down to us, offering glimpses of this land and its natural wealth. One of the earliest such descriptions belongs to the ancient Egyptian nobleman Sinuhe, who wrote about Canaan nearly four thousand years ago. This is how he described it: "It was a good land… Figs were in it, and grapes. It had more wine than water. Plentiful was its honey, abundant its olives. Every (kind of) fruit was on its trees. Barley was there, and emmer. There was no limit to any (kind of) cattle" (Pritchard J. *Ancient Near Eastern Texts*, p.19).

According to the biblical Book of Numbers, the spies sent by Moses to explore the land of Canaan described it as a land that "flows with milk and honey." As tangible proof of its fertility, they brought back "a branch with a single cluster of grapes, and they carried it on a pole between two of them" (Num. 13:23, 27). The Bible explicitly names seven species of plants and fruits for which this land was renowned: wheat, barley, grapes, figs, pomegranates, olives, and dates. The Book of Deuteronomy places particular emphasis on Moses' final instructions to the people on the eve of their entry into the land of Canaan, underscoring not only its agricultural abundance but also its distinctiveness among the lands of the ancient Near East: "For the Lord your God is bringing you into a good land, a land with flowing streams, with springs and underground waters welling up in valleys and hills, a land of wheat and barley, of vines and fig trees and pomegranates, a land of olive oil and honey, a land where you may eat bread without scarcity, where you will lack nothing, a land whose stones are iron and from whose hills you may mine copper" (Deut. 8:7-9).

The most detailed description of this land in antiquity was left to us by the Roman-Jewish historian Flavius Josephus. He knew it better than anyone else, for it was his homeland – Judea. Writing in the first century CE, Josephus described the northern part of the country, Galilee, in the following terms:

"This country is exceedingly fertile and rich in pastures, and it is planted with trees of every kind. Its abundance is such that it invites even the laziest to cultivate it. It is therefore no wonder that the entire land is densely populated: not a single part lies uncultivated or uninhabited. On the contrary, it is thickly studded with cities, and the villages, owing to the extraordinary fertility of the soil, are everywhere so populous that even the smallest of them contains more than fifteen thousand inhabitants. In short, although Galilee is smaller in extent than Perea (Transjordan), it surpasses it in strength and importance, for the whole of Galilee is cultivated and has the appearance of one vast, continuous garden" (*Jewish War*, 3.3.2–3).

No less interesting are Josephus' remarks about the Jewish population of Galilee in his own time. Despite living on the frontier and being surrounded on all sides by foreign peoples – Phoenicians to the west and

Syrians to the north and east – the Galileans, according to Josephus, possessed exceptional resilience and military preparedness. He writes: "Despite the foreign population surrounding them on all sides, the inhabitants nevertheless always steadfastly withstood any enemy attack. From their earliest youth they prepared themselves for war, and they were always numerous. These fighters could never be reproached for a lack of courage, nor the country for a lack of men" (*Jewish War,* 3.3.2–3).

When speaking of Galilee, no ancient author could bypass Lake Kinneret (the Sea of Galilee), known in the Greco-Roman world as Lake Gennesaret. Flavius Josephus left the most detailed and vivid description of this remarkable body of water:

"Lake Gennesaret received its name from the region that lies along its shores. Its waters are sweet and very pleasant for drinking, for they are finer than the thick waters of marshes and clear to the eye. The lake is surrounded on all sides by gently sloping shores, so that the water may easily be drawn. It is cooler than one would expect from so large a body of water. If it is exposed to the open air, it becomes cold, almost like snow; therefore, in summer the inhabitants commonly leave it outside overnight. Various kinds of fish live in the lake, differing in form and taste from those found elsewhere. The river Jordan flows through the middle of the lake… Along Lake Gennesaret stretches a region of the same name, remarkable for the richness of its nature and its extraordinary beauty. The soil here, owing to its exceptional fertility, is receptive to every kind of vegetation, and the inhabitants have cultivated it with astonishing diversity. The mildness of the climate further contributes to the growth of the most varied plants. Nut trees, which require a cooler environment, flourish in abundance alongside palm trees, which usually grow only in hot countries. Fig and olive trees, which prefer a more temperate climate, also thrive nearby.

Here, nature seems deliberately to have brought together opposites; here, too, unfolds a marvelous contest of the seasons, each striving to assert its dominance in this single region. The land produces its fruits not once a year, but continuously, without interruption. The most prized fruits – grapes and figs – ripen for ten months of the year, while other fruits succeed one another in unbroken sequence throughout all seasons.

In addition to the gentle climate, this extraordinary fertility is further sustained by irrigation from a powerful spring, called by the inhabitants *Kfar Nahum*. Some even suppose it to be a branch of the Nile, since the same species of fish are found in it as in the lake near Alexandria. Such, then, is the nature of that region" (*Jewish War* 3.10.7–8).

Samaria lay to the south of Galilee and constituted the historical inheritance of the "house of Joseph," belonging to two of the most prominent Israelite tribes – Ephraim and Manasseh. This region formed the political and administrative heart of the Kingdom of Israel. Its capital, Shomron (Samaria), was founded here, and from it the entire territory took its name. Josephus describes Samaria in the following terms:

"The country of the Samaritans lies midway between Galilee and Judea. Its nature closely resembles that of Judea. Both regions are rich in mountains and plains; they are easily cultivated, fertile, planted with trees, and abundant in fruits, both wild and cultivated. They are not particularly well supplied with natural irrigation, but they receive plentiful rainfall. All their waters are exceptionally fresh, and thanks to the abundance of excellent pasture, the cattle produce more milk here than anywhere else. The strongest proof of the excellence and fertility of both countries – Samaria and Judea – is the density of their population" (*Jewish War,* 3.3.4).

Josephus speaks in a markedly different tone when describing Perea, that is, central Transjordan – the ancestral territory of the Israelite tribes of Reuben and Gad. In contrast to Galilee and Samaria, he emphasizes its harsher natural conditions:

"Perea, though much larger in extent than Galilee, is for the most part wild, uncultivated, and too rugged for the production of delicate fruits. Those areas that are not entirely deserted and possess a certain degree of fertility, together with the plains that are under cultivation, are used chiefly for olive trees, vineyards, and palm groves. These lands are abundantly watered by mountain streams, and when these dry up during the hot winds, by ever-flowing springs. Perea extends in length from the fortress of Machaerus to the city of Pella, and in breadth from Philadelphia (Rabbath-Ammon) to the Jordan River" (*Jewish War,* 3.3.3).

All ancient authors – and Josephus in particular – paid special attention to the Jordan River Valley and the Dead Sea basin, through which the river flows. From a geological and natural perspective, this region is truly unique and has no equal anywhere else on Earth: it represents the lowest area on the planet's land surface. The entire Jordan Valley, beginning at Lake Hula in the north, continuing through Lake Kinneret, and extending southward to the southern extremity of the Dead Sea, lies within the deepest tectonic depression on Earth, known in antiquity as the Ghor. From north to south, this depression stretches for nearly 250 kilometers. The floor of the Ghor Depression lies approximately 395 meters below sea level, while in the area of the Dead Sea basin it reaches a depth of about 751 meters below sea level. This makes it the lowest exposed land surface on Earth. According to some geologists, tectonic processes in this region have not ceased, and the depression may still be slowly subsiding.

This extraordinary geological formation – encompassing both the Jordan River Valley and the Dead Sea – never failed to impress ancient observers. As a result, classical, biblical, and Near Eastern authors left us numerous descriptions of how this region appeared two thousand years ago, often emphasizing its otherworldly character, extreme climate, and striking contrasts with the surrounding lands. Josephus describes the Jordan Valley in the following terms:

"Through the middle of this land flows the Jordan, which divides it between two lakes of entirely opposite nature: Asphaltitis (Dead Sea) and Tiberias (Kinneret). The first is salty and barren, the second fresh and life-giving. In summer, the whole valley appears scorched, and the air, because of the excessive heat, is harmful to health. Apart from the Jordan, the valley has no sources of water. For this reason, palm trees grow especially luxuriantly and bear abundant fruit along the riverbanks, while those farther away flourish much less. Above the valley rise mountain ranges, completely devoid of vegetation and stretching over a great distance – northward as far as the outskirts of Scythopolis (Beth She'an), and southward to the place where Sodom once stood, reaching the shore of the Asphalt Lake. Along their entire length these mountains are barren and uninhabited, for their sterility allows no plant life to grow" (*Jewish War*, 3. 8. 2).

The most favorable part of the Jordan Valley was considered to be the region of Jericho, which lay within its own enclosed oasis-like basin. This valley attracted human attention from the earliest times. Fertile alluvial soil, a warm and stable climate, abundant springs suitable for irrigation, and rich – sometimes unique – vegetation turned this area into the true pearl of Canaan. Human settlement here began as early as the Mesolithic period, and Jericho is rightly regarded as the oldest city in the world. The first urban settlement arose here approximately 11–12 thousand years ago, making Jericho the site of the earliest known human civilization – one that emerged in Canaan, not in Sumer or the Nile Valley. However, this blessed land also bore a fatal flaw: powerful and recurrent earthquakes. Located directly on the Syrian–African tectonic fault, Jericho was repeatedly destroyed by seismic catastrophes. For this reason, its inhabitants were periodically forced to abandon this earthly paradise and resettle in less fertile, but more geologically stable, regions.

Jericho was the first city conquered by the Israelites under the leadership of Joshua. However, its walls fell not as the result of a conventional military assault, but due to a catastrophic earthquake, which claimed the lives of most of its inhabitants. This natural disaster left such a deep impression on collective memory that Joshua issued a solemn warning against rebuilding the city: "Cursed before the Lord be anyone who tries to build this city, Jericho! At the cost of his firstborn, he shall lay its foundation, and at the cost of his youngest he shall set up its gates!" (Josh. 6:26).

The warning was not merely symbolic. Centuries later, during the reign of King Ahab of Israel, a man named Hiel of Bethel rebuilt Jericho – and, as the Bible notes with grim precision, he lost his sons in accordance with Joshua's curse (1 Kings 16:34). Thus, in biblical consciousness, Jericho became not only a symbol of ancient prosperity and human beginnings, but also a reminder of the destructive forces hidden beneath the most fertile and alluring landscapes.

Throughout ancient history powerful earthquakes repeatedly destroyed Jericho, claiming lives and forcing its inhabitants to abandon the city. Yet people returned here again and again, even after losing their loved ones, drawn by the irresistible attraction of this earthly paradise – fertile soil, abundant springs, and a climate unmatched elsewhere in Canaan. One such catastrophe appears to have caused the pollution and poisoning of the main water source of the Jericho Valley. Eventually, the water was restored, and life once again flourished in the Jericho Valley. According to the Bible, this recovery was brought about by the prophet Elisha, who healed the polluted spring and removed its curse (2 Kings 2:19–22).

Josephus describes it as follows: "Near Jericho there is an exceptionally abundant spring, highly suitable for irrigation, rising close to the ancient city – the first in the land of Canaan to be captured by force of arms by Joshua, the leader of the Jews. In former times, this spring, it is said, was destructive: it damaged crops and trees, harmed women, and was generally deadly to all living things. But the prophet Elisha, the disciple and successor of Elijah, purified it and rendered it completely wholesome and life-giving… He utterly transformed the spring, so that the water which had once caused sterility and famine thereafter produced abundant and prosperous offspring.

The spring irrigates a greater area than any other and nourishes magnificent gardens planted close together. The soil yields many varieties of palm trees, irrigated by the spring's waters and differing in name and flavor. The juiciest fruits are pressed to produce a honey so fine that it scarcely falls short of true honey; nevertheless, bees also thrive in the region. Trees producing balsam – the most precious of substances – grow here as well, along with henna and myrobalan. This land, which yields rare and valuable products in remarkable abundance, may justly be called an earthly paradise. Few regions can rival it in fertility, so generously does the soil repay cultivation... Even in winter the climate is so mild that the inhabitants wear linen garments, while snow falls elsewhere in Judea" (*Jewish War,* 4. 8. 3).

Jericho – or, more precisely, the valley in which it lies – was also described by the ancient Greek geographer Strabo (64 BCE-24 CE). He writes: "Hiericunt (Jericho) is a valley enclosed by a ring of mountains, which slope downward toward it and form a kind of natural amphitheater. Within it lies a palm grove; although other fruit-bearing and garden trees grow there as well, palms predominate. Here too are located the royal palace and the balsam garden. Balsam is a fragrant shrub whose bark is cut in order to collect its sap, which resembles thick milk. This sap is gathered in vessels and, when poured into shells, gradually hardens. The juice possesses remarkable healing properties: it alleviates headaches, cures incipient cataracts, and improves poor eyesight. For this reason, balsam is highly prized, especially since it grows nowhere else but here" (*Geographica* XVI, 2, 34–46).

The healing properties of Judean balsam were admired by many ancient authors, among them the Greek historian Diodorus Siculus, the Roman naturalist Pliny the Elder, and the Greek physicians Dioscorides and Nicander of Colophon. Pliny the Elder, in particular, speaks of balsam with unmistakable admiration: "All perfumes are inferior to the fragrance of balsam, which has been granted to Judea alone among all lands... Today balsam is a subject of Rome and pays tribute together with its people." Pliny, who devoted an entire section of his *Natural History* to palm trees in different countries, likewise considered the Judean palms to be unrivaled:

"Judea is most renowned for its palms. The palms of Judea are not only abundant and productive, but also the most celebrated – not those found everywhere, but above all those of Hiericunt (Jericho). Their distinctive quality lies in the thick juice they exude, whose taste resembles wine blended with the sweetest honey" (*Naturalis Historia,* XIII, 26–45).

Yet it was the Dead Sea that impressed ancient authors more than anything else. Like the Ghor tectonic depression in which it lies, it had no equal in the ancient world. It was the saltiest lake known to Hellenistic geographers, with a concentration of salt eight to nine times higher than that of the Mediterranean Sea – so great that it rendered the water utterly hostile to life. For this reason, Greek and Roman writers commonly referred to it as the *Dead Sea* or the *Asphalt Lake.* The Judeans themselves, however, used a different name. In biblical and Jewish tradition, it was called the *Salt Sea,* a designation that emphasized not death, but its defining natural characteristic and its economic value rather than its sterility.

This is how Josephus described the Dead Sea:

"Its water is bitter and sterile, yet so light that it supports even the heaviest objects cast upon it. It is difficult for a person to sink into it, even with the most strenuous effort. Vespasian, who once visited the lake and examined its properties, ordered that several men who could not swim be thrown into it with their hands bound behind their backs; yet all of them, as if lifted by a gust of wind, immediately rose to the surface and remained floating. The lake also exhibits a remarkable changeability of color: three times a day its surface alters its hue, reflecting the sun's rays in a shifting play of colors. In many places, black lumps of asphalt rise from its depths and float upon the water, resembling in shape and size headless oxen. The inhabitants collect these masses from boats, using them as a means of livelihood… This asphalt is employed not only in shipbuilding, but also for medicinal purposes, as it is mixed into various remedies" (*Jewish War,* 4.8.4).

It is noteworthy that Scribonius Largus, the personal physician of the Roman emperor Claudius, referred to the asphalt of the Dead Sea as *Judean resin* and actively employed it in the preparation of his medicinal remedies. This testimony confirms that the products of the Dead

Sea were not merely objects of curiosity, but also valued components of Roman pharmacology. Josephus Flavius, in turn, connects the geological peculiarities of the region with its biblical past and offers the following description of Sodom and Gomorrah:

"The territory of Sodom borders upon this lake. It was once a land remarkable for its fertility and the prosperity of its cities, but it is now entirely scorched. According to tradition, because of the impiety of its inhabitants, it was destroyed by divine lightning. Even now there remain visible traces of the fire sent by God, and the shadows of five cities may still be discerned" (*Jewish War,* 4.8.4).

The ancient geographer Strabo, referring to accounts current among the local inhabitants, records a widespread legend according to which "thirteen cities, the chief among them Sodom, were destroyed by an earthquake and by fires; as a result, the lake overflowed its banks, and the surrounding rocks were set ablaze." At the same time, Strabo also cites the opinion of the earlier Greek geographer Eratosthenes of Cyrene (276-194 BCE), who proposed a more strictly geological interpretation. According to Eratosthenes, "the whole of this region was originally the bed of the lake and later emerged as a result of an earthquake and the upheaval of deeper strata to the surface" (*Geographica,* XVI, 2, 34–46).

According to the biblical tradition, four thousand years ago the region of the Dead Sea presented a far more favorable and fertile landscape than it does today. The Book of Genesis describes the area as exceptionally well-watered: "It was well watered everywhere, like the garden of the Lord, like the land of Egypt, in the direction of Zoar; this was before the Lord destroyed Sodom and Gomorrah" (Gen. 13:10). What is now the Dead Sea was not a salty lake at that time, but a large freshwater lake. The Jordan River flowed into it from the north, while several smaller streams – which often dried up in the summer – fed it from the east. A dozen prosperous Canaanite cities lined the shores of this lake, and the irrigated coastal lands were famous for their fertility. The Book of Genesis identifies this area as "the Valley of Siddim, that is the Dead Sea" (Gen. 14:3). In the Valley of Siddim, there were not only Sodom and Gomorrah but also the Canaanite cities of Admah, Zeboiim, and Bela (Zoar). The biblical patriarch Abraham found this area to be prosperous and densely populated. The Bible testifies that Abraham and his allies helped these local cities resist a raid by a coalition of Syrian rulers. However, even during Abraham's time, alarming seismic activity was evident: "The Valley of Siddim was full of bitumen pits, and as the kings of Sodom and Gomorrah fled, some fell into them" (Gen. 14:10). Following a powerful earthquake and the eruption of subterranean layers into the freshwater lake, the valley was transformed into the hypersaline, lifeless Dead Sea, while the coastal cities were completely destroyed and potentially submerged.

The ancient Greek geographer Eratosthenes was remarkably accurate when he attributed the origin of the Dead Sea to tectonic processes. These forces persist today, though they are largely limited to the periodic discharge of asphalt (bitumen) masses. This ancient ecological catastrophe led to the flooding of the fertile Siddim Valley and transformed southeastern Canaan into a semi-desert. It is plausible that a portion of the displaced Canaanite population migrated to the Nile Delta, drawn by available land and familiar environmental conditions. If so, the unprecedented growth of the Hyksos capital, Avaris, may be explained not only by the influx of Amorite semi-nomadic tribes but also by the exodus of sedentary Canaanites fleeing the devastation of the Dead Sea region.

This region attracted the ancestors of modern humans even in prehistoric times; one of the most advanced Epipaleolithic cultures, the Natufians, established their home here. Flourishing in Canaan during the Mesolithic period (approximately 12,000–9,500 BCE), the Natufians were among the first to adopt a sedentary lifestyle and construct permanent dwellings. They pioneered the transition from nomadic foraging to proto-agriculture and, subsequently, from hunting to animal husbandry. Notably, they were among the first to domesticate the dog. The Natufians also demonstrated early artistic sophistication, creating some of the oldest known musical instruments and achieving remarkable skill in the production of jewelry and pigments. While the Natufian culture extended into Lebanon and parts of Syria, its heartland remained centered in Canaan. This culture was named after the Wadi Natuf, a dry riverbed located 27 km northwest of Jerusalem, where archaeologists first discovered one of their settlements.

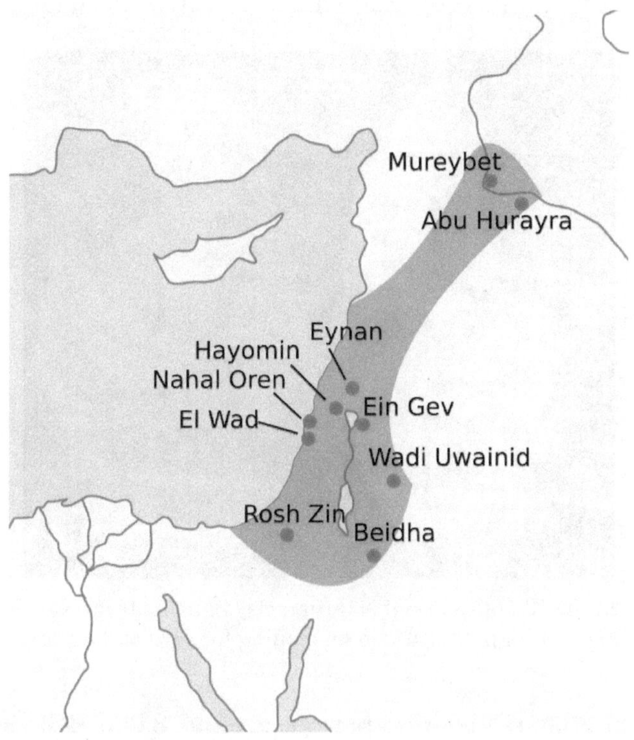

1. Region of the Natufian culture

The Natufians were relatively short in stature; even the tallest among them did not exceed 165 cm. They possessed slender limbs and thin bones, yet their elongated heads had a cranial capacity that was often greater than that of many modern humans. Notably, genomic analysis of their remains has revealed very little Neanderthal admixture, suggesting a lineage rooted in early modern humans (Cro-Magnons). Anthropologists classify the Natufians as ancient representatives of the Indo-Mediterranean race. Their culture persisted for approximately three millennia, marking a gradual transition from the Mesolithic to the Neolithic period. Over time, the late Natufian culture diverged into two distinct groups: the Khiamite, which predominated in northern Canaan, and the Harifian, which was concentrated in the south. Despite their differences, both cultures remained linked by their shared Natufian heritage.

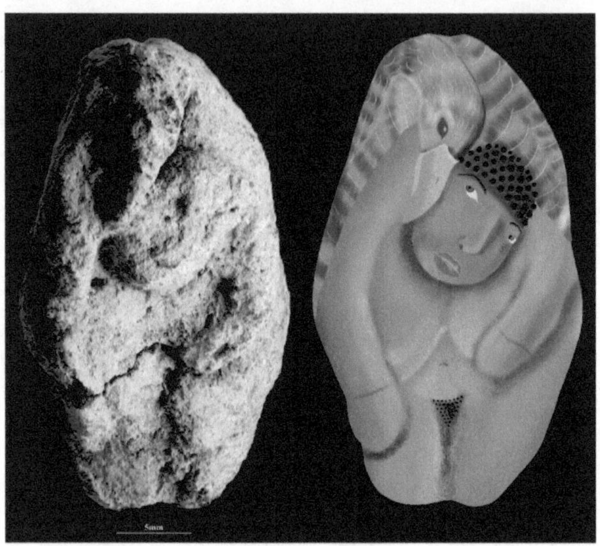

2. The 12,000-year-old Natufian clay figurine from Nahal Ein Gev, depicting a woman leaning forward and a goose

During the later Neolithic period, around 8,000 BCE, new groups of people arrived in Canaan, bringing with them the Tahunian culture. Originating from southern Asia Minor, these people shared cultural roots with the inhabitants of famous sites like Çatalhöyük and Hacilar. The culture takes its name from Wadi Tahun near Bethlehem, where its distinct characteristics were first identified. The Tahunian culture gradually displaced the two late Natufian cultures (the Khiamite and Harifian). It became most widespread in the Jordan Valley and is closely linked to the rise of Jericho as a major Neolithic center. Archaeologists believe that the people of Pre-Pottery Neolithic B Jericho were culturally and genetically related to the inhabitants of Çatalhöyük, which was established around 7,500 BCE in the Konya region of modern-day Turkey.

The people of the Tahunian culture arrived from Anatolia, but they did not settle in a vacuum. In the Jericho area, a Neolithic city – Pre-Pottery Neolithic A – already existed, built by the Natufians. The Tahunian culture was distinguished from the Natufian by a completely different stone-processing technique, a new style of dwelling, and the definitive transition to full-scale agriculture and animal husbandry. It is highly probable that these two groups gradually intermixed, particularly as they shared similar physical characteristics. This integration is supported by the burial findings in Jericho from that period. Archaeologists discovered skulls where the facial features had been meticulously reconstructed with clay and shells had been placed in the eye sockets. These artifacts provide a unique glimpse into the appearance of the people of the Tahunian culture who inhabited Jericho around 7000 BCE. Both the Natufian and Tahunian populations represented early modern humans (Cro-Magnons) of the Indo-Mediterranean type, and neither was related to the later Semitic groups.

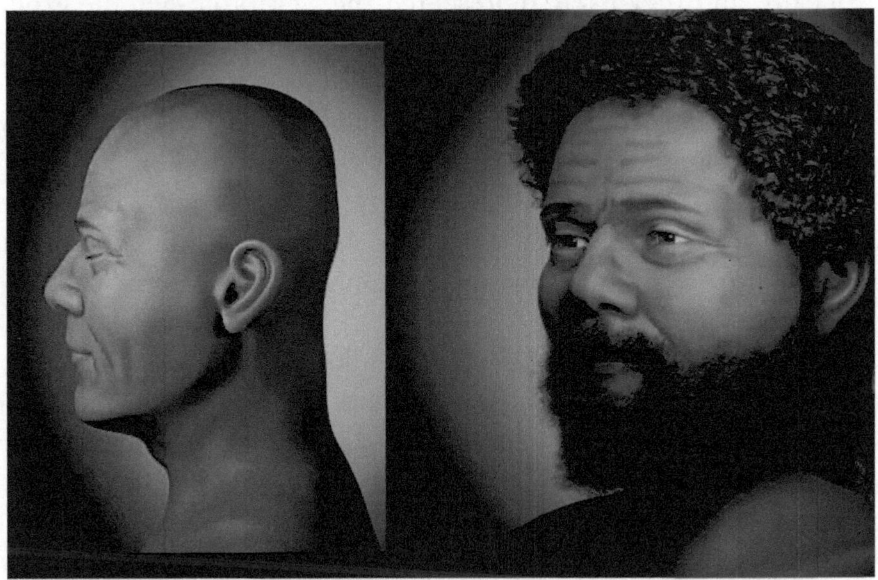

3. Jericho skull reconstruction. 7000 BCE

The Tahunian culture dominated Canaan for two to three thousand years; however, beginning in the 7th to 6th millennia BCE, it was superseded by a fundamentally different Neolithic culture: the Yarmukian. This archaeological culture takes its name from the Yarmuk River, a tributary of the Jordan, where its remains were first identified. Unlike the Natufians and Tahunians, the Yarmukian people utilized handmade ceramics fired in open pits, though the potter's wheel had not yet been invented. At Sha'ar HaGolan, the largest known settlement of this period, archaeologists have unearthed hundreds of art objects. Most notable among these are fired clay figurines depicting women. Consequently, the Yarmukian culture represents a major historical milestone – the onset of the Pottery Neolithic.

The newcomers represented not only a fresh culture but a new ethnic group as well. Anthropologically, they differed significantly from the Natufians and Tahunians; they were considerably taller, with medium-long (mesocephalic) skulls and very prominent noses. These physical characteristics align them with the Near-Eastern (Armenoid) type of Europeans, and they likely represented the first proto-Semitic groups to arrive in Canaan. While the Yarmukians also originated from the north, they did not come from southwestern Anatolia like their predecessors, but rather from southeastern Anatolia – the upper reaches of the Tigris and Euphrates rivers. Their persistent connection to Anatolia is evidenced by the abundance of obsidian artifacts, a material sourced exclusively from that region. Naturally, the distribution of the Yarmukian culture was not limited to Canaan; it extended across Lebanon and Syria as well.

In the 5th millennium BCE, the Yarmukian culture was succeeded – or perhaps merely supplemented – by another Pottery Neolithic group: the Wadi Rabah culture. Its people were of the same proto-Semitic stock as the Yarmukians, sharing a similar anthropological profile. The most significant distinction between the two lay in their architecture; while Yarmukian settlements featured varied or rounded designs, the Wadi Rabah culture showed a strict preference for rectangular dwellings.

The 4th millennium BCE brought yet another distinct archaeological culture to Canaan: the Ghassulian. This culture represented Canaan's transition from the Stone Age to the Bronze Age, a period commonly known as the Copper Age, or the Chalcolithic (Eneolithic). As is standard in archaeology, the culture was named after the site where it was first identified – Tulaylat al-Ghassul, located in the Jordan Valley, east of Jericho. Archaeologists and anthropologists generally agree that the bearers of this culture were definitively Semitic. While the Ghassulians were accomplished farmers and livestock breeders, they were distinguished from all preceding cultures by their mastery of metallurgy. They were the first to mine copper and craft it into tools and weapons, establishing the earliest mines at Timna in southeastern Canaan. Furthermore, Ghassulian pottery was noted for its sophistication, characterized by graceful forms, skillful coloring, and technical perfection.

Many archaeologists view the bearers of the Ghassulian culture as the vanguard of the Western Semites. Over time, as they merged with the populations of preceding archaeological cultures, they became known as the "Canaanites." The Ghassulian culture was concentrated primarily in southern Canaan and flourished for roughly five hundred years, from 3800 to 3300 BCE. However, some scholars argue for an earlier arrival, placing their emergence at the end or even the middle of the 5th millennium BCE. Regardless of their exact start date, the Ghassulian period was eventually succeeded by a new wave of Western Semites. This new group established the "Canaanite civilization" – a society characterized by the development of fortified, walled cities, marking the definitive start of the Early Bronze Age (2900–2300 BCE).

In the 23rd century BCE, the urban Canaanite culture also came to an end, superseded by the semi-nomadic culture of the Amorites. This new wave of Western Semites originated from the upper reaches of the Tigris and Euphrates rivers. At the conclusion of this migratory wave, around the 20th century BCE, the final group of Amorite semi-nomads arrived in Canaan, led by the biblical patriarch Abraham. His descendants were destined to eventually conquer the land and, by fully integrating with the local population, provide the region with its enduring name, history, and religion.

The land where the patriarch Abraham arrived has been known by several names throughout history. The earliest and most ancient was Retenu – the name used by the ancient Egyptians to describe the territory separated from them by the Sinai Desert. This designation was associated with the "Rapha" (Rephaite), a tall people who had inhabited the region neighboring Egypt since the Neolithic period. Later, beginning in the 3rd millennium BCE, the region became known as Canaan (*Kenaan*), named after the Canaanites, the first Semitic groups to settle there. Although the Canaanites were Western Semites, the name "Canaan" is likely not of Semitic origin; rather, it referred to the local autochthonous population. As these original inhabitants intermixed with the arriving Semites, the name was adopted by the new population.

From the end of the 3rd millennium BCE, the northern part of Canaan became known by a different name: Amurru, or the "Land of the Amorites." Semi-nomadic Amorite tribes settled there, and between the 23rd and 20th centuries BCE, they spread across the entirety of the Fertile Crescent, with Amurru being just one of their territories. Eventually, the name "Canaan" returned as the standard designation for the region.

For a brief period during the 17th and 16th centuries BCE, Canaan acquired a new name – the Land of Haru. This was due to the invasion of the Hurrians from the Kingdom of Mitanni, who briefly seized control of several Canaanite cities. The name *Haru* encompassed both Canaan and Syria, as both territories were under Hurrian influence at the time. However, from the 15th to the 13th centuries BCE, Egypt asserted dominance over the region and restored its ancient name: Canaan.

At the beginning of the 12th century BCE, the Hebrew tribes conquered Canaan, and from that time forward, the land became known as Israel. Following the later division of the United Monarchy, two distinct Hebrew states emerged, giving the land two simultaneous names: Israel in the north and Judah in the south. After the fall of the Northern Kingdom of Israel, the name Judah came to represent the entire region.

The arrival of Alexander the Great's army in 333 BCE and the subsequent Hellenization of the Levant introduced a new designation: for two centuries, the region was known as Coele-Syria. However, the Maccabean Revolt eventually restored both national sovereignty and the ancestral name of Judea to the entire country.

In the middle of the 2nd century CE, the Romans – infuriated by the persistent rebellions of the Jewish people – officially renamed the country "Palestine." Under the threat of death, they sought to erase the name "Judea" from public memory and official records. While the geographical term "Palestine" eventually took root in medieval and modern history, only three names truly dominated in antiquity: Canaan, Israel, and Judea. These are the only three names utilized within biblical history across both the Old and New Testaments.

Today, this ancient land is divided between the territories of two modern states: Israel and Jordan. Historical Canaan also encompassed the regions of Judea and Samaria – often referred to in contemporary political discourse as the West Bank – as well as the Gaza Strip. Furthermore, parts of modern-day Lebanon and southern Syria, specifically the Golan Heights, were integral to historical Canaan. Because the borders of Canaan and Palestine were never strictly defined and remain a subject of debate, modern historians frequently employ the politically neutral and more precise term "Southern Levant" to describe this region.

The fate of the people of Canaan is as unique as the role this land has played in the history and culture of humanity. Of all the peoples who inhabited the earliest cradles of civilization – the dwellers of the Nile Valley, the Sumerians, Akkadians, and Hittites – only fragile mummies and museum artifacts have survived to our day. A similarly unenviable fate befell even much "younger" peoples – the Achaeans, Etruscans, and Romans. They, too, remain only in history textbooks and museums, while entirely different nations, with other cultures, religions, and languages, now live on lands that once belonged to them.

Yet the contemporaries of those ancient peoples – the Jews, direct descendants of the inhabitants of Canaan – did not vanish into oblivion. They managed to carry their culture, religion, and language, their historical memory and even their physical appearance, through the crucible of millennia. Moreover, they succeeded in returning to their homeland and restoring their ancient country. No other people in the world has known or endured anything like this.

CHAPTER I.

Pre-Israelite Canaan

IN ETHNIC TERMS, PRE-ISRAELITE CANAAN was as diverse as its natural counterpart. The Old Testament is the only written source that mentions the most ancient ethnic groups of Canaan. Their full list is given in the biblical book of Genesis, which names ten of them: "the Kenites, and the Kenizzites, and the Kadmonites, and the Hittites, and the Perizzites, and the Rephaim; and the Amorites, and the Canaanites, and the Girgashites, and the Jebusites" (Gen. 15:19–21). In later biblical books, for example in Deuteronomy, only seven peoples are mentioned: "the Hittites, and the Girgashites, and the Amorites, and the Canaanites, and the Perizzites, and the Hivites, and the Jebusites" (Deut. 7:1). In addition to them, the Bible also names the Philistines, Geshurites, and Maachatites.

Over time, almost all the peoples of pre-Israelite Canaan completely mixed with the Hebrews and became an integral part of the Israelites and Judahites. It was these peoples – both autochthonous and newly arrived, of both Semitic and non-Semitic origin – who became the flesh and blood of their common descendant, the Jewish people, formed in the land of Canaan. The "biblical Hebrews," having taken possession of Canaan, completely dissolved into its population, giving it their name, history, and religion.

1. The Pre-Semitic Population

We know nothing about the ethnicity and language of the most ancient inhabitants of Canaan. The archaeological cultures known to us, discovered in the territory of the Southern Levant, cannot answer this question. However, judging by the skulls found in the Jordan Valley, we can confidently say that the bearers of the Natufian and Tahunian cultures were not Semites. The situation is much more complicated with the Yarmukian and Wadi Rabah cultures. They already represent the Near Eastern Caucasoid type and, most likely, were proto-Semites. Only with regard to the latest – the Ghassulian archaeological culture – can we say that its bearers were Semites.

1.1 The People of Rapha (Rephaim)

This people was the most ancient known population of Canaan. The Rephaim had lived in this country at least since the Neolithic period. Their distinctive feature was their tall stature, incomparably greater than the average height of the Semitic peoples. It was this unusual height that made the strongest impression on the scouts of the "house of Jacob" sent by Moses to "spy out" the Promised Land. They reported that, "We are not able to go up against this people, for they are stronger than we... The land that we have gone through as spies is a land that devours its inhabitants, and all the people that we saw in it are of great size. There we saw the Nephilim (the Anakites come from the Nephilim), and to ourselves we seemed like grasshoppers, and so we seemed to them" (Num. 13:31–33).

The Hebrews considered the Rephaim, or Anakites (giants), to be descendants of the "Nephilim." According to the earliest biblical narratives, the Nephilim were giants born from the union of fallen angels with the daughters of men. Later, the name *Nephilim* came to mean simply human giants, who were called Anakim or Rephaim. This ancient people lived in all parts of Canaan: both west of the Jordan River and east of it, in Transjordan. The Rephaim inhabited both the Golan Heights and Mount Hermon in the north, as well as the areas of historical Judea, Moab, and Ammon. According to ancient Canaanite epics from Ugarit, the Rephaim lived not only in Canaan, but also along the Lebanese coast and in Syria.

The Semites who came to Canaan called their tall neighbors by different names: the Israelites called them "Anak" and "Rephaim," the Moabites "Emim," and the Ammonites "Zamzummim." In the southwest, in the Gaza region, they were known as the "Avim." Of these many names, only one – Rephaim – had any relation to the self-designation of this people, whose mythical ancestor was Rafa. According to the books of Judges and Joshua, the entire area of modern Hebron once belonged to the leaders of the tall Rephaim – Sheshai, Ahiman, and Talmai – the sons of the legendary Anak, and the city of Hebron itself was founded by the same people and was previously called "Kiriath-arba," after "the greatest man among the Anakim" (Judg. 1:10; Josh. 14:15; 15:13–14). The king of the northern Transjordanian region of Bashan, Og, also came from them. The giant Goliath, whom the Philistines sent out to duel with young David, was likewise a descendant of the same people. However, this ancient autochthonous people of Canaan very quickly dissolved among the West Semitic peoples who came there. By the time of the conquest of Canaan by the Israelites, the Neolithic giants had become Semites in language and culture.

This circumstance confused the authors of the biblical books, so in some cases they still call them "Rephaim," and in others already "Amorites" or "Canaanites." The best example in this regard is the Hebron region, whose population is alternately described as Rephaim, Amorites, and Hittites. The last mentions of the Rephaim are associated with the Philistines. In the southwest of Canaan, later known as Philistia, there lived many Rephaim who had adopted the language and culture of the Canaanites even before the arrival of the Sea Peoples. The Bible particularly emphasizes that the Philistines did not expel the Rephaim and, judging by later reports, actively used their outstanding physical abilities in their army. The best warriors of the Philistine army came from the Rephaim. The Book of Kings mentions among them not only the famous Goliath from the city of Gath, but also the then-famous warriors Yishbi and Saph, who also came from the "descendants of Rapha," the legendary ancestor of these people. The Book of Chronicles reports that in a battle with the Philistines near the city of Gezer, one of King David's brave men killed Sippai, a giant from the Rephaim. In another war with the Philistines from the city of Gath, another of David's brave men defeated Lahmi, the brother of the famous Goliath, and King David's nephew threw to the ground another giant Rephaim. "Again there was war at Gath, where there was a man of great size who had six fingers on each hand and six toes on each foot, twenty-four in number; he also was descended from the giants. When he taunted Israel, Jonathan, son of Shimea, David's brother, killed him. These were descended from the giants in Gath; they fell by the hand of David and his servants" (1 Chr. 20:4–8). It is difficult to say why these tall and physically strong people retreated so quickly before the Semitic newcomers, but they probably stood at a much lower level of social organization and were inferior to them in numbers.

Unlike many ancient peoples of Canaan, the Rephaim were luckier: they are mentioned not only in the Bible, but also in extra-biblical sources. Thus, in the ancient Egyptian curse texts of the Middle Kingdom (19th century BCE), mention is made of the "people of Anak" (*Iy Anaq*) and its three rulers, "Erum, Abi-yamimu, and Akirum" (*Ancient Near Eastern Texts,* p. 328). Another, later ancient Egyptian document, *Papyrus Anastasi I,* already from the time of the New Kingdom (12th century BCE), speaks of the semi-nomads Shasu from Canaan, among whom there were real giants. This papyrus also names the places where these giants lived: Kiryat Anab, that is, Kiryat Arba (Hebron), and Kiryat Sefer (Devir).

The existence of the Rephaim is also confirmed by another extra-biblical source: the Ugaritic tale *Aqhat,* where the ruler of the city and the main character, Danel, is called the man of Rapha. The recording of this Canaanite myth from the city of Ugarit dates to about 1350 BCE.

Finally, there is yet another extra-biblical confirmation of the existence of the Rapha people. At the end of the fourth and in the third millennia BCE, the ancient Egyptians called Canaan by a completely different name – the land of Retenu, that is, the land of the Rephaim, who were the main population of this country before the arrival of the West Semitic peoples.

It is quite possible that the rite of circumcision of male infants originated precisely among the Rapha people in southern Canaan, even during the Neolithic era. Be that as it may, ancient Egyptian palettes from the end of the fourth millennium BCE depict the inhabitants of southern Retenu (Canaan) as circumcised. The Western Semites who came to southern Canaan inherited this custom from the Rephaim, with whom they completely mixed.

Judging by the unusual height of the Rephaim and their clearly non-Semitic origin, this ethnic group cannot be classified as bearers of any of the known archaeological cultures of Canaan, whether Mesolithic, Neolithic, or Eneolithic. This is so even though the Rephaim lived not only in Canaan but also in parts of Lebanon and Syria. Probably, this tall ethnic group was very small in number, although scattered over a large territory. This, in turn, highlights how many blank spots still exist in our knowledge of prehistoric Canaan.

By the time the Hebrew tribes returned from Egypt, this autochthonous people had mostly merged with the surrounding West Semitic populations. The remnants of the Rephaim mixed with the Israelites so quickly that their name in Hebrew became a synonym for something long gone and forgotten. The Book of Joshua already noted: "None of the Anakim was left in the land of the Israelites; some remained only in Gaza, in Gath, and in Ashdod" (Josh. 11:22–23). Later, the only reminder of them was the presence of unusually tall Jews who had inherited the genes of this legendary people of Canaan. Such was the Israelite king Saul, who owed his exceptional height and physical strength to ancestors who came from the Rephaim. A descendant of the Anak was also mentioned by the first-century CE Roman author Lucius Columella, who wrote about "a Jewish man who was taller than the tallest German." Josephus likewise mentioned the Jewish giant Eleazar, whom the Parthian king Artabanus sent as a gift to the Roman emperor Tiberius (*Antiquities of the Jews,* 18.4.5). There is little doubt that the leader of the anti-Roman revolt, Bar Kokhba – whose height and physical abilities frightened even experienced Roman soldiers – also had ancestors among the Rephaim.

1.2. The People of Hori (Horites)

Due to the similarity of their ethnonyms, many authors confuse this autochthonous people of southern Canaan with the Hurrians, the indigenous people of eastern Anatolia and southern Transcaucasia. Perhaps, if anything united these two different ethnic groups, it was their non-Semitic origin and their existence surrounded by Semitic peoples. The Horites, like the Rephaim, were among the most ancient, indigenous inhabitants of Canaan, inhabiting it at least since the Neolithic period. Unfortunately, we know nothing about their ethnicity or their language. The Old Testament is the only written source that mentions a people named Hori.

Unlike the Rephaim, the Horites lived only in southern Canaan – more precisely, in southeastern Transjordan (in the area of Mount Seir), in the Negev, and in northern and central Sinai. Most likely, this people settled in such difficult places to live at a time when the climate in the Near East was much more humid and favorable than it is today. After all, according to archaeological data, about 9-10 thousand years ago there was so much rainfall that today's deserts in the Negev and northern Sinai had abundant vegetation, and human settlements existed there. Why did these people, who had inhabited Sinai and southern Canaan since the Neolithic period, not leave these regions when, beginning in the 5th millennium BCE, the climate became increasingly arid, and Sinai and the Negev gradually turned into deserts and semi-deserts? Oddly enough, in ancient times, before the domestication of the camel, deserts protected people from enemies better than any fortress. In addition, the inhabitants of the semi-deserts of Sinai and Canaan knew all the hidden water sources very well and were able to survive in such harsh conditions. All those who remained in Sinai, the Negev, and Mount Seir belonged to the Hori people.

Around the 19th century BCE, the Edomites – the closest relatives of the Hebrews – settled in the area of Mount Seir in southeastern Canaan. They subjugated the Horites but did not drive them out; instead, they became neighbors and began to intermarry. The first example was set by Esau, the brother of the patriarch Jacob and the forefather of the Edomites. He took Oholibamah, the great-granddaughter of the Horite leader Seir-Hori, as his wife. Esau's eldest son, Eliphaz, followed his father's example, although he did not marry her but took Timna, the youngest daughter of the same Seir-Hori, as his concubine. It was from this prominent concubine that Amalek was born, who was destined to become the ancestor of the Amalekites, a nomadic people who were often at odds with the southern Hebrew tribes.

Why does the Bible, when listing all the peoples who lived in Canaan, never name the people of Hori? First, this is because the descendants of Esau (the Edomites) completely assimilated the people of Seir-Hori even before the Hebrew conquest of Canaan. The same thing happened to the Hori people as to the Rephaim: they were completely absorbed by their West Semitic neighbors, and much earlier than the famous Anakites. Second, the Hori people merged with the closest relatives of the Hebrews – the Edomites – and therefore the Book of Genesis provides the genealogy of the Hori, beginning with their patriarch Seir-Hori. Only the Hebrews themselves or their closest relatives were accorded this distinction. However, despite the inclusion of the genealogy of Seir-Hori, the biblical books are completely silent about the origin and history of this people.

Apart from the Edomites, only the Amalekites could claim the right to be heirs of the Hori people. These nomads, although they belonged to the West Semitic peoples in language and culture, were descended from a mixture of Edomites and Horites. It is possible that the latter played an even more significant role in their ethnogenesis than the Edomites. It is no coincidence that their ethnonym, *Amalek*, is not of Semitic origin, and that their excellent knowledge of every corner of Sinai and the Negev was passed on to them by their ancestors, the Horites, who had lived there for many generations.

In its narrative of the conquest of southern Canaan, the Bible once again mentions the Horites, whom the Hebrew tribe of Simeon encountered in the Beersheba region. It appears that some groups of the Horite people managed to survive in the semi-desert regions of the Negev until the middle of the 12th century BCE, when the Hebrews settled there.

All attempts to uncover the history of this people of southern Canaan have so far been unsuccessful. Although Oxford University professor Archibald Sayce claimed as early as 1915 to have found ancient Egyptian inscriptions mentioning a people called 'Khar' in southern Canaan, and the Midrash (Genesis Rabbah) interprets the name 'Hori' as meaning 'free people,' neither source is considered entirely reliable by modern standards.

2. West Semitic Peoples

By the end of the 3rd millennium BCE, the majority of Canaan's inhabitants were West Semitic peoples. Ethnically, they were closely related and spoke different dialects of the same language. Their primary differences lay in their ways of life, levels of economic and cultural development, and the timing of their arrival in Canaan.

All Western Semites in Canaan were divided into three groups: Canaanites, Amorites, and Arameans. Two of these – the Canaanites and the Amorites – were the most prominent. The Canaanites were descendants of the Western Semites who had arrived as early as the 4th millennium BCE and had completely merged with the indigenous Neolithic population. All Canaanites led a sedentary lifestyle and were engaged in agriculture.

The Amorites arrived about a thousand years later, at the end of the 3rd millennium BCE, and were initially semi-nomadic tribes. Unlike the

Canaanites, who occupied the lowlands and plains suitable for farming, the Amorites settled in the hills and mountainous regions of inner Canaan. The Amorites living west of the Jordan River quickly adopted a sedentary lifestyle and took up agriculture. The "Hittites, Jebusites, Perizzites, and Hivites" mentioned in the Bible belonged to these sedentary Amorite populations. Those who lived east of the Jordan in Transjordan and continued a semi-nomadic lifestyle were referred to in the Bible simply as "Amorites."

The third and smallest group of Western Semites were the Arameans. They appeared in Canaan relatively late – about a thousand years after the Amorites – and settled only in the northeastern regions of the country (today's Golan Heights).

2.1. Canaanites

The Canaanites were the first of the West Semitic peoples to leave their ancestral homeland in northwestern Mesopotamia. Moving southwest during the 4th millennium BCE, they gradually settled throughout the territories of modern-day Syria, Lebanon, Israel, and Jordan. They were also the first Western Semites to appear in the land of Retenu, as the ancient Egyptians called the region.

Arriving before other Semitic groups, the Canaanites occupied the most favorable areas for agriculture: the Mediterranean coastal strip, the Jordan River Valley, the fertile Jezreel Valley, and parts of the Shephelah – a hilly upland in the southwest that they later shared with the Perizzites, an Amorite people. The name of the region, Canaan, is derived from these inhabitants. Originally, this name did not apply to the entire territory, but only to the areas where the Canaanites specifically resided, primarily the coastal strip and the Jordan Valley. Although Canaanite populations also lived along the Lebanese coast and in Syria, the name "Canaan' did not take hold beyond these specific southern areas.

Those whom the Greeks later called the "Phoenicians" also considered themselves Canaanites, as did the inhabitants of Phoenician colonies like

Carthage. The Bible also refers to the Canaanites as "Sidonians," a name derived from the Canaanite port city of Sidon (modern Saida). They were not only a sedentary agricultural people but also the most socio-economically and culturally advanced ethnic group in the region. Archaeological excavations have provided significant evidence that the Canaanites arrived from the north at the end of the 4th millennium BCE. Furthermore, their predecessors – the bearers of the Ghassulian culture who appeared in southern Canaan around 4000 BCE – were also Western Semites. They acted as a vanguard for the Canaanites and also migrated from the north.

4. Canaanite figurine of mourner from the funerary equipment of a warrior, c. 1800-1600 BCE. Yehud, Israel.

The Canaanites – or rather, the first West Semitic people known to us by that name – completely assimilated the original Neolithic inhabitants of the Mediterranean coast, the Jordan Valley, the Jezreel Valley, and the Shephelah. The autochthonous population of these regions, who built the famous "Neolithic cities," consisted of the descendants of the Natufian, Tahunian, Yarmukian, Wadi Rabah, and Ghassulian cultures, which had already partially merged. This new ethnic group, arising from the blending of Semitic newcomers and the indigenous inhabitants, inherited the ethnonym "Canaanites" and the Semitic language. However, they also acquired distinct features that differentiated them from other Western Semites, as well as from the Rephaim and Horites who inhabited the highlands of Canaan.

It is noteworthy that the biblical patriarchs often preferred to deal with the Amorite peoples of Canaan rather than the Canaanites, even though both were West Semitic. Later, when the Hebrews returned from Egypt, it was the Canaanites who displayed the greatest hostility toward them, offering more serious resistance than most of the Amorite tribes. Joshua was unable to conquer the most desirable areas of the country inhabited by the Canaanites; in the open terrain of the valleys, he had no defense against their iron chariots, and he lacked the battering rams necessary to storm their fortified cities.

The famous Song of Deborah recounts the difficult war between the northern Hebrew tribes and the Canaanite army of King Jabin. While Sisera, Jabin's commander, possessed 900 iron chariots, Barak, the Israelite commander, had none. He secured a victory over the Canaanites only through a tactical ruse, luring the enemy chariots onto the muddy banks of the Kishon River, where they became immobilized (Judges 4:3–17).

5. Canaanite relief, depicting a lion and lioness. 14th century BCE, Beth Shean.

During the prolonged military confrontation between the Philistines and the Israelites, the Canaanite city-states maintained a strictly neutral position. In contrast, the Amorites supported the Israelites, with whom they shared close ethnic ties (1 Sam. 7:14). The Canaanite regions only submitted to Israelite rule during the reign of King David in the early 10th century BCE; his campaigns effectively completed the conquest of Canaan that had begun under Joshua in the early 12th century BCE. Following the division of the United Monarchy (931–928 BCE), nearly all territories inhabited by Canaanites became part of the Northern Kingdom of Israel.

Given the significant distinctions between the Amorites and the Canaanites, the latter should be defined specifically as the descendants of the initial West Semitic migrations intermixed with the indigenous Neolithic populations of the Southern Levant.

2.2. Amorites

The semi-nomadic Amorite tribes appeared in Syria, Mesopotamia, and Canaan in the 23rd–20th centuries BCE. The arrival of a large mass of nomads led to the collapse of the entire system of city-states created by the Canaanites. Some cities were destroyed, while others were abandoned by their inhabitants, who moved to the southern regions of Canaan, which were least affected by the invasion.

Archaeological evidence indicates the rapid and violent nature of the destruction of the entire urban culture of western Canaan in the Early Bronze Age (3050–2300 BCE), and that it was replaced by a completely different culture that had nothing in common with the previous one (Mazar, A., *Archaeology of the Land of the Bible*, pp. 144–151). The new culture – the culture of semi-nomadic tribes – dominated northern and central Canaan for three centuries, from the 23rd to the 20th centuries BCE. During this period, the country was characterized by semi-nomadic tribes and small agricultural settlements. Similar processes took place on the Lebanese coast and in southern Syria. Unlike these regions, southern Canaan and Transjordan were almost unaffected. There, archaeologists trace complete continuity with the previous Canaanite urban culture. Probably, the southern and eastern regions served as a refuge for the former population of northern and central Canaan.

The well-known ancient Egyptian document of the 20th century BCE, *The Tale of Sinuhe*, fully confirms the predominance of semi-nomads in northern Canaan. Sinuhe, an Egyptian dignitary at the court of the pharaoh, fled his country during the troubled interregnum and left a detailed description of northern and central Canaan, where he spent many years. According to his account, in the country of Retenu – as the Egyptians then called Canaan – semi-nomadic tribes lived everywhere. During his long stay there, he never mentioned seeing or visiting any large city, which is no accident, since, judging by archaeological data, such cities had long been destroyed or abandoned by their inhabitants (*Ancient Near Eastern Texts*, pp. 18–22).

The Amorites came to Canaan from southern Syria and the Lebanese coast, and there, in turn, from northwestern Mesopotamia – the ancestral homeland of all Western Semites. Around the same time, another powerful stream of Amorite tribes moved southeast along the river valleys of the Tigris and Euphrates, and many cities of Mesopotamia suffered the same fate as those of Canaan. However, in terms of territory and population, Mesopotamia was clearly superior to Canaan and southern Syria, and therefore the Amorites there very quickly dissolved among the local population and adopted its culture. As a result, the period of chaos and destruction was much shorter – only about a hundred years (2230–2130 BCE).

Canaan, however, did not become the final refuge for all nomadic Amorites. Later, most of them moved further southwest, to the Nile Delta. The climatic conditions of the Nile Delta, and above all the abundance of water throughout the year, proved to be far more suitable for semi-nomadic cattle breeders than Canaan, with its periodic droughts leading to famine. It is no coincidence that the Book of Genesis equates the land of Egypt with the "garden of God" (Gen. 13:10). The first groups of semi-nomadic Amorites reached the Nile Delta precisely because of drought and famine in Canaan. Over time, West Semitic nomads began to come to Egypt more frequently and to remain there for longer periods. This marked the beginning of the permanent presence of the Amorites – called *'aamu* by the Egyptians – in the Nile Delta.

Hivites

The Hivites were the most numerous sedentary Amorite people of pre-Israelite Canaan. Their ancestors came to this region from the north (via Syria and Lebanon) around the 23rd century BCE, like most of the Amorite tribes that settled in Canaan. They settled primarily in the highlands of Samaria and northern Judea, but the Bible also mentions groups of Hivites living in Galilee, in the region of Mount Hermon, and in what is now southern Lebanon (Judg. 3:3; Josh. 11:3).

The Hivites probably inhabited most of northern and central Canaan, with the exception of the coastal areas and the fertile Jezreel Valley, which remained in Canaanite hands. The first detailed mention of the Hivites appears in the biblical account of the patriarch Jacob's stay near the city of Shechem in central Canaan (Gen. 33:18; 34:31). Although this narrative was recorded no earlier than the 11th–10th centuries BCE, it most likely reflects events of the 18th–17th centuries BCE, that is, the period of Jacob's life in Canaan. It shows the following:

1. The Hivites had already transitioned from a semi-nomadic lifestyle to a sedentary one, and their principal occupation had become agriculture rather than cattle breeding.
2. The main city of central Canaan, Shechem, was founded by and belonged to the Hivites. The city of Shechem was probably named after its founder, the ruler of the Hivites.
3. Relations between the Hivites and the Hebrews were friendly; otherwise, the Hivites would not have allowed Jacob to set up his

camp directly in front of their city, nor would they have sold him a plot of land on which he erected an altar to his God.

4. The Hivites did not yet practice the rite of circumcision, although at that time it was widely used in southern Canaan, for example by the Rephaim, Hittites, and Jebusites.
5. It was no coincidence that the Hivites were willing to intermarry with the Hebrews, since, in ethnic and linguistic terms, both represented the same broader group – West Semitic peoples of Amorite origin.
6. The complete rout of Shechem by Simeon and Levi (the southern Hebrew tribes) caused a serious conflict within the "house of Jacob" and significantly complicated its relations with the peoples of Canaan.

The Book of Joshua confirms that the patriarch Jacob purchased land from the Hivites of Shechem. Moreover, it reports that Joseph's bones, brought from Egypt, were later buried on this land (Josh. 24:32–33). This would, of course, have been possible only if there had been good, neighborly relations between the Hivites and the Hebrews. This explains Jacob's extreme indignation when he learned of the attack by Simeon and Levi's people on the friendly city of Shechem.

The second, rather extensive mention of the Hivites relates to the period of the conquest of Canaan by the Hebrew tribes at the beginning of the 12th century BCE. It concerns the peace concluded with the Hivites of Gibeon, the making of which nearly undermined the unity of the Israelite tribal confederation. The Book of Joshua presents this peace treaty as the result of a fraudulent ruse by the Hivites, who allegedly pretended to be envoys from a distant city seeking an alliance with the Israelites. According to the narrative, the leaders of Israel did not know that Gibeon was only about twenty kilometers away and, therefore, sealed peace with the Hivites with an oath. When the deception was revealed, nothing could be changed, since the conquest of Gibeon would have meant breaking a sworn oath. In reality, this story appears to have been intended to conceal serious disagreements among the leaders of the Israelite alliance.

The Hivites were the most numerous Amorite people inhabiting northern and central Canaan, including its largest city, Shechem. As can be inferred from the Amarna archive correspondence, the "House of Joseph" was in alliance with the Hivites of Shechem. At that time, the ruler of the city, Labayu, and his sons hoped to shake off Egyptian power over Canaan with the help of the Habiru, the name under which the "House of Joseph" was then operating. However, their plan failed, and assassins sent by the Egyptians dealt with the rebellious ruler. Despite this, friendly relations between the Hivites of Shechem and the "House of Joseph" remained. It is no coincidence that Shechem is never mentioned as a conquered city, even though it would have been impossible to gain a foothold in central Canaan without taking possession of it. However, not all the Hivites of Canaan became allies of the Israelites. While the Hivites in the center of the country (Shechem) and in the southern regions (Gibeon) supported the conquests of Joshua, the Hivites in the north, in Galilee, sided with his enemies – the Amorite kingdom of Hazor and the Jabin dynasty that reigned there. It is highly probable that the population of Hazor itself – the largest city and kingdom in northern Canaan – also consisted mainly of Hivites.

The Hivites of Shechem reemerged during the period of the Judges, when, after the long rule of Judge Gideon, one of his sons, Abimelech – whose mother came from the Hivites of Shechem – seized power over the northern Hebrew tribes. It was to the Hivites of this city that Abimelech appealed when he struggled for power against Gideon's other sons. "Now Abimelech son of Jerubbaal went to Shechem to his mother's kinsfolk and said to them and to the whole clan of his mother's family, "Say in the hearing of all the lords of Shechem, 'Which is better for you, that all seventy of the sons of Jerubbaal rule over you or that one rule over you?' Remember also that I am your bone and your flesh." So, his mother's kinsfolk spoke all these words on his behalf in the hearing of all the lords of Shechem, and their hearts inclined to follow Abimelech, for they said, "He is our brother." They gave him seventy pieces of silver out of the temple of Baal-Berith with which Abimelech hired worthless and reckless fellows who followed him. He went to his father's house at Ophrah and killed his brothers the sons of Jerubbaal, seventy men, on one stone...Then all the lords of Shechem and all Beth-millo came together, and they went and made Abimelech king, by the oak of the pillar at Shechem" (Judges 9:2-6). However, the elders of the city were not satisfied with Abimelech's dubious origin, since his mother was only Gideon's concubine. At that point, a rival appeared – Gaal, son of Ebed, from the Hivite nobility. "Gaal son of Ebed said, "Who is Abimelech, and who are we of Shechem, that we should serve him? Did not the son of Jerubbaal and Zebul his officer serve the men of Hamor father of Shechem? Why then should we serve him? If only this people were under my command! Then I would remove Abimelech; I would say to him, 'Increase your army and come out" (Judges 9:28-29).

Internal Hivite strife brought an end to Abimelech's three-year reign, led to the destruction of Shechem, and resulted in the death of its inhabitants. Abimelech himself was killed by a woman who crushed his head with a fragment of a millstone. The Book of Judges concludes: "Thus God repaid Abimelech for the crime he committed against his father in killing his seventy brothers; and God also made all the wickedness of the people of Shechem fall back on their heads" (Judges 9:56–57).

The Hivites possessed not only Shechem, but also more southerly cities: Gibeon, Kephirah, Beeroth, and Kiriath-Jearim. Joshua, the leader of the "house of Joseph," was interested in preserving peace and alliance with them, but the tribe of Benjamin laid claim to the entire territory of the southern Hivites, including their principal city of Gibeon. Perhaps, prior to the descent into Egypt, part of this region had belonged to the tribe of Benjamin. In the end, the conflict was settled, but its very fact reminded us that the "house of Joseph," having returned to Canaan two and a half centuries earlier than the other Hebrew tribes, had managed to create a system of relationships with neighboring peoples there, which they sought to preserve even during the conquest of the country. The alliance with the Hivites of Gibeon became further evidence that, contrary to the claims of biblical sources, the Israelite conquest of Canaan did not lead to the expulsion or extermination of the local peoples, but to mixing and merging with them. The authors of the Bible could not help but recognize this fact, but they considered it a violation of the alliance with Yahweh and placed all responsibility for it on their people: "But you have not obeyed my command. See what you have done! S o now I say, I will not drive them out before you, but they shall become adversaries to you, and their gods shall be a snare to you" (Judges 2:2-3).

However, the southern Hivites soon found another, more reliable ally – the southern tribe of Judah. It became the principal defender of the southern Hivites against encroachments on their lands by the tribe of Benjamin. During the rule of Judge Othniel (late 12th century BCE), the Hebrews fought at least twice with the tribe of Benjamin over the latter's attempts to seize the cities of the southern Hivites. The formation of the United Monarchy and the reign of Saul, a Benjaminite, led to the subordination of all the lands of the southern Hivites to the native tribe of the first Israelite king. However, the triumph of the Benjaminites was short-lived. The accession of David, who came from the tribe of Judah, restored the rights of the southern Hivites to their lands. Moreover, the rebellion of the Benjaminite Sheba against David's authority provided the Gibeonites with a convenient opportunity to exact revenge on the Benjaminites – and specifically on Saul's royal family – for years of oppression and insult. David easily found a pretext to physically eliminate the descendants of the first Israelite king, who posed a threat to his own dynasty. When a three-year drought occurred, David's prophets interpreted it as divine punishment for the crimes committed by the House of Saul against the Gibeonites. The king's advisers suddenly "remembered" that the Benjaminites, led by Saul, had violated the peace treaty concluded between Joshua and the inhabitants of Gibeon two centuries earlier. Ever the savvy politician, David did not execute the surviving descendants of Saul himself; instead, he handed nearly all of them over – two sons and five grandsons – to their enemies, the Gibeonites.

The eventual split of the United Monarchy into Israel and Judah also divided the Hivite populations. Those living in the north and center, such as in Shechem, remained in Israel under the protection of the "House of Joseph." Meanwhile, the southern groups – specifically those in Gibeon, Kephirah, Beeroth, and Kiriath-Jearim – unhesitatingly aligned with Judah and the reigning Davidic dynasty. In the following years, the Hivites quickly assimilated into the surrounding Israelite and Judahite populations, becoming an integral part of those peoples.

The Book of Nehemiah indirectly records the fate of the southern Hivites. According to these records, the first wave of Judeans returning from the Babylonian captivity included inhabitants of the former Hivite cities: 95 people from Gibeon (Neh. 7:25) and 743 from Kiriath-Jearim, Kephirah, and Beeroth (Neh. 7:29). The southern Hivites also played an active role in the restoration of Jerusalem's fortifications during the 5th century BCE. Nehemiah notes: "The repairs were made by Melatiah the Gibeonite and Jadon the Meronothite – men of Gibeon and Mizpah – who were under the jurisdiction of the governor of the province Beyond the River" (Neh. 3:7). Furthermore, Nehemiah identifies the Gibeonites as "the temple servants living on Ophel," noting that they "made repairs up to a point opposite the Water Gate on the east and the projecting tower" (Neh. 3:26).

Hittites

The West Semitic people known as the Hittites, who lived in southern Canaan, are often confused with the Indo-European Hittites of the same name who inhabited Asia Minor. Whereas the Semitic Hittites appeared in Canaan as part of a large group of Amorite tribes around the 23rd century BCE, the Indo-European Hittites at the same time settled far from Canaan, in central Anatolia.

According to the Semitic genealogy in the Book of Genesis, the name "Heth" belonged to one of the sons of Canaan, the ancestor of all the Canaanite peoples. By contrast, the Indo-European newcomers called themselves by an entirely different name – *Nesites.* The designation "Hittites" was later applied to them after they mixed with and dominated the local population, who called themselves *Hatti.* Could the Indo-European Hittites of central Anatolia have appeared in southern Canaan during the lifetime of the biblical patriarch Abraham in the 20th–19th centuries BCE? Absolutely not. In the 20th–18th centuries BCE, the Hittites had not yet expanded beyond central and southeastern Anatolia. Only in the late 17th to early 16th centuries BCE did the Hittite king Hattushili I gain a foothold in northern Syria, and his grandson Murshili I went on to capture Babylonia. All of this, however, occurred far from Canaan, and even farther from its southern regions. Moreover, these were military campaigns aimed at the acquisition of booty rather than the colonization of conquered territories.

From the 15th to the early 12th centuries BCE, all of Canaan was under Egyptian rule – the Hittites' principal rival in the Near East – making it highly unlikely that the Egyptians would have permitted any significant Hittite settlement activity in the region. Finally, no extra-biblical sources attest to Hittite settlement in Canaan, let alone in its southern part. Only in the 14th–13th centuries BCE did Hittite military units appear in southern Syria and in the land of Amurru (present-day Lebanon), but again not in Canaan. Thus, neither the Indo-European Hittites nor the indigenous Hatti people of Anatolia had any connection with the West Semitic people of Amorite origin known as the "Hittites." The similarity of the ethnonyms of these entirely different peoples is accidental. By the 20th century BCE, the semi-nomadic Amorite tribe known as *Hit* had finally settled in the Hebron region. At that time, this area was known by a different name – Kiryat Arba – and was inhabited by the Rapha (Rephaim), an indigenous non-Semitic people who had lived throughout Canaan since the Neolithic period. Despite their different ethnic origins, the Hittites quickly found common ground with the tall Rephaim. The latter, in turn, adopted the language and culture of the newcomers and rapidly merged into the dominant West Semitic population. The Hittites were the first to accept the patriarch Abraham and to become his allies. It was in the Hebron region, on the land of the Hittite ruler Mamre, at a place called *Elonei Mamre*, that both the religious center and the residence of all three biblical patriarchs – Abraham, Isaac, and Jacob – were located.

The ruler Mamre himself, together with his brothers Eshkol and Aner, were Abraham's closest allies. All of them took part with Abraham in the war against the coalition of Syrian kings, which ended with the rescue of Lot, Abraham's nephew. Despite his frequent movements throughout southern Canaan, Abraham spent most of his life in the region of Hebron among the Hittites. He himself described his status there in the following words: "I am a stranger and an alien residing among you" (Gen. 23:4). For their part, the Hittites regarded the Hebrews not merely as close allies, but as members of their own community. When Sarah, the patriarch's wife, died, the Hittites offered Abraham the best of their burial places, entirely free of charge. Abraham, however, insisted on purchasing the well-known cave of Machpelah near Hebron, so that it would be his undisputed property and would serve as a burial place for his family and descendants. As the Book of Genesis records: "His sons Isaac and Ishmael buried him in the cave of Machpelah, in the field of Ephron son of Zohar the Hittite, east of Mamre – the field that Abraham purchased from the Hittites. There Abraham was buried with his wife Sarah" (Gen. 25:9–10). It was there, at Mamre in Hebron (formerly Kiryat Arba), that Abraham's son Isaac also ended his days. This tomb became the burial place of all three biblical patriarchs and their wives.

The Hittites were the first people of Canaan with whom Esau, the beloved son of the patriarch Isaac and grandson of Abraham, became related by marriage. The Book of Genesis testifies to this: "When Esau was forty years old, he married Judith daughter of Beeri the Hittite, and Basemath daughter of Elon the Hittite" (Gen. 26:34). Elsewhere, however, the same Basemath is identified as a daughter of Ishmael, while another wife of Esau, Adah, is again described as the daughter of Elon the Hittite.

The Hittites reacted ambiguously to the return of the Hebrews from Egypt. They treated with hostility the three northern tribes of the "House of Joseph," who found themselves in a position of the *Habiru* in Canaan during the 15th–13th centuries BCE. Even later, at the beginning of the 12th century BCE, when the leader of the northern tribes, Joshua, sought hegemony in Canaan, the Hittites and their territories were not conquered. By contrast, the Hittites renewed their alliance with the southern tribe of Judah, which returned to Canaan in the mid-12th century BCE. The entire Hebron region, with the exception of Debir, surrendered without resistance to Caleb, the leader of the tribe of Judah. Caleb did not attempt to storm the city of Hebron itself, but simply "drove out from there Sheshai, Ahiman, and Talmai, the descendants of Anak." In other words, the Hittites opened the gates of the city without resisting their long-standing allies, and the latter, for their part, harmed no one and merely replaced the ruling elite (Josh. 15:13–14). This provides a clear example of how the population of Canaan was transformed not through the extermination or expulsion of the defeated, but through the mixing and assimilation of victors and vanquished. Only one city, Debir (formerly Kiryat Sefer), offered resistance. Its population was perhaps not Hittite, but Canaanite or Perizzite, groups that had no alliance with the southern tribes. Debir was eventually captured by Othniel, Caleb's nephew and the future judge of the tribe of Judah. Once again, however, its population was neither killed nor expelled.

Hittite Hebron passed into the hands of the Kenizzites of Caleb, an Edomite tribe that joined the tribe of Judah after its exodus from Egypt. The influence of the Kenizzites and their leader Caleb was so great that, even before the conquest of southern Canaan, they had seized real power within the tribe. The wealthy nobleman Nabal, encountered by the future King David, was a descendant of the Kenizzites of Hebron, whereas David himself came from the older Judahite aristocracy that had settled in Ephrath (Bethlehem) and had been pushed into the background by the Kenizzites.

The Hebron region became the center of settlement for the tribe of Judah, and the city of Hebron itself became the capital of Judah and the residence of King David until his conquest of Jerusalem. Many Hittites became loyal servants and close confidants of the king. One of them was Uriah the Hittite, one of David's warriors, from whom the king took his wife Bathsheba; he was precisely one of those Hittites from the Hebron region. Although three different groups settled in the Hebron area – the Hittites, the Kenizzites (Edomites), and the Judahites – they all belonged to the same West Semitic peoples of Amorite origin and spoke the same language. It is therefore not surprising that by the 9th–8th centuries BCE these peoples had intermingled so thoroughly that no distinct traces of either the Hittites or the Kenizzites can be discerned within the consolidated Judahite population of Hebron. As for the Rephaim, the indigenous inhabitants of the region, they had been completely assimilated by the Hittites even before the return of the Hebrews from Egypt.

Although the Hittites disappeared as a distinct people, becoming the flesh and blood of the Judahite population, their name continued to live on in the biblical books. By that time, however, these were already different Hittites – not Semites, but Indo-Europeans, natives of Asia Minor – who served as mercenaries at the courts of the kings of Judah and Israel and in their armies. The term "Hittites" came to denote foreign mercenaries in general, encompassing not only actual Hittites, but also natives of Anatolia and northern Syria, such as Palaians, Luwians, or even Hurrians. Under this designation, even Greeks could be included, and later the broader term "Kittim" came into use.

The original Hittites, who had absorbed the indigenous inhabitants of Hebron, were not merely allies and neighbors of the Hebrews. They became one of the ancestors of the Jewish people – one of its formative roots, reaching deep into the history of Canaan.

Jebusites

The Jebusites were a West Semitic people of Amorite origin who lived exclusively in Jerusalem and its immediate surroundings. In terms of both population and territory, they were clearly inferior to the Canaanites and to other Amorite peoples of Canaan. Jerusalem was often called Jebus – the city of the Jebusites – after the name of this people. It was not only their principal city, but in fact their only city. The name of Jebusite Jerusalem is first attested in ancient Egyptian execration texts of the 20th century BCE. In these texts, the Egyptians listed the enemies of the pharaoh and sought to harm them through ritual curses. This indicates that Jebusite Jerusalem had arisen at least four thousand years ago and had already managed, in some way, to attract Egyptian hostility. The execration texts even preserve the names of two rulers of the city: Shas'an and Y'qar'am.

The Jebusites were closely related to their Hittite neighbors of Hebron, and it is quite possible that both groups originally constituted a single Amorite people, later divided for political or dynastic reasons. In any case, this is suggested by the words of the prophet Ezekiel: "Thus says the Lord God to Jerusalem: Your origin and your birth were in the land of the Canaanites; your father was an Amorite and your mother a Hittite" (Ezek. 16:3). In the time of the biblical patriarch Abraham, however, Jerusalem – or Jebus – was better known as Shalem (or *Yerushalimu*), a name given in honor of the local pagan deity who served as the city's patron. Only much later, when the city came under the rule of King David, a committed Yahwist and monotheist, was its name reinterpreted and adjusted, becoming *Yerushalayim*, "the city of peace."

The Jebusites, being a small people, required strong allies for protection, and the Hebrews became such allies. The Book of Genesis relates that in the time of the patriarch Abraham, Canaan was attacked by a coalition of Syrian rulers who, after plundering the cities of southern Canaan, attempted to flee northward with their spoils. Abraham's people, together with their Amorite allies, pursued the enemy as far as Damascus and, after recovering the booty, returned home victorious.

Among Abraham's grateful allies in southern Canaan was Melchizedek, the king of Jebusite Salem. He not only blessed Abraham but also gave him a tithe of everything that had been recovered (Gen. 14:1–20). It is noteworthy that the faith embraced by Abraham in Canaan corresponded to that practiced in his allied city of Salem. Both the patriarch Abraham and Melchizedek, king and high priest of Jebusite Jerusalem, worshiped the same "God Most High, maker of heaven and earth," who at that time was understood as the supreme deity of the Canaanite pantheon, El (Gen. 14:18–22).

The departure of the Hebrews to Egypt left Jebus without its traditional defenders, and in the second half of the 16th century BCE the city came under the influence of the Hurrian state of Mitanni, where the Indo-Aryan warrior elite known as the *maryannu* held power. Although Hurrian and Indo-Aryan dominance in Canaan was relatively brief – lasting only until the 15th century BCE – it nonetheless resulted in the establishment of Hurrian and Indo-Aryan ruling dynasties in a number of Canaanite cities. Among these was Jebusite Jerusalem, where the local ruling dynasty of the Zadokites was compelled to relinquish political authority to the newcomers, retaining only its priestly functions. The correspondence of the Jerusalem ruler Abdi-Heba, preserved in the Amarna archive of the 14th century BCE, indirectly confirms this dynastic change in the city.

After the return of the Hebrews from Egypt, their alliance with the Jebusites of Jerusalem was renewed. This time, the primary defender of Jebus was the main southern tribe of Judah. This explains why Jerusalem was not among the cities conquered either by Joshua, the leader of the northern Hebrew tribes, or by Caleb, the head of the southern tribes. Nevertheless, tensions persisted. The northern tribe of Benjamin laid claim to the city and the surrounding lands of the Jebusites. Having returned from Egypt as part of the "House of Joseph" more than two centuries earlier than the other Hebrew tribes, Benjamin – probably identified under the term *Habiru* – repeatedly attempted to capture Jebusite Jerusalem. The Book of Judges attests that the tribe of Benjamin frequently encroached on Jebusite territory and sought to seize Jerusalem during Joshua's campaigns. It is also possible that even earlier, King Abdi-Heba, who ruled the city in the second half of the 14th century BCE, was referring to the tribe of Benjamin when he complained to the Egyptian pharaoh about the aggressive intentions of the *Habiru*.

With the return of the large tribe of Judah from the Sinai wilderness in the mid-12th century BCE, the situation changed, and the Jebusites once again gained a reliable ally and protector. During the judgeship of Othniel, at the beginning of the period of the Judges, the tribe of Judah inflicted several defeats on the tribe of Benjamin, thereby ending its claims to the lands of the Jebusites. In turn, Jebusite Jerusalem assisted the two southern Hebrew tribes, Judah and Simeon, in conquering the territories of the Perizzites and Canaanites in the Shephelah and in defeating their ruler, Adoni-Bezek. Notably, the captured ruler was brought to Jebusite Jerusalem, where he was executed by the city's allies (Judges 1:3–7).

Before David's conquest of Jerusalem, the Bible repeatedly refers to this city as belonging to, or at least associated with, the tribe of Judah. For example, in the episode describing David's victory over Goliath, the text states: "David took the head of the Philistine and brought it to Jerusalem" (1 Sam. 17:54). Many biblical scholars regard this passage as a historical anachronism. However, the biblical text may simply reflect the fact that Jebusite Jerusalem was the closest ally of the southern tribes and took part with them in repelling the Philistine offensive.

By virtue of its alliance with the tribe of Judah, Jebusite Jerusalem managed to preserve its independence until David's accession to the throne and his restoration of the United Monarchy. At the same time, the lands of the Jebusites separated the territories of the northern and southern tribes, so one of David's first steps (c. 1004–965 BCE) was the territorial unification of Israel and Judah through the annexation of Jebus into the United Monarchy. Moreover, David sought to transform this enclave into his personal domain, one not tied to the tribal territories of either the northern or the southern tribes. The very fact that the supposedly "impregnable" city – claimed to have resisted conquest for centuries – was taken swiftly and with little resistance suggests that the southern tribe of Judah neither wished to seize the city itself nor permitted others to do so, in order to protect its Jebusite allies. It is also possible that within Jebusite Jerusalem there existed an influential faction sympathetic to the "House of Jacob," which facilitated the peaceful transfer of the city into David's hands. It is noteworthy that the conquest was not followed by reprisals: there was no revenge by the victors, no massacre of the besieged, and no destruction of the city. King David did not lay a hand on its inhabitants, the Jebusites. The original population remained in place and was soon fully integrated into the tribe of Judah. The Jebusite priesthood later merged with the Aaronite priesthood and became part of the Jerusalem Temple clergy. It is quite possible that Zadok himself – the high priest at the court of David and later Solomon – did not originate from the Aaronites, but rather from the Jebusite royal and priestly dynasty of the Zadokites. This ancient ruling house, to which Melchizedek, mentioned in the Bible as an ally of Abraham, is traditionally assigned, had been removed from political power when Jerusalem, like several other cities of Canaan, fell under the control of an Indo-Aryan elite (the *maryannu*). It was probably the Zadokites who led the pro-Judahite faction within the city and assisted David's warriors in taking control of Jerusalem. At the same time, the biblical tradition emphasizes that the Indo-Aryan elite of Jerusalem, which had earlier displaced the Zadokites, was likewise left unharmed by David. From one of its representatives – Araunah (Aravennah) – David purchased the site on which the Jerusalem Temple was later built.

In general, the Jebusites, as long-standing allies – first of the patriarch Abraham and later of the southern tribe of Judah – were rapidly absorbed into the population of Judah and became an indistinguishable part of the Judahite people well before the fall of the First Temple in 586 BCE. Yet the most intriguing aspect lies elsewhere. The religious concepts of the Jebusite kings–high priests appear to have been identical to the new faith adopted by Abraham – a belief system that represented an early step toward genuine monotheism. Moreover, there is reason to believe that the Jebusite royal dynasty of the Zadokites (later known as the Sadducees) played a significant role in the formation and institutional consolidation of the priesthood of the First Jerusalem Temple.

Perizzites

The Perizzites were the second most important – and perhaps the most numerous after the Hivites – of the Amorite peoples in pre-Israelite Canaan. In terms of their economic and cultural development and their way of life, the Perizzites were closer to the Canaanites than any other Amorite group in the region. They appear to have been the first of the Amorites to enter Canaan, as they occupied the most favorable agricultural areas after the Canaanites themselves. They were also the first among the semi-nomadic Amorites to adopt a fully sedentary, agrarian way of life. It is noteworthy that the Perizzites not only sought to settle in close proximity to the Canaanites but also maintained allied relations with them rather than with the Amorite groups to whom they were ethnically closer.

The Perizzites inhabited the Shephelah, a fertile hilly region in the southwestern part of Canaan, as well as the most agriculturally suitable areas of the northern Negev. Their main settlement zone lay between the territory of the modern Gaza Strip – occupied at that time by the Canaanites and Rephaim – and the Hebron region, where the Hittites and the same Rephaim lived. Among the Perizzite cities, the most notable were Lachish, Libnah, Bezek, Eglon, Ziklag, and Sharuhen. The small town of Ziklag, for example, is well known as the residence of the future King David during his period of service among the Philistines. The city of Sharuhen entered history as the last stronghold of the Hyksos rulers of Egypt. It is also quite possible that the large city of Gerar at that time was Perizzite rather than Canaanite. Because of their close cultural and economic proximity to the Canaanites, biblical authors often confused the Perizzites with the Canaanites or failed to distinguish clearly between them.

The Perizzites, unlike the Hittites, Jebusites, and Hivites, were never allies of the Hebrews; on the contrary, they often displayed open hostility toward them. Nevertheless, the Book of Genesis repeatedly mentions the presence of the biblical patriarchs in Perizzite lands. Thus, Abraham concluded an agreement with the Perizzite ruler Abimelech, according to which the patriarch paid him with livestock for the right to use his land (Gen. 21:27). The very name Be'er Sheva ("well of the oath") recalls this agreement with the Perizzites in the northern Negev, as well as the conflicts with them over wells. Another biblical patriarch, Isaac, spent even more time in Perizzite territory. Here the Hebrews – or at least some of them – attempted to settle on the land and engage in agriculture. "Isaac sowed seed in that land and in the same year reaped a hundredfold. The Lord blessed him, and the man became rich; he prospered more and more until he became very wealthy" (Gen. 26:12–13). Most likely, this passage refers to the Shephelah region bordering Gaza. The mention of the Philistines in this episode is a historical anachronism, since in Isaac's time it was not the Philistines who inhabited this area, but the Perizzites and the Canaanites. Isaac's conflict, once again over water, occurred precisely with the Perizzites, who were unwilling to share their land with the newcomers. The hostile attitude of the Perizzites prevented the Hebrews from settling permanently in the Shephelah, forcing them to continue their semi-nomadic way of life in the northern Negev. Unlike Abraham, who spent most of his life among the friendly Hittites of Hebron, Isaac was compelled to reside primarily in the northern Negev and the Shephelah, repeatedly clashing with the Perizzites over land and water resources. It is therefore no coincidence that he chose to spend his final years in Hebron, among his allied Hittites.

During the conquest of southern Canaan by the Hebrew tribes, the Perizzites and the Canaanites were the only peoples who put up serious resistance. The outcome of the war with them was decided in a battle with the Perizzite ruler Adoni-Bezek in the Shephelah region. The forces of the two southern Hebrew tribes, Judah and Simeon, with the support of the Midianite tribe of the Kenites, inflicted a crushing defeat on the combined army of the Perizzites and Canaanites led by Adoni-Bezek. Having lost ten thousand warriors, Adoni-Bezek attempted to flee, but he was captured and executed. The Book of Judges preserves the final words of the Perizzite ruler: "Adoni-Bezek said, 'Seventy kings, with their thumbs and big toes cut off, used to pick up scraps under my table; as I have done, so God has paid me back'" (Judges 1:4–7).

The appearance of the Philistines in the southwest of Canaan at the beginning of the 12th century BCE complicated the situation of the Perizzites, their closest neighbors. Later, in the 11th century BCE, the Perizzites became one of the first victims of the expansion of this war-like Indo-European people. In the long-term confrontation between the Philistines and the Hebrews for hegemony in Canaan, the Perizzites, like all the Amorite peoples, clearly chose the side of the latter. Perhaps their choice was influenced by their West Semitic origin, culture, and language in the face of the alien Indo-European newcomers. As it turned out, they were not mistaken in taking the side of the winner. King David inflicted such crushing defeats on the Philistines that they abandoned their policy of expansion in Canaan once and for all. From then on, the Perizzite Shephelah became part of the United Monarchy, and after its split (931-928 BCE) it passed to Judah.

Indeed, some Perizzite cities along the border between Judah and Philistia often shifted their political allegiance depending on which of their neighbors was stronger. For example, during the reign of the Judahite king Jehoram (849–842 BCE), when his kingdom was weakened by internal political strife and a prolonged war with Edom, the city of Libnah – a powerful fortress situated on the strategically important route from Philistia to Jerusalem – rebelled against Judah. "At that time Libnah also revolted against his rule because he had forsaken the Lord, the God of his ancestors" (2 Chr. 21:10). Libnah was one of Judah's western outposts on the border with the Philistines, and its defection represented a significant loss for Jehoram's kingdom. Although the city was assigned to the Levites for settlement following its conquest by the Hebrew tribes, the majority of its population remained Perizzite. The city's leaders evidently preferred to change their political orientation and entered into an alliance with their western neighbors, the Philistines.

However, the majority of the Perizzites merged so rapidly with the Judahite population that they became fully Judaized, demonstrating not only loyalty to Judah but also remarkable heroism during the devastating Assyrian invasion of 701–700 BCE. The Assyrian army became bogged down for an extended period near Lachish, the principal city of the former Perizzite Shephelah. The siege proved exceptionally difficult, as the city's defenders inflicted heavy losses on the Assyrian forces. The Assyrian king Sennacherib was so impressed by the scale of the battle that he commissioned bas-reliefs in his palace at Nineveh depicting the storming of Lachish. Even after Lachish fell, the Judaized Perizzites continued to resist. The city of Libnah, which had by that time once again become part of Judah, successfully withstood Assyrian attacks for many months, providing crucial support to the besieged Jerusalem.

6. Sennacherib's siege of Lachish. Relief from Nineveh.

Archaeological evidence confirms the terrible devastation inflicted by the Assyrians on the Shephelah, the most fertile region of Judah. Its population, which had constituted nearly half of Judah's total population, was reduced by roughly threefold. Most cities, including Lachish – the second most important city in the kingdom – were left in ruins (Finkelstein I. and Silberman N.A. *The Bible Unearthed,* pp. 263-264). Assyrian sources likewise speak of the forced resettlement of part of the Shephelah's population to Assyria and even give the figure of 200,115 deportees. Of course, this number is a clear exaggeration, highly characteristic of Assyrian victory reports, but it nevertheless testifies to the deportation of a significant portion of the Judahite population of Perizzite origin. None of the available sources, either biblical or extra-biblical, report their return to Judah.

More than a century later, the cities of the Perizzite Shephelah were once again besieged by conquerors from Mesopotamia – this time by the Babylonians – and once again became a serious obstacle for them. The most stubborn resistance to the Babylonian army was offered by two cities, Lachish and Azekah. Both were powerful fortresses located in the Shephelah region and guarded this fertile area as well as the approaches to Jerusalem from the south and west. To date, twenty-one fragments of correspondence between the commander of the Lachish garrison and his superior in Jerusalem have been discovered in the ruins of ancient Lachish.

Judging by this fragmentary evidence, the defenders of the Judahite cities maintained contact with one another by means of fire signals from fortress towers. The absence of a signal fire at night indicated the fall of a city. Thus, for example, it became known that Azekah was the first to fall to the Babylonian onslaught. One of the fragments of correspondence states that during this difficult time for Judah, the Lachish garrison continued to maintain contact with Egypt, Judah's ally, in the hope that the Egyptians would sooner or later come to its aid.

The complete merging of the Perizzites with the Judahites had occurred long before the destruction of the First Jerusalem Temple and the fall of Judah in 587–586 BCE. Therefore, those descendants of the Perizzites who found themselves in the half-century Babylonian captivity entered it already as Judahites.

Transjordanian Amorites (Kingdoms of Sihon and Og)

The eastern half of Canaan – Transjordan – was a vast territory dominated by semi-nomadic Amorite groups. They appeared there at approximately the same time as their brethren to the west of the Jordan River, in the 23rd–20th centuries BCE. Unlike the western Amorites, however, they did not settle permanently for a long time and continued to lead a semi-nomadic way of life until the 12th–11th centuries BCE. The southern and eastern regions of Transjordan, which were more arid and sparsely populated, belonged to peoples related to the Hebrews – the Edomites, Moabites, and Ammonites. The central and northern parts of Transjordan, especially the areas adjacent to the Jordan River, were more fertile and richer in water resources. It was in these lands that the Amorite kingdoms of Sihon and Og, mentioned in the biblical books of Numbers and Deuteronomy, were located.

The kingdom of Sihon occupied the central Transjordanian region between the Arnon stream, which flowed into the Dead Sea, and the Jabbok River, a tributary of the Jordan. Most of the population of this kingdom consisted of semi-nomadic Amorites, who were little different from their immediate neighbors – the Moabites and Ammonites. It is true that the land on which the kingdom of Sihon was located had been taken from Moab and Ammon, and this became the cause of constant strife between them. However, the indigenous population of these territories were not Amorites at all, but the people known as the Rapha (Rephaim), who, despite mixing with West Semitic newcomers, managed to survive there at least until the 10th century BCE. The Book of Numbers reminds us of this: "For Heshbon was the city of King Sihon of the Amorites, who had fought against the former king of Moab and captured all his land as far as the Arnon. Therefore the singers say, 'Come to Heshbon; let it be built; let the city of Sihon be established. For fire came out from Heshbon, flame from the city of Sihon. It devoured Ar of Moab and swallowed up the heights of the Arnon. Woe to you, O Moab! You are undone, O people of Chemosh! He has made his sons fugitives and his daughters captives to an Amorite king Sihon" (Num. 21:26–29).

The second wave of Hebrew tribes, led by Moses out of Egypt at the beginning of the 12th century BCE, inevitably encountered the borders of Sihon's kingdom on their way to Canaan. This is how the biblical text describes this encounter: "Then Israel sent messengers to King Sihon of the Amorites, saying, "Let me pass through your land; we will not turn aside into field or vineyard; we will not drink the water of any well; we will go by the King's Highway until we have passed through your territory." But Sihon would not allow Israel to pass through his territory. Sihon gathered all his people together and went out against Israel to the wilderness; he came to Jahaz and fought against Israel. Israel put him to the sword and took possession of his land from the Arnon to the Jabbok, as far as to the Ammonites, for the boundary of the Ammonites was strong. Israel took all these towns, and Israel settled in all the towns of the Amorites, in Heshbon, and in all its villages" (Num. 21:21-25).

To the north of Sihon's lands was the second Amorite kingdom, ruled by Og, a descendant of the Rephaim. Its territory extended from the Jabbok River in the south to the sources of the Jordan in the north and included not only the northern part of the Jordan Valley but also the present-day Golan Heights, which were then known as the regions of Bashan and Argov. In addition to the semi-nomadic Amorites, Og's kingdom still contained a significant population of Rephaim who, as in the land of Sihon, represented the autochthonous inhabitants of these territories. In the 12th century BCE, new groups of Western Semites – the Arameans – began to penetrate Og's lands from the northeast, initially in a peaceful manner, though they still constituted a clear minority of the population. The Bible mentions the fate of the legendary king Og and his country in a markedly laconic manner: "Then they [Israelites] turned and went up the road to Bashan, and King Og of Bashan came out against them, he and all his people, to battle at Edrei. But the Lord said to Moses, "Do not be afraid of him, for I have given him into your hand, with all his people and his land. You shall do to him as you did to King Sihon of the Amorites, who lived in Heshbon. So, they killed him, his sons, and all his people, until there was no survivor left, and they took possession of his land" (Num. 21:33-35).

The possessions of Sihon were divided between two Hebrew tribes: the southern tribe of Reuben and the northern tribe of Gad. Since Moab and Ammon regarded these lands as their own, Reuben found itself in chronic conflict with the Moabites, and Gad with the Ammonites. As for the territory of Og's kingdom, it passed primarily to the northern tribe of Manasseh, from the "House of Joseph." Following the settlement of the Hebrews in Transjordan, the northeastern part of the Jordan Valley came to be known by a new name – Gilead – and the term "Gileadites" began to be used to refer to the inhabitants of this region, primarily members of the two northern Hebrew tribes of Gad and Manasseh.

The Bible provides contradictory information regarding the fate of the Transjordanian Amorites and Rephaim. The Book of Deuteronomy states unequivocally: "At that time we captured all his towns, and in each town we utterly destroyed men, women, and children. We left not a single survivor. Only the livestock we kept as spoil for ourselves, as well as the plunder of the towns that we had captured" (Deut. 2:34–35). However, the earlier Book of Numbers speaks of the intention of the tribes of Reuben, Gad, and Manasseh to build fortified cities in order to protect their families from the local inhabitants before departing to conquer Canaan: "Then they came up to him and said, 'We will build sheepfolds here for our flocks and towns for our little ones, but we will take up arms as a vanguard before the Israelites until we have brought them to their place. Meanwhile, our little ones will remain in the fortified towns because of the inhabitants of the land'" (Num. 32:16–17).

Thus, if it was necessary to provide protection from the local population, such a population must certainly have remained in place. Most likely, the Book of Numbers, as the earlier source, preserves more reliable historical information, whereas the later Book of Deuteronomy was guided less by a factual presentation of events than by didactic considerations – namely, how idolaters should be treated so that they would not lead monotheists astray from the true faith. Consequently, the Amorites and Rephaim of these territories remained entirely in their places and quickly merged with the Hebrew population.

2.3. Aramean Peoples: Geshurites and Maachatites

The Arameans represented the third and final wave of West Semitic tribes that filled the lands of Fertile Crescent. Like the two earlier waves of Western Semites – the Canaanites and the Amorites – they were displaced from their common Semitic homeland in the upper reaches of the Tigris and Euphrates by the movement of Indo-European tribes. Climate change, which caused drought and famine across vast areas of Eurasia in the late 13th–early 12th centuries BCE, led not only to the invasions of the Sea Peoples and the collapse of the Hittite Empire, but also pushed large numbers of Aramean tribes southward into Syria and Mesopotamia. As a result, all of Syria and Mesopotamia gradually came to speak Aramaic, and this language became the lingua franca of the entire ancient Near East for a long period. Only two regions of the Levant – the Lebanese coast and Canaan – managed to avoid Aramaization and to preserve their Canaanite–Amorite population. The Arameans ultimately settled along the northeastern borders of Canaan. The Aramean tribe of the Geshurites settled in the area of what is today the Golan Heights, while another group of Arameans – the Maachatites – established themselves in the region of Mount Hermon and the Beqaa Valley. It would not be entirely correct to include the Geshurites and Maachatites among the peoples of pre-Israelite Canaan, since they appeared in the northeastern part of Canaan at approximately the same time as the Hebrews returned to the country from Egypt. Moreover, their numbers were relatively small. Nevertheless, the Aramean peoples, along with their language and culture, played such a significant role in the history of the Israelite and Judahite kingdoms that it is worth mentioning all the Aramean tribes that were present in Canaan.

At the end of the 11th century BCE, the Geshurites and Maachatites established small kingdoms of their own – Geshur and Maacah – which became vassals and tributaries of King David. The mother of David's favored son, Absalom, was the daughter of the ruler of Geshur, and it was there, in Aramean Geshur, that Absalom hid from his father's wrath for several years. After the division of the United Monarchy, Geshur and Maacah became integral parts of the Kingdom of Israel and completely lost their autonomy. The territories of these former kingdoms constituted the only area in Canaan at that time where Aramaic was spoken.

In the 12th–10th centuries BCE, the population of what is now the Golan Heights and the Mount Hermon region (then known as Bashan and Argov) was highly mixed and consisted of four ethnic components: the remnants of the Rephaim (the indigenous inhabitants of these areas), the semi-nomadic Amorites, the Hebrew tribe of Manasseh, and the Arameans (the Geshurites and Maachatites). All of these groups, with the exception of the Rephaim, represented closely related West Semitic peoples. It is noteworthy that the Book of Genesis classifies the Arameans and the Hebrews as descendants of Shem, whereas it assigns the peoples of Canaan (for example, the Canaanites, Hivites, Hittites, and Jebusites) to the descendants of Ham. Thus, for the biblical authors, the Arameans were considered much closer to the Hebrews than were the peoples of Canaan (Gen. 10:21–23). Moreover, the Book of Genesis reports that Milka – the wife of Nahor and sister-in-law to the patriarch Abraham – bore him eight sons. Among them was Kemuel, the forefather of the Arameans. Thus, while Genesis defines Abraham as a "Hebrew," it also clearly identifies his Aramean origins (Gen. 22:21–23). Furthermore, the text identifies both Bethuel (Abraham's nephew) and Laban (Rebekah's brother) as Arameans. The name of Harran, Abraham's homeland where his relatives remained, was eventually changed to Aram-Naharaim and later to Padan-Aram; both names are directly linked to the Aramean people (Gen. 24:10; 25:20; 27:2, 5). Finally, Deuteronomy explicitly states that the ancestors of the Hebrews were nomadic Arameans: "A wandering Aramean was my ancestor" (Deut. 26:5).

Consequently, biblical sources indirectly confirm the assumption that the Amorites and Arameans were originally a single West Semitic people that later split. One group, the Amorites, departed their common homeland between the 23rd and 20th centuries BCE, while the Arameans followed a millennium later. The cultural and linguistic differences between them developed primarily due to their separation over that thousand-year period.

3. Hurrians

The southward and eastward migration of Indo-Europeans led to the large-scale displacement of Semitic tribes from their ancestral homelands in northwestern Mesopotamia. However, the Semites were not the only group uprooted by this movement; a similar fate befell the Hurrians of Eastern Anatolia. Forced southward, the Hurrians settled in northern Syria and Mesopotamia, significantly displacing the Semitic populations already established there. Hurrian names begin to appear in northern Mesopotamian records as early as the late 3rd millennium BCE. This ethnic group established several independent states, the most prominent of which was Mitanni. The Hurrians were ethnically and linguistically distinct from the Semites, the Indo-Europeans, and the Neolithic inhabitants of Canaan; their precise origins and language remain an enigma to this day. It is highly probable that the Hurrians were an autochthonous people of the Southern Trans-Caucasus and Eastern Anatolia, closely related to the groups that later founded the state of Urartu.

The presence of the Hurrians in Canaan is irrefutably evidenced by the Amarna letters, which mention Canaanite rulers with names of clear Hurrian origin, even though these individuals represented West Semitic culture and language. This situation is echoed by another historical fact: during the reign of Pharaoh Amenhotep II (1427–1397 BCE), the Egyptians referred to Canaan as the "land of Haru", using the same term for both the Hurrians and their territories. Furthermore, a significant number of seals characteristic of the Hurrians of Mitanni have been unearthed throughout Canaan; interestingly, many of these date to the period following the collapse of the Mitanni state. Additionally, archaeological evidence of this ethnic presence extends to southern Canaan, where a tablet inscribed with Hurrian names was discovered in the city of Gezer (Mazar A. *Archaeology of the Land of the Bible,* p.192). Unfortunately, we lack contemporary written sources that explicitly explain the arrival of the Hurrians or their specific role within Canaan. The most probable window for their appearance is the second half of the 16th century to the early 15th century BCE. This period marked the zenith of Mitanni military power – the preeminent Hurrian state – when its borders expanded into southern Syria. It is unlikely the Hurrians arrived much later, as Canaan soon fell under prolonged Egyptian hegemony. Had the Hurrians invaded during that time, the Egyptians surely would have recorded such incursions in their victory steles or temple bas-reliefs. Conversely, a pre-16th-century arrival is equally improbable, as the Hurrian southern frontier had not yet extended beyond Northern Syria. It was during the second half of the 16th century BCE, at the height of Mitanni's expansion, that numerous cities across southern Syria and Canaan were destroyed. While some historians attribute this wave of devastation to Egyptian military campaigns – allegedly aimed at eliminating the remaining Hyksos and their allies – the Canadian Egyptologist Donald Redford challenges this narrative. Redford argues that the Egyptian army under Pharaoh Ahmose I and his immediate successors was simply too weak to inflict such widespread destruction. He points out that the Egyptians struggled to capture the Hyksos capital of Avaris by direct assault. Furthermore, it took them three years to seize Sharuhen, a relatively minor city in southern Canaan. Even sixty years later, Thutmose III – often called the "Napoleon of Ancient Egypt"

– required a seven-month siege to take Megiddo, a mid-sized Canaanite city. Consequently, Redford rightly notes that we have absolutely no reason to attribute the destruction of Canaanite cities to the Egyptian army during this period. In turn, Redford suggested that these devastations should either be attributed to a later period – specifically the campaigns of Thutmose III – or that the responsibility lies with Mitanni. If we assume that the Hurrians invaded Canaan during the second half of the 16th century BCE, the ultimate defeat of the Hyksos (the West Semitic rulers of Egypt) becomes far more understandable. They would have been forced to wage a war on two fronts; at the decisive phase of their struggle against the Theban pharaohs, they were likely cut off from the vital support of their Canaanite allies.

During this upheaval, Hurrian groups from Mitanni successfully penetrated Canaan, seizing power in several key cities. These invaders were likely a small military elite rather than a mass migration, as there is no archaeological evidence of a large-scale Hurrian ethnic presence or a complete cultural displacement in Canaan. Moreover, the frequency of Hurrian names in written documents does not by itself indicate the degree of Hurrianization of the Canaanite population, since writing was generally used by the local elite, who were the group most closely integrated with the newcomer conquerors. Judging by the letters from the Amarna archive, the Hurrians formed the ruling elite only in certain Canaanite city-states, which suggests that their penetration into Canaan occurred not by peaceful means, but through the conquest of some of its cities. Later, in the 14th–13th centuries BCE, the defeats of Mitanni in its wars with the Hittites, and subsequently with the Assyrians, led to the arrival in Canaan of a new wave of Hurrians – this time not as conquerors, but as refugees. Be that as it may, it is necessary to acknowledge the obvious fact that from the second half of the 16th to the early 15th centuries BCE, part of the ruling elite of Canaan became Hurrian in origin. These changes in the composition of the country's population took place during the period when the Hebrews were in Egypt; therefore, the appearance of the Hurrians could not be reflected in biblical sources. In any case, by the time the Hebrews returned from Egypt, the Hurrian groups had already been largely assimilated into the surrounding West Semitic population.

Several researchers associate the Hurrians with the biblical Horites, based on the obvious similarity of their ethnonyms. However, they are unable to offer any satisfactory explanation of how the Hurrians, who lived in northern Mesopotamia in the 20th–18th centuries BCE, could simultaneously have ended up in the region of Seir, more than a thousand miles from their area of settlement. Moreover, according to the Bible, the people of Hori inhabited Mount Seir long before the arrival of Esau. This fact excludes any connection between them and the Hurrians, who at that time were still located in northern Mesopotamia. In addition, unlike the biblical Horites, who occupied a subordinate position in the semi-desert regions of Edom, the historical Hurrians – who appeared in Canaan much later – became part of the ruling class. Moreover, they were present not among nomadic groups on the periphery of the country, but in the flourishing urban centers of Canaan. A similar confusion can be observed here as in the case of the Indo-European Hittites and the Semitic Hittites of the Bible. It is possible that in some biblical texts the Hurrians are referred to as Hittites. In general, the ethnonym "Hittites," which is mentioned many times in the Bible, appears to be a collective designation that concealed not so much the Hittites proper as various Hurrian and Indo-European groups present in Canaan.

4. Indo-Europeans

4.1. Philistines

The Philistines can be regarded as a people of pre-Israelite Canaan only conditionally, bearing in mind that they appeared in the southwest of the country shortly before its conquest by the Hebrews. At the same time, it should be noted that the northern Hebrew tribes arrived in Canaan about a thousand years earlier, and the southern tribes about eight hundred years earlier, than the Philistines. Nevertheless, the Philistines succeeded in establishing themselves in Canaan around 1200 BCE, just before the return of the second wave of Hebrew tribes from Egypt, and for this reason they came to be considered one of the peoples of the land. Initially, the Philistines appeared as invaders and enemies of Egypt, and later as its mercenaries and colonists, who were allotted the Gaza region for settlement.

The Philistines were part of the so-called Sea Peoples, a group of peoples of Indo-European origin who arrived by sea from the northwest. The reasons that caused the mass migration of various Indo-European tribes from north to south at the end of the 13th century BCE are unknown, but it can be assumed that this movement was the result of natural phenomena that led to drought and famine in their former areas of settlement. It is also possible that these groups were forcibly pushed southward by other Indo-European peoples advancing from the north. At that time, Asia Minor suffered from such a severe and prolonged drought that the Hittite Empire was compelled to request large shipments of grain from Egypt. The few written monuments discovered at Philistine sites – such as seal inscriptions from Ashdod – belong to the so-called Minoan Linear A script. Unfortunately, this ancient writing system, which originated on Crete, has not yet been fully deciphered. Nevertheless, some information about the Philistines can be derived from their material culture, particularly their ceramics, which display clear features of the Mycenaean style. This points to an Aegean, and more specifically Achaean, origin of the Philistines.

The Bible gives different names for the country from which these people came: in one case, Cyprus; in another, Crete. However, it is most likely that Cyprus or Crete were only stopovers for the ancestors of the Philistines. Their probable homeland was Mycenae in southern Greece – the hometown of the legendary King Agamemnon. In the second half of the 13th century BCE, Dorian tribes invaded the Peloponnese from the north and, over the course of a century, destroyed not only Mycenae but the entire Achaean civilization. Part of the population was enslaved (for example, the helots in Sparta), while others emigrated to the islands of the Aegean Sea, Crete, and Cyprus. In search of a new homeland, the Achaean Greeks, along with other displaced tribes, set their sights on the Nile Delta and Canaan, which were then under Egyptian rule. Bas-reliefs and frescoes from the temple of Ramesses III at Medinet Habu, located within ancient Egyptian Thebes, depict the warriors of these nations alongside carts carrying their families. This was not a predatory raid, but the forced migration of an entire people. However, in the decisive battle against the army of Ramesses III, the coalition of the Sea Peoples was defeated. Consequently, the Philistines (the *Peleset*, as the Egyptians called them) appeared in southwest Canaan not as victors, but as mercenaries and colonists in the service of the pharaoh.

7. Philistine captives, relief at the temple of Ramesses III at Medinet Habu.

A few years after the death of Ramesses III, Egypt's rule over southern Canaan came to an end, and the Philistines became masters of the southern coast. Before their arrival, the local population consisted of Canaanites and the Rephaim – the most ancient inhabitants of the land.

Although the newcomers were outnumbered, they possessed superior military organization and higher-quality weaponry. It was the Philistines who effectively brought the Iron Age to Canaan; they possessed the secrets of iron smelting and utilized the metal for mass-producing weapons. While West Semitic peoples, including the Israelites, were aware of iron centuries before the Philistines arrived, they lacked the efficient production methods the Philistines used. Consequently, for the Israelites, iron remained a luxury – more expensive than if it had been cast from gold. Iron weapons were far more effective than bronze, and their mass adoption in battle provided a decisive advantage. Furthermore, the Philistines possessed incomparably greater military experience. This expertise was forged both through protracted wars to defend their original homelands and through their tenure as elite mercenaries in the service of the Egyptian pharaohs and Hittite rulers.

The Philistines captured Canaanite cities and established their own communities, governed by leaders known as "seranim" ("lords" or "tyrants"). The Philistine territory was organized as a confederation of five cities: Gaza, Ashkelon, Ashdod, Ekron, and Gath. Over time, the Philistines assimilated quickly with the local Semitic population; they adopted the Canaanite language, and their deities began to take on Semitic names. It is noteworthy that purely Mycenaean pottery has been found only in Ashdod and Ekron – the earliest Philistine settlements. In later strata, the pottery style becomes a hybrid Aegean-Canaanite form.

Between 1985 and 2016, archaeological excavations were conducted in the Ashkelon area under the direction of Lawrence Stager, a professor at Harvard University. During these digs, archaeologists discovered Philistine burials dating from the 12th to the 7th centuries BCE. Analysis of the skeletal remains led to several remarkable discoveries. Specifically, DNA extracted from the bones of 12th-century BCE Philistine children clearly indicated an Aegean (specifically Cretan) origin. The artifacts found within these graves further corroborated their Aegean roots. However, DNA from skeletons dating to the 10th–9th centuries BCE revealed a complete physical assimilation of the Philistines with the local Canaanites – a shift that was equally evident in their evolving material culture.

8. Philistine pottery example

The Philistine threat was already well known to both Moses and Joshua. The former, not wanting a military clash with them, refused to lead his people from Egypt along the shortest route to Canaan, which ran along the seacoast through the lands of the Philistines. The latter, as the Bible admits, "could not drive them out." The initial blow of the overseas aliens was taken by the Israelite tribe of Dan, the Philistines' closest neighbor. Its leader and judge, Samson, dedicated his life to repelling Philistine aggression; however, the tribe could not withstand the pressure of its warlike neighbors and, leaving its tribal territory, was forced to find a new homeland in northern Galilee.

The second major clash occurred during the time of the judge Shamgar, son of Anath, "who killed six hundred of the Philistines with an oxgoad" (Judges 3:31). However, this was only a trial run. Their main expansion began later, in the 11th century BCE. From the story of the high priest Eli, we already know about a major battle with the Philistines at Ebenezer and Aphek, which ended with the defeat of the Israelites and the capture of the shrine of the Hebrew tribes – the Ark of the Covenant. Under the last judge and high priest, Samuel, the situation stabilized somewhat: the northern and southern Hebrew tribes managed to successfully repel several attacks by the Philistines, although wars with them continued throughout the years of Samuel's reign. On this occasion, the biblical text contains a short but very significant phrase: "The towns that the Philistines had taken from Israel were restored to Israel, from Ekron to Gath, and Israel recovered their territory from the hand of the Philistines. There was peace also between Israel and the Amorites" (1 Sam. 7:14). It is probable that the clashes for the lands of Canaan between the Hebrew tribes and the Amorite (and Canaanite) peoples ended, and the Western Semites united to fight their most dangerous enemy: the Philistines.

The first king of Israel, Saul, won an important victory over the Philistines at Michmash in the center of the country. This was achieved even though his army was incomparably worse-armed than the Philistines. Fearing rebellion, the Philistines forbade the Hebrew tribes dependent on them from engaging in blacksmithing. As a result of this policy, "there was no smith to be found throughout all the land of Israel, for the Philistines said, 'The Hebrews must not make swords or spears for themselves,' so all the Israelites went down to the Philistines to sharpen their plowshares, mattocks, axes, or sickles… So, on the day of the battle neither sword nor spear was to be found in the possession of any of the people with Saul and Jonathan, but Saul and his son Jonathan had them" (1 Sam. 13:19–22). This largely explains why biblical heroes and judges fought the Philistines with unusual weapons ill-suited for warfare, such as Samson with a donkey's jawbone and Shamgar, son of Anath, with an oxgoad.

The Hebrews not only fought the Philistines but also served them in the military. The future King David, fleeing from Saul's persecution, was forced to hide among his enemies. While in the service of Achish, the ruler of the prominent Philistine city of Gath, David and his men lived as military settlers in the border town of Ziklag, guarding Philistine lands from invasions by nomadic tribes from the Negev and northern Sinai. It is probable that these military settlers enjoyed sufficient freedom in choosing the targets of their campaigns; otherwise, David would not have been able to avoid clashes with his own tribe. However, David and his detachment were far from the only Hebrews in the military service of the Philistines. The Bible also mentions other Hebrews who were in the Philistine camp on the eve of battles with Saul's army. As follows from the biblical text, however, they proved unreliable in the war against their fellow tribesmen and often went over to their side during the battles.

Wars between the Philistines and the Hebrews continued throughout the period of the Judges and the reign of Saul, the first Israelite king. These conflicts were fought with varying degrees of success; neither side could achieve a decisive victory to establish total hegemony over Canaan. Only Saul's defeat at the Battle of Mount Gilboa – where the king and three of his sons perished – seemed to radically shift the balance in favor of the Philistines. Following this, the United Monarchy collapsed, allowing the Philistines to briefly assert power over all of Canaan. However, David's accession to the throne in Judah and the subsequent re-establishment of his alliance with the northern tribes provoked renewed Philistine attacks and the resumption of their "hundred-year war." This time, leading the reunited monarchy, David inflicted such crushing defeats on the Philistines that they ceased to pose a threat to the Israelites or their Amorite allies.

The split of the United Monarchy eased the pressure on Philistine cities, allowing them to regain independence from their Israelite and Judahite neighbors. However, discord and mutual strife affected more than just the Hebrews; internal conflict also struck the Philistine pentapolis, and the union of the five cities dissolved permanently. Each city began to pursue its own foreign policy and, eventually, to war with one another. The collapse of the Philistine alliance coincided with the final Canaanization of these Indo-European newcomers. They merged completely with the local Canaanites and Rephaites (Rephaim), who significantly outnumbered them. By the 9th century BCE, this originally Aegean-Achaean ethnic group had become effectively West Semitic and Canaanite in physical, cultural, and linguistic terms. In the end, only the ethnonym "Philistines" and the regional name "Philistia" remained as vestiges of their past. A millennium later, the Romans used this name to rename Judea "Palestine," an intentional effort to erase the traditional name of the homeland of the rebellious Jews.

The Philistine cities themselves did not retain their independence for long. As early as the reigns of the first Israelite kings – Nadab, Baasha (909–886 BCE), and Elah – Israel began conducting military campaigns into Philistia. This military onslaught intensified under the Israelite kings Omri and Ahab (873–852 BCE). Simultaneously, the Judahite king Jehoshaphat (870–846 BCE) reduced several Philistine cities to tributaries. Only the sudden strengthening of Aram-Damascus saved these cities from total subordination to Israel and Judah. However, this relief did not bring freedom; instead, the Philistine cities were utterly defeated by the invading forces of Hazael, the most powerful king of Aram-Damascus.

Later, the weakening of Aram-Damascus due to its wars with Assyria allowed the Israelites and Judahites to re-establish control over the coastal Philistine cities. The Hebrew kingdoms divided Philistia between them: the northern territory fell to Israel, while the southern portion went to Judah. In 770 BCE, the Judahite king Azariah (Uzziah) captured Ashdod – then the preeminent Philistine city – dismantled its walls and stationed a garrison there. Judah's dominance over southern Philistia endured until the Assyrian invasion. In 734 BCE, the Assyrians seized the Philistine cities and subsequently the entire Southern Levant. Decades later, in 711 BCE, King Hezekiah of Judah led a regional uprising against Assyrian rule. While most Philistine cities joined the rebellion, others – led by Ekron – remained loyal to the Assyrians. In response, Hezekiah conquered Ekron, deposed its ruler, and compelled the remaining

Philistine cities to expel the Assyrian forces. However, the anti-Assyrian rebellion ultimately failed, and Hezekiah was forced to withdraw from Philistia. The Assyrians retaliated harshly against the rebellious cities; Ashdod and Ashkelon, in particular, were destroyed, and the majority of their inhabitants were deported to Assyria. Yet Assyrian dominance over Philistia proved short-lived. Half a century later, exhausting wars with neighboring powers forced the Assyrians to abandon the Southern Levant permanently. Egyptian Pharaoh Psammetichus I moved to exploit this power vacuum, attempting to seize Philistia. His progress, however, was painstakingly slow – he reportedly spent twenty-nine years on the siege of Ashdod alone.

Ultimately, it was not the Egyptians, but the Babylonians, who dealt the fatal blow to Philistia. In 605–604 BCE, the Babylonian king Nebuchadnezzar II razed most of the Philistine cities – including Ashdod – and deported their populations to Mesopotamia, from which they never returned. In doing so, he eradicated the final remnants of Philistine ethnic and cultural identity, effectively ending the history of the Philistines in Canaan. Although the geographical name "Philistia" persisted for the southwestern region of the land, its subsequent inhabitants had no historical or ancestral connection to the Philistine people.

4.2. Tjeker and Sherdanu

The Philistines were not the only Sea People to settle in Canaan. Another group of Aegean origin, the Tjeker, established themselves on the northern coast in the city of Dor. A third people, the Sherdanu (Sherden), also secured territory in northern Canaan.

Historians rely on a significant ancient Egyptian document from approximately 1100 BCE, known as "The Report of Wenamun," to understand this period. The text details the journey of an official from the Temple of Amon at Karnak to the Phoenician city of Byblos to procure cedar for the god's ceremonial barge. During his travels, Wenamun stayed in Dor and confirmed that the city was ruled by the Tjeker.

His narrative suggests that the rulers of other coastal Canaanite cities were also of Aegean or Anatolian origin. Together with the Phoenicians, these groups maintained a monopoly over maritime trade in the Eastern Mediterranean (*Ancient Near Eastern Texts,* pp. 25-29).

It can be assumed that Wenamun's information regarding the Sea Peoples in northern Canaan is highly reliable. The Egyptians were intimately acquainted with these groups; many had served as mercenaries in the Egyptian army as early as the 14th century BCE. The Amarna letters specifically mention the Sherden in the service of the Pharaoh, and they later participated in the Battle of Kadesh under Ramesses II. Furthermore, Rib-Hadda, the ruler of Byblos (Gubla), makes early mention of the Sherdanu presence on the Lebanese coast.

Later, during the reign of Pharaoh Merneptah, a coalition of Sea Peoples – including the Sherden, Shekelesh, Lukka, Tursha, Akawasha, and Denyen – allied with the Libyans to launch repeated attacks on Egypt. However, it was during the reign of Ramesses III that the Egyptians gained their most comprehensive knowledge of these groups, as the Sea Peoples began a mass migration toward the Eastern Mediterranean, encompassing Anatolia, Syria, Canaan, and the Nile Delta.

If the Lebanese and Syrian coasts suffered extensively from the attacks of the Sea Peoples, and if several groups settled in southwestern Canaan, it is unsurprising that they were present on the northern Canaanite coast as well. Of the three groups recorded in Canaan – the Philistines, Tjeker, and Sherdanu – the Philistines played by far the most significant role. The other Sea Peoples were numerically inferior and left a less substantial mark on the region's history.

It is possible that many of these Sea Peoples were categorized under the general label of "Hittites" on the eve of the Israelite conquest. Ultimately, these Indo-European groups were relatively small and were completely assimilated into the surrounding West Semitic population, eventually becoming part of the fabric of the Israelites and Judahites.

4.3 Maryannu (Indo-Aryans)

The Amarna tablets identify several rulers of Canaanite and Syrian city-states with distinctly Indo-Aryan names, such as Biridashwa of Yanoam, Shuvardata of Keilah, Yashdata of Taanakh, and Artamanya of Zir-Bashan. Furthermore, biblical texts contain names like the Jebusite Araunah (Aravenna) of Jerusalem, which also suggest an Indo-Aryan or Hurrian-Mitanni origin. How and when did these Indo-Aryans reach Canaan? The most plausible timeline involves the military expansion of the Hurrian state of Mitanni during the late 16th and early 15th centuries BCE. Although the Hurrians and Indo-Aryans were ethnically and linguistically distinct, both groups penetrated into Canaan simultaneously as part of the general military forces of Mitanni.

It is known that the Kingdom of Mitanni, located in northern Syria and southeastern Anatolia, was ruled by a royal dynasty of Aryan origin. Moreover, the entire military elite – especially the charioteers – consisted of Indo-Aryans. This class of Aryan warriors was called the *maryannu* (maryanu). They constituted the main military force and the ruling class in a state whose population consisted predominantly of Hurrians, who had nothing in common with either the Aryans or the Indo-Europeans. The *maryannu*, having captured several Canaanite cities, founded their own ruling dynasties there, but over time they adopted the language and culture of the surrounding population. By the time the Hebrews returned from Egypt, only Aryan personal names remained from the Indo-Aryans (*maryannu*); their bearers had already become Western Semites.

5. Unidentified Peoples: Girgashites and Kadmonites

Among all the pre-Israelite peoples of Canaan mentioned in the Bible, two of them remain particularly elusive: the Girgashites and the Kadmonites. The Book of Genesis identifies the Girgashites as descendants of Canaan – the legendary progenitor of the region's inhabitants – which underscores their deep roots in the land's history. This lineage suggests they were likely indigenous, distinguishing them from the Hurrians or Indo-European groups who arrived in the region much later. Yet, despite frequent mentions across several biblical books, the text remains silent on exactly where the Girgashites lived. Moreover, the Bible does not mention any clashes or direct contact between the Hebrews and the Girgashites. Given that the name "Girgashite" is likely not of Semitic origin, it is reasonable to assume they were an indigenous Canaanite group that had assimilated so thoroughly with their West Semitic neighbors that they had virtually disappeared by the time the Hebrews entered the land.

There are two notable attempts to link the Girgashites with other known ethnonyms. The first is based on a Hittite cuneiform tablet describing the Karkisha (either a people or a city-state) who fought alongside the Hittites against Ramesses II at the Battle of Kadesh. However, this theory faces a major obstacle: the Karkisha were allies from distant Anatolia, not from within the land of Canaan.

The second version appears in New Testament commentary, where the Girgashites are associated with the non-Jewish inhabitants of the "country of the Gadarenes" on the northeastern shore of the Sea of Galilee (Lake Kinneret). In the Gospel of Mark, Jesus visits this Hellenistic settlement and casts a "legion" of demons out of a possessed man into a herd of swine (Mark 5:1–20). Local pagans, unsettled by the event, urged Jesus to depart. Proponents of this version suggest "Gergesenes" (a variant reading in some manuscripts) refers to the ancient Girgashites. However, this overlooks the fact that the ethnic landscape of the first century CE was vastly different from that of 12th-century BCE Canaan. By the Roman period, the indigenous population of Canaan had long been fully assimilated into the Judeans, becoming an integral part of the Jewish people. Moreover, not a single source – biblical or extra-biblical – reports the presence of Girgashites on the shores of the Sea of Galilee or within Judea. Attempts to 'fit' the New Testament toponym 'Gadara' to the Old Testament ethnonym 'Girgash' are frankly unconvincing.

However, there is a find more compelling than this pseudo-scientific theory: a 13th-century BCE Ugaritic document mentions an individual (perhaps representing a group) named 'grgš' (Girgash). If this is not merely a coincidence, it provides the first extra-biblical confirmation of the Girgashites' existence in Canaan or on the Lebanese coast. Beyond this, however, practically nothing is known of the people themselves.

The situation regarding the 'Kadmonites' is somewhat simpler. Unlike the Girgashites, this group is mentioned only once in the Hebrew Bible (Gen. 15:19). Among biblical scholars, there is a much broader consensus regarding the interpretation of this ethnonym; as a rule, they identify them as the 'Bnei Kedem' ('Sons of the East'), referring to the nomadic and semi-nomadic tribes moving between Canaan and the Euphrates. If this identification is correct, it remains unclear why the specific name 'Kadmonites' was used only once, given that nomads from the northeast were a constant presence in the region. Furthermore, the biblical authors were well aware of these nomadic groups, identifying them specifically as Ishmaelites, Midianites, Amalekites, Kenites, or simply nomadic Amorites. Must we interpret the name 'Kadmonites' solely through the lens of *kedem* ('east')? An alternative translation of the root denotes 'ancient' or 'primordial.' It is possible that this overarching designation referred to the remnants of the land's most archaic population – perhaps even predating the Rephaim – whom only the biblical patriarchs would have encountered four millennia ago. If this is the case, it explains why the name appears only once: it describes a group that had already vanished from the historical stage by the time of later biblical writers.

CHAPTER II

Hebrews and Their Relatives

The Hebrews were Western Semites of Amorite origin, or simply Amorites. In the 23rd-20th centuries BCE semi-nomadic Amorite tribes flooded all of Mesopotamia, Syria, and Canaan. They came to these lands from the common Semitic homeland, located in the upper reaches of the Euphrates and Tigris rivers. But who of this huge mass of Amorites was subsequently considered Hebrews? Only those who came to the land of Canaan and, having lived there for two or three centuries, migrated further due to droughts and famine – to the Nile Delta, to Egypt. The Nile Delta, abundant in water, gradually became the land of Western Semites. By the 18th century BCE, semi-nomadic Amorite tribes gathered in the Nile Delta in such numbers that they became the full masters of the country, and their leaders ruled Egypt under the name of the Hyksos for more than a century. Later, the Egyptians managed to restore their power over the country and, fearing the Western Semites, tried first to oust them from the Nile Delta, and later to enslave those who remained. But can all the Amorites who lived in Egypt be considered the ancestors of the Hebrews? Of course not. Only a part of them, only those who returned to Canaan, began to be called Hebrews. Other Amorites returned to the Lebanese coast and to Syria, that is, to the regions from which they had come to Egypt. All Western Semites who returned from Egypt were called *abiru* (Akkadian) or *'apiru* (Egyptian). In the ancient

Near East, this name usually meant newcomers who had lost their tribal territory and home. According to one version, the ethnonym *'ivri/ibri* ("Hebrew") originated precisely from the word *'abiru*. If so, this term is unfortunate, since it has nothing to do with ethnicity and denotes only a temporary social status.

It was Egypt, or rather their long stay in the Nile Delta, first under the rule of their own, West Semitic pharaohs, and then Egyptian ones, that united and bound together two groups of Amorite tribes from Canaan: the "House of Joseph" and the "House of Jacob." They went to Egypt as semi-nomadic Amorites and returned to Canaan as Hebrews. The mission of Moses, the dramatic exodus from Egypt, the acceptance of the Ten Commandments at Mount Sinai turned these Amorite tribes into related Hebrew tribes. And finally, - the reconquest of their lands in Canaan - returned the displaced Hebrews to their homeland.

By the way, from the ethnic point of view, the Transjordanian peoples – the Edomites, Moabites and Ammonites – much more closely represented the very same ethnos that the biblical patriarch Abraham brought into Canaan. If the tribal group of the patriarch should be called the Hebrews, then Edom, Moab and Ammon deserve this ethnonym incomparably more than the Judahites and Israelites themselves, because these ethnic groups, having settled in the sparsely populated and semi-desert Transjordan, intermixed far less with the local Canaanite peoples than the Hebrew tribes.

To find out what the "original" Hebrews looked like, we must pay attention to their closest nomadic relatives, whom the Egyptians called "Shasu" and neighboring West Semitic peoples called "Sutu."

They are depicted on the bas-reliefs of the northern wall of the Great Hypostyle Hall at Karnak in Egypt. Most likely, under the general name "Shasu", these bas-reliefs depict the Edomites, against whom Pharaoh Seti I (1290-1279 BCE) repeatedly carried out military campaigns. In anthropological, ethnic and linguistic terms, the Edomites, along with the Moabites and Ammonites, were one whole with the Hebrew tribes. However, when the "House of Jacob" returned to Canaan after four centuries of settled life in the Nile Delta, the Hebrews led a different way of life and dressed differently from their brothers - the nomadic Shasu.

1. Northern Hebrew tribes

The ancestors of the northern Hebrew tribes, like most of the Amorites, appeared in Canaan around the 23rd century BCE, that is, three hundred years before Abraham and the southern tribes. They occupied northern and central Canaan and pushed aside other Western Semites - the Canaanites, who had arrived there even earlier, about a thousand years before them. The northern tribes came from northwestern Mesopotamia, but they did not wander through Mesopotamia and were not in Sumer, like their southern brothers. They moved directly to the southwest, through Syria, to Canaan. Although the northern Hebrew tribes, like the southern ones, belonged to the Western Semites of Amorite origin, they, probably, were not closely related to the southern tribes and, unlike them, did not initially trace their genealogy to Abraham, Isaac and Jacob. The authors of the Bible attributed them to the "House of Jacob" much later, when both tribal groups, northerners and southerners, found themselves in the United Monarchy.

The northern tribes, known as "Israel", consisted of two main parts. The first and most important were three closely related tribes: Ephraim, Manasseh, and Benjamin. The first two tribes traced their genealogy directly to the legendary Joseph, who was considered the favorite son of the forefather of the northern tribes - Israel. It is not for nothing that both these tribes were called the "House of Joseph." The third tribe - Benjamin was significantly inferior to them and was considered their junior partner. As a rule, the tribe of Ephraim always claimed leadership in the "House of Joseph," and it also imposed its hegemony on the other northern tribes. The other part of the northern tribes consisted of the tribes of Dan, Naphtali, Gad and Asher, who played a secondary, subordinate role, which was reflected in the biblical canon - the ancestors of these tribes were also considered the sons of the patriarch, but from women with a low social status. The tribes of Zebulun and Issachar stood on an intermediate position between the first and second. At the same time, all these tribes, both the "House of Joseph" and the secondary ones, traced their origins to a common patriarch - Israel.

Somewhere at the end of the 18th century BCE, the northern tribes leave Canaan and go to Egypt, to the Nile Delta. Apparently, the departure of the northern tribes or some of them was explained not so much by drought as by intertribal conflicts. The narrative about Joseph and his brothers sheds light on this problem. The conflict of the "House of Joseph" with the other tribes forced him to leave Canaan for the Nile Delta, where many Amorite tribes had already settled. Later, it was the privileged position of the "House of Joseph" in Hyksos Egypt that attracted the rest of the northern tribes there. In contrast, the southern tribes - the "House of Jacob" - appeared in the Nile Delta much later, only in the second half of the 17th century BCE, and their fate in Egypt was different from that of their northern brothers.

1.1. "House of Joseph"

The "House of Joseph" occupied a special position among all the Hebrew tribes. Unlike the other tribes, it was part of the Hyksos rulers of Egypt, held a privileged position under the Hyksos pharaohs, and patronized the "House of Jacob" and other Amorite tribes that later came to the Nile Delta. The Book of Genesis especially singled out the "House of Joseph" among the other tribes, firstly, as the main military force among the northern tribes, and secondly, for its special position in Egypt. Here are the words of the patriarch Jacob-Israel about his favorite son: "The blessings of your father are stronger than the blessings of the eternal mountains, the bounties of the everlasting hills; may they be on the head of Joseph, on the brow of him who was set apart from his brothers" (Gen. 49:26). The patriarch-father, addressing Joseph, once again singles him out: "I now give to you one portion more than to your brothers, the portion that I took from the hand of the Amorites with my sword and with my bow." (Gen. 48:22).

The "House of Joseph" was not only the first of the Hebrew tribes to go to Egypt, but also the first to return from there to Canaan in the middle of the 15th century BCE. At that time, the Western Semites were not forcibly kept in Egypt, but on the contrary, were expelled as potential enemies and heirs of the Hyksos pharaohs. The Bible points to the same time, reporting that the Temple of Solomon was built 480 years after the arrival of the sons of Israel from Egypt. Knowing that the Temple of Solomon was erected around 960 BCE, we get 1440 BCE as an approximate date of the Exodus from Egypt of several northern tribes.

The "House of Joseph" represented the same Habiru in Canaan that we know about from the letters of the Amarna archive of the 14th century BCE. It was the "House of Joseph" that created the tribal union of Israel, which was mentioned in his stele by Pharaoh Merneptah (1213-1203 BCE). At that time, the area of the Israelite tribal union was limited to the areas of the city of Shechem and later Samaria, that is, the tribal territory of the "House of Joseph." However, Israel, mentioned in the stele of Merneptah, represented a union of only those northern Hebrew tribes that made up the "House of Joseph." Other northern tribes, not to mention the southern ones - the "House of Jacob," were at that time in the Nile Delta, in Egypt, and continued to suffer from forced labor for the Pharaoh. Only later, at the beginning of the 12th century BCE, when the second wave of Hebrew tribes, led by Moses, returned to Canaan from Egypt, the northern tribes of Zebulun, Issachar, Naphtali, Asher, Gad and Dan were able to join the Israelite tribal union. The Israelite alliance included only those tribes that, before their departure to Egypt, had their tribal territories in central and northern Canaan. However, there were exceptions. One southern Hebrew tribe, Reuben, which had been "disadvantaged" in the "House of Jacob," also requested to join the northern Israelite tribal alliance. This new, significantly expanded Israelite tribal alliance was led by Joshua, son of Nun, the leader of the tribe of Ephraim. He carried out the biblical conquest of Canaan in the first half of the 12th century BCE. In reality, this conquest concerned only central and northern Canaan. The southern regions of the country were conquered exclusively by the forces of two southern Hebrew tribes - Judah and Simeon, and much later, in the second half of the 12th century BCE.

After conquering part of Canaan and settling on the land, the Israelite tribal confederation weakened and even temporarily disintegrated. These years are known to us as the biblical period of the Judges, "when everyone did what they wanted." But even during this period of disintegration, the tribe of Ephraim from the "House of Joseph" constantly vied for the role of leader of the northern tribes. It not only refused to recognize the authority of Judge Gideon, who came from the closely related tribe of Manasseh, but also threatened him with war. The Ephraimites' claims to supremacy led them to a fratricidal war with another judge - Jephthah from Gilead (the tribes of Manasseh and Gad). The Gileadites not only defeated the Ephraimites but also massacred them at the Jordan River crossing. The leaders of the tribe of Ephraim did not give up their claims to leadership even at the height of the Philistine aggression, when the elders of all the northern tribes elected Saul to the throne. The Ephraimites were the only ones who did not recognize the first Israelite king Saul, even though he came from the tribe of Benjamin, the closest relative of the same "House of Joseph." Later, Jeroboam, the head of the tribe of Ephraim, organized a rebellion against the king Solomon, and having suffered a defeat, found refuge with the Egyptian pharaoh. The same Jeroboam led the uprising of the northern tribes against the power of Rehoboam, the son of King Solomon. This time he was successful - he split the United Monarchy and became the first king of Israel. The tribe of Ephraim initially dominated the Israelite kingdom. It was not for nothing that the Israelite prophet Hosea noted: "When Ephraim spoke, there was trembling; he was exalted in Israel..." (Hosea 13:1).

1.2. The Tribe of Dan: Semites or Indo-Europeans?

Of all the northern tribes the most enigmatic was Dan. This tribe is not mentioned in the pre-Egyptian period when the Hebrews were living in Canaan. The only exception is the official genealogy, in which the forefather of the tribe, Dan, is named as the son of Jacob-Israel and, moreover, as the son not from his wives, but from the slave girl Bilhah. Thus, it is relegated to the very bottom of the tribal hierarchy. The first information about the tribe of Dan appears only during the period of stay in the desert after the exodus from Egypt. Thus, Oholiab, the son of Ahisamach from the tribe of Dan, is named as a master who helped build and decorate the Ark of the Covenant (Exod. 35:34-35). Another, much more important episode tells of the son of an Egyptian man and an Israelite woman from the tribe of Dan who insulted and cursed the name of God, for which he was put to death by stoning (Lev. 24:10-11). Thus, we have indirect evidence that the tribe of Dan left Egypt not with the "House of Joseph" in the 15th century BCE, but later, together with Moses at the beginning of the 12th century BCE.

Some information about the tribe of Dan is provided by the story about its leader Samson and his uncompromising fight against the Philistines during the period of the Judges. For some reason, none of the Hebrew tribes treated the Philistines with such hostility and did not fight them with such ferocity as the tribe of Dan. After all, the Philistines, having settled in the southwestern part of Canaan, did not exterminate or expel the local population - the Canaanites and the even more ancient Rephaim (or Avvim, as they were called there). That is, the Semitic and pre-Semitic population remained untouched there, and the Bible clearly states this. Why did only the tribe of Dan have to leave its allotted land, adjacent to the territory of the Philistines? Isn't the irreconcilability between the Philistines and the Danites explained by their common Indo-European, or more precisely, Achaean/Aegean origin? As is known, related peoples conflict with each other much more fiercely than with foreigners. And Samson's fight with the Philistines is more like the exploits of the Achaean heroes than the wars of the Israelite judges.

In the victory Song of Deborah there are words that shed light on the origin of the tribe of Dan. In condemning those Israelite tribes that refused to help their brothers in the battle with Sisera, the military chief of King Jabin of Hazor, the Song of Deborah names the tribe of Dan and asks: "And Dan, why did he abide with the ships?" (Judges 5:17). How did the Israelite tribe, former semi-nomads who settled on land, suddenly become seafarers? After all, at that time only the Phoenicians and the Sea Peoples "abide with the ships." If belonging to the Phoenicians immediately disappears, then the Achaean/Aegean origin seems the most plausible.

A Sea People by the name of Danuna are mentioned in Egyptian sources of the 14th century BCE during the reign of the pharaohs Amenhotep III and Akhenaten. During the reign of Ramesses II, mercenaries from the Sea Peoples took part on the side of the Egyptians in the famous Battle of Kadesh against the Hittites. But the first attack of these peoples on Egypt occurred only at the end of the 13th century BCE during the reign of Merneptah. Much later, during the reign of Ramesses III (in the 8th year of his reign), the Sea People by the name of Denyen was named among those who attacked the Egyptian army in the Nile Delta region. Perhaps this is the same people which were called somewhat differently by Hittite sources as Daniya-wana. Finally, Homer spoke of the Danaoi (another name for the Achaeans) who inhabited Argolis and Argos on the Peloponnese peninsula in southern Greece. If all these similar names are not a mere coincidence, and the Israelite tribe of Dan really represented some part of this Aegean people, then its appearance in the Nile Delta dates to the end of the 13th century BCE, when the mass migration of the Sea Peoples to the east and southeast began. If the Danites are directly related to the legendary Danaoi of Argolis, then they were the closest neighbors of the Mycenaeans, who, according to archaeologists, made up a significant part of the Philistines. It is difficult to say how the inhabitants of ancient Argos came to Egypt: were they mercenaries and military settlers in the service of the pharaoh or captives who were taken into slavery with their families. At least, ancient Egyptian sources confirm the existence of a large number of mercenaries and military settlers from the Sea Peoples in the Nile Delta during the reign of Ramesses II and Merneptah. Later, there were even more captives from these people. Be that as it may, in the troubled years, on the eve of the rise to power of Pharaoh Setnakht, when there was a civil war in Egypt, this Sea People could have left Egypt in the same way as the Hebrew tribes of Moses. They could have been part of that numerous "rabble" mentioned in the Bible, which caused so much anxiety and trouble to Moses. If this was so, then in search of their place in Canaan, the Danites joined the Israelite alliance created by the northern tribes. The memory of their stay in Egypt and forced homelessness in Canaan turned out to be stronger than ethnic kinship, and it was this factor that united this group of Indo-Europeans with the Western Semites. Their main enemies became their old neighbors and adversaries from their former homeland – the Philistines, who prevented the Danites from gaining access to the Mediterranean coast. The former seafarers could not confine themselves to agriculture and livestock farming and moved to the northernmost part of Canaan. There, after capturing the Canaanite city of Laish (Leshem), they renamed it Dan and finally settled in their new location. By the way, 3,000-year-old archaeological finds in Tel Dan show Aegean artifacts that may indicate the Aegean origin of the Dan tribe (*Haaretz,* Dec. 4, 2016).

The northern coast of Canaan was controlled by the Phoenicians and the people of Aegean origin Tjeker, with whom the Dan tribe was able to quickly find a common language. Later, all the Sea Peoples who settled in Canaan - the Danites, the Tjeker, the Sherdanu (Sherden), and the Philistines themselves - assimilated with the Western Semites and became an integral part of them. Interestingly, the biblical account of the Danite tribe's migration from the south to the north of Canaan does not mention a single name of any Danite, not even their leaders, although at the same time it names Micah, the head of the Ephraimite clan who gave them temporary refuge. From the episode of the migration of the Danites, it becomes clear that there was not a single Levite priest among them, which once again distinguished them from other Hebrew tribes. One can argue whether the Israelite tribe of Dan was Semitic or Indo-European in origin, but one cannot deny that it was an affiliated tribe, which before the exodus from Egypt had no direct relation to the Hebrews.

2. Southern Hebrew Tribes

The southern Hebrew tribes were part of the last wave of Amorite tribes that appeared in Canaan around the 20th century BCE. These were the nomadic Amorites who, for some reason, were unable to settle in other lands of the Fertile Crescent and therefore decided to join their fellow tribesmen in Canaan. This group of tribes was led by the biblical patriarch Abraham and included the ancestors of not only the southern Hebrew tribes, but also their closest relatives: the Edomites, Moabites, and Ammonites. This group also included the ancestors of the Midianites, Ishmaelites, and those desert peoples who traced their origins to Abraham. Initially, all or some of these Amorite tribes tried to settle in southern Mesopotamia, in particular in the area of the ancient Sumerian city of Ur. But, for some reason unknown to us, they were forced to return to their homeland, to the area of the city of Haran in northwestern Mesopotamia. Unlike the northern Hebrew tribes, the tribes of Abraham settled in the remaining free lands of Canaan, namely in the south and in Transjordan, and later in Sinai.

The southern Hebrew tribes, later known as the "House of Jacob," initially numbered only four tribes: Reuben, Simeon, Levi and Judah. The birthright, that is, seniority, belonged to Reuben, below him in rank were Simeon, then Levi and, finally, Judah came last. During the four-century stay in Egypt, other Amorite tribes that had come from central and northern Canaan also became kin with the "House of Jacob," above all Issachar and Zebulun, and later Gad, Asher, and Naphtali. The last to join them was the small tribe of Dan. All these tribes "adopted" in Egypt will later become known as the northern Hebrew tribes and will leave Egypt as part of the "House of Jacob" under the leadership of Moses. It is noteworthy that the Book of Genesis, which tells about the pre-Egyptian period of the life of the Hebrews, is completely silent about the "adopted", mentioning them only in the official genealogy.

Before leaving for the Nile Delta, the tribe of Reuben managed to maintain its privileges as the eldest in the "House of Jacob." However, after the exodus from Egypt, the leadership in the "House of Jacob" passed to Judah, as the most numerous and powerful southern tribe. Then Reuben, deprived of power, aligned himself with the northern tribes – especially since already in the pre-Egyptian period the tribe of Reuben had the best relations among all the southern tribes with the "House of Joseph," the leader of the northerners. With their assistance, the tribe of Reuben received its allotment in central Transjordan, on lands that had previously belonged to the Amorite kingdom of Sihon. After the split of the United Monarchy, the southern tribe of Reuben remained with the northerners - in Israel.

The tribe of Simeon was considered the second in seniority after Reuben but never claimed primacy. Moreover, in the pre-Egyptian period, and especially after returning from Egypt, it was considered a junior partner of the tribe of Judah. This tribe followed the example of its incomparably more powerful brother in everything. Thus, before leaving for the Nile Delta, the tribe of Simeon, like Judah, became close and even related to the Canaanites of the southern part of the country. For example, the son of the forefather of the tribe of Simeon, Shaul, was descended from a Canaanite woman. After returning from Egypt, both tribes entered into an alliance with the Midianite tribes. This time, the leader of the tribe of Simeon, Zimri, son of Salu, took as his wife Kozbi, daughter of Tzur, leader of a whole group of Midianite tribes. Together with Judah and the Midianites, the tribe of Simeon lingered in the Sinai deserts for four decades, and then, together with the same allies, but separately from the other Hebrew tribes, conquered most of southern

Canaan. And finally, after the conquest, they settled in the Beersheba region in the northern Negev, next to Judah. Already during the period of the United Monarchy (11th-10th centuries BCE), the tribe of Simeon completely merged with the tribe of Judah.

The tribe of Levi was the smallest of all the Hebrew tribes, both southern and northern. In the pre-Egyptian period, this tribe did not stand out in any way. It "distinguished itself" only by the fact that together with another southern tribe - Simeon, it massacred the Hivites of Shechem, which caused extreme indignation of the patriarch Jacob. The tribe of Levi was made famous by Moses, who came from the family of the leader of this tribe. Moses turned his fellow tribesmen, the Levites, not just into priests, but into bearers of the monotheistic tradition and historical memory of the Hebrews. It was the Levites who became the creators of the book of books - the Bible. Moses managed to introduce the Levites into most of the Hebrew tribes and thereby ensure them influence disproportionate to their numbers. However, the "House of Joseph" did not give the Levites even a single allotment in their tribal territories, and this later led to a chronic conflict between northern Levites and the kings of Israel. Unlike most Hebrew tribes, the Levites and their descendants did not leave the pages of Jewish history for a long time. It is the Levites who are credited with the victory of monotheism in Judah; they were the main fighters against all forms of paganism and idolatry. There is an assumption that the so-called "Hasideans" ("righteous"), who led the struggle of the Jews for freedom and faith during the Maccabean wars (167-142 BCE) against the Seleucid Empire, were descendants of the Levites. Perhaps many famous Pharisees in Hasmonean Judea also came from them.

The southern tribe of Judah played an even more important role in Jewish history. It is no coincidence that its name first became the designation of the southern part of Canaan and its population (Judah and Judahites), then passed on to the entire country (Judea) and its people (Judeans). Moreover, this ethnonym also determined the name of the first monotheistic religion in the world (Judaism). How did this unremarkable tribe in the pre-Egyptian period become a determining factor in Jewish history?

Firstly, after the exodus from Egypt, the size of this tribe increased sharply, and it turned into a mega-tribe. During four decades of wandering through the deserts of Sinai and Midian, at least one Midianite tribe, the Kenites, and one Edomite tribe, the Kenizzites, joined him. Moreover, a considerable number of individual Midianite and Edomite clans were incorporated into it, for example the Rechabites and the Maonites. These were the same West Semitic nomads who worshipped Yahweh, whom the Egyptians called the "Shasu of Yahweh." All of them, together with the Hebrews, wanted to conquer southern Canaan. In general, the tradition of assimilation with the local indigenous population was started in the pre-Egyptian period by Judah himself, the forefather of this tribe. He had a Canaanite wife, and all the leaders of this tribe traced their lineage to his son Shelah. And finally, another southern Hebrew tribe, Simeon, quickly merged with the tribe of Judah. The Bible stops mentioning it very early, from the time of King Saul's accession to the throne (late 11th century BCE).

Secondly, the central role of this tribe was strengthened by the priestly clan of the Aaronites. There is reason to believe that the Aaronites were the traditional priestly clan of the "House of Jacob," and they did not come from the tribe of Levi, as stated in the Bible, but rather from the tribe of Judah. The high priest Aaron was not Moses' brother, otherwise the rebellion of the Levite Korah against the Aaronites in the Sinai desert would have lost all meaning. The Aaronites always enjoyed the support of the leaders of the tribe of Judah and, for their part, in every way defended and promoted the interests of this tribe: first in the "House of Jacob," and then in the United Monarchy.

Thirdly, the importance of this tribe was always supported by the fact that the dynasty of King David, which ruled for more than 400 years, came from this tribe. It is not surprising that the Aaronites, who were the same compilers of the Bible as the Levites, did everything to prove the right of the tribe of Judah to leadership in the "House of Jacob."

However, the matter was not simple, because above Judah in rank stood three older brothers - Reuben, Simeon and Levi. Therefore, for each of them, the Aaronites chose from the oral epic such narratives that cast doubt on their right to leadership in the southern tribal group. The right to choose belonged only to their forefather Jacob, and it was in his mouth that the words were put, depriving the eldest sons of claims to leadership. Thus, the eldest, Reuben, was accused of his former relationship with his father's concubine Bilhah: "Reuben, you are my firstborn, my might and the first fruits of my vigor, excelling in rank and excelling in power. Unstable as water, you shall no longer excel because you went up onto your father's bed; then you defiled it – you went up onto my couch!" (Gen. 49:3-4). Simeon and Levi were reminded of the massacre in Shechem, which they carried out in revenge for the fact that the son of the city's ruler dishonored their sister Dinah. "Simeon and Levi are brothers; weapons of violence are their swords. May I never come into their council; may I not be joined to their company, for in their anger they killed men, and at their whim they hamstrung oxen. Cursed be their anger, for it is fierce, and their wrath, for it is cruel! I will divide them in Jacob and scatter them in Israel" (Gen. 49:5-7). After the claims of the elder brothers to leadership have been brushed aside, Judah's right to power follows: "Judah, your brothers shall praise you; your hand shall be on the neck of your enemies; your father's sons shall bow down before you... The scepter shall not depart from Judah, nor the ruler's staff from between his feet, until tribute comes to him, and the obedience of the peoples is his" (Gen. 49:8,10).

The "House of Jacob," which had grown greatly in Egypt due to the Amorite tribes that had joined it, experienced its rise and fall in the Sinai desert. Here at Mount Sinai, the Ten Commandments and the Covenant with the One Lord of Moses were adopted – that is, the religious and political union of the Amorite tribes that had left Egypt was formed. From that moment on, all of them became sons of the "House of Jacob," bound together by Moses' monotheistic idea, which later developed into the first monotheistic religion in the world. However, in this

Sinai desert, the "House of Jacob" also experienced a split. The civil war in Egypt, which had allowed the tribes of Moses to leave this country, ended, and the last great Egyptian pharaoh, Ramesses III (1186-1155 BCE), came to power. Egypt's military strengthening brought southern Canaan back under its control, so the two southern tribes, Judah and Simeon, were unable to begin reconquering their territories in southern Canaan. They were forced to linger in the desert for four decades until the heirs of Ramesses III finally lost all of their father's and grandfather's possessions. However, the remaining tribes of Moses, who were returning to central and northern Canaan, could not remain in the harsh conditions of the wilderness for an indefinite period. Evidently, the schism occurred after the rebellion of Korah. The northern tribes, together with the Levites, under the leadership of Moses and Eleazar, departed for central Canaan. The southern tribe of Reuben, deprived of seniority in favor of the tribe of Judah, joined the northerners. Thus, the original core of the "House of Jacob" was split. The southern tribes of Judah and Simeon, along with their Edomite and Midianite allies, remained in the desert for forty years. Almost the entire Aaronite clan remained with them, except for Eleazar and his family.

The fact that the two southern tribes (Judah and Simeon) were absent from Canaan until at least the middle of the 12th century BCE is confirmed by the Song of Deborah (this is possibly the earliest monument of Hebrew literature, dating back to the 12th century BCE). It lists all the Hebrew tribes except for the two southern ones: Judah and Simeon are eloquently absent there. Thus, if the northern tribes under the leadership of Joshua conquered part of northern and central Canaan in the first half of the 12th century BCE, then the southern ones took possession of the southern part of the country only in the second half of the 12th century BCE. Archaeological data confirm the fact that southern Canaan (historical Judah) was populated by Hebrews only at the end of the 12th – in the 11th centuries BCE, that is, much later than the central and northern parts of the country. According to the Book of Judges, only two southern tribes – Judah and Simeon – fought together for southern Canaan; there is not a single word about assistance from their northern brethren: "Judah said to his brother Simeon, "Come up with me into the territory allotted to me, that we may fight against the Canaanites; then I, too, will go with you into the territory allotted to you." So, Simeon went with him" (Judges 1:3). And the southerners were led not by Joshua, but by Caleb, the son of Jephunneh, a Kenizzite. The true ally of the southern tribes turned out to be the Midianite tribe of the Kenites, with whom Moses became related after fleeing from Egypt, and which repeatedly helped them during their stay in the desert. "The descendants of Hobab the Kenite, Moses's father-in-law, went up with the people of Judah from the city of palms into the wilderness of Judah, which lies in the Negeb near Arad. Then they went and settled with the Amalekites" (Judges 1:16). This part of the Kenites, like the Kenizzites, very quickly became part of the tribe of Judah.

The two priestly clans of southern origin also found themselves separated from each other: the Aaronites almost entirely remained in the south - in Judah, and almost all the Levites in the north - in Israel. Thus, historically, two independent Yahwistic centers developed: the southern, Aaronite at the Jerusalem Temple and the northern, Levitical in Shiloh. Each of them created their own books, which were then integrated into a single Bible. Only after the fall of the Kingdom of Israel in 722 BCE both priestly corporations were reunited in Judah, although not on equal terms: the Levites again found themselves as assistants to the Aaronites.

3. Edomites

The Edomites were the closest people to the Hebrews. Both were of the same ethnic origin, spoke the same language, had a common tribal origin, lived next to each other and were at the same level of social and cultural development. If we take the pre-Egyptian period, then both peoples had a common history and common gods. In a word, before the departure of the "House of Jacob" to Egypt, the Hebrews and the

Edomites were one people, or rather two parts of the same people, which were only called differently: "Jacob" and "Edom". The progenitor of Edom was Esau, the brother, moreover, the twin of Jacob - the forefather of the Hebrews. Of all the nomadic Amorite peoples brought to Canaan by the biblical patriarch Abraham, only two of them - the Hebrews and the Edomites - traced their genealogy back to two patriarchs at once: Abraham and Isaac. The Bible does not hide the fact that Isaac, the father of the twins, clearly preferred Esau, not because he was considered the eldest, but because he was spiritually closer to him. This circumstance compelled the authors of the Bible – the descendants of Jacob – to downplay the role of Isaac in the genealogy of their forefathers. By contrast, they devoted incomparably more attention to his wife Rebekah, who zealously defended the interests of her favored son Jacob. It was precisely at this level of the tribal hierarchy that the compilers of the Bible had to make significant changes to the narratives they had inherited. The first difficulty was connected with Esau's birthright. According to the law of that time, the eldest son, or the firstborn of the principal wife, received not only his father's entire inheritance but also leadership over the whole clan or tribe. This is why a struggle for the birthright arose between Jacob and Esau.

Being born of the same mother as Jacob, Esau was considered the elder, and moreover the favored son of Isaac. However, the idea of Edomite seniority over the Hebrews was unacceptable to the compilers of the Bible, especially since they were engaged in this work at a time when Edom was a tributary of the United Monarchy. Therefore, two narratives were included in the biblical canon, the purpose of which was to justify Jacob's right to the birthright. The first of these was the story of Esau selling his birthright for a bowl of lentil pottage, and the second was how Jacob fraudulently obtained his father's blessing, intended for Esau. Both of these portray the cunning Jacob in a far from flattering light, even though they attempt to place all the responsibility on his mother, Rebekah, who favored the younger son. Be that as it may, the birthright acquired by Jacob in this way looks unconvincing. The attempts of the editors of the Old Testament to prove the right of Jacob, their ancestor, to the birthright were continued in the later rabbinic tradition, which views Esau and his descendants in a frankly negative light.

Jacob's return from Haran to Canaan, his fear of Esau, and Esau's unexpectedly cordial reception of his brother, who had offended him, testify to several facts at once. Firstly, despite the stories about the transfer of birthright, in reality it was Esau, not Jacob, who became Isaac's heir and the main one in their tribal hierarchy. Secondly, Esau was clearly stronger than Jacob, that is, in the pre-Egyptian period, the tribes of Jacob were inferior to the ancestors of the Edomites in military terms. It was not for nothing that Jacob was frightened by the number of Esau's warriors (Gen. 32:6-7). Thirdly, Esau showed nobility and generosity not only by forgiving his brother, but also by offering him all kinds of help. "But Esau ran to meet him and embraced him and fell on his neck and kissed him, and they wept" (Gen. 33:4). And Jacob himself admitted that "for truly to see your face is like seeing the face of God, since you have received me with such favor" (Gen. 33:10). All this speaks of very good relations between the ancestors of the Hebrews and the Edomites in the pre-Egyptian period of their life in Canaan. And finally, even before the departure of the "House of Jacob" to the Nile Delta, Esau settles on Mount Seir in southeastern Canaan. In doing so, Esau cedes to his twin brother the "family nest" of their father Isaac in the Hebron region, as well as pastures with dug wells in Beersheba in the northern Negev.

The early history of the Edomites is connected with two more ethnic groups: the Hori people, the indigenous inhabitants of southeastern Canaan, and the Amalekites, the West Semitic nomads of the Negev and northern Sinai. The Hori people were of non-Semitic origin and had lived in the area of Mount Seir since the Neolithic period. When the Edomites arrived there, they pushed back the local inhabitants but did not expel them. Over time, friendly and even kinship relations developed between the newcomers and the indigenous inhabitants of Mount Seir. One of Esau's wives, Oholibamah, came from the clan of the leader of the Hori people. Subsequently, the Horites quickly assimilated with the Edomites. A second people, the Amalekites, likely emerged from the mixing of nomadic Edomites with those Horites who lived in the Negev and in northern Sinai. The Book of Genesis traces the origin of Amalek, the progenitor of the Amalekites, to Eliphaz, the eldest son of Esau, and his concubine Timna from the Horites. Because the Old Testament characterizes the Amalekites as enemies of the "House of Jacob," some of this negativity is inevitably projected onto the Edomites themselves, who gave birth to this ethnic group.

Edom and Jacob became different peoples only after the return of the Hebrews from Egypt. During the 430 years of the "House of Jacob's" sojourn in the Nile Delta, other Amorite tribes joined it. Together with the "House of Jacob," they lived for centuries under the influence of Egyptian culture and traditions; together they experienced a period of prosperity under the rule of the West Semitic (Hyksos) pharaohs and a time of enslavement under Ramesses II. In addition to all this, the dramatic exodus from Egypt and the acceptance of the Covenant with the one God of Moses turned the Hebrews into a people distinct from their Edomite brethren, who never left their tribal territory in southeastern Canaan. Upon their return from Egypt, Jacob-Israel's encounter with the closely related Edom took a very different turn. Here is how the Book of Numbers describes it: "Moses sent messengers from Kadesh to the king of Edom, "Thus says your brother Israel: You know all the adversity that has befallen us... and here we are in Kadesh, a town on the edge of your territory. Now let us pass through your land. We will not pass through field or vineyard or drink water from any well; we will go along the King's Highway, not turning aside to the right hand or to the left until we have passed through your territory. But Edom said to him, "You shall not pass through, or we will come out with the sword against you." The Israelites said to him, "We will stay on the highway, and if we drink of your water, we and our livestock, then we will pay for it. It is only a small matter; just let us pass through on foot." But he said, "You shall not pass through." And Edom came out against them with a large force, heavily armed. Thus, Edom refused to give Israel passage through their territory, so Israel turned away from them" (Num. 20:14, 16-21). Thus ended the friendship between the descendants of Esau and Jacob.

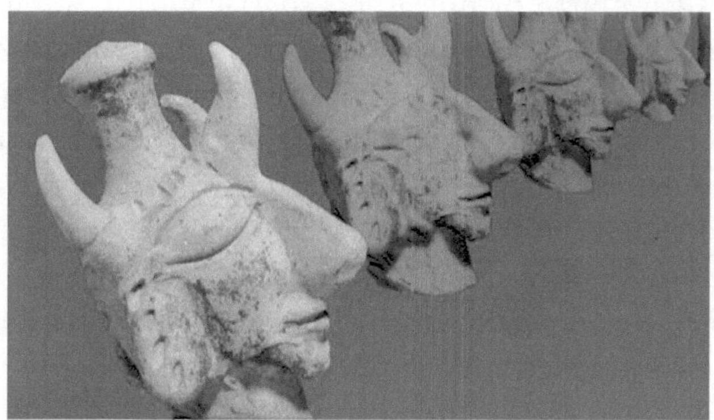

9. Edomite goddess.

Over time, the relationship between the brotherly peoples - the Edomites and the southern Hebrew tribes became even worse. At the same time, their relations with the northern tribes, in particular with the "House of Joseph," were incomparably better than with each other. The hostility of the Edomites to the Judahites was obvious even in those times. For example, it was the Edomite Doeg who handed over to King Saul those who helped the Judahite David escape, although the king's fellow tribesmen, his own Benjaminites, refused to do so.

During the years of the existence of the United Monarchy, King David subjugated Edom, making it his tributary. The conquest of Edom was entrusted to David's general, Abishai. "Abishai son of Zeruiah killed eighteen thousand Edomites in the Valley of Salt. He put garrisons in Edom, and all the Edomites became subject to David" (1 Chr. 18:12-13; 2 Sam. 8:14). But Hadad, the heir to the Edomite king, managed to escape to Egypt. As the Book of Kings reports, "Hadad fled to Egypt with some Edomites who were servants of his father. He was a young boy at that time. They set out from Midian and came to Paran; they took people with them from Paran and came to Egypt, to Pharaoh king of Egypt, who gave him a house, assigned him an allowance of food, and gave him land. Hadad found great favor in the sight of Pharaoh, so that he gave him his sister-in-law for a wife, the sister of Queen Tahpenes. The sister of Tahpenes gave birth by him to his son Genubath, whom Tahpenes weaned in Pharaoh's house; Genubath was in Pharaoh's house among the children of Pharaoh" (1 Kings 11:17-20). The reason for such a warm welcome to the heir to the Edomite throne was the intention of the Egyptians to use Edom against the sharply strengthened United Monarchy. The kingdom of David, which had become their closest neighbor, inspired them with serious concerns, so the Egyptians considered Hadad as their potential ally. During the reign of David's son Solomon, the Edomite king Hadad tried to restore the independence of his country but was defeated and fled to Egypt again.

The split of the United Monarchy did little to help the Edomites: submission to the United Monarchy was replaced by even greater dependence on Judah. The younger brother enslaved the elder for a long time. From time to time, the Edomites managed to free themselves from the rule of the younger brother, but only either during wars between Israel and Judah or in years when Judah was weakened. Such a period was precisely the reign of the Judahite king Joram. "In his days Edom revolted against the rule of Judah and set up a king of their own" (2 Kings 8:20). Joram's war with the Edomites was very protracted and went on with varying success. In open battles the Judahite army was victorious, then the Edomites switched to guerrilla warfare in the desert terrain they were familiar with. "Then Joram crossed over to Zair with all his chariots. He set out by night and attacked the Edomites and their chariot commanders who had surrounded him, but his army fled home" (2 Kings 8:21). In the end, Joram chose to abandon the endless and costly war for power over Edom, and the "elder" brother became independent of the "younger" again. However, the kings of Judah viewed this small neighboring kingdom as their traditional vassal and perceived its independence as a challenge to themselves. That is why the Judahite king Amaziah considered organizing a military campaign against Edom the primary goal of his reign. This time, unlike the times of Joram, the successes of the Judahite army exceeded all expectations. "He killed ten thousand Edomites in the Valley of Salt and took Sela by storm; he called it Jokthe-el, which is its name to this day" (2 Kings 14:7). Among the rich spoils he brought from Edom were statues of the Edomite gods, numerous objects of their cult, and even priests of the main Edomite god Kaus. Trying to weaken the influence of the Yahwist priests, he allowed the worship of Edomite deities in Judah.

10. Edomite ritual vessels from Ein Hazeva, 7th century BCE.

Amaziah's power over Edom did not last long. Overestimating his strength, the Judahite king started a war with Israel and suffered a crushing defeat, which gave the Edomites the opportunity to restore their independence from Judah. However, Amaziah's son, Azariah (who later changed his name to Uzziah), managed to conquer Edom again and make it his tributary. The Edomites had another chance to free themselves from the rule of Judah only during the reign of the Judahite king Ahaz, when the Israelites and the Arameans of Damascus tried to force him to join their alliance against Assyria. The allies besieged Jerusalem and once again helped Edom free itself from the rule of the Judahites. However, Ahaz, finding himself in a hopeless situation, turned to Assyria for help. The subsequent invasion of the Assyrians put the Edomites in an even more difficult position: dependence on Judah was replaced by an incomparably heavier tribute to the Assyrian kings. The arrival of the Babylonians did not bring relief to the Edomites either. The yoke of the Mesopotamian rulers turned out to be much heavier and humiliating than the rule of the Judahites.

4. Moabites

The Moabites were not merely relatives of the Hebrews in ethnic, linguistic, and even tribal terms; they were in fact the very same people as the Hebrews. All differences between them emerged only after the four-century sojourn of the "House of Jacob" in Egypt. The closeness of these two peoples is no coincidence. After all, the progenitor of the Moabites was considered to be Lot, the nephew of the patriarch Abraham, the son of his brother Haran. After the death of his father in the city of Ur in Sumer, Lot accompanied his uncle everywhere. Together with Abraham (then he was still simply called Abram) he set out for the distant land of Canaan, and when famine struck there, he went with him for a short time to the Nile Delta. And he returned with him as well. It was for the sake of freeing his nephew Lot, who had been taken captive, that Abraham and his allies entered the war against the coalition of Syrian rulers and saved his relative. In those days, the nomadic Amorites, who lived by grazing cattle on arid lands, needed large areas, so the separation of relatives with their herds of cattle was a common and necessary occurrence. Here is how the Book of Genesis describes the separation of the biblical family, that is, the future Hebrews and Moabites: "Now Lot, who went with Abram, also had flocks and herds and tents, and the land could not support both of them living together because their possessions were so great that they could not live together. Thus, strife arose between the herders of Abram's livestock and the herders of Lot's livestock... Then Abram said to Lot, "Let there be no strife between you and me and between your herders and my herders, for we are kindred. Is not the whole land before you? Separate yourself from me. If you take the left hand, then I will go to the right, or if you take the right hand, then I will go to the left." So, Lot chose for himself all the plain of the Jordan, and Lot journeyed eastward, and they separated from each other" (Gen. 13:5-9,11).

The ancestors of the Moabites occupied the region of southern Transjordan, adjacent to the eastern shore of today's Dead Sea. However, four thousand years ago this sea did not exist yet. The deep depression occupied by this sea today was then called the Siddim Valley, through which the Jordan River flowed. The ecological catastrophe that occurred during the time of Abraham and Lot destroyed entire cities and turned this area into a lifeless desert with a few oases. The most ancient known population of these places were the tall Rephaim, a people of non-Semitic origin who lived throughout Canaan since the Neolithic period. The Moabites called them "emim." Before the ecological catastrophe that created the Dead Sea, the Siddim Valley was home to Canaanite cities, of which only two - Sodom and Gomorrah - became known thanks to the Bible. After the formation of the Dead Sea, the surviving Canaanites left the area, ceding it to the semi-nomadic Moabites.

According to the biblical version, the progenitor of the Moabites was Moab, born from Lot and his elder daughter, who resorted to incest because of the absence of men (Gen. 19:31–34, 37). However, one cannot rule out that the story of incest among the ancestors of the Moabites was deliberately added to the Pentateuch by the later editors of the Bible, for example by the lawgiver Ezra in the 5th century BCE, in order to halt the wave of marriages between Judeans and Moabites. As is well known, Jews were forbidden to intermarry with peoples who had ever practiced incest.

The Moabites, like the other two Transjordan peoples – the Edomites and the Ammonites – were ethnically the same group of nomadic Amorite tribes that the patriarch Abraham brought to Canaan. But, unlike the Hebrews, they did not live in Egypt for hundreds of years and did not mix to such an extent with the peoples of Canaan. This is what the prophet Jeremiah meant when he spoke of the Moabites: "Moab has been at ease from his youth, settled like wine on its dregs;

he has not been emptied from vessel to vessel, nor has he gone into exile; therefore his flavor has remained, and his aroma is unspoiled" (Jer. 48:11).

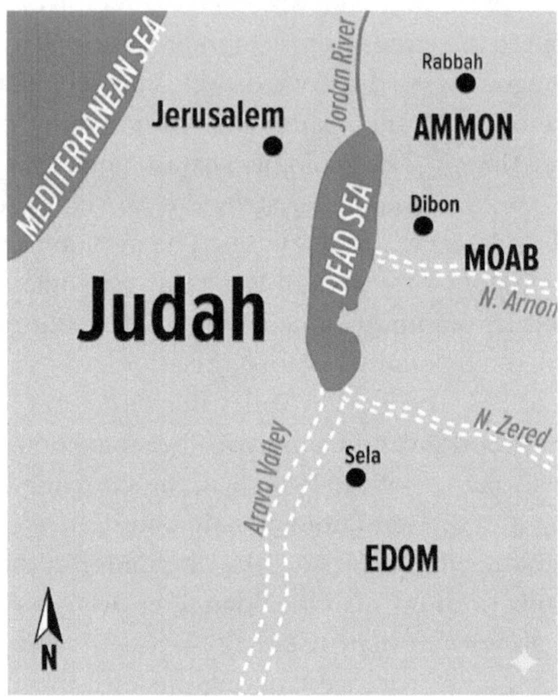

11. A map of Judah, Ammon, Moab and Edom

The ancestors of the Moabites settled in the territory between the Arnon stream in the north and the Zered stream in southern Transjordan. In winter, during the rainy season, the dry beds of these streams turn into rivers flowing into the Dead Sea. South of Moab, in the very southeast of Transjordan, another relative of the Hebrews settled – Edom. North of Moab, the situation turned out to be more complicated. First, the Amorite kingdom of Sihon arose there, which periodically attacked the Moabites and even captured part of their territory. Later, when the Hebrew tribes of Moses returned from Egypt, they defeated the kingdom of Sihon, and its lands, including those captured from

Moab, were given to the tribe of Reuben. Thus, a territorial dispute arose, complicating the relations of the Moabites with this tribe.

The Hebrews who returned from Egypt turned out to be much more numerous and stronger than their ancestors who had left four centuries earlier. The Moabites were frightened by the appearance of their relatives, who had once been close and friendly to them. "Now Balak son of Zippor saw all that Israel had done to the Amorites. Moab was in great dread of the people, because they were so numerous; Moab was overcome with fear of the Israelites. And Moab said to the elders of Midian, "This horde will now lick up all that is around us, as an ox licks up the grass of the field." Now Balak son of Zippor was king of Moab at that time" (Num. 22:2-4). However, the kinship that connected the two peoples did not allow them to come into conflict with each other at that time. Deuteronomy contains an important warning on this matter: "Do not harass Moab or engage them in battle, for I will not give you any of its land as a possession, since I have given Ar as a possession to the descendants of Lot" (Deut. 2:9). But the refusal of the Moabites to help their relatives - the Hebrews in a difficult time for them, in turn, gave rise to condemnation and rejection of Moab in the same Deuteronomy: "No Ammonite or Moabite shall come into the assembly of the Lord even to the tenth generation. None of their descendants shall come into the assembly of the Lord forever, because they did not meet you with food and water on your journey out of Egypt and because they hired against you Balaam son of Beor, from Pethor of Mesopotamia, to curse you" (Deut. 23:3-4).

The Moabites treated the northerners (Israelites) and southerners (Judahites) differently. If they were at enmity with the former, then, as a rule, they maintained good-neighborly relations with the latter. This was because Moab directly bordered the lands of the Israelites, but the lifeless Dead Sea separated it from the Judahites. The first serious conflict occurred with the "House of Joseph" in the period of the Judges (12th-11th centuries BCE). The collapse of the Israelite tribal union and civil strife among the Hebrews prompted the Moabites to take advantage of the weakness of their neighbors. "The Israelites again did what was evil in the sight of the Lord, and the Lord strengthened King Eglon of Moab against Israel, because they had done what was evil in the sight of the Lord. In alliance with the Ammonites and the Amalekites, he went and defeated Israel, and they took possession of the city of palms. So, the Israelites served King Eglon of Moab for eighteen years. But when the Israelites cried out to the Lord, the Lord raised up for them a deliverer, Ehud son of Gera, a Benjaminite, a left-handed man" (Judges 3:12-15). The Israelite judge Ehud, having arrived with gifts to the ruler of Moab, was able to take advantage of the fact that he was left-handed and dealt a mortal blow to Eglon. Confusion among his enemies allowed him to leave Moab and safely reach his home. "When he arrived, he sounded the trumpet in the hill country of Ephraim, and the Israelites went down with him from the hill country, having him at their head. He said to them, "Follow after me, for the Lord has given your enemies the Moabites into your hand." So, they went down after him and seized the fords of the Jordan against the Moabites and allowed no one to cross over. At that time they killed about ten thousand of the Moabites, all strong, able-bodied men; no one escaped. So Moab was subdued that day under the hand of Israel. And the land had rest eighty years" (Judges 3:27-30).

At the time when the Israelites fought with the Moabites, the Judahites had peaceful and neighborly relations with them. If the Book of Judges tells about the wars of the northern tribes with Moab, then the Book of Ruth (Megillat Ruth) speaks of the closeness between the Moabites and the Judahites, emphasizing the devotion of the Moabite woman to her Judahite relatives. The words of the Moabite Ruth, the great-grandmother of King David, became the answer to those who urged them not to intermarry with the Moabites: "But Ruth said, "Do not press me to leave you, to turn back from following you! Where you go, I will go; where you lodge, I will lodge; your people shall be my people and your God my God. Where you die, I will die, and there will I be buried. May the Lord do thus to me, and more as well, if even death parts me from you!" (Ruth 1:16-17). These words became prophetic at least for that part of the Moabites who later became part of the Jewish people. The close relations between the Judahites and the Moabites are confirmed by the fact that the future King David, hiding from Saul's persecution, hid his parents with the Moabites, with the assistance of the ruler of Moab.

12. The Balua Stele (1400-1100 BCE) depicts a Moabite king flanked by the god Chemosh on the left and a goddess on the right.

The formation of the United Monarchy turned all its neighbors into tributaries of this powerful kingdom. Moab did not escape a similar fate. The split of this kingdom changed little for the Moabites; they remained tributaries of the Israelites, but maintained good relations with the Judahites. The hostility and wars between Israel and Judah turned the latter into a potential ally of Moab. However, Moab looked similarly at the Aram-Damascus, which was Israel's main enemy. Aram-Damascus, waging constant wars with Israel, constantly incited Moab and Ammon to "secede" from the Israelites, and promised Judah help in its confrontation with its stronger northern neighbor.

The entire system of political and military alliances in Canaan literally turned upside down when the Omri dynasty came to power in the Kingdom of Israel. The Israelite kings from this dynasty (885-842 BCE) established peaceful and even kinship relations with Judah, making it their main ally. But this same step turned Judah into an enemy of Moab, Ammon and Damascus. From now on, the Judahite kings, together with the Israelite kings, punished Moab for its attempts to free itself from paying tribute. Thus, the Judahite king Jehoshaphat took part in the campaign of the Israelite king Jehoram against the Moabite ruler Mesha, who decided to break away from Israel. "So King Jehoram marched out of Samaria at that time and mustered all Israel. As he went, he sent word to King Jehoshaphat of Judah, "The king of Moab has rebelled against me; will you go with me to battle against Moab?" He answered, "I will; I am as you are; my people are your people; my horses are your horses" (2 Kings 3:6-7). During the difficult and exhausting war, the Moabites, despite stubborn resistance, found themselves on the verge of complete defeat. The Moabite king Mesha in despair turned to the main Moabite god Kemosh for help and even sacrificed his firstborn son right on the fortress wall of his capital Kir-hareseth. "He took his firstborn son who was to succeed him and offered him as a burnt offering on the wall" (2 Kings 3:27). And indeed, salvation came, though in the person of the Arameans of Damascus, who unexpectedly attacked Israel from the north and thereby forced the allies to abandon the siege of Kir-hareseth.

The history of Moab was lucky. It is mentioned not only in the biblical books but also has a very important non-biblical source - the stele of Mesha, the same Moabite king against whom the Israelites and Judahites jointly fought. The Mesha Stele tells us that Moab was conquered by the Israelite king Omri and remained a tributary of Israel for 40 years. According to the text of the stele, King Mesha thanks the supreme Moabite god Kemosh for freeing him from the power of Omri's son and for the opportunity to subjugate the lands that belonged to the Israelite

Transjordanian tribes. The Mesha Stele was erected around 840 BCE and is now kept in the Louvre. However, it was badly damaged by the local Arabs, who broke it into pieces to sell it for more.

13. Mesha Stele

The sharp rise of Aram-Damascus, which reached its peak under King Hazael (842-796 BCE), tied down all the forces of Israel and allowed the Moabites not only to free themselves from its power, but even to seize part of the lands from the Israelite tribes of Reuben and Gad. These areas once belonged to Moab but were captured by the Amorite kingdom of Sihon. The Hebrews, having defeated Sihon, transferred these areas to the tribes of Reuben and Gad. Thus arose a centuries-old territorial dispute between Moab and these Israelite tribes. However, the freedom won by King Mesha did not last long. Hazael, the king of

Aram-Damascus, gradually imposed tribute on almost all the states of Syria and Canaan, including Moab.

Preoccupied with wars with Israel, the Arameans of Damascus put together a coalition of Moab, Ammon, and Edom against Judah, Israelite ally. Apparently, this happened in 850-849 BCE, in the last year of the reign of the Judahite king Jehoshaphat. Intending to march on Judah, all three allied armies united at the Ein Gedi oasis on the western shore of the Dead Sea. But discord between the allies ruined the entire undertaking. Fierce disputes turned into fierce battles. First, the Moabites together with the Ammonites, dealt with the army of Edom, and then, failing to reach an agreement, actually killed each other. Thus, even before beginning, the war of the Transjordanian kingdoms against Judah ended. However, this was not surprising, because Moab had long been in conflict with both Ammon and Edom over border lands. On the other hand, if Edom longed for the death of its younger brother, then Moab and Ammon only wanted to tear Judah away from their enemy - Israel.

Using the confrontation between Israel and Aram-Damascus, Moab managed to remain independent until the coming to power of the Israelite king Jeroboam II (788-747 BCE). During his reign, Israel defeated Aram-Damascus and subjugated not only all of Syria, but also the Transjordanian kingdoms of Moab and Ammon. Dependence on Israel continued until Assyria returned to this region. The Assyrian king Tiglath-Pileser III (746-727) became the new master of all of the Levant, and the tribute to the Assyrians turned out to be incomparably heavier than the Israelite one. The fall of the hated Assyria in 612 BCE gave only a short respite: the Assyrians were soon replaced by other Mesopotamian conquerors – the Babylonians. The resistance to the Neo-Babylonian Kingdom was led by Judah, and the Transjordanian kingdoms and Egypt promised to help it at the decisive moment. But in 587 BCE, Judah fell under the blows of the Babylonians and help never came. In 582 BCE, the Babylonians invaded Canaan again. This time, the main blow fell not on the destroyed Judah, but on its neighbors – Ammon, Moab and Edom. The Transjordanian kingdom of Moab suffered the same sad fate as Judah. Hoping to free themselves from the heavy hand of the Chaldeans, the Moabites vainly relied on Egypt for help. But the Egyptians again proved too weak and indecisive. As a result, the Babylonians not only destroyed and ravaged Moab, but also took part of the country's population captive. The Judahite prophet Jeremiah wrote: "Therefore I wail for Moab; I cry out for all Moab; for the people of Kir-heres I mourn. More than for Jazer I weep for you, O vine of Sibmah! Your branches crossed over the sea, reached as far as Jazer; upon your summer fruits and your vintage the destroyer has fallen... Therefore, my heart moans for Moab like a flute, and my heart moans like a flute for the people of Kir-hereseth, for the riches they gained have perished" (Jer. 48:31-32,36).

The fall of Moab and Edom facilitated the penetration into southern Transjordan of the Nabataeans – Arab nomadic tribes from Arabia – who gradually displaced the Moabites and Edomites from their ancestral lands and forced them to resettle westward, into southern Judah. In the 5th–4th centuries BCE, the Nabataeans finally seized the territory of Moab, and the name of the Moabites ceased even to be mentioned. Most likely, the majority of the Moabites, having adopted Jewish monotheism, were assimilated with the Judeans.

5. Ammonites

The ancestors of the Ammonites were part of the tribal group of the patriarch Abraham, who, in search of a new homeland, first tried to settle in southern Mesopotamia, and then went to Canaan. The ethnic origin and genealogy of the Ammonites almost completely repeat the history of their brothers - the Moabites. The Ammonites, just like the Moabites, considered Lot, Abraham's nephew, to be their forefather and patriarch, that is, their ancestors were part of the biblical family. As in the case of the Moabites, the Bible traces the origin of the Ammonites to incest between Lot and his daughter. If the eldest daughter of Lot, who gave birth to a son Moab, was considered the foremother of the Moabites, then the foremother of the Ammonites was the youngest daughter, who gave birth to another son from Lot, whom she named Ben-Ami ("son of my people"). Biblical tradition explains the fact of incest by the lack of choice, since Lot's daughters lost their grooms and were left without men at all because of an ecological catastrophe. This was the same geological cataclysm that destroyed the cities of Sodom and Gomorrah and led to the appearance of the Dead Sea. Be that as it may, it remains a mystery whether the ancestors of the Moabites and Ammonites really allowed incest or whether the editors of the Bible, wanting to prevent marriages of Jews with idolaters in the post-Babylonian period, included this narrative in the book of Genesis. In any case, the Ammonites and Moabites were fraternal peoples and had a common origin with the Hebrews. Moreover, both of these peoples settled next to each other: Ammon in central Transjordan, and Moab in the south. The northern border of Ammon was the Jabbok River, a tributary of the Jordan River, and the southern - the Arnon stream, flowing into the Dead Sea. The indigenous population of these territories was the Rapha (Rephaim) people, who were known to the Ammonites under the name "Zamzummim." The Ammonites, like their fellow Moabites, not only did not touch the tall inhabitants of these places, but on the contrary, quickly got closer and mixed with them. Although Ammon, like Moab, was closely related to the Hebrews, Moab had better relations with them than Ammon. Both Moab and Ammon were constantly at odds with the Israelites over the lands of the Transjordanian tribes of Reuben and Gad. On the other hand, the Ammonites, like the Moabites, tried to maintain peace with the Judahites, with whom they did not have any territorial disputes and even a common border.

Ammon, like Moab and Edom, also did not show hospitality to its relatives, the Hebrews who returned from Egypt, for which it was severely condemned in Deuteronomy (Deut. 23:4-7). For this unseemly act, the Ammonites were punished by not having returned them the lands that the Amorite kingdom of Sihon seized from them. Israel, having defeated this kingdom, gave the former Ammonite lands to the Hebrew tribe of Gad. At that time, the Ammonites did not dare to conflict with the Hebrew tribes, but they remembered this later, during the period of the Judges, when Israelite alliance fell apart and the Hebrews were weakened as a result of civil strife. Around the middle of the 11th century BCE, taking advantage of the Philistine attack on the Hebrew tribes, the Ammonites captured Gilead (the Transjordanian lands of the Israelite tribes of Gad and Manasseh). The resistance to the Ammonites was then led by Judge Jephthah, who came from Gilead himself. "So, Jephthah crossed over to the Ammonites to fight against them, and the Lord gave them into his hand. He inflicted a massive defeat on them from Aroer to the neighborhood of Minnith, twenty towns, and as far as Abel-keramim. So, the Ammonites were subdued before the Israelites" (Judges 11:32-33).

14. Milcom, the main god of the Ammonites.

However, this was far from the last time that the Ammonites contested the Gilead region from Israel. The next time the Ammonites attacked Gilead was at the very beginning of the reign of King Saul, when he had not yet time to strengthen his power over the Israelite tribes. "Nahash the Ammonite went up and besieged Jabesh-gilead, and all the men of

Jabesh said to Nahash, "Make a treaty with us, and we will serve you." However, the Gileadites' attempt to negotiate with the Ammonites about paying them a moderate tribute failed. Nahash, the ruler of Ammon, knowing that the Israelites were busy fighting the Philistines, demanded incomparably more: "But Nahash the Ammonite said to them, "On this condition I will make a treaty with you, namely, that I gouge out everyone's right eye and thus put disgrace upon all Israel" (1 Sam. 11:1-2). Young Saul, whose power was still very shaky — for example, the tribe of Ephraim did not recognize him as king — was forced to take extreme measures: "He took a yoke of oxen and cut them in pieces and sent them throughout all the territory of Israel by the messengers, saying, "Whoever does not come out after Saul and Samuel, so shall it be done to his oxen!" Then the dread of the Lord fell upon the people, and they came out as one" (1 Sam. 11:7). Thus, with the help of threats, Saul was able to gather a large army and defeat the Ammonites. "At the morning watch they came into the camp and cut down the Ammonites until the heat of the day, and those who survived were scattered, so that no two of them were left together" (1 Sam. 11:11).

The Ammonite ruler Nahash (1010-990 BCE?) was an enemy of King Saul and the Israelite tribes living in Gilead, but at the same time he had good relations with the Judahites and, moreover, "dealt loyally" with Saul's enemy, David (2 Sam. 10:2). However, as soon as David became the king of the United Monarchy, the Ammonites' attitude towards him changed dramatically, and not by chance: David did not hide his intention to subjugate all three Transjordanian kingdoms. While this was done quickly with Edom and Moab, the war with the Ammonites dragged on for a long time. After the death of Nahash, one of his sons, Hanun, an enemy of the United Monarchy, seized power in Ammon. But David considered himself entitled to intervene in the succession dispute: his military leaders, Joab and Abishai, were Nahash's grandsons, since their mother, Zeruah, was the Ammonite king's own daughter. There were also other Judahite families directly connected to Nahash; for example, the military leader Amasa was the son of another daughter of the Ammonite ruler. "So, David gathered all the people together and went to Rabbah and fought against it and took it. He took the crown of Milcom from his head; the weight of it was a talent of gold, and in it was a precious stone, and it was placed on David's head. He also brought forth the spoil of the city, a very great amount" (2 Sam. 12:29-30). Having won a complete victory, David placed his protege Shovi, another son of Nahash, on the throne of Ammon. However, the war with the Ammonites brought him into conflict with a much more serious enemy – the Arameans. The Aramean kingdoms in Syria saw David's growing power as a direct threat to their interests, so supporting Ammon was just a convenient pretext for a war with the United Monarchy. But unexpectedly for everyone, David's army defeated the Aramean kingdoms of Zobah, Rehob, Maacah, Tov and Damascus, thus taking control of all of Syria up to the Euphrates River. Thus, the war for the subjugation of the modestly sized Ammon led to the creation of King David's regional empire.

However, the Ammonites once again played an important role during the reign of King David. It was they who helped David regain power when his beloved son Absalom rebelled against him. At the most difficult moment for David, the Ammonite ruler Shobi, one of the sons of Nahash, whom David placed on the throne after long wars, came out on his side. It was the Ammonites and David's mercenaries who became the main fighting force that won the battle with Absalom's army in the Ephraim Forest.

The Ammonites were represented not only in the army of the United Monarchy, but also in its palaces and harems. The daughters of the Ammonite kings were the wives of Judahite military leaders and aristocrats, moreover, one of them, the Ammonite Naamah, became the favorite wife of King Solomon, and their common son, Rehoboam, became the first king of Judah after the split of the United Monarchy. For the noble Ammonites living in Jerusalem, an altar was built to their main god Milcom, which caused discontent among the Yahwist priests.

The split of the United Monarchy did not free Ammon from the need to pay tribute to its stronger neighbors. As a rule, the Ammonites were subordinate to either Israel or Aram-Damascus, depending on which of them was militarily dominant at a given time. For example, during the reign of the Omri dynasty, Ammon was a tributary of Israel. According to the Assyrian stele of Shalmaneser III (the Kurkh Monolith), during the reign of Ahab, the Ammonite ruler Baasha son of Rehob took part as an Israelite vassal in the Battle of Qarqar (853 BCE) against the army of the Assyrian king Shalmaneser III. On the other hand, during the reign of Hazael and his successors, Ammon was a tributary of Aram-Damascus. But during the reign of the Israelite king Jeroboam II, the Ammonites, like the Arameans of Damascus themselves, were subordinated to Israel.

15. The Ammonite king Yarh-Azar. A limestone statuette dates to the late 8th century BCE.

Assyria's arrival in the Levant put an end to the Israelite-Aramean rivalry and turned all the kingdoms of the region, including Ammon, into tributaries of that empire. True, Ammon, together with its neighbors, tried more than once to free itself from the heavy hand of Assyria. The most significant anti-Assyrian coalition was created in the 730s BCE. It was initiated by the Israelite king Pekah and the king of Aram-Damascus - Rezin. Ammon, like the other Transjordanian kingdoms, became an active participant in this coalition, but, as it turned out, made the wrong choice, and its tribute to Assyria only increased. The defeat of Assyria by the Babylonians and Medes in 612 BCE gave too short a respite, because the place of the hated Assyria was taken by the Neo-Babylonian kingdom. The siege of Jerusalem by the Babylonians and the fall of Judah in 586 BCE was a bad omen for the Ammonites, who, like the Judahites, vainly relied on Egyptian aid.

At the same time, Ammon played a fatal role in the fate of Gedaliah, a Judahite official appointed by the Babylonians as governor of Judah after the destruction of Jerusalem and the Temple. Gedaliah's efforts to quickly restore Judah and unite it with the population of the former Israelite kingdom ran counter to the interests of the Ammonites, who had been laying claim to the Israelite lands (Gilead) in central Transjordan since the time of the Judges. As is well known, the formation of a powerful kingdom of Israel forced Ammon not only to renounce its claims to its lands, but eventually to become its tributary. The fall of the Israelite kingdom and the subsequent destruction of Assyria revived the old claims of the Ammonites. However, this time they were confronted by the Neo-Babylonian kingdom and its Judahite governor Gedaliah. Baalis, the then king of Ammon, not wanting to allow Judah to grow stronger, hoped to use for his own purposes the members of the Davidic dynasty who had taken refuge in his kingdom from the Babylonian invasion. One of them, Ishmael, son of Netanya, "of the royal family and of the royal dignitaries," with the assistance of the Ammonite king Baalis, plotted to murder Gedaliah. During a feast, he and his warriors killed Gedaliah and slaughtered his entire court, including the Babylonian garrison. Having found no support among the population, the conspirators captured many prisoners, including the daughters of the last king of Judah, and tried to escape to King Baalis in Ammon. However, the Judahite troops that remained loyal to Gedaliah overtook them near the city of Gibeon and blocked their way to Ammon. Then Ishmael, along with several accomplices, abandoned everything and was forced to secretly flee to his patron in Ammon.

In 582 BCE, the army of the Babylonian king Nebuchadnezzar II once again fell upon the lands of Southern Levant. This time, the main target of the Babylonians was not Judah, but the Transjordanian kingdoms. The first to suffer was Ammon, whose king Baalis was accused of secretly conspiring with Egypt and harboring the enemies of Babylonia. He was probably also accused of aiding the murderers of Gedaliah. The Judahites and Samaritans viewed the defeat of the Ammonites with a certain degree of satisfaction, as they well remembered that after the fall of the Kingdom of Israel, Ammon had seized part of its lands belonging to the Israelite tribes east of the Jordan. Jeremiah expressed this as follows: "Thus says the Lord: Has Israel no sons? Has he no heir? Why then has Milcom dispossessed Gad and his people settled in its towns? Therefore, the time is surely coming, says the Lord, when I will sound the battle alarm against Rabbah of the Ammonites; it shall become a desolate mound, and its villages shall be burned with fire; then Israel shall dispossess those who dispossessed him, says the Lord" (Jer. 49:1-2). The Ammonites shared the same fate as the Judahites: their country was destroyed, and the most noble and wealthy part of the people were carried away into captivity in Babylonia. "Wail, O Heshbon, for Ai is laid waste! Cry out, O daughters of Rabbah! Put on sackcloth, lament, and slash yourselves with whips! For Milcom shall go into exile, with his priests and his attendants" (Jer. 49:3).

6. Ishmaelites

The Ishmaelites were West Semitic nomads who traced their origins to the biblical patriarch Abraham. Their ancestors came to Canaan from the upper Euphrates River with the tribes of Abraham but later settled in the Paran and Shur deserts in central Sinai, where trade routes to and from Egypt passed (Gen. 21:21). Unlike other Amorite nomads, they were not pastoralists, but traders between Egypt, Syria and Mesopotamia. They brought spices, incense (balsam, frankincense), as well as copper, silver and precious stones to Egypt. From Egypt they exported grain, fabrics, gold and ivory items. Their special place among the nomadic Amorites was explained by two circumstances. Firstly, by the nobility of origin: the founder of this people, Ishmael, was considered the firstborn of the patriarch Abraham and was his favorite son before the birth of Isaac. As the Book of Genesis acknowledges, when Abraham made a covenant with God, he thought first about the well-being of Ishmael. "And Abraham said to God, "O that Ishmael might live in your sight!" (Gen. 17:18). The desire of Sarah, Abraham's wife, to remove Ishmael from the house greatly saddened the patriarch (Gen. 21:11). The Bible also emphasizes another fact, that of all the sons of Abraham, only Isaac and Ishmael buried their father. Both Jacob and Ishmael had 12 sons, who became the forefathers of their tribes and roamed between Egypt and northern Mesopotamia (Gen. 25:16,18). The compilers of the Bible placed Ishmael's genealogy in an honorable second place after their own line of Isaac-Jacob. No other nomadic West Semitic peoples who traced their origins to Abraham were honored with such a distinction. It must be admitted that the line of Ishmael and his mother Hagar was somewhat obscured by the authors of the Bible, who were interested in highlighting only their own branch - from Sarah and Isaac. However, this was also explained by the more important role of Sarah in Abraham's family. After all, she was the daughter of his father Terah, albeit from another woman, while Hagar was a stranger of low social status. Hagar's lineage was important because it connected the patriarch Abraham with the Amorites of the Nile Delta. Although the Book of Genesis calls Hagar "an Egyptian," in reality she came from the Amorites who lived in Egypt. Incidentally, Ishmael's wife was also from Egypt, but not Egyptian. Family ties with the Amorites of the Nile Delta became the second important advantage of the

Ishmaelites. This gave them the opportunity to monopolize all trade with Egypt, at least during the period of domination of the Western Semites there.

The Hebrews considered the Ishmaelites as their close relatives and preferred to intermarry with them rather than with the peoples of Canaan. In this regard, the act of Esau, the eldest son of the patriarch Isaac, is very characteristic. "So, when Esau saw that the Canaanite women did not please his father Isaac, Esau went to Ishmael and took Mahalath daughter of Abraham's son Ishmael and sister of Nebaioth to be his wife in addition to the wives he had" (Gen. 28:8-9). The special kinship between the Hebrews and the Ishmaelites continued until the departure of the "House of Jacob" to Egypt. Four centuries of residence in the Nile Delta consigned to oblivion both the kinship and friendship between the two peoples.

The Bible also recalled the Ishmaelites in later times. For example, the Book of Judges, narrating the victory of Judge Gideon over the Midianites, noted that some of them were Ishmaelites (Judges 8:24). Another biblical book, Chronicles, reported that the father of one of King David's commanders, Amasa, was an Ishmaelite named Jether (1 Chr. 2:17). However, later biblical sources cease to mention this people at all. Probably, over time, the Ishmaelites dissolved among other nomadic Semitic peoples, and above all, among the Midianites and Arabs.

7. Kenites

During the Exodus from Egypt, the Hebrews found an important ally - the Midianite tribes of the Kenites. They were West Semitic nomads of Amorite origin, who, like the "House of Jacob," traced their origins to the patriarch Abraham. If the Hebrews traced their lineage back to the patriarch Isaac, the son of Abraham and Sarah, then the Midianites considered their ancestor to be Midian, Abraham's son from Keturah, the second wife whom the patriarch took after Sarah's death. The ancestors of the Midianites came to Canaan together with the tribes of Abraham, but not finding a place for themselves in this country, they began to roam around southern Sinai and northwestern Arabia. Since then, these areas have become known as the country of Midian. The Midianites were not a single people, they were divided into several nomadic tribal groups, which periodically united for joint campaigns, and then fought with each other. One of these Midianite tribal groups was the Kenites.

The Kenites played an important role in the most dramatic period of Jewish history. They sheltered Moses, who fled from the Egyptians, and after the exodus of the Hebrews from Egypt, they helped them cope with the difficulties of living in the desert. The Book of Exodus captures several important fragments of meetings with the Kenites. One of them concerns the arrival of Moses' father-in-law, Jethro, the ruler of Midian, to the camp of Moses. He arrived with his daughter, Moses' wife, Zipporah, and their two sons. Jethro's visit was a gesture of goodwill and represented support for the "House of Jacob" who found themselves in the unfamiliar conditions of the barren desert. As an experienced man in nomadic life, Jethro helped Moses organize his tribes in the desert and establish legal proceedings. The fact that Jethro participated in the joint worship and brought sacrifices to the one Lord of Moses speaks of the formalization of the allied relations between the Kenites and the "House of Jacob," which strengthened the kinship between Jethro and Moses. Another episode is associated with Moses' request to his brother-in-law, the Midianite Hobab: "He said, "Do not leave us, for you know where we should camp in the wilderness, and you will serve as eyes for us. Moreover, if you go with us, whatever good the Lord does for us, the same we will do for you" (Num. 10:31-32). During the years of wandering in the desert, the tents of the Kenites stood alongside the tents of the Hebrews. These Midianite tribes became a strategic ally of the "House of Jacob." The Kenites were guides, advisers and assistants in the vast lifeless desert. Moses wanted to see the Kenites in his new tribal union. Family ties with this part of the Midianites strengthened the position of the tribe of Levi and helped Moses during the unrest of the Amorite tribes that left Egypt together with the

"House of Jacob." Two other southern tribes, Judah and Simeon, also sought an alliance with the tribes of the desert. It was at this time that they were joined in large numbers by Midianite and Edomite nomadic clans, who wanted to go with Moses to conquer southern Canaan. Alliances with nomadic clans and tribes were cemented through marriages of their leaders. Thus, the leader of the tribe of Simeon - Zimri, following the example of Moses, took as his wife Cozbi, the daughter of Zur, the ruler of one of the Midianite tribal groups. It is possible that the southern tribes of Levi, Simeon and Judah saw in the alliance with the Midianites a counterweight to the growing influence of the northern Hebrew tribes, who left Egypt at the same time. In any case, while the "House of Jacob" was in the desert, the alliance with the Midianites remained a vital necessity.

The Kenites were the main ally of the two southern Hebrew tribes of Judah and Simeon when they conquered southern Canaan. Later, the Kenites settled in the region of Arad and gradually merged with the tribe of Judah (Judges 1:16). At the same time, not all the Kenites settled on the land immediately after the conquest of Canaan; some of them continued to roam both in the south and in the north of Canaan. Nevertheless, the Hebrew tribes regarded them as their allies and distinguished them from other nomadic peoples.

In the first half of the 12th century BCE, during the wars of the northern tribes with the Jabin dynasty, who ruled the powerful Hazor kingdom, the Kenites, who were then roaming around Galilee, took the side of the Israelite tribes. As the Song of Deborah relates, the wife of the leader of the Kenites, Jael, lured the commander of Jabin, Sisera, into her tent and killed him there (Judges 4:21). Another mention of the Kenites dates to the second half of the 11th century BCE, when the Israelite king Saul waged war with the Amalekites. At that time, there were Kenite clans in the Amalekite camp, and Saul, not wanting to inadvertently harm them, asked them to leave the territory of the Amalekites, whom he was going to defeat. "Saul said to the Kenites, "Go! Leave! Withdraw from among the Amalekites, or I will destroy you with them, for you showed kindness to all the Israelites when they came up out of Egypt." So, the Kenites withdrew from the Amalekites" (1 Sam. 15:6). It is difficult to say whether all the Kenites joined the Hebrew tribes, but most of them became part of the tribe of Judah.

The last mention of the fate of the Kenites refers to the invasion of the Assyrian army of King Sennacherib on Judah about 701 BCE. It is put into the mouth of the soothsayer Balaam: "Then he looked on the Kenite and uttered his oracle, saying, "Enduring is your dwelling place, and your nest is set in the rock, yet Kain is destined for burning. How long shall Asshur take you away captive? "Again, he uttered his oracle, saying, "Alas, who shall live when God does this?" (Num. 24:21-23). The descendants of the Kenites in Judah suffered greatly from the Assyrian invasion, and some of them were taken into Assyrian captivity. According to the victorious report of King Sennacherib, the Assyrians then deported two hundred thousand Judahites to Mesopotamia. (*Ancient Near Eastern Texts,* p. 288).

8. Midianites

The Kenites were only a small part of the Midianite tribes, who roamed the arid territories of southern Sinai, northwestern Arabia and the Syrian Desert. The Kenites belonged to those West Semitic nomads who worshiped Yahweh. It was them that the ancient Egyptians called "the Shasu of Yahweh." In contrast, most Midianites adhered to traditional Canaanite beliefs, among which the cult of Baal, the god of thunder, dominated. The Midianite nomads also had different political orientations. If the Kenites were allies of the Hebrews, then other Midianite tribes helped their enemies, for example, the Amorite ruler Sihon in central Transjordan. The first military clash between the Hebrews and the Midianites occurred in Moab on the eve of crossing the Jordan and conquering Canaan. The formal reason for the war was the cult of Baal-Peor, with which the Midianites tried to tempt some of the Israelites. However, the real reason for the war was the long-standing alliance of some of the Midianite tribes with the Amorite kingdom of Sihon. "They did battle against Midian, as the Lord had commanded Moses, and killed every male. They killed the kings of Midian: Evi, Rekem, Zur, Hur, and Reba, the five kings of Midian, in addition to others who were slain by them, and they also killed Balaam son of Beor with the sword" (Num. 31:7-8). This battle with the Midianites was the first, but, as it turned out, far from the last for the Hebrews.

After the conquest of Canaan, "in the days when there was no king in Israel," the Midianite nomads carried out devastating raids on the lands of the Hebrew tribes for seven years in a row. This probably happened at the beginning of the 11th century BCE, and the Book of Judges describes these events as follows: "For whenever the Israelites put in seed, the Midianites and the Amalekites and the people of the east would come up against them. They would encamp against them and destroy the produce of the land, as far as the neighborhood of Gaza, and leave no sustenance in Israel, nor any sheep or ox or donkey. For they and their livestock would come up, and they would even bring their tents, as thick as locusts; neither they nor their camels could be counted, so they wasted the land as they came in. Thus, Israel was greatly impoverished because of Midian, and the Israelites cried out to the Lord for help" (Judges 6:3-6). The resistance to the nomads was led by Judge Gideon from the northern tribe of Manasseh, the same one who was the first in his tribe to speak out against the worship of the pagan cult of Baal. He managed to gather a military militia from his own tribe, which was joined by military detachments from the northern tribes of Asher, Zebulun and Naphtali. The decisive battle took place in the Jezreel Valley, where Gideon routed the nomads and put the remnants of their army on flight. Some of the fleeing nomads, including the Midianite leaders Oreb and Zeeb, were finished off by warriors from the tribe of Ephraim, who were "offended" at Gideon for not calling them to battle and not sharing with them the glory of victory and rich spoils. The remaining fugitives, led by their rulers Zebah and Zalmunna, managed to cross to the eastern bank of the Jordan and they tried to escape to the east, to the Syrian Desert. However, after several days of difficult pursuit, Gideon and his warriors overtook the nomads and destroyed them. "So, Midian was subdued before the Israelites, and they lifted up their heads no more. So, the land had rest forty years in the days of Gideon" (Judges 8:28).

Later, during the period of the United Monarchy, first Saul and then David repeatedly undertook military campaigns against the Midianite nomads, who became their tributaries. However, the split of the United Monarchy weakened the pressure on the Midianites and allowed them to free themselves from tribute. However, they posed a real threat only to the southern regions of Judah and dared to attack its lands only during periods of sharp weakening of Judah, for example, during the reign of King Jehoram. It was precisely at that time, when the Judahite army together with the king was away on yet another military campaign, that detachments of Philistines and nomads from Midian penetrated deep into the country: "The Lord aroused against Jehoram the anger of the Philistines and of the Arabs who are near the Cushites. They came up against Judah, invaded it, and carried away all the possessions they found that belonged to the king's house, along with his sons and his wives, so that no son was left to him except Jehoahaz, his youngest son" (2 Chr. 21:16-17). Most likely, this refers to those Philistines and Midianites who were tributaries of Judah. As a result of the weakening of the Southern Kingdom, they considered it possible not only to free themselves from vassal dependence but also to attack their former suzerain. It cannot be ruled out that behind the attack of the Philistines and Midianites at that time stood Aram-Damascus, which was trying to weaken Judah as much as possible, since it had then become an ally of Israel. During periods of Judah's military strengthening – for example, in the reigns of Jehoshaphat or Azariah (Uzziah) – the Midianites once again became tributaries of the Judahite kings. The fall of Judah in 586 BCE eased the situation of the Midianites, but not for long.

The invasion of the Nabataean Arabs deprived Midianites of their nomadic encampments and made them tributaries of these Arabian tribes. The subsequent fate of the Midianites, who roamed southern Sinai and northwestern Arabia, differed little from that of their nomadic neighbors, the Amalekites: both, having lost their freedom, merged with the Nabataeans and lost their ethnic identity. The group of Midianite tribes that wandered in the Syrian Desert preserved its distinctiveness for much longer, but it too lost it with the arrival of the Arab conquerors there in the 7th century CE.

9. Amalekites

No other people of Canaan aroused such hostility among the Hebrews as the Amalekites. The forefather of this nomadic people, Amalek, was considered the grandson of Esau, Jacob's brother, therefore, in terms of genealogy, he was closer to the Hebrews than, for example, Moab, Ammon or Midian. However, Amalek's mother, Timna, was only a concubine of Esau's eldest son, Eliphaz, and because of this, Amalek's status in the tribal hierarchy of Edom was considered low. In addition, Timna was not an Edomite, but from the people of Hori, who inhabited Mount Seir in southern Transjordan. The Horites were descendants of the ancient pre-Semitic population of Canaan and Sinai. It is noteworthy that the very name *Amalek* is clearly not of Semitic origin, which supports the view that the Amalekites were a mixed people – Edomites, that is, West Semites, combined with the Neolithic non-Semitic population of southern Canaan and Sinai.

The tribal territories of the Amalekites were in the Negev and northeastern Sinai. The Amalekites viewed the "House of Jacob" as a potential enemy, believing that after returning from Egypt, it would try to occupy its former tribal territories in southern Canaan, which included their own areas in the central Negev. The Amalekites considered many of the wells and oases in northern Sinai to be their monopoly and were jealous of the presence of strangers there. No one could roam there or use the wells without the consent of the Amalekites. It is also possible that the Egyptians incited the Amalekites to attack the Hebrew tribes, which they viewed as potential enemies of Egypt. Without waiting for the arrival of the Hebrew tribes, the Amalekite leaders decided to attack first to catch them by surprise. A clash with the Amalekites posed a great danger for the fugitives from Egypt, who were unprepared for war. In the first half of the 12th century BCE Amalek was at the height of its short-lived power and was then a serious military force in southern Canaan and Sinai. The Bible quotes Balaam, a magician and oracle of those times: "First among the nations was Amalek, but its end is to perish forever" (Num. 24:20).

The first battle between the two peoples took place in Rephidim, on Sinai, but it did not reveal a winner. The Amalekites' attack was successfully repelled, but they were able to freely retreat to the east. The Book of Numbers speaks only of "the weakening of the Amalekites by the power of the sword." This unexpected attack was perceived by the Hebrews as a violation of all norms of West Semitic tribal morality. After all, the Amalekites were relatives, and, unlike the Midianites, quite close: Amalek was the grandnephew of the forefather of the Hebrews, Jacob. It is no coincidence that the southern Hebrew tribes for a long time did not allow themselves to fight with either Moab or Ammon, and especially not with Edom, since they were related to them. They expected the same from the Amalekites, but this did not happen. The memory of the treachery of Amalek, who attacked the "House of Jacob" at the most difficult moment of its history, was preserved for a long time, so the Book of Exodus contains an unprecedentedly harsh judgment about it: "Then the Lord said to Moses, "Write this as a remembrance in a book and recite it in the hearing of Joshua: I will utterly blot out the memory of Amalek from under heaven." ...The Lord will have war with Amalek from generation to generation." (Exod. 17:14,16). The second battle with the Amalekites took place on the border of the Negev. This time, Amalek allied with the Canaanites and forced the "House of Jacob" to retreat to the Sinai desert. The Amalekite attacks forced the Hebrews to stick to the southern half of the Sinai Peninsula, where the Midianites and Ishmaelites, loyal to them, dominated. The subsequent history of relations between the two peoples was characterized by the same hostility and dislike.

Unlike the southern Hebrew tribes, the northern ones suffered much less from the attacks of the Amalekites and at times had quite friendly relations with them. We have indirect evidence that some Amalekite clans took part in the military militia of the largest northern tribe, Ephraim (Judges 5:14). The memory about them is also preserved in the name of one of the mountains in the tribal territory of Ephraim. The Book of Judges specifically mentions Mount Amalek, indicating that it was there that the Israelite judge Abdon, son of Hillel, was buried (Judges 12:15). Although the northern Hebrew tribes had significantly better relations with the Amalekites than the southern ones, they also suffered greatly from the raids of these nomads. During the period of the Judges, approximately at the beginning of the 11th century BCE, the Amalekites, having united with a group of Midianite tribes, carried out devastating raids on the lands of the northern tribes for seven years. Only Judge Gideon from the tribe of Manasseh managed to defeat the nomads and thus put an end to these raids. It is noteworthy that three other northern tribes helped him defeat the Amalekites - Asher, Zebulun and Naphtali, but not the brotherly tribe of Ephraim from the same "House of Joseph."

A new serious conflict with the Amalekites arose at the beginning of the reign of Saul, the first king of the United Monarchy. In the first years of his reign, the Israelite Saul was heavily dependent on Judge Samuel, the de facto ruler and high priest of the southern Hebrews (Judah and Simeon). Due to their geographical location, the southern tribes suffered the most from the raids of these nomads based in the Negev and Sinai. The old feud between the "House of Jacob" and Amalek, dating back to the Exodus from Egypt, was also making itself felt. Therefore, Samuel demanded from Saul's army not just their military defeat, but their destruction. However, Saul, a northerner, harbored no hatred toward the Amalekites and showed them mercy, sparing the lives and property of the defeated (1 Sam. 15:24). This provoked the wrath of the high priest Samuel, who personally put the Amalekite ruler Agag to death and threatened Saul with a complete break with him.

In general, the attitude of the Israelites (northerners) and the Judahites (southerners) towards the Amalekites was fundamentally different from each other. While Saul, a northerner, actively employed Amalekites in his army, David, a southerner who succeeded him on the throne, felt hostility toward them and did not admit them into his forces. Moreover, David blamed an Amalekite for Saul's death and had him executed merely for having, at Saul's command, helped him end his life after the defeat in the battle with the Philistines at Mount Gilboa. Even before his accession to the throne, while in the service of the Philistines, David repeatedly fought against the Amalekites. The enmity between him and the descendants of Amalek was mutual. Seizing the moment when David and his warriors had gone on campaign with the Philistines, the Amalekites attacked his patrimony – the town of Ziklag. "Now when David and his men came to Ziklag on the third day, the Amalekites had made a raid on the Negeb and on Ziklag. They had attacked Ziklag, burned it down, and taken captive the women and all who were in it, both small and great; they killed none of them but carried them off and went their way. When David and his men came to the city, they found it burned down and their wives and sons and daughters taken captive." David and his men pursued the Amalekites and overtook them. "When he had taken him down, they were spread out all over the ground, eating and drinking and dancing, because of the great amount of spoil they had taken from the land of the Philistines and from the land of Judah. David attacked them from twilight until the evening of the next day. Not one of them escaped, except four hundred young men, who mounted camels and fled. David recovered all that the Amalekites had taken, and David rescued his two wives. Nothing was missing, whether small or great, sons or daughters, spoil or anything that had been taken; David brought back everything. (1 Sam. 30:1-3,16-19).

For centuries, the nomadic Amalekites attacked the southern Hebrew tribes, until, at the end of the 8th century BCE, the Judahite king Hezekiah completely defeated them. Two centuries later, the nomadic camps of the Amalekites were captured by the Arab tribes of the Nabataeans. Having mingled with the Arabs, the Amalekites disappeared from the pages of history. But the memory of their hatred for the "House of Jacob" remained: the name of Amalek became synonymous with the sworn enemy of the Jewish people. The Book of Deuteronomy calls: "Remember what Amalek did to you on your journey out of Egypt, how he attacked you on the way, when you were faint and weary, and struck down all who lagged behind you; he did not fear God. Therefore when the Lord your God has given you rest from all your enemies on every hand, in the land that the Lord your God is giving you as an inheritance to possess, you shall blot out the remembrance of Amalek from under heaven; do not forget" (Deut. 25:17-19).

10. Kenizzites

The Bible mentions the Kenizzites as a people who lived in Canaan. The Kenizzites were an Edomite nomadic tribe, the forefather of which was considered to be Kenaz, the grandson of Esau, the twin brother of the patriarch Jacob (Gen. 36:10-11). The Kenizzites joined the Hebrews almost immediately after their exodus from Egypt. They belonged to those Shasu tribes who, according to ancient Egyptian sources, worshiped Yahweh. This circumstance was decisive for the nomadic West Semitic tribes of Sinai, Midian and Canaan. After all, the Midianite tribes of the Kenites, who joined the Hebrews, were also guided by a common faith. Of all the Hebrew tribes, the Kenizzites formed kinship ties specifically with the southern tribe of Judah. Moreover, for unclear reasons, they very quickly seized the leadership of this tribe. Thus, at the Exodus from Egypt, the Bible names Nahshon, the son of Aminadab, as the leader of the tribe of Judah. He was also the brother-in-law of the high priest Aaron. However, starting with the episode about the spies sent to Canaan, the new leader of the tribe of Judah is constantly called the head of the Kenizzites - Caleb, the son of Jephunneh. But the episode with the spies occurred at the very beginning of the forty-year stay in the desert. But that is not all. The Book of Exodus, listing the genealogy of the southern tribes of Reuben, Simeon and Levi, who were in Egypt, does not do the same with respect to the fourth southern tribe - Judah. And it is no coincidence, because the Kenizzites and their leaders, who displaced the old tribal aristocracy, were never in Egypt. Their rise to leadership of the tribe of Judah may be explained by the fact that part of the northern Negev was the tribal territory of the Kenizzites, and they knew better than anyone the living conditions and geography of both the Negev itself and southern Canaan in general.

During the period of Egypt's resurgence under Ramesses III, when the conquest of Canaan threatened a direct confrontation with the Egyptian army, the Kenizzites and Kenites imposed their own decision upon the two southern tribes, Judah and Simeon: to remain in the familiar desert until the Egyptians withdrew from southern Canaan. It was the leader of the Kenizzites, Caleb, who headed and executed the conquest of southern Canaan in the mid-12th century BCE, while the leader of the northern Hebrew tribes, Joshua, conquered a significant portion of northern and central Canaan at the beginning of the same century.

The Bible highly values the merits of Caleb and places him next to Joshua. These two leaders were the only ones among all the spies sent by Moses to Canaan who were not afraid of the difficulties of conquering this country. Caleb himself recalled it this way: "I was forty years old when Moses the servant of the Lord sent me from Kadesh-barnea to spy out the land, and I brought him an honest report. But my companions who went up with me made the heart of the people melt, yet I wholeheartedly followed the Lord my God. And Moses swore on that day, saying, 'Surely the land on which your foot has trodden shall be an inheritance for you and your children forever, because you have wholeheartedly followed the Lord my God.' And now, as you see, the Lord has kept me alive, as he said, these forty-five years since the time that the Lord spoke this word to Moses, while Israel was journeying through the wilderness, and here I am today, eighty-five years old. I am still as strong today as I was on the day that Moses sent me; my strength now is as my strength was then, for war and for going and coming" (Josh. 14:7-11). For their loyalty to the Lord and the common cause, Caleb and the Kenizzites were rewarded with the region of Hebron, the best land in the lot of the tribe of Judah, and in southeastern Canaan in general. "So, Hebron became the inheritance of Caleb son of Jephunneh the Kenizzite to this day, because he wholeheartedly followed the Lord, the God of Israel. Now the name of Hebron formerly was Kiriath-arba; Arba was the greatest man among the Anakim. And the land had rest from war" (Josh. 14:14-15).

The Kenizzites continued to play a leading role within the tribe of Judah. Suffice it to say that during the period of the Judges, the son of Caleb's younger brother – Othniel – became the leader not only of the tribe of Judah but of the entire Israelite tribal confederation (or at least of a portion of the tribes). The support of the Kenizzites was of vital importance for the first Israelite king, the northerner Saul, especially when the prophet and judge Samuel – the de facto ruler of the southern tribes – rose against him. The Kenizzites supported Saul as well in his confrontation with David, who represented the old tribal aristocracy of Judah that had been pushed aside from power by the Kenizzites. The conflict between the future king David and the influential Kenizzites – the masters of Hebron – is best reflected in the episode involving the wealthy Nabal. When David, hiding with his men from Saul's army, humbly asked Nabal to send him some food, he arrogantly refused. "But Nabal answered David's servants, "Who is David? Who is the son of Jesse? There are many servants today who are breaking away from their masters. Shall I take my bread and my water and the meat that I have butchered for my shearers and give it to men who come from I do not know where?" (1 Sam. 25:10-11). Nabal was a descendant of Caleb and considered himself to be far more noble and important than David, who came from the impoverished Judahite aristocracy. The Kenizzites preferred to see the Benjaminite Saul on the royal throne rather than the Judahite David, who competed with them for power in the tribe. David took Nabal's insulting refusal as a personal challenge and a declaration of war: "Now David had said, "Surely it was in vain that I protected all that this fellow has in the wilderness, so that nothing was missed of all that belonged to him, but he has returned me evil for good. God do so to David and more also if by morning I leave so much as one male of all who belong to him" (1 Sam. 25:21-22). This conflict ended with the death of Nabal, and his young wife, the beautiful Abigail, became one of David's wives.

David's accession to the throne in Judah and his restoration of the United Monarchy meant the complete defeat of the Kenizzites. The descendants of Caleb felt left out in David's kingdom. They tried to take revenge on David during the rebellion of his beloved son Absalom. The Kenizzites anointed Absalom to the throne in Hebron and helped him take Jerusalem and all of Judah. However, the defeat of Absalom's rebellion put an end to all the ambitions of the Kenizzites once and for all. The entrenchment of David's dynasty in Judah and its four-hundred-year rule over the country caused everyone to forget how serious the Kenizzites' claims to supreme power in Judah had once been.

11. Maonites

The Bible calls the inhabitants of the semi-desert regions of Maon and Ziph, located near the southwestern shore of the Dead Sea, "Maonites." This inaccessible area abutted the Judean Desert in the north and merged with the deserted Negev in the south. The eastern border of Maon and Ziph was the shore of the lifeless Dead Sea. These harsh places were inhabited by tribes (or tribe?) of Edomite origin, the so-called "Maonites." It is possible that some of the inhabitants of Maon and Ziph, especially in the north, also belonged to the Edomite tribe of Kenizzites, who eventually merged with the tribe of Judah. In any case, the Maonites were very close to the Kenizzites and, as a rule, supported them in everything. The Book of Judges mentions the Maonites among those peoples who attacked the Hebrew tribes and even ruled over them for some time (Judges 10:12). It is difficult to say whether this referred to the dominance of the Kenizzites over the tribe of Judah. However, the power of the Maonites could hardly have extended beyond the territory of the southern tribes.

David and his men hid in these harsh and difficult-to-access places for a long time. It is noteworthy that the Maonites, like the Kenizzites, did not support David. Moreover, they were the first to express their willingness to help Saul catch his enemy. "Then some Ziphites went up to Saul at Gibeah and said, "David is hiding among us in the strongholds of Horesh, on the hill of Hachilah, which is south of Jeshimon. Now, O king, whenever you wish to come down, do so, and our part will be to surrender him into the king's hand... Saul and his men went to search for him. When David was told, he went down to the rock and stayed in the wilderness of Maon. When Saul heard that, he pursued David into the wilderness of Maon" (1 Sam. 23:19-20, 25). Here in Maon, David encountered the rich and noble Kenizzite Nabal, the de facto owner of Maon. "There was a man in Maon whose property was in Carmel. The man was very rich; he had three thousand sheep and a thousand goats. He was shearing his sheep in Carmel. Now the name of the man was Nabal, and the name of his wife was Abigail. The woman was clever and beautiful, but the man was surly and mean; he was a Calebite" (1 Sam. 25:2-3). Nabal, like all the Kenizzites and Maonites, was ill-disposed toward David. Whether this reflected a historical resentment of the elder brother toward the younger (the Edomites toward the Judahites), or an intratribal struggle for power within the tribe of Judah, in any case the conflict between David and Nabal ended with the latter's death. From that time on, David's relations with the Maonites were irreparably damaged, and his presence in Maon became mortally dangerous. The inhabitants of Ziph and Maon watched his every move and reported everything to King Saul. There was a moment when Saul's warriors almost captured him, but unexpected news of a Philistine attack on Israel forced them to abandon everything and rush to meet the enemy. It was impossible to remain in Maon any longer, and David decided to seek refuge among the Philistines. "David said in his heart, "I shall certainly perish one day by the hand of Saul; there is nothing better for me than to escape to the land of the Philistines; then Saul will despair of seeking me any longer within the borders of Israel, and I shall escape out of his hand" (1 Sam. 27:1).

The remote, semi-desert areas and the pastoral way of life of the Maonites kept them away from political events both in Judah and in Southern Levant in general. Later, after the fall of Judah and during the Babylonian captivity of part of the Judahites, the regions of Ziph and Maon were intensively populated by the Edomites, who were literally squeezed out of their homeland by the Arab tribes of the Nabataeans.

The Maonites, who lived in hard-to-reach areas in the southeast of Judah, retained their isolation until the Maccabean wars. The First Book of Maccabees mentions "the wickedness of the sons of Baean" (Maean?), "who were a trap and a snare to the people and ambushed them on the highways." Judah Maccabee "shut up them in towers, and he encamped against them, vowed their complete destruction, and burned with fire their towers and all who were in them" (1 Macc. 5:4-5). The Maonites, as in the case of David, preferred to support the central authority rather than Judean rebels. However, later, when Jonathan succeeded his fallen brother Judah, the Maonites did help the Maccabees defeat the army of the Seleucid general Bacchides, especially since the fighting was taking place on their territory (1 Macc. 9:62-68).

Being Edomites by origin, the Maonites had a difficult relationship with the Judeans. The regions of Maon and Ziph returned to Judea only after the Maccabean Wars (167-142 BCE). At the same time, the Maonites, like all the Idumeans, accepted Judaism and became an integral part of the Jewish people.

12. Rechabites

The Rechabites were just a large clan belonging to the Midianite tribe of the Kenites. The progenitor and lawgiver of this clan was Jonadab (Jehonadab), who was also a contemporary and mentor of the Israelite king Jehu (841–814 BCE). However, the clan derived its name – the

Rechabites – not from Jonadab himself, but from his father or even a more distant ancestor, Rechab, about whom virtually nothing is known. Jonadab himself traced his lineage back to Jethro, the chieftain of the Kenite tribe and the father-in-law of Moses. Unlike the rest of the Kenites, who settled in the Arad region in the northern Negev, the Rechabites continued to lead a nomadic lifestyle, not only in the territory of Judah, but also in the north, in Israel.

The Rechabites drew attention for two distinctive features. First, they were convinced Yahwists – zealous devotees of the God of Israel and fierce opponents of all pagan cults. In this respect, they surpassed even the Levites and the Aaronites. Second, they led an ascetic and righteous way of life, arousing both amazement and admiration among those around them. It is no coincidence that some Jewish and Christian authors linked the origins of all righteous ascetics – the Hasideans, Nazarenes, and Essenes – to the Rechabites. The Rechabites explained their strictly nomadic way of life by arguing that the comforts of settled life corrupt people and lead them away from God's covenants. For this reason, they lived only in tents and did not touch wine, for which they were nicknamed "sons who drink water." The best description of the Rechabites' rules of life was given by the Judahite prophet Jeremiah at the beginning of the 6th century BCE: "Then I set before the Rechabites pitchers full of wine and cups, and I said to them, "Have some wine." But they answered, "We will drink no wine, for our ancestor Jonadab son of Rechab commanded us, 'You shall never drink wine, neither you nor your children, nor shall you ever build a house or sow seed, nor shall you plant a vineyard or even own one, but you shall live in tents all your days, that you may live many days in the land where you reside.' We have obeyed the charge of our ancestor Jonadab son of Rechab in all that he commanded us, to drink no wine all our days, ourselves, our wives, our sons, or our daughters, and not to build houses to live in. We have no vineyard or field or seed, but we have lived in tents and have obeyed and done all that our ancestor Jonadab commanded us. But when King Nebuchadrezzar of Babylon came up against the land, we said, 'Come, and let us go to Jerusalem for fear of the army of the Chaldeans and the army of the Arameans.' That is why we are living in Jerusalem" (Jer. 35:5-11).

The Book of Kings testifies that the Rechabite lawgiver Jonadab enjoyed deep respect from the Israelite king Jehu, the Yahwist, who, having seized power, killed all the priests of Baal, as well as the members of the Omri dynasty, who supported this pagan cult. "When he left there, he (Jehu) met Jehonadab son of Rechab coming to meet him; he greeted him and said to him, "Is your heart as true to mine as mine is to yours?" Jehonadab answered, "It is." Jehu said, "If it is, give me your hand." So, he gave him his hand. Jehu took him up with him into the chariot. He said, "Come with me and see my zeal for the Lord." So, he had him ride in his chariot" (2 Kings 10:15-16). Jehonadab, as an honored and respected guest of King Jehu, was also present at the slaughter of the priests of Baal in Samaria (2 Kings 10:23).

The Rechabites helped rebuild Jerusalem and its fortress walls after the return of the Judahites from the Babylonian captivity. This is briefly mentioned in the Book of Nehemiah, the Persian governor of Judah: "Malchijah son of Rechab, ruler of the district of Beth-haccherem, repaired the Dung Gate; he rebuilt it and set up its doors, its bolts, and its bars" (Neh. 3:14).

The Rechabites did not become an isolated religious sect in Judaism, like the Essenes, for example. They not only recognized the Jerusalem Temple and the temple priests, but also participated in the temple service themselves. According to the Mishnah (Oral Torah), the descendants of Jonadab even had their own day for work in the Temple - the 7th of Abba (Ta'an 4:5). All this echoes the prophecy of Jeremiah about the Rechabites: "Thus says the Lord of hosts, the God of Israel: Because you have obeyed the command of your ancestor Jonadab and kept all his precepts and done all that he commanded you, therefore thus says the Lord of hosts, the God of Israel: Jonadab son of Rechab shall not lack a descendant to stand before me for all time" (Jer. 35:18-19).

According to Jewish tradition, the Rechabites merged with the Levites. Nevertheless, the asceticism and righteousness of the Rechabites left such a deep imprint on history that in the Middle Ages and in modern times travelers and explorers periodically encountered "Rechabites" among Bedouin tribes of Sinai, Arabia, Palestine, and even Yemen. As a rule, this involved mere coincidences of names, although there were also cases of outright fraud.

13. Jerahmeelites

The Bible twice mentions some "Jerahmeelites" who lived in the northern Negev, next to the tribe of Judah and the Kenites. Both episodes relate to the service of the future King David among the Philistines and with his relations with the tribes and clans of the northern Negev. In the first case, David, trying to lull the vigilance of the Philistine king Achish, reported on imaginary attacks on the enemies of the Philistines. "When Achish asked, "Against whom have you made a raid today?" David would say, "Against the Negeb of Judah," or "Against the Negeb of the Jerahmeelites," or "Against the Negeb of the Kenites" (1 Sam. 27:10). The second episode lists the tribes and clans friendly to David, with whom he shared the spoils taken from the Amalekites: "When David came to Ziklag, he sent part of the spoil to his friends, the elders of Judah, saying, "Here is a present for you from the spoil of the enemies of the Lord. It was for those in Bethel, in Ramoth of the Negeb, in Jattir, in Aroer, in Siphmoth, in Eshtemoa, in Racal, in the towns of the Jerahmeelites, in the towns of the Kenites..." (1 Sam. 30:26-29). It is noteworthy that the Bible distinguishes and separates the Jerahmeelites from the Judahites and their allies, the Kenites. In addition, there is also an extra-biblical source that confirms the location of the Jerahmeelites in the northern Negev in the region of Arad. We are talking about the inscriptions of the Egyptian Pharaoh Sheshonq I (the biblical Shishak) at the southern entrance to the Temple of Amun in Karnak. These inscriptions list 150 places that Pharaoh Shoshenq captured or plundered during his campaign in Canaan in 925 BCE. As is known, the Egyptians attacked Judah and Israel immediately after the split of their United Monarchy. Among the places captured by the Egyptians, Sheshonq names "Arad Bet Yrhm," that is, "Arad of the House of the Jerahmeelites."

Who were the Jerahmeelites, friendly to David and the Judahites, whose settlements were located on the southern borders of the tribes of Judah and the Kenites? Most likely, it was an Edomite or Midianite nomadic clans that joined the Hebrews after their exodus from Egypt. The basis of the union between them was not ethnic identity, although both were Western Semites of Amorite origin, but a common faith - Yahwism. The Jerahmeelites, like the Kenites and Kenizzites, belonged to the same "Shasu of Yahweh" that were repeatedly mentioned in ancient Egyptian sources. Probably, Yahwism, though still in a pagan form, was brought by the Hebrews and their relatives from the common Semitic homeland in northern Mesopotamia, and only Moses gave it an unambiguously monotheistic character. Why did the biblical authors prefer not to call their allies and fellow believers – the Kenizzites, the Kenites, the Jerahmeelites, the Rechabites and the Maonites - by their true names: the Edomites and Midianites, which in fact they were? The explanation lies in Jewish history, in which the Edomites and Midianites usually acted as enemies and adversaries, first of the Hebrew tribes, and later of their kingdoms – Israel and Judah.

There is another point of view on the origin of the Jerahmeelites. According to it, the Jerahmeelites were a purely Judahite clan, named after Jerahmeel, the great-grandson of Judah – the forefather of this southern Hebrew tribe. From the books of Genesis and Chronicles we know that Judah, the son of the patriarch Jacob, had a common son Peretz with his daughter-in-law Tamar. Peretz was the father of Hezron, and Hezron in turn became the father of Jerahmeel (Gen. 38:6-29; 1 Chr. 2:4-5,9). Some biblical scholars make this unremarkable Jerahmeel the progenitor of the Jerahmeelite clan. This version gives rise to serious objections. Firstly, not a single biblical book, including all the apocrypha, calls Jerahmeel the ancestor of any clan, and especially not of the Jerahmeelites. Secondly, how did the descendants of one of the most important lineages of the tribe of Judah end up outside the territory of their own tribe? After all, the old Judahite tribal aristocracy, like the families of Judge Samuel, King David and the same Jerahmeel, settled not in the outskirts of the northern Negev, but in the center of Judah, in Bethlehem (former Ephrat). Thirdly, the Bible clearly distinguishes between the Hebrew tribes, the Kenites and the Jerahmeelites, making it clear that these are different groups of the population, although they are all friendly to David.

14. Habiru

The Habiru were known in the ancient Near East already very early – almost five thousand years ago. Although the etymology of this term is unknown, it was used to denote "outsiders" or "alien newcomers" who, for various reasons, had left their homeland. They either remained in the country that had given them refuge or moved on in search of a better life. As a rule, these were nomadic or semi-nomadic groups that could be of very different ethnic origins: Western or Eastern Semites, Hurrians, or Indo-Europeans. The Habiru tribes and clans usually traveled with large herds of livestock and led a pastoral way of life. But livestock products were not always enough for life, and the Habiru, in search of a livelihood, hired themselves out as workers to the local population. Being free people, they became mercenary warriors in the armies of local rulers, craftsmen, servants and even tenant farmers. There are cases when Habiru occupied the posts of the high dignitaries at the courts of the ancient Near Eastern rulers. It also happened that, having failed to find sources of food, the Habiru engaged in robbery, attacking local rulers and their cities. In a word, everywhere - in Anatolia, Mesopotamia, Syria and Canaan - the Habiru were considered outsiders, from whom both a threat and help could come for local rulers.

However, the traditional image of Habiru, characteristic of the 3rd millennium BCE, underwent significant changes in the 15th-12th centuries BCE. During this period, almost all the Amorite tribes who had lived there for several centuries, left the Nile Delta. The beginning of the exodus was set in motion by the fall of the Hyksos kingdom – the West Semitic pharaohs who had ruled Egypt for more than a century. Fearing a repetition of their domination over the country, the Egyptians sought to expel as many Amorite tribes as possible from the Nile Delta. As a result, large numbers of Amorites appeared in Canaan, along the Lebanese coast, and in southern Syria, and the local population began to call them by the old name – "Habiru." However, there was a major difference between the earlier Habiru and the new ones. Firstly, the newcomers belonged exclusively to the Western Semites, or more precisely, to the Amorites. Secondly, they were all forced to leave the same country - Egypt - and the same region - the Nile Delta. Thirdly, having come to Egypt as nomads, they became sedentary residents after several centuries of stay there. Finally, fourthly, the Amorites from the Nile Delta returned to the countries where they lived before leaving for Egypt and had their own tribal territories there. Thus, unlike the traditional Habiru, the new arrivals were refugees who had returned to their former homeland.

Most of these Habiru in Canaan were the "House of Joseph," which consisted of the tribes of Ephraim and Manasseh, as well as the closely related tribe of Benjamin. The "House of Joseph" had been associated with the Hyksos rulers of Egypt, so after the fall of the Hyksos kingdom it was forced to leave the Nile Delta together with them or shortly thereafter. The "House of Joseph" returned to Canaan no later than the middle of the 15th century BCE. This was the first exodus of the Hebrew tribes from Egypt, about which the Bible is completely silent. Most of the Hebrew tribes, however, were not associated with the Hyksos and were therefore allowed to continue living in the Nile Delta. As for the "House of Joseph," it found itself in the position of the Habiru in Canaan, since its tribal lands were occupied by local peoples. However, the terms "Habiru" and "Hebrews" cannot be equated. The Hebrews represented only a part of the numerous Amorite tribes that found themselves in the position of the Habiru. The latter, having been forced out of the Nile Delta, spread throughout the territories of Canaan, Amurru, and Syria. The Habiru who fought against the local rulers in northern Lebanon had no relation to the Israelite tribes. By contrast, the Habiru in the region of Shechem clearly belonged to the "House of Joseph," and central Canaan was the main sphere of activity of the Israelite tribes. The position of the Habiru was further complicated by the fact that the "occupiers" of their tribal territories – the rulers of the local city-states – were tributaries of the pharaoh and enjoyed Egyptian protection. Consequently, the reconquest of Canaan in the 15th–13th centuries BCE was impossible due to Egypt's indisputable military superiority at that time.

Almost all our knowledge of the Habiru in Canaan comes from letters sent by Canaanite rulers to their overlord, the Egyptian pharaoh, which were preserved in the so-called Amarna archive. The archive takes its name from the el-Amarna valley, located about 300 kilometers south of modern Cairo. This was the site of the ancient Egyptian capital Akhetaten, founded by the reformist pharaoh Amenhotep IV, better known as Akhenaten. The Amarna archive consists of nearly four hundred cuneiform clay tablets, most of which are written in the international diplomatic language of the time – Akkadian. Chronologically, the archive most likely dates to the second half of the 14th century BCE.

Unfortunately, none of the letters in the Amarna archive provides even the slightest indication of who the Habiru were or how they appeared in Canaan. However, judging by the tone and character of the correspondence, the Egyptian pharaoh was so well informed about this matter that the local rulers did not consider it necessary to explain anything to him. It is therefore obvious that the Habiru did not emerge in the middle of the 14th century BCE, but much earlier, and that their arrival was connected with events in Egypt itself.

A common feature of all the messages from the rulers of Canaan is the firm conviction that the Habiru represented a force hostile to Egypt, and that their anti-Egyptian character was regarded as obvious and long established. Accordingly, in their efforts to discredit their opponents in the eyes of the Egyptians, each ruler considered it sufficient simply to report that they were connected with the Habiru and enjoyed their support. At the same time, the Habiru themselves, at least during the period of the Amarna archive, declared their loyalty to Egypt and did not display any open hostility. This suggests that they had been involved in a serious conflict with Egypt at a much earlier time, a fact of which the rulers of Canaan were clearly aware.

The hypothesis that the Habiru were of social origin is not supported by the texts of the Amarna letters. None of the rulers of Canaan, Amurru, or Syria even mentions that the Habiru, or any part of them, were landless peasants or impoverished townspeople, nor is there any reference to popular uprisings driven by social causes. On the contrary, the information contained in the letters of the local rulers points in the opposite direction.

The Amarna archive contains several letters from Biridiya, the ruler of the Canaanite city of Megiddo, in which he complains about the difficulties of the war against the Habiru. In one such letter, he submits a complaint to the pharaoh against the sons of Labayu, the ruler of the city of Shakmu (Shechem), accusing them of having hired the Habiru and the Sutu for silver in order to wage war against him (EA 246:1–11).

Another Canaanite ruler, Milk-ilu of the city of Gazru (Gezer), found himself in an incomparably worse position. He appealed to the pharaoh to rescue both himself and Shuwardatu, the ruler of the city of Quiltu, from the power of the Habiru (EA 271:9–27). Yet another Canaanite ruler, whose name is illegible on the tablet, wrote quite bluntly: "Let it be known to the king, my lord, that the mayors of the major cities of my lord have fled, and the whole land of the king, my lord, has gone over to the Habiru" (EA 272:1–17).

He is echoed by the ruler of Jerusalem, Abdi-Heba, who warns the pharaoh that "the king no longer has any lands; the Habiru have plundered all the king's lands. If the archers arrive this year, the lands of the king, my lord, will be preserved; but if the archers do not arrive, the lands of the king, my lord, will be lost" (EA 286:53–60). Abdi-Heba, for his part, accused Milk-ilu and the sons of Labayu of handing over the king's lands to the Habiru (EA 287:4–32). At the same time, Labayu himself was also blamed for surrendering the land of Shechem to the Habiru

(EA 289: 18–24). Most likely, these accusations were driven by the fact that the ruler of Jerusalem was at war with these Canaanite kings.

We have reason to believe that the Habiru who supported Labayu and his sons belonged to the "House of Joseph." Probably, in return for their support, the ruler of Shechem restored to them part of the tribal territory that had belonged to them prior to their departure for Egypt. This is precisely what the ruler of Jerusalem, Abdi-Heba, accused him of doing.

From the letters of the Canaanite rulers, it is clear that, from a military point of view, the Habiru were markedly superior to them, and that without the threat of Egyptian intervention all of Canaan would have fallen into their hands. Thus, the new governor of the city of Gazru, Yapahu, openly acknowledged his military impotence. "Let the king, my lord," he wrote to the pharaoh, "the sun in the sky, take thought for his land. Since the Habiru are stronger than we are, let the king, my lord, come to our aid; otherwise the Habiru will destroy us" (EA 299:12–21). A similar appeal was voiced by Canaanite ruler Shub-Andu, who likewise acknowledged the superiority of the Habiru (EA 305:15–24).

16. Amarna Letter (EA 299), written on behalf of Yapahu, ruler of Gezer.

To what extent do the Amarna letters reflect the history of the northern Hebrew tribes in Canaan in the fourteenth century BCE? After all, not a single Israelite tribe or biblical figure is mentioned anywhere in them. Nevertheless, they can help us in three ways. First, wherever the Habiru are mentioned in central Canaan, there is a high probability that the Israelite tribes are concealed under this name. Second, the letters of the local rulers provide an idea of the political situation in Canaan one and a half to two centuries before its conquest by the Hebrews. Finally, the Amarna archive contains important information about the Habiru as such.

Having been driven out of the Nile Delta, the Amorite tribes dispersed under the name *Habiru* throughout Canaan, Syria, and Mesopotamia. However, they were concentrated in the greatest numbers in Canaan and in the land of Amurru – that is, in the regions from which they had originally gone to Egypt. There they constituted a significant part of the population and therefore exercised a decisive influence on the subsequent fate of the region.

The exodus of the Amorites from the Nile Delta came to an end only in the thirteenth century BCE, a development associated with the accession of Ramesses II (1279–1213 BCE), the third pharaoh of the Nineteenth Dynasty. Unlike his predecessors, who had expelled Western Semites from Egypt, he began to compel them to perform large-scale labor on the construction of new cities in the Nile Delta and forbade them to leave the country. The son of Ramesses II, Pharaoh Merneptah (1213–1203 BCE), and his grandson Seti II (1203–1197 BCE), continued the policy of enslaving the Western Semites who remained in the Nile Delta. From this point onward, the Amorite tribes – later known as the Hebrew tribes – began to wait for a favorable moment to leave Egypt, which had become hostile to them.

Such an opportunity arose quite soon, at the beginning of the twelfth century BCE, when a civil war broke out in Egypt between rival claimants to the pharaonic throne. It was during this period of turmoil, when the Nineteenth Dynasty collapsed and was replaced by the Twentieth, that the well-known biblical exodus from Egypt, led by Moses, took place. The biblical exodus thus represents the final stage in the history of the return of the Amorite tribes from Egypt.

The process of the Amorite exodus from the Nile Delta began at the end of the sixteenth century BCE, with the collapse of Hyksos rule in Egypt, and ended only at the beginning of the twelfth century BCE with the departure of the tribes led by Moses. However, the exodus under Moses is presented in the Bible as a single, unified event involving all the Hebrew tribes. In reality, at least three northern Hebrew tribes were already present in Canaan, where they appear in the messages of Canaanite rulers from the Egyptian Amarna archive as part of the so-called *Habiru/Apiru*. It is these tribes of the "House of Joseph" that are mentioned again on the stele of Pharaoh Merneptah (c. 1207 BCE) under the name "Israel," which at that time was located in central Canaan. The return of the tribes led by Moses from Egypt and their alliance with the "House of Joseph" made possible the Hebrew conquest of Canaan in the twelfth century BCE.

15. Sutu

The sedentary agricultural populations of Canaan referred to all nomads by a single term, *Sutu*. In reality, the Sutu were not a single nomadic people, but rather a group of West Semitic tribes of Amorite origin who roamed the semi-desert regions of Sinai, the Negev, and Transjordan. The Egyptians used a slightly different term for them, *Shasu*.

In the documents of the Amarna archive, the Sutu are often mentioned alongside the Habiru. However, the rulers of Canaan clearly distinguished between the Sutu and the Habiru, although they did not explain the nature of this distinction. The principal difference was that the Sutu/Shasu had not gone to Egypt, had not adopted a sedentary life in the Nile Delta, and had no connection with the Hyksos. They were not dispossessed like the Habiru, having managed to retain their tribal territories in Sinai and Canaan. Despite occasional clashes with Egypt, the Sutu did not experience the same deep conflict with that country as the Habiru and therefore were not regarded as an anti-Egyptian force in the region. Moreover, some Sutu/Shasu tribes even entered Egyptian service. None of the rulers of Canaan complained to the pharaoh about their rivals' contacts with the Sutu, whereas they frequently accused one another of forming alliances with the Habiru. Another important difference concerned their way of life. The Sutu remained nomadic, while the Habiru had led a sedentary existence before leaving the Nile Delta and sought to return to it at the first opportunity.

In the messages of the rulers of Canaan, the Sutu are most often portrayed as nomadic raiders who attacked trade caravans passing through their territories. They showed little respect for local authorities or even for Egypt itself and, like many nomadic groups, were regarded as unpredictable and difficult to control. The settled population therefore treated them with caution and distrust. The Canaanite rulers and the Egyptians adopted an ambivalent attitude toward the Sutu. On the one hand, they periodically employed them as mercenaries; on the other hand, they were compelled to organize military expeditions to pacify the most aggressive tribes.

Many Sutu groups in Canaan appear to have arrived as part of a large tribal confederation traditionally associated with the patriarch Abraham around the twentieth century BCE. This confederation included not only the ancestors of the Hebrews, but also those of the Edomites, Moabites, Ammonites, Ishmaelites, and Midianites. At the time of the patriarchs, all of these groups belonged to the same West Semitic ethnic continuum of Amorite origin. Before their migration to Egypt, the Hebrews themselves were regarded as Sutu-like nomads, no different from their relatives.

All Sutu peoples in Canaan, with the exception of the semi-nomadic Amorites of Sihon, traced their lineage to Abraham or to his closest kin. However, unlike the Hebrews, the ancestors of these groups occupied a subordinate position within the Amorite tribal hierarchy. As a result, they inherited less favorable territories – primarily semi-arid lands

– which encouraged the preservation of a predominantly nomadic way of life. The Book of Genesis attributes the Sutu nomads either to the descendants of Abraham by the slave Hagar, such as the Ishmaelites, or to the offspring of the sons from Abraham's second wife, Keturah, such as the Midianites. And finally, Genesis reminds us, there were nomadic clans from the unnamed concubines of the patriarch (Gen. 25:1–6). The Sutu included not only the secondary descendants of Abraham himself, but also the tribes that traced their lineage back to his nephew Lot, such as the Moabites and Ammonites in Transjordan.

The Edomites were considered the most noble nomads, since their ancestor Esau was the elder brother of the patriarch Jacob and the favorite son of the patriarch Isaac. They were also the closest relatives of the "House of Jacob." All the Sutu, unlike the Hebrews, did not live in Egypt for hundreds of years, but roamed their tribal territories in the Negev, Transjordan, Sinai, and Midian (northwestern Arabia). A long sedentary life in the Nile Delta and a hasty departure from there turned the Hebrews from the Sutu into the Habiru.

Starting from the 11th century BCE, the Transjordanian Sutu (Ammonites, Moabites, and Edomites) began to settle on the land and became sedentary inhabitants. At the same time, the Sutu in Sinai, the Negev, and Midian, such as the Midianites, Ishmaelites, and Amalekites, continued to maintain their nomadic way of life for a very long time.

CHAPTER III.

The United Monarchy – the First Pan-Canaanite State

1. The Myth of the Expulsion and Destruction of the Peoples of Canaan

The conquest of Canaan by the Hebrews in the 12th century BCE was far from complete. The most fertile and agriculturally convenient areas, such as the Jordan Valley, the Jezreel Valley, and the Mediterranean coastal plain, remained in the hands of the Canaanites. Some inland areas and their cities, such as Jerusalem, were still in the power of the Amorite peoples. Allied relations with the Hivites – the most numerous Amorite people in Canaan – left their cities untouched, such as Shechem, Gibeon, Kephirah, Be'erot, and Kiriath-Jearim. The Hebrew tribes had neither battering rams nor experience in storming heavily fortified cities, so when it came to cities, the authors of the Book of Joshua openly admitted that "Israel burned none of the towns that stood on mounds except Hazor, which Joshua did burn" (Josh. 11:13). The same was true of the valleys: "all the Canaanites who live in the plain have chariots of iron" (Josh. 17:16), which the Israelites did not have at that time, so for a long time they were unable to take control of the most convenient areas for agriculture. The incomplete nature of the conquest of Canaan by the Hebrews is recognized by the Bible itself: "Now Joshua was old and advanced in years, and the Lord said to him, "You are old and advanced in years, and very much of the land still remains to be possessed"" (Josh. 13:1).

But the most important thing was something else: the local peoples of Canaan were not exterminated, nor were they driven out of their lands. Biblical texts contain obvious contradictions regarding the fate of the population in the conquered areas. On the one hand, their authors claim that "Joshua defeated the whole land, the hill country and the Negeb and the lowland and the slopes and all their kings; he left no one remaining but utterly destroyed all that breathed" (Josh. 10:40). On the other hand, the Bible provides a wealth of evidence that the Hebrew tribes in all areas of Canaan settled next to the local peoples without causing them any harm:

"The people of Judah could not drive out the Jebusites, the inhabitants of Jerusalem, so the Jebusites live with the people of Judah in Jerusalem to this day" (Josh. 15:63).

"They did not, however, drive out the Canaanites who lived in Gezer, so the Canaanites have lived within Ephraim to this day but have been made to do forced labor" (Josh. 16:10).

"Within Issachar and Asher, Manasseh had Beth-shean and its villages, Ibleam and its villages, the inhabitants of Dor and its villages, the inhabitants of En-dor and its villages, the inhabitants of Taanach and its villages, and the inhabitants of Megiddo and its villages (the third is Naphath). Yet the Manassites could not take possession of those towns, but the Canaanites continued to live in that land. But when the Israelites grew strong, they put the Canaanites to forced labor but did not utterly drive them out" (Josh.17:11-13).

"Zebulun did not drive out the inhabitants of Kitron or the inhabitants of Nahalol, but the Canaanites lived among them and became subject to forced labor" (Judges 1:30).

"Asher did not drive out the inhabitants of Acco or the inhabitants of Sidon, or of Mahalab, or of Achzib, or of Helbah, or of Aphik, or of Rehob, but the Asherites lived among the Canaanites, the inhabitants of the land, for they did not drive them out" (Judges 1:31-32).

"Naphtali did not drive out the inhabitants of Beth-shemesh or the inhabitants of Beth-anath but lived among the Canaanites, the inhabitants of the land; nevertheless, the inhabitants of Beth-shemesh and of Beth-anath became subject to forced labor for them" (Judges 1:33).

"Yet the Israelites did not drive out the Geshurites or the Maacathites, but Geshur and Maacah live within Israel to this day" (Josh. 13:13).

The same situation developed in the eastern part of Canaan, in central and northern Transjordan, where the Hebrews defeated the Amorite kingdom of Sihon and the Amorite-Rephaite kingdom of Og. Their lands were divided between the Hebrew tribes of Reuben and Gad, as well as half of the tribe of Manasseh. The Bible again gives contradictory information about the fate of the Transjordanian Amorite population. Deuteronomy clearly states the following: "At that time we captured all his towns, and in each town we utterly destroyed men, women, and children. We left not a single survivor. Only the livestock we kept as spoil for ourselves, as well as the plunder of the towns that we had captured" (Deut. 2:34-35). However, the earlier Book of Numbers speaks of the intention of the tribes of Reuben, Gad and Manasseh to build city walls to protect their families from the locals before leaving to conquer Canaan: "We will build... towns for our little ones, but we will take up arms as a vanguard before the Israelites, until we have brought them to their place. Meanwhile our little ones will stay in the fortified towns because of the inhabitants of the land" (Num. 32:17). Thus, if it was necessary to think about protection from the local population, then there certainly remained such. Which of the biblical books gives a more reliable picture? Most likely, the earlier one - Numbers, written during the time of the United Monarchy, while Deuteronomy was created much later, in the 7th century BCE.

Cases of extermination and expulsion of residents of captured cities were an exception to the rule. From an economic point of view, it was more profitable to leave them in their places and make them tributaries, which is what happened. The claims of the authors of the Book of Joshua about the total destruction of the population of many Canaanite cities are included in the Old Testament from a purely didactic point of view - to demonstrate how to treat idolaters. The authors of the biblical books - the bearers of the idea of monotheism - were afraid of the influence of the pagans on their people, so they always warned their fellow tribesmen: "You shall not enter into marriage with them, neither shall they with you, for they will surely incline your heart to follow their gods" (1 Kings 11:2). In fact, as the Book of Judges admits, in life, the exact opposite happened: "So the Israelites lived among the Canaanites, the Hittites, the Amorites, the Perizzites, the Hivites, and the Jebusites, and they took their daughters as wives for themselves, and their own daughters they gave to their sons, and they served their gods" (Judges 3:5-6). Thus, the Hebrew tribes not only lived in peace with the conquered peoples, but also quickly assimilated with them.

17. The Conquest of Canaan and the allotment of conquered territories to Hebrew tribes. Yohanan Aharoni, The Land of the Bible.

The alliance with the Hivites of Gibeon became another evidence that, contrary to the claims of the biblical authors, the Israelite conquest of Canaan did not lead to the expulsion or destruction of the local peoples, but to mixing and merging with them. The authors of the Book of Judges could not help but acknowledge this fact, but they considered it as a violation of the covenant with Yahweh and placed all responsibility for this on their people: "But you have not obeyed my command. See what you have done! So now I say, I will not drive them [Canaanites] out before you, but they shall become adversaries to you, and their gods shall be a snare to you" (Judges 2:2-3).

The expansion of the Philistines in the 11th century BCE forced all the West Semitic peoples in Canaan to reconcile and unite. The Book of Samuel describes this change as follows: "There was peace also between Israel and the Amorites" (1 Sam. 7:14). Peaceful relations between former enemies contributed to even greater rapprochement and mixing between the West Semitic peoples. However, sometimes even wars were not an obstacle to close contacts between the opposing peoples of Canaan. This is indicated at least by the example of the Israelite judge Samson, who took a fancy to a girl from the Philistines. Despite their different origins and faith, and most importantly, the hostile relations between the two peoples, he was able to marry the girl he liked without any difficulty. If it was so easy to arrange a marriage between the Israelites and their enemies, the Philistines, then what can we say about the closely related West Semitic peoples - the Canaanites and Amorites - all of them over time completely mixed with the Hebrew tribes. The repeated reminders in the Pentateuch and the Book of Joshua about the need to expel the peoples of Canaan seem like a mockery of reality. The authors of these books called for the expulsion or destruction of those who had long since become an integral part of their own people.

According to Hebrew Bible, in the song of Deborah, a judge and prophetess of the era of the Judges, there is another impressive example of assimilation. Listing the tribes that helped their brothers, the authors claim that "some came from Ephraim, whose roots were in

Amalek" (Judges 5:14). Thus, in Ephraim - the most important northern tribe of the "House of Joseph" - there was a clan or clans that traced their origins to Amalek - the sworn enemy of the "House of Jacob". The memory of them remained even in the name of one of the mountains in the tribal territory of Ephraim – "the mount of Amalek" (Judges 12:15).

All these facts suggest that the Hebrews, who traced their ancestry to the biblical patriarchs, were far from the sole ancestors of the Jewish people. The flesh and blood of this people were not so much the newcomers – the descendants of Abraham, Isaac, and Jacob – but rather all the peoples of Canaan, including its indigenous inhabitants. The Hebrews, who represented a minority among the peoples of Canaan, did not exterminate or expel the conquered peoples, as was long believed, but completely assimilated among them, giving them their name, their history, and, most importantly, their religion. Thus, Canaan was transformed into the Land of Israel (Eretz Israel), and the autochthonous inhabitants of this land came to identify themselves as Jews.

This means that the history of the people we now call the Jewish people is much older than four thousand years. It dates back not only to the biblical patriarchs, but rather to the first Neolithic cities of Canaan, which appeared about ten thousand years ago, long before the rise of the ancient Egyptian and Sumerian civilizations.

Recent breakthroughs in the field of genetics have fully confirmed what archaeologists had long suspected: the Israelites and Judahites, who once inhabited the kingdoms of Israel and Judah, are in fact the direct descendants of Canaan's most ancient population. DNA extracted from Canaanite remains dating to the 4th and 3rd millennia BCE matches, in every essential detail, the DNA found in the bones of Israelites and Judahites from the 1st millennium BCE (*Cell*, May 2020; *Bible History Daily*, June 2020).

2. The Rule of Saul - the Rise of Israelite Power

In the history of Canaan, the 11th century BCE was a time of Philistine expansion. This people of Achaean origin, who captured the southwestern part of Canaan a century earlier, quickly converged and then mixed with the indigenous population of those places - the Canaanites and Rephaim. By the beginning of the 11th century BCE the five main cities where the Philistines had settled – Ashdod, Ashkelon, Gaza, Ekron and Gath – managed to unite, and their rulers, the seranim ("tyrants"), began a systematic conquest of all of Canaan. However, the main obstacle to taking over the country were the Hebrew tribes, who had returned to Canaan from Egypt at about the same time that the Philistines appeared there. Protracted wars began between the two peoples, which lasted, with breaks, for almost a century. The advantage of the Philistines was the massive use of iron weapons and a much better organization of their army, because they were hereditary warriors and constantly served as mercenaries in Egypt. The Philistines also made full use of the extraordinary physical qualities of the Rephaim, whom they strenuously attracted to their army. One of many such giant warriors was the famous Goliath, who fought in a duel with the future King David. The Israelite judges, who ruled over one or even several tribes, were unable to withstand the experienced, battle-hardened Philistine army, consisting of professional warriors of enormous height and physical strength. A completely new organization of power and army was needed, which would cover all the tribes without exception; a king was needed who would have much greater powers than any judge. A serious external threat and the "voice of the people" forced the Hebrew tribes to unite around their own king. The first step was taken by the tribal aristocracy of the northern tribes – the Israelites – who chose Saul from the tribe of Benjamin. Obviously, the main role in their choice was played by the military merits and personal qualities of Saul himself. The Bible admits that "there was not a man among the Israelites more handsome than he; he stood head and shoulders above everyone else." The prophet and judge of the southerners, Samuel, also paid tribute to him, claiming that "there is no one like him among all the people" (1 Sam. 9:2; 10:24). But, as expected, the tribal nobility of the tribe of Ephraim, who always claimed leadership, refused to recognize him as their king. The Bible indignantly reports: "But some worthless fellows said, "How can this man save us?" They despised him and brought him no present" (1 Sam. 10:27).

Judge Samuel, the de facto ruler of the two southern tribes - Judah and Simeon - was faced with an unpleasant alternative: either to end up under the rule of the Philistines, or to enter into an alliance with the Israelites and give up some of his powers. In the end, he settled on the second option. He recognized Saul's supreme authority over him, and Saul, in turn, made him the high priest of the entire union – both Israelites and Judahites. But Samuel, having become a forced ally of the Israelite king, did everything to discredit him in the eyes of the people and the tribal nobility. Samuel had his own candidate for the throne of the king – David, who, like the high priest himself, represented the old tribal aristocracy of the tribe of Judah. Both of them came from Ephrath, as Bethlehem was called at that time, and were possibly distant relatives. However, as long as a serious external threat existed, Saul, Samuel, and David were forced to unite and act together.

The first king of Israel proved himself to be an outstanding military leader. In a short time, he defeated almost all of his neighbors who encroached on the lands of the Hebrew tribes. "When Saul had taken the kingship over Israel, he fought against all his enemies on every side: against Moab, against the Ammonites, against Edom, against the kings of Zobah, and against the Philistines; wherever he turned he routed them" (1 Sam. 14:47). But his most important victories were over the Philistines at Michmash, over the Ammonites in Gilead, and over the Amalekites in the Negev. Thanks to his military successes, Saul created the largest territorial kingdom in Canaan. It included not only all the Hebrew tribes, both northern and southern, but also the main Amorite peoples west of the Jordan: the Hivites, Hittites, and Perizzites. Jebusite Jerusalem and the Canaanites of the Jezreel Valley and the

Mediterranean coast remained outside Saul's control. At the same time, the Philistines in the southwest and the Transjordanian kingdoms in the east continued to challenge the Israelite king's power over Canaan. But within his kingdom, Saul no longer encountered serious opposition. Even the Ephraimites recognized Saul's right to the throne thanks to his impressive victories over his enemies. Saul was the first to create a small but permanent army of professional warriors. Unlike the tribal militias of the period of the Judges, recruited only from Israelites and Judahites, Saul's army included warriors from all the peoples of Canaan, even the Amalekites. The Bible testifies: "There was hard fighting against the Philistines all the days of Saul, and when Saul saw any strong or valiant warrior, he took him into his service." (1 Sam. 14:52). In essence, the Israelite king created a prototype of the first pan-Canaanite state, where there was a place for all the peoples of Canaan. It is noteworthy that after a complete victory over the Amalekites, Saul, despite Samuel's ultimatum demands, refused to exterminate them, moreover, he tried to save the life of their ruler Agag.

Over time, Saul's position became so strong that he decided to get rid of his main competitor, David, who commanded the army of the southern Hebrew tribes. He was worried about David's growing popularity every day, not only among the Judahites, but also among the northern tribes - the Israelites. "But all Israel and Judah loved David, for it was he who marched out and came in leading them... And the women sang to one another as they made merry, "Saul has killed his thousands and David his ten thousands." Saul was very angry, for this saying displeased him. He said, "They have ascribed to David ten thousands, and to me they have ascribed thousands; what more can he have but the kingdom?" (1 Sam. 18:6-8). It was not for nothing that Saul reminded his son and heir Jonathan that "for as long as the son of Jesse lives upon the earth, neither you nor your kingdom shall be established" (1 Sam. 20:31). The attempts of the Israelite king to deal with a potential rival led to David's flight to his native Judah, where he and his detachment of warriors took refuge in a hard-to-reach area near the Dead Sea. The strengthening of Saul's power and authority allowed him to push aside the high priest Samuel and the Judahite aristocracy that stood behind him. The main allies and helpers of the Israelite king in Judah were the Kenizzites – the rulers of Hebron, as well as their relatives, the Maonites, inhabitants of the places where David was hiding. As is known, both the Kenizzites and the Maonites were Edomites who had joined the tribe of Judah on the eve of the conquest of southern Canaan.

With the assistance of the Kenizzites and the Maonites, Saul's army found and surrounded David's detachment, and only an unexpected attack by the Philistines forced the Israelites to lift the siege and hurry to meet the enemy. For his part, David, not finding support in the territory of his own tribe, was forced to seek refuge and protection from his enemies, the Philistines. Perhaps David would have remained in the service of the Philistines until the end of his life, if the Israelites had not suffered an unexpected military catastrophe. Saul's army suffered a serious defeat in the battle with the Philistines at Mount Gilboa, the king and his three sons, including his heir Jonathan, were killed. This event completely changed the balance of power among the Hebrew tribes. From now on, the hegemony of the northern tribes was put to an end for a long time. David's small but battle-hardened army turned out to be the main military force in the territory of the southern tribes, a fact he wasted no time in exploiting. David entered the Kenizzite city of Hebron without a fight, where the elders of the tribe proclaimed him king of Judah.

3. The Reign of David and Solomon – the Dominance of the Judahites

The death of Saul and his three sons, on the one hand, and the proclamation of David as the king of Judah, on the other, led to the split of the United Monarchy into its original two halves: Israel and Judah. If Judah had already found its king, then Israel had to find its own again. Saul's family was represented by Abner, the cousin and military commander of the deceased king. He managed to convince the leaders and elders of the northern tribes of the need to recognize Ishbosheth (Ishbaal), the last surviving son of Saul, as the new king of Israel. At that moment, the tribal nobility of the Israelite tribes preferred the royal dynasty of the Benjaminites to the dominance of the Judahites. Abner brought Ishbosheth to Mahanaim, the Transjordanian center of the Israelite tribes, where the official ceremony of anointing him as king took place. After this, the struggle between the two contenders, Ishbosheth and David, began for the right to lead the United Monarchy. Ishbosheth's army was primarily composed of members of his own tribe, Benjamin, while the military forces of Judah consisted of David's troops, with whom he had served among the Philistines. The other tribes adopted a wait-and-see approach, ready, as was customary at the time, to switch allegiance to the strongest side when the time was right. The battle took place near Gibeon, on the land of the southern Hivites, but it did not reveal a winner, so negotiations between the Israelites and the Judahites resumed again.

However, Ishbosheth proved to be a weak king; he was unable to protect the Israelites from the attacks of the Philistines and thus failed to live up to the expectations of the elders of the northern tribes. Moreover, the actual ruler was not even him, but the military commander Abner, in whose hands the real military power lay. Ishbosheth's unpopularity contrasted sharply with the charisma of David – a talented military leader and politician. No one except David, who had both fought against the Philistines and served in their ranks, knew the weaknesses and strengths of their army so well. Two years of Ishbosheth's unsuccessful reign ended with the assassination of this king, and then the leaders of the northern tribes chose a southern candidate – David. However, David himself did not just want to gain power over the Israelites, but to somehow inherit it from Saul. To do this, he demanded the return of his wife Michal, Saul's daughter, who legitimized his inheritance of the dynasty of the deceased king. Moreover, David ordered the execution of Ishbosheth's murderers and brought Mephibosheth, the son of his friend Jonathan, closer to him. Thus, David conquered the northern tribes not by military force, but by skillful diplomacy, giving them hope of liberation from the rule of the Philistines.

David's first step as the king of the united state was the conquest of Jebusite Jerusalem (Jebus), which, wedged between Israel and Judah, actually divided the northern and southern Hebrew tribes. The Jebusites were an Amorite people who had been an old neighbor and ally of the southern tribes, just as, for example, the Hivites of Shechem had been for the northern tribes. Friendly ties between them dated back to the time of the patriarch Abraham and the king of Shalem (Jerusalem) Melchizedek, when they entered into an alliance and fought together against common enemies. The return of the Hebrews from Egypt led to the renewal of allied relations with the Jebusites. However, David was no longer satisfied with the allied relations with the Jebusites and wanted to turn this enclave in the center of the Hebrew tribes into his own fiefdom, in no way connected with the tribal territories of the Israelites and Judahites. The very fact of the swift and painless capture of the well-fortified city indicates that there was an influential party of David's supporters within Jebusite Jerusalem, which facilitated the city's surrender. It is noteworthy that there was no revenge by the victors or destruction of the city whatsoever. The Jebusites remained in their places and quickly became an integral part of the tribe of Judah. The Jebusite priesthood later merged with the Aaronites and Levites.

The reunification of the Israelites and Judahites, and the proclamation of David as their king, as expected, led to war with the Philistines. From now on, David, who had previously been their protected vassal, became their main enemy. Unfortunately, the Bible tells very little about the two military campaigns that led to the liberation of the United Monarchy from the Philistines. David hesitated between defensive and offensive tactics. At first, he locked himself in the newly conquered fortress of Jerusalem, but later his experience as a commander suggested the advantage of active action, and he hurried to meet the enemy. The outcome of both wars with the Philistines was decided near Jerusalem, in the Valley of Rephaim, named after the original inhabitants of Canaan. Here, more than ever before, David's service with the Philistines and his knowledge of their military strategy and tactics proved invaluable.

The first battle resulted in such a crushing defeat of the Philistines that even their gods and priests were captured by the Israelites. The second battle ended even more disastrously for them: David's warriors, having defeated the Philistines, pursued the remnants of their army to the city of Gezer. These two victories completely and finally freed the Hebrew tribes from the power of the Philistines. But David did not stop there, he himself went on the offensive and captured the main Philistine city of Gath. However, he did not seek revenge on his former patrons, but instead negotiated a moderate tribute. From that time on, the Philistines no longer posed a serious military threat either to the United Monarchy or to Israel and Judah separately after its split. Most likely, this was connected not so much with David's campaigns, but with internal processes in the Philistine cities themselves: their former alliance finally fell apart, and alone they were too weak to threaten their neighbors. Moreover, the gradual cultural and physical Canaanization of the Philistines made them more similar to the neighboring West Semitic peoples than to their Achaean and Aegean ancestors. The complete victory over the Philistines led to some cities and regions with a predominantly Canaanite population, which had remained independent under Saul, voluntarily recognizing David's authority over themselves. This primarily concerned the Canaanites of the Jezreel Valley and the Mediterranean coast, as well as cities such as Gezer and Beth-Shean.

David's second most significant achievement was his victories over the Aramean kingdoms of Syria, which tried to prevent him from subjugating the Transjordan region. The first war with the Arameans occurred after David's conquest of the Transjordanian kingdoms of Moab and Edom. "David also struck down the king of Zobah, Hadadezer son of Rehob, as he went to restore his monument at the River Euphrates. David took from him one thousand seven hundred horsemen and twenty thousand foot soldiers. David hamstrung all the chariot horses but left enough for a hundred chariots. When the Arameans of Damascus came to help King Hadadezer of Zobah, David killed twenty-two thousand men of the Arameans. Then David put garrisons among the Arameans of Damascus, and the Arameans became servants to David and brought tribute" (2 Sam. 8:3-6).

The second war with the Arameans of Syria was over Ammon. "When the Ammonites saw that they had become odious to David, the Ammonites sent and hired the Arameans of Beth-rehob and the Arameans of Zobah, twenty thousand foot soldiers, as well as the king of Maacah, one thousand men, and the men of Tob, twelve thousand men. When David heard of it, he sent Joab and all the army of the warriors...When all the kings who were servants of Hadadezer saw that they had been defeated by Israel, they made peace with Israel and became subject to them. So, the Arameans were afraid to help the Ammonites any more" (2 Sam. 10:6-7, 19). These two victories of David led to the expansion of the territory of the United Monarchy all the way to the Euphrates River. It is interesting that, having conquered almost all of Syria, David did not touch the neighboring cities of Phoenicia, although they were much weaker militarily than the Aramean kingdoms. The reasons for such a "merciful" attitude towards the Phoenician cities of Tyre and Sidon were purely economic: their ruler Hiram was the main supplier of materials, such as cedars, precious metals and stones, as well as skilled craftsmen for the United Monarchy. "King Hiram of Tyre sent messengers to David, along with cedar trees and carpenters and masons who built David a house" (2 Sam. 5:11). Trade with Phoenicia gained even greater scope during the time of King Solomon, who needed skilled craftsmen and a huge amount of materials to build the Jerusalem Temple.

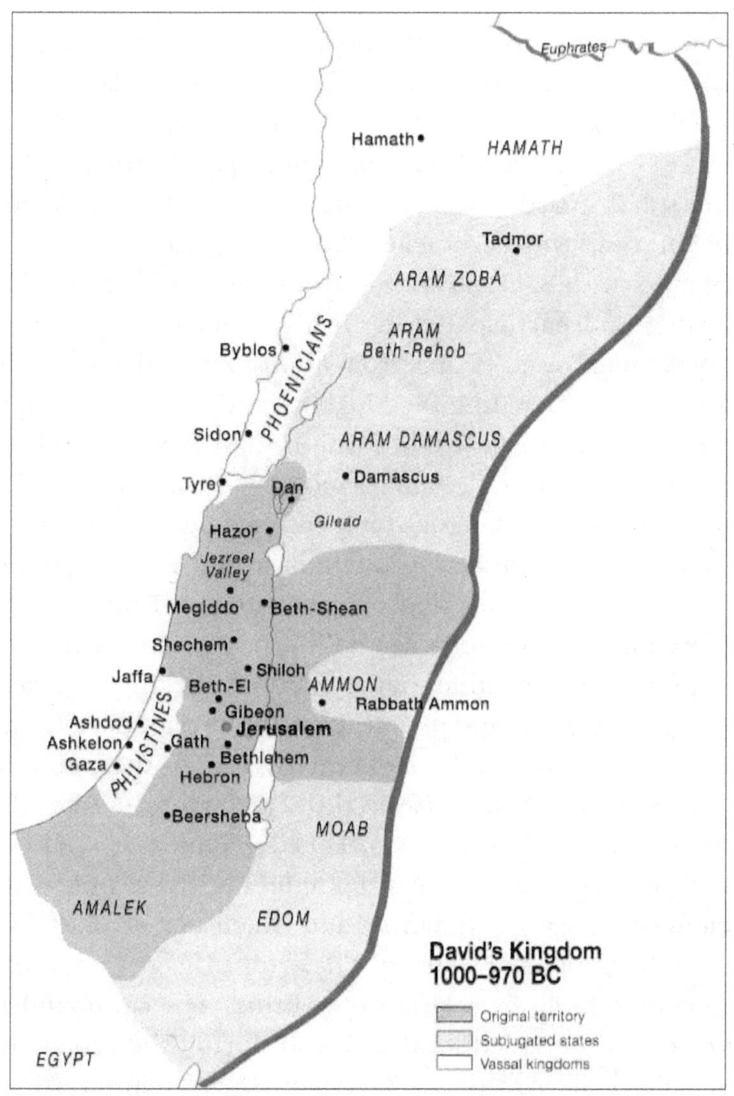

18. United Monarchy during the reign of King David. Mcmillan Bible Atlas.

Under David, a permanent mercenary army gained great importance. Unlike the tribal troops of Israel and Judah, this army was subordinate only to the king and had no connection to the tribal organization. Compared to the times of Saul, the permanent army under David was significantly increased. Like Saul, David recruited people not only from the Hebrew tribes, but from all the peoples of Canaan. However, unlike Saul, who trusted only his fellow tribesmen - the Benjaminites, David showed preference for mercenaries of Achaean, Aegean and Hittite origin. The most combat-ready and experienced part of the standing army was his personal guard – several hundred men, the so-called "brave men" and "heroes," who accompanied him always and everywhere: they fought together with Saul's army, hid from it, served with David among the Philistines and participated in all his military campaigns. Among David's "brave men" were people from almost all the Hebrew tribes and peoples of Canaan, including the Moabites and Ammonites. In particular, these chosen ones included the Hittite Uriah, from whom David took his future wife Bathsheba, Solomon's mother (1 Chr. 11:11-47; 12:16-17). Over time, David's personal guard increasingly began to consist of mercenary warriors of Aegean and Asia Minor origin. The king paid tribute to their military experience and organization, and most importantly, he considered them more reliable and loyal to him than his own fellow tribesmen. The pan-Canaanite character of David's kingdom was evident in everything. Foreigners and people from all the nations of Canaan predominated at the court, in the royal guard, and in the standing army: Cretans, Pelasgians, Achaeans (from the Sea Peoples), Gittites (from the Philistine city of Gath), Arameans, Hittites, Canaanites, Hivites, and Jebusites. It is no coincidence that the names of the people who served David belonged not only to Judahites and Israelites, but also to representatives of all the nations of Canaan. The army officer from whom David takes the woman he loves is Uriah the Hittite. The commander of the mercenaries who remained loyal to David during the rebellion is Ittai the Gittite. Even the Ark of the Covenant David temporarily entrusts not to the Levites or Aaronites, but to his loyal Gittite, Obed-Edom. His military commanders, Joab and Abishai, are grandsons of Nahash, the Ammonite king; the king's chief advisor and friend, Hushai the Archite, is also not a Judahite, as are most of David's wives and concubines. One of the two high priests, Abiathar, came from a northern priestly dynasty, and the second, Zadok, was probably of Jebusite origin.

The Kingdom of David was not just a union of northern and southern Hebrew tribes, it was a pan-Canaanite state, which for the first time in the history of this country included all of its historical regions: Israel, Judah, Moab, Ammon, Edom, the Canaanite and Amorite city-states and partly Philistia. The creation of such a state was of exceptional importance for all of Canaan. For the first time, the endless inter-Canaanite wars came to an end, and the country ceased to be an object of plunder and expansion by its aggressive neighbors. The Hebrew tribes, who returned to Canaan from Egypt at different times, acted as the unifiers. Although they were a minority among the population of Canaan, being scattered throughout different parts of this country, they sought to unite and dominate its entire territory. The kingdom of David was mostly inhabited by closely related West Semitic peoples who spoke different dialects of the same language and had common ethnic and cultural roots. The unification of the country accelerated the process of creating a single people of Canaan based on the Hebrew ethnic group.

However, David's enormous empire was undermined from within by a serious disease - an extremely unequal distribution of duties and unfair taxation. Almost all the burdens of maintaining the regional empire were placed on the northern Hebrew tribes and the Canaanite-Amorite population of the country. The king's native Judah was in a privileged position: it paid the least, but decided everything and ruled everyone. And this is despite the fact that the Judahites were significantly inferior to the Israelites both in terms of numbers and in economic development. As long as the Philistine threat existed, the northern tribes were ready to put up with the hegemony of the southerners. But as the external danger receded, the Israelites began to feel burdened by the power of the Judahites and their privileges, especially since they contradicted the original terms of their alliance. The first alarming sign of trouble in David's kingdom was the rebellion of Absalom, the king's beloved son. Absalom simply wanted to ascend to his father's throne as quickly as possible, but as soon as he promised to reduce the taxes of the northern tribes, he immediately gained the support of the Israelites. The influential Kenizzites, to whom he was ready to grant high positions at his court, anointed him king in Hebron. Although the rebellion was suppressed by David's personal guard, and Absalom himself was killed, the discord between the Israelites and the Judahites only worsened. This was facilitated both by David's concessions to the Kenizzites and his unwillingness to compromise with the Israelites. The circumstances of the king's return to Jerusalem after the defeat of the rebels further fueled the conflict between the northerners and the southerners. "Then all the people of Israel came to the king and said to him, "Why have our kindred the people of Judah stolen you away and brought the king and his household over the Jordan and all David's men with him?" All the people of Judah answered the people of Israel, "Because the king is near of kin to us. Why then are you angry over this matter? Have we eaten at all at the king's expense? Or has he given us any gift?" But the people of Israel answered the people of Judah, "We have ten shares in the king, and in David also we have more than you. Why then did you despise us? Were we not the first to speak of bringing back our king?" But the words of the people of Judah were fiercer than the words of the people of Israel" (2 Sam. 19:41-43).

The second rebellion against David was essentially an uprising of the northern tribes against the dominance of the southerners in the United Monarchy, and moreover, a rejection by the Israelites of any alliance with the Judahites whatsoever. It was led by a man from the tribe of the deceased king, a Benjaminite named Sheba, son of Bichri. "Now a scoundrel named Sheba son of Bichri, a Benjaminite, happened to be there. He sounded the trumpet and cried out, "We have no portion in David, no share in the son of Jesse! Everyone to your tents, O Israel!" So, all the people of Israel withdrew from David and followed Sheba son of Bichri, but the people of Judah followed their king steadfastly from the Jordan to Jerusalem" (2 Sam. 20:1-2). However, the uprising was spontaneous, unprepared, and was quickly suppressed by David's mercenary guard and the Judahites. The inhabitants of the city of Abel Beth Maacah, the last stronghold of the rebels in Upper Galilee, preferred to hand over the head of Sheba rather than die in the destroyed city.

David ruled for forty years: for the first seven years he was king only of Judah, and his residence was in Hebron, but for the following thirty-three years he reigned over the United Monarchy and made Jerusalem his capital. Having subjugated his allies – the Israelites – he transformed his kingdom into a regional empire. But the hegemony and privileges of the Judahites were not supported by their numbers or economic power. This imbalance between the Judahites and the Israelites represented the main danger to the United Monarchy. Its future depended entirely on how well David's successor could mitigate the contradictions between the Judahites and the Israelites. However, the transfer of power from David to his successor was very dramatic. With the support of David's personal guard, the high priest Zadok, and the prophet Nathan, one of the king's sons, Solomon, managed to bypass his brother and the direct heir to the throne, Adonijah. David, who was on his deathbed, was forced under pressure from his courtiers to change his will and appoint a new heir – Solomon. Upon gaining power, the new king dealt ruthlessly with his rival and all those who had supported him.

Solomon's reign was significantly different from everything his father did. While David pursued an active offensive policy and created a regional power from the Nile to the Euphrates, Solomon limited himself to a peaceful, defensive strategy and gradually lost the territories conquered by his father. The Book of Kings emphasizes: "He [Solomon] had peace on all sides. During Solomon's lifetime Judah and Israel lived in safety, from Dan even to Beer-sheba, all of them under their vines and fig trees" (1 Kings 4:24-25). However, even this purely peaceful policy did not relieve him from the need to fight. Firstly, Solomon had to wage a long war with the Edomite king Hadad, who after David's death returned from Egypt to restore his kingdom. Secondly, he was forced to repel attacks from the Aramean ruler Rezon, whom he had previously allowed to capture Damascus and fortify himself there. From then on, Aram-Damascus became the worst enemy of the United Monarchy, and then of the Kingdom of Israel.

Despite the peaceful policy and the rejection of any conquests, the tax burden and duties under Solomon increased noticeably compared to the period of David's reign. Solomon spent a lot of money on building fortresses and defensive structures, such as those in Hazor, Megiddo, Gezer, and also in Baalat and Tadmor. He rebuilt the walls and fortress of David in Jerusalem. He had to maintain a large mercenary army, with 12,000 horsemen and 1,400 chariots alone. Each chariot cost as much as the entire household of a wealthy landowner (1 Kings 10:26-29). But incomparably greater funds were spent on building the Jerusalem Temple and the palace for Solomon himself. The Temple took seven years to build, and the royal palace even longer – thirteen. Both buildings were constructed of expensive stones and precious woods, and the inside was covered with gold. To decorate the palace and the Temple, Solomon ordered the creation of two hundred large and three hundred small shields made of beaten gold (1 Kings 6:20-23; 7:1; 10:16-17). The construction was supervised by the best craftsmen of Phoenicia, and precious metals and stones were also brought in large quantities from there. To pay for all these materials and work, Solomon annually supplied the Phoenician king Hiram with large quantities of wheat and olive oil. Moreover, twenty Israelite cities in Galilee were given to Hiram as payment (1 Kings 9:11). To provide labor for his grandiose plans for the construction of cities, fortresses, palaces, and the Temple, "King Solomon conscripted forced labor out of all Israel; the levy numbered thirty thousand men. He sent them to the Lebanon, ten thousand a month in shifts; they would be a month in the Lebanon and two months at home... Solomon also had seventy thousand laborers and eighty thousand stonecutters in the hill country, besides Solomon's three thousand three hundred supervisors who were over the work, having charge of the people who did the work" (1 Kings 5:13-16).

All these duties fell on the shoulders of the northern Israelite tribes and the Amorite-Canaanite population of the United Monarchy. The Book of Kings reports that labor duties and taxes were imposed on the descendants of the Amorites, Hittites, Perizzites, Hivites and Jebusites who remained in Canaan after its conquest by the Hebrews (1 Kings 9:20-21). Thus, the Bible once again confirms that the numerous Amorite peoples and Canaanites were not only not exterminated or expelled, but remained untouched in their places. And yet, according to the same Bible, they outnumbered the Hebrews. The pan-Canaanite character of Solomon's kingdom was felt even in the king's harem, which consisted of "Moabite, Ammonite, Edomite, Canaanite and Hittite women" (1 Kings 11:1). Likewise, the religious life of the United Monarchy reflected the cults and beliefs of all the peoples of Canaan. "For Solomon followed Astarte the goddess of the Sidonians and Milcom the abomination of the Ammonites...Then Solomon built a high place for Chemosh the abomination of Moab and for Molech the abomination of the Ammonites on the mountain east of Jerusalem" (1 Kings 11:5,7).

A significant increase in taxes and duties under Solomon, and most importantly, their unfair distribution among the population became the main reason for the new uprising of the northern tribes. This time, the Israelites were led by Jeroboam, one of the leaders of the tribe of Ephraim. As the Bible testifies, "he rebelled against the king." At the same time, the Book of Kings acknowledges that "the man Jeroboam was very able, and when Solomon saw that the young man was industrious, he gave him charge over all the forced labor of the house of Joseph" (1 Kings 11:28). However, the rebellion failed. "Solomon sought therefore to kill Jeroboam, but Jeroboam promptly fled to Egypt, to King Shishak of Egypt, and remained in Egypt until the death of Solomon" (1 Kings 11:26,40). Thus, the Egyptian pharaoh Shoshenq I (the biblical Shishak) gave shelter to Solomon's enemies - the Edomite king Hadad and the rebellious Ephraimite Jeroboam. At the same time, impressed by David's great victories, he wanted to establish good relations with his rapidly strengthening neighbor. To this end, he gave his daughter in marriage to Solomon, and as a dowry for her, he granted the Canaanite city of Gezer, which the Egyptians had previously captured (1 Kings 9:16).

4. The Division of the United Monarchy into Israel and Judah

The United Monarchy lasted for about a hundred years. It disintegrated immediately after the death of King Solomon, approximately in

931-922 BCE. The formal reason for the split was the refusal of Solomon's son, Rehoboam, to reduce the tax burden on the northern tribes. In response, the northerners refused to submit to him and recognize him as their legitimate king. Rehoboam tried to suppress their rebellion militarily, but they outnumbered the southerners to such an extent that he quickly abandoned any attempts to restore his power by force. This third rebellion of the northern tribes against the power of the Davidic dynasty was successful, and the United Monarchy was forever split into two unequal halves: the Northern Kingdom - Israel and the Southern Kingdom - Judah. Both of them were separate states of the northern and southern Hebrew tribes. Rehoboam, the son of Solomon, was destined to become the first king of Judah, and Jeroboam, one of the leaders of the tribe of Ephraim, was chosen as the first king of Israel. The common capital, Jerusalem, remained the main city of Judah, and Jeroboam made his residence in Shechem, the largest city in central Canaan, which had been a stronghold of the "House of Joseph" even before the conquests of Joshua.

Israel significantly exceeded Judah in territory and especially in population. Ten Hebrew tribes and the majority of the pre-Israelite Amorite-Canaanite population ended up in the Northern Kingdom. In the south of Canaan, in Judah, only two Hebrew tribes remained: Judah and Simeon, which by the time of the breakup of the United Monarchy had in fact merged into a single whole and were called by the same name – the Judahites. The territory of the northern tribe of Benjamin was divided between Judah and Israel: the southern, Hivite regions (for example, Gibeon) passed to Judah, while the northern ones, including Bethel and Mizpah, went to Israel. Probably those Benjaminites who, according to the Bible, acted jointly with the Judahites against the seceding northern tribes in reality belonged not so much to the tribe of Benjamin itself as to the southern Hivites. On the other hand, the southern tribe of Reuben, which had settled in Transjordan, preferred to preserve its alliance with the northern tribes and remain in the Kingdom of Israel, which once again confirms the fact of a serious struggle for power with the principal tribe of the southerners – Judah. Another Hebrew tribe, Levi, was divided between the two kingdoms. It had always been the smallest among its brethren, and its fate was determined by Moses: to serve God and uphold the idea of monotheism. The majority of the Levites remained in Israel, where they created their own religious center at Shiloh. The northern Levitical dynasty that headed the center at Shiloh traced its origin to the sons of Moses. On the other hand, almost all the Aaronite priests found themselves in the south, in Judah. Their center became the Jerusalem Temple. It was they – the heirs of the high priests Aaron and Zadok – who became the priests of the Temple in Jerusalem.

This split was inevitable. And the fact that during the two hundred years (928-722 BCE) of their separate existence, Israel and Judah never tried to unite again, even during the best period of relations between them, once again testifies to the objective nature of their division. Despite the fact that both the northern tribes (Israelites) and the southern (Judahites) were Western Semites of Amorite origin, they had different genealogy. The biblical patriarchs known to us - Abraham, Isaac and Jacob, as well as the entire biblical family, including Lot, Ishmael, Esau and Midian, in reality represented the forefathers of only the southern tribes (Judahites) and their close relatives: the Edomites, Moabites, Ammonites, Ishmaelites and Midianites. The northern tribes, and above all the "House of Joseph", traced their origins to the legendary Israel and had a completely different history before leaving for Egypt. Staying in Egypt and conquering Canaan brought the two groups of Western Semites together. Memories of the vicissitudes of fate in Egypt turned out to be such an important circumstance for both groups that even after the split of the united state in both kingdoms, in Judah and Israel, the main holiday remained Passover - the holiday associated with the exodus from Egypt. It was during the period of the United Monarchy that the authors of the initial books of the Bible linked the genealogy of the Israelites and the Judahites. Thus, the patriarch Jacob simultaneously became Israel, and the number of his sons (the tribes) increased to twelve. However, the skillful interweaving of the narratives and genealogies of the Israelites and the Judahites could not turn them into a single whole. The main factor pushing them to unite was an external threat - the expansion of the Philistines, which they could not withstand alone. After the external danger had receded, the northern tribes began to feel burdened by the union with the southern ones, or rather, by their hegemony over them. This is evidenced by both the rebellion of Sheba in the last years of David's reign and the attempt of a similar uprising by Jeroboam during the period of Solomon. The southern Davidic dynasty clearly infringed on the interests of the northern tribes; it imposed on them and the Canaanite-Amorite population of Canaan a whole mass of taxes and labor duties. At the same time, David's own tribe, Judah, had a privileged status and was exempted, if not from all, then from most of the tax burdens and duties. The situation of the northern tribes worsened even more during the reign of Solomon, who carried out large-scale and expensive construction throughout the country. The famous Jerusalem Temple, Solomon's own palace, numerous defensive structures, barracks and warehouses were built primarily at the expense of the northern tribes, who also had to support Solomon's magnificent court and his large mercenary army. Solomon gave Hiram, the king of Tyre, "20 cities in the land of Galilee" only for his help in building the Jerusalem Temple and decorating his palace. This was done against the wishes of the Israelites themselves and only increased their discontent with the power of the southern king. The interests of the northerners were also infringed in foreign policy. Solomon paid primary attention to protecting the south of the country; for example, he spared no expense in waging war against the Edomite ruler Hadad, but looked with indifference at the growing Aramean threat from the north. His passivity on the northern borders led to the fact that he allowed Aram-Damascus to strengthen, which became the main enemy of the northern tribes. If Solomon's military power and authority had been weaker, the alliance of the northern and southern tribes would have fallen apart during his reign.

Perhaps this union would have been more viable if it had been led by representatives of the northern tribes, for example, the "House of Joseph", and not the southern dynasty of David. After all, no matter how numerous the southern tribe of Judah was, it still represented a clear minority among the Hebrew tribes. If the northern dynasty of Saul had managed to stay in power, it would have had more chances to pursue a balanced policy than the Davidic line. The dynasty of Saul successfully expressed the interests of both the northern tribes in general and the "House of Joseph" in particular. At the same time, being represented by the smallest tribe, it was forced to consider the interests of other tribes, on relations with which its fate entirely depended. In addition, the Benjaminites were not only the southernmost part of the northern tribes, but also the immediate neighbors of Judah, so they took its interests into account more than others. Perhaps these were the considerations that guided the leaders of the Hebrew tribes when they initially chose Saul.

Economically and socially, Israel was much more developed than Judah. The northern and central areas of Canaan, which it occupied, were densely populated agricultural areas with a large number of cities. In contrast, the southern areas of the country, which belonged to Judah, had a much sparser population, mainly engaged in cattle breeding. There were incomparably fewer cities here, and those that did exist, with the exception of Jerusalem, were smaller in size than the cities of the north and center. This contrast in development between the north and south of Canaan was explained primarily by different natural conditions. The most fertile and agriculturally convenient regions were located in the northern part of Canaan; it was there that the greatest amount of rainfall occurred, and the main sources of water were found, whereas the south of the country consisted of mountainous, arid areas better suited to livestock breeding than to agriculture. The contrast was just as great in population numbers: the northern tribes outnumbered their southern brethren by two to three times. Yet Israel's numerical superiority over Judah was not limited to this. The Israelite tribes proper constituted only the ruling minority among the population of the Northern Kingdom. Along the Mediterranean coast, in Galilee, in the Jezreel Valley, and in the Jordan Valley, Canaanite and Amorite peoples predominated, further increasing the disparity between Israel and Judah. Of course, the same peoples also lived in the territory of Judah, but because of the harsher natural conditions their numbers there were small. For this reason, the southern Hebrew tribes constituted a higher proportion in Judah than the northern ones did in Israel, though probably still no more than half of the total population. On the basis of archaeological data on the population density of Canaan at that time, it may be assumed that in terms of the number of inhabitants Israel surpassed Judah by at least five to six times. In light of such a significant disparity between the two parts of the United Monarchy, the de facto hegemony of the southern tribes over the northern ones was unnatural and doomed to an inevitable end.

The collapse of the union between the Israelites and the Judahites also led to a religious schism between them. As an alternative to the Temple of the Lord in Jerusalem, the Israelite king Jeroboam established two specifically Israelite religious centers of his own: one in the south, at Bethel, and another in the north, at Dan, where he set up golden calves. They were akin to the golden calf fashioned by the high priest Aaron in the Sinai wilderness. Identical calves likewise represented the traditional Canaanite cult of Baal, which at that time was so widespread among the northern tribes and their Canaanite neighbors. Jeroboam, and after him all the Israelite kings, legalized the already existing Canaanite cults of the northern tribes, as well as their priests of non-Levitical origin. Yahwism remained, but no longer as the principal religion – only as one cult among others, and moreover in the old pagan form against which Moses had fought. This explains the extreme hostility of the Levites and the Aaronites toward all the Israelite kings.

The revolt of the northern tribes and the collapse of the United Monarchy gave rise to hostile relations between the Israelites and the Judahites, which periodically led to wars. The split had serious consequences not only for the Hebrew tribes but for the whole of Canaan as well, which once again became vulnerable to foreign invasions.

CHAPTER IV

Ethnic Evolution of the Kingdoms of Israel and Judah

1. The Assimilation of the Hebrew Tribes with the Peoples of Canaan

The primary successor to the United Monarchy was its smaller part, Judah. This southern Hebrew kingdom, remaining under the rule of the Davidic dynasty, maintained Jerusalem as its capital and Yahwism as its official religious cult. The main religious center of the former United Monarchy, the Temple of Jerusalem, along with its treasury, also remained in the Judahite capital. In addition to the Hebrew tribes of Judah, Simeon, and part of Benjamin, the Kingdom of Judah also included pre-Israelite Amorite peoples: the Jebusites, Hittites, Perizzites, and southern Hivites. The ancient, tall people of Rapha (Rephaim), who lived in various regions of Judah, had by that time almost completely mixed with the pre-Israelite Amorite peoples. By the time of the split of the United Monarchy the Rephaim remained mostly in southwestern Canaan, in Philistia, where they were known as "Avvim." The Kingdom of Judah also inherited small enclaves of purely Canaanite populations, located in the Shephelah region near the Perizzites.

The semi-desert Negev, which became the southern part of Judah, was home to the nomadic Amalekites, who maintained their nomadic lifestyle throughout the history of the country. Other nomads, the Kenite tribe from Midian, who had joined the Hebrews before the conquest of Canaan, settled on the land in the northeastern Negev near Arad. South of the Kenites were the Jerahmeelites, who, like the Amalekites, were also nomadic. However, unlike the Amalekites, they were Yahwists and allies of the Judahites. Further north, in the hard-to-reach areas of the western Dead Sea coast, lived the Maonites and Ziphites, Edomite clans that had joined the tribe of Judah. Even further north, in Hebron, was a region dominated by the Kenizzites, an Edomite tribe that had allied with the tribe of Judah almost immediately after its exodus from Egypt. This was the ethnic composition of Judah's population after the split of the United Monarchy. It should be added that Judah also maintained its rule over its close neighbor and brother, Edom.

Over the three and a half centuries of Judah's existence (10th to 6th centuries BCE), the process of forming a single ethnic and cultural community progressed even further than in the Kingdom of Israel. This was because the Southern kingdom existed for a century and a half longer than the Northern one, and because Judah was significantly smaller in size and population than Israel. The Southern kingdom did not have the same number of Canaanite and Amorite inhabitants as the Northern one. Moreover, among the Hebrew tribes in the south, the dominance of the tribe of Judah was undisputed, which was not the case for the tribe of Ephraim or Manasseh in the north. The higher proportion of the tribe of Judah and the much longer period of Judah's existence as a Hebrew state allowed for the almost complete assimilation and Judaization of the local peoples. As a result, the population of the Southern kingdom became much more homogenous than in the north. This factor played a crucial role in the restoration of Judah's statehood and, consequently, prevented the revival of Israel in the north.

One piece of evidence of how far the process of forming a single Judean people had progressed is the census of Babylonian captives intending to return home. It showed that very few of them could not provide proof of their belonging to the Judean people, even though at the time of the conquest of Canaan, the southern Hebrew tribes constituted no more than half of the entire local population. Another piece of evidence comes from the biblical sources themselves. While narratives from the period of the Judges and the United Monarchy frequently mention Canaanite and Amorite peoples and non-Israelite and non-Judahite names, such mentions become fewer and fewer later on, until they disappear completely. Thus, all the peoples in the territory of Judah, both Semitic and non-Semitic, gradually transformed into Judeans. Wars and droughts, expulsions and captivities, which led to population movements, accelerated the mixing and assimilation.

By the end of the First Temple period, the entire conglomerate of settled and nomadic ethnic groups had finally merged into a homogeneous people under the common name "Judeans." At least in cultural, linguistic and physical terms, the assimilation of all these ethnic groups was complete. Thus, by the 6th century BCE, the Judeans were not so much the descendants of the southern Hebrew tribes as they were the heirs of the local autochthonous peoples of Southern Canaan, who had lived there even before the arrival of the "House of Jacob" and constituted the majority of the population. As the prophet Ezekiel said to Jerusalem and its inhabitants: "Your origin and your birth were in the land of the Canaanites; your father was an Amorite and your mother a Hittite" (Ezek. 16:3). The southern Hebrew tribes played a very important role: they united all these southern Canaanite ethnic groups and were themselves absorbed into them, giving their name, history and religion to a new, Judean people – their common heir.

The Northern Kingdom of Israel presented a more complex ethnic picture. Unlike the Southern Kingdom, where only one Hebrew tribe, Judah, reigned supreme, the Northern Kingdom contained ten Israelite tribes, each of which demanded its share of power. And although the tribe of Ephraim always claimed leadership, neither it nor the "House of Joseph" as a whole had enough "weight" to impose its rule on the large population of Israel. Moreover, all the Hebrew tribes, as the Bible itself repeatedly acknowledged, constituted a minority of the population of Canaan. The Northern Kingdom included many areas populated by Canaanites, especially the Jezreel and Jordan valleys, as well as the Mediterranean coast. Among the pre-Israelite Amorite peoples, the Hivites predominated, living in both the central interior regions, such as Shechem, and in Galilee. In the northeast, particularly on the Golan and in the Mount Hermon area, Aramean peoples – the Geshurites and Maachatites – had settled (starting from the 12th century BCE). Furthermore, the Kingdom of Israel always sought to rule over its Transjordanian neighbors, Ammon and Moab.

Jeroboam, the first true Israelite king, failed to establish his own dynasty. Similarly, the tribe of Ephraim was unable to hold its power over the Kingdom of Israel. Jeroboam's son, Nadab, fell victim to a bloody coup led by his own commander in the second year of his reign. "Baasha son of Ahijah, of the house of Issachar, conspired against him, and Baasha struck him down at Gibbethon, which belonged to the Philistines, for Nadab and all Israel were laying siege to Gibbethon...As soon as he was king, he killed all the house of Jeroboam; he left to the house of Jeroboam not one who breathed, until he had destroyed it" (1 Kings 15:27, 29).

The new king had no connection to either the tribe of Ephraim or the "House of Joseph" in general; he was from the tribe of Issachar, whose lands were located near the then-Israelite capital, Tirzah. This northern tribe left Egypt with the southern tribes of Moses and Aaron and, due to its large size and high position in the Amorite tribal hierarchy, was "adopted" in the desert by the "House of Jacob": its lineage was traced back to the sons of Leah, the senior wife of the patriarch Jacob. It is likely that the rise of a king from this tribe was made possible by the support of opponents of Ephraimite hegemony. Baasha's enthronement showed that, unlike the monopoly of the tribe of Judah among the southern tribes, neither the "House of Joseph" nor the tribe of Ephraim possessed the exclusive influence needed to claim power among the northern tribes.

Baasha succeeded in taking away from Judah all the disputed areas in the territory of the tribe of Benjamin and, moreover, encircling Jerusalem. However, the Judahite king Asa, with the help of rich gifts, drew the Aramean kingdom of Damascus into a war on his side. This prolonged the confrontation between Israel, Judah, and the Arameans of Damascus for many years. The fate of Baasha's heir was no better than that of Jeroboam's son. Upon his ascension to the throne, Elah, son of Baasha, was killed by his own commander: "But his servant Zimri, commander of half his chariots, conspired against him. When he was at Tirzah drinking himself drunk in the house of Arza, who was in charge of the palace at Tirzah, Zimri came in, struck him down, and killed him, in the twenty-seventh year of King Asa of Judah, and succeeded him. When he began to reign, as soon as he had seated himself on his throne, he killed all the house of Baasha; he did not leave him a single male of his kindred or his friends" (1 Kings 16:9-11). However, Zimri only managed to hold power for seven days. Upon learning of the palace coup in the capital, the Israelite commanders, who were at the time besieging Philistine cities, hurried with their troops to Tirzah and, quickly taking it, killed the usurper. This was followed by new disputes over which of the Israelite commanders should occupy the vacant throne.

The civil war that erupted in the Kingdom of Israel after the overthrow of Zimri brought another commander, Omri, to power. Although the Bible provides detailed information about the origins of Saul, David, Jeroboam, and Baasha – all kings who founded or tried to found their own dynasties – it is silent about the lineage of Omri, one of the most famous Israelite kings. Given Omri's and his son Ahab's particular devotion to the Canaanite cult of Baal, as well as their close ties to the Canaanites of the Jezreel Valley, it is highly probable that the new king was of Canaanite origin from that very region.

Omri fundamentally changed Israel's policy toward Judah: he abandoned the hostility and wars that characterized the reigns of Jeroboam and Baasha and began to build good neighborly relations. The genuine peace with Judah was another indirect piece of evidence for Omri's Canaanite origin. All other kings from the Israelite tribes were characterized by overt hostility toward their southern brothers. A new direction in foreign policy was also an alliance with the king of the Phoenician city of Sidon, Ethbaal. The Sidonians, like all Phoenicians, were also Canaanites. This alliance guaranteed a friendly rear to the north and opened up new opportunities for participation in international trade, including maritime trade, which was of greatest interest to the Canaanites. Omri and his son Ahab undertook extensive construction projects and needed a large number of highly skilled craftsmen, who could be obtained, once again, from the Phoenician cities. Of all the Israelite kings, Ahab went the furthest in strengthening the alliance with the Phoenicians: he married Jezebel, the daughter of the Sidonian king Ethbaal.

The kings of the Omride dynasty (c. 880-841 BCE), of whom there were only four, did not manage to stay on the Israelite throne for long. Taking advantage of an injury sustained by Jehoram, the last king of this dynasty, in a battle with the Arameans of Damascus, his commander Jehu seized power and began the rule of his own dynasty. Unlike the Canaanite Omride dynasty, which served the cult of Baal, Jehu was from the Hebrew tribes and supported the Yahwists. He brutally dealt with the priests of Baal, brought the Rechabites (nomadic Yahwist-ascetic clans) closer to him, but did not allow the northern Levites to lead the Yahwist worship in the main Israelite religious centers – Bethel and Dan. All five kings of the Jehu dynasty waged constant wars with Aram-Damascus and sought to make peace with Assyria. Jehu's son, Jehoahaz, had the hardest time, as his reign coincided with the peak of Aram-Damascus's military power. In contrast, his successors, the Israelite kings Jehoash and especially Jeroboam II, repeatedly defeated the Arameans of Damascus and captured all of Syria up to the Euphrates River.

19. Kingdoms of Israel and Judah in 9th-8th centuries BCE

The Jehu dynasty ended as a result of another military coup. The biblical sources again provide no information about the new king's origin. This is another confirmation that the ethnic factor had lost its former significance due to the merging of the Hebrew tribes with the peoples of Canaan. The new ruler became the commander Menahem, who dealt with the conspirators who had killed the king but did not return power to the Jehu dynasty. Menahem's reign was short and was overshadowed by a new Assyrian advance on the countries of the Levant. Due to the clear imbalance of power, Menahem chose to buy off the Assyrians and cede to them the Israelite lands in Syria and Transjordan. Neither he nor his heir was forgiven for this. Menahem's son was overthrown almost immediately upon his ascension to the throne. This time, power was seized by people from Gilead, from the Hebrew tribes of Gad and Manasseh, whose Transjordanian lands Menahem had ceded to the Assyrians.

The Gileadite commander, Pekah, became the new Israelite king. He, like part of the Israelite aristocracy, was extremely dissatisfied with the concessions to Assyria, and therefore, in order to create a new anti-Assyrian coalition, he entered into an alliance with his former enemy, Aram-Damascus. The cities of Phoenicia and Philistia, as well as Ammon and Moab, joined the Israelite-Aramean coalition against Assyria. Judah's refusal to participate in this coalition led to a new war between the Israelites and the Judahites. The Judahite king Ahaz, hard-pressed on all sides by the Israelites and Arameans, turned to Assyria for help. Assyria again descended upon the countries of the Levant, and the numerous anti-Assyrian coalition collapsed like a house of cards, leaving Israel and Aram-Damascus to face the huge Assyrian army alone.

The first to fall was Aram-Damascus. Its army was defeated, its king was killed, and the city's population was deported to Assyria. Trying to avoid the sad fate of Damascus, the Israelite commanders, along with the courtiers, overthrew Pekah and proclaimed commander Hoshea as king. He hurried to the Assyrian king Tiglath-Pileser III, who was then in the fallen Damascus, and managed to negotiate peace, albeit on harsh terms for Israel. The new Israelite king Hoshea was likely from the "House of Joseph" and, most remarkably, was not just a Yahwist but was closer than any other Israelite king to the northern Levites. Hoshea proved to be the last Israelite king in the history of the Northern Kingdom. Trying to reclaim the original Israelite lands in Transjordan and Syria, as well as to get rid of his dependence on Assyria, he sought an alliance with Egypt.

Upon learning of the secret negotiations between the Israelite king and the Egyptian pharaoh, the Assyrians decided to preempt their opponents. "Then the king of Assyria invaded all the land and came to

Samaria; for three years he besieged it" (2 Kings 17:4-5). The main forces of the Assyrian army, led by King Shalmaneser V himself, participated in the siege of the Israelite capital. However, Samaria offered such stubborn resistance that the siege lasted for more than three years. The Israelites not only defended themselves but also carried out unexpected sorties into the Assyrian camp. In one of these, the Assyrian king Shalmaneser V was killed. The storming of Samaria was completed by the new Assyrian king, Sargon II (721–705 BCE). Infuriated by the unusually long and fierce resistance of Samaria and the death of his brother, he ordered, in revenge, that part of the city's inhabitants be deported to Assyria and that captives from other conquered Assyrian cities be settled in their place.

The supreme power in Israel was characterized by chronic instability. While in Judah the same Davidic dynasty ruled for almost three and a half centuries, in Israel a single ruling dynasty never emerged. During the two centuries of the Northern Kingdom's existence, 19 kings succeeded each other on the throne, representing both different Hebrew tribes and the peoples of pre-Israelite Canaan. However, only two of the Israelite kings, Omri and Jehu, managed to establish dynasties that ruled for a relatively long period. The other rulers could not establish their own dynasties; their sons were overthrown almost immediately after ascending the throne. As a rule, most Israelite kings were successful military commanders who seized power under various circumstances. The main challenge was to hold on to this power and protect their heirs from other power-hungry commanders just like themselves. The absence of an established dynasty and, consequently, the instability of supreme power in the Northern Kingdom had their objective reasons. Unlike Judah, which was represented primarily by one large tribe, Israel consisted of a dozen Hebrew tribes that vied with each other for supreme power. The weight of even such significant tribes as Ephraim or Manasseh was not great enough to monopolize power in the Northern Kingdom. Therefore, unlike the tribe of Judah in the Southern Kingdom, none of the northern tribes possessed the "critical mass" that would have allowed it to set the tone in Israel. Furthermore, the territory of the Northern Kingdom was home to particularly numerous

Canaanite and Amorite peoples, who had successfully remained there after all the conquests of Joshua. As they became culturally and physically assimilated with the Hebrew tribes, they too began to participate in the governance of the Kingdom of Israel.

In the United Monarchy, the transfer of power from the Israelite dynasty of Saul to the Judahite dynasty of David was explained by the struggle for hegemony in Canaan between the northern and southern Hebrew tribes. These same inter-tribal conflicts were the reasons for the rebellions of the northern tribes led by Sheba and Jeroboam against the Davidic dynasty. And again, the tribal feuds between the Northerners and Southerners eventually split the United Monarchy.

However, as biblical sources testify, all the coups d'état in the Kingdom of Israel were not caused by tribal or ethnic conflicts but were political, religious, and social in nature, or were explained by the personal ambitions of commanders who craved power. For example, the commander Baasha from the Hebrew tribe of Issachar removed Jeroboam I's son from power not because he was dissatisfied with the rule of the tribe of Ephraim, but because of ambition and a thirst for power. For the same reason, the commander Zimri overthrew Elah, Baasha's heir, from the throne. On the other hand, the Israelite king Ahab, from the Canaanite Omride dynasty, took the life of the innocent Naboth, his own countryman from the Jezreel Valley, for a piece of land he desired. But Naboth's fellow Canaanites did not stand up for him; only the Hebrew prophet Elijah, who protested against the social injustice, did.

The commander Jehu dealt with the Omride dynasty not because it was of Canaanite origin, but as an ambitious Yahwist who wanted to seize supreme power from the worshipers of the pagan cult of Baal. And again, the Gileadite Pekah from the Hebrew Transjordanian tribes overthrew King Menahem's son primarily because of excessive concessions to Assyria. Finally, the coup d'état carried out by Hoshea was explained exclusively by the foreign policy failures of King Pekah, and not by his origin from Transjordanian Gilead. It is noteworthy that after the reign of Baasha, the authors of the biblical books ceased to indicate the tribal or ethnic origin of the next Israelite king altogether, although they continued to mention his father's name. This is an indirect confirmation that by this time the difference between the northern tribes themselves, as well as between them and the Canaanite-Amorite population, had become so blurred that the emphasis shifted to the territorial affiliation of the new kings. By the end of the Kingdom of Israel's existence, all the peoples living in it – the Hebrews, Canaanites, Hivites, Geshurites, and Maacathites – had gradually merged into one large ethnic group: the Israelites.

The fall of the Kingdom of Israel to the Assyrian Empire changed Judah's attitude toward its northern neighbor. In an attempt to extend their political influence over the population of the former Northern Kingdom, the Judahite kings began to appeal to the shared traditions and historical past of the northern and southern tribes, seeking to attract residents from the most war-torn areas to the south, and inviting them to the Temple of Jerusalem to celebrate common holidays. This policy had some success and led to a significant influx of people into Judah and a strengthening of Yahwism's influence in central and northern Canaan.

The Judahite king Hezekiah was the most active in this direction. He spared no effort to spread Judah's religious influence throughout the territory of the former Kingdom of Israel, which had been divided into four Assyrian provinces. He used common traditional holidays, and above all, the most important of them, Passover, as a pretext for reconciliation with the elders and religious leaders of the northerners. "Hezekiah sent word to all Israel and Judah and wrote letters also to Ephraim and Manasseh, that they should come to the house of the Lord at Jerusalem, to keep the Passover to the Lord the God of Israel" (2 Chr. 30:1). The king attached such great importance to establishing relations with the northern tribes that he even took an extraordinary step: he postponed the celebration of Passover until the arrival of the Israelites (2 Chr. 30:2-3). However, as the Book of Chronicles acknowledges, these efforts were at best only partially successful: "So the couriers went from city to city through the country of Ephraim and Manasseh, and as far as Zebulun, but they laughed them to scorn and mocked them. Only a few from Asher, Manasseh, and Zebulun humbled themselves and came to Jerusalem" (2 Chr. 30:10-11). Hezekiah's envoys met with the greatest resistance in the land of the tribe of Ephraim. It was this tribe that had suffered the most from the forced deportation of the population to Assyria and was, in the literal sense, decapitated. However, the remaining Ephraimites, along with the settlers from Syria and Babylonia who had been brought there, refused to accept Jerusalem's spiritual hegemony. The old rivalry between the "House of Joseph" and the "House of Jacob" prevented the creation of a religious union between the northerners and the southerners. Nevertheless, the military and political fall of the "House of Joseph" revived Judah's hope of leading all the Hebrew tribes, as it had been in the time of King David.

During the reign of Hezekiah, large numbers of economically active people from the former Kingdom of Israel, which had been devastated by the Assyrians, migrated to Judah. This significantly accelerated the economic and social development of the Southern Kingdom. According to archaeological data, within a few decades after the fall of Samaria, the population of Jerusalem grew by 15 times, and its area increased by 10–12 times; the city was enclosed by new, more powerful walls. Another large city, Lachish, also experienced rapid growth. The results of excavations indicate a sharp increase in the number of cities and agricultural settlements in both the most fertile valley of the country, the Shephelah, and in the more arid areas south of Jerusalem (Finkelstein I. and Silberman N., *The Bible Unearthed*, pp. 243-45). There is no doubt that in the late 8th century BCE, Judah was experiencing a demographic explosion accompanied by the rapid development of its economy, and the main reason for its prosperity was the overflow of population from the territory of the former Kingdom of Israel. The invasion of the Assyrian army interrupted this process and set Judah back in every respect. However, later, after the Assyrians left the country, its development accelerated again, though unlike the period before the war with Assyria, the growth of population and the economy occurred not so much in the Shephelah region as in the areas located south of Jerusalem.

Later, after the fall of the hated Assyria, the Judahite king Josiah (640-609 BCE) extended his authority over the territory of the former Kingdom of Israel. It is difficult to say whether he managed to annex all the lands of the northern tribes to Judah, but he certainly controlled Samaria and part of Galilee; otherwise, he would not have been able to carry out his religious reform there with such authoritarian and cruel methods, which imply the presence of political and military power. The Book of Chronicles specifically lists the areas of the Israelite tribes where Josiah destroyed idolatry: "In the towns of Manasseh, Ephraim, and Simeon, and as far as Naphtali, in their ruins all around, he broke down the altars, beat the sacred poles and the images into powder, and demolished all the incense altars throughout all the land of Israel. Then he returned to Jerusalem" (2 Chr. 34:6-7).

Unlike the actions of the more cautious Hezekiah, Josiah's religious reform caused outright discontent in the lands of the former Kingdom of Israel, where the influence of traditional religious cults was felt much more strongly than in Judah. Josiah's warriors killed the priests of pagan cults, destroyed their temples and altars, and desecrated the graves of their revered prophets. The Samaritans, being part of the "House of Joseph," felt even more humiliated by the fact that their new ruler, Josiah, represented the very "House of Jacob" which was their traditional competitor in the struggle for power over the Hebrew tribes. Unlike the Judahite king, the Assyrians had never imposed their gods and had tried not to interfere in the religious life of the peoples under their rule.

Thus, during the reign of King Josiah, Judah annexed a significant part of the former Israelite lands, including lower Galilee. However, the political and military vacuum that arose after the collapse of the Assyrian Empire was very quickly filled by another military power, Babylonia, and Judah's rule over the territory of the former Northern Kingdom proved to be short-lived.

By the end of the existence of the Kingdom of Israel (722 BCE) and the Kingdom of Judah (586 BCE), two closely related ethnic groups had formed in most of the territory of Canaan: the Israelites (in the center and north) and the Judahites (in the south). Both of these peoples were the result of the physical and cultural assimilation of the Hebrews with all the indigenous inhabitants of Canaan who had populated the country since prehistoric times. The eastern part of Canaan, Transjordan, was at that time inhabited by relatives of the Israelites and Judahites: the Ammonites, Moabites, and Edomites. All these peoples of the former Canaan were ethnically close to one another, spoke dialects of the Hebrew language, but differed in their level of socio-economic development and religious beliefs.

The fall of the Kingdom of Israel, and then of Judah, did not change the demographic situation in the territory of the former Canaan. This is because only a small percentage of the population of these kingdoms was taken to Assyria and Babylonia. Moreover, half a century after the destruction of Jerusalem and the First Temple, many Judahites returned to their homeland and rebuilt their Temple and capital. On the other hand, it was the destruction of both Hebrew kingdoms that accelerated the convergence and assimilation of the two closely related peoples – the Israelites and the Judahites.

2. The Myth of the Ten Lost Tribes of Israel

In 722 BCE, after a grueling three-year siege, the Assyrians stormed Samaria and deported its inhabitants to three different regions of the Assyrian Empire. The Book of Kings states: "In the ninth year of Hoshea the king of Assyria captured Samaria; he carried the Israelites away to Assyria. He placed them in Halah, on the Habor, the river of Gozan, and in the cities of the Medes… The king of Assyria brought people from Babylon, Cuthah, Avva, Hamath, and Sepharvaim and placed them in the cities of Samaria in place of the people of Israel; they took possession of Samaria and settled in its cities" (2 Kings 17:6, 24). The Bible unambiguously claims: "So Israel was exiled from their own land to Assyria until this day… None was left but the tribe of Judah alone" (2 Kings

17:18, 23). These words have always been understood as a total relocation of the Israelites to Assyria, which gave rise to the myth of the disappearance of the ten northern tribes, whose traces are still sought everywhere.

However, the Assyrian king Sargon II, in his inscriptions made in the palace at Khorsabad (Dur-Sharrukin), says nothing about the exile of all the Israelites. He only reports the following: "I besieged and conquered Samaria, led away as booty 27,290 inhabitants of it. I formed from among them a contingent of 50 chariots and made remaining (inhabitants) assume their (social) positions. I installed over them an officer of mine and imposed upon them the tribute of former king" (*Ancient Near Eastern Texts*, pp. 284-285).

If you add the 27,290 captives taken by Sargon II to the 13,500 residents previously deported by the Assyrian king Tiglath-Pileser III from Galilee and Gilead (from the territories of the tribes of Naphtali, Zebulun, Manasseh, Gad, and Reuben), the total number of deportees does not exceed 41,000 people. The Assyrians' accounts that they only deported the Israelites twice – a smaller part under Tiglath-Pileser III and a larger part under Sargon II – are indirectly confirmed by a contemporary of these events, the Judahite prophet Isaiah: "In the former time he brought into contempt the land of Zebulun and the land of Naphtali, but in the latter time he will make glorious the way of the sea, the land beyond the Jordan, Galilee of the nations" (Isaiah 9:1).

But what was the total population of the Kingdom of Israel at that time? The biblical and archaeological data at our disposal suggest that on the eve of Samaria's fall, the Kingdom of Israel had a population of no less than half a million people, and most likely much more. Thus, those who were deported to Assyria actually constituted only a negligible part of the Northern Kingdom's total population.

In fact, the biblical sources themselves indirectly acknowledge that the vast majority of Israelites remained in their homes. For example, the Judahite king Hezekiah, who ruled after the fall of the Northern Kingdom, "wrote letters to Ephraim and Manasseh, that they should come to the house of the Lord in Jerusalem to keep the Passover to the Lord, the God of Israel" (2 Chr. 30:1). If both of these tribes had been completely taken to distant Assyria, why would the Judahite king have invited them to a festival in Jerusalem? As it turns out, not only Ephraim and Manasseh but also other northern tribes were in their places. "So, the couriers went from city to city through the country of Ephraim and Manasseh, and as far as Zebulun, but they laughed them to scorn and mocked them. Only a few from Asher, Manasseh, and Zebulun humbled themselves and came to Jerusalem" (2 Chr. 30:10-11). The Book of Chronicles then adds that "for a multitude of the people, many of them from Ephraim, Manasseh, Issachar, and Zebulun, had not cleansed themselves, yet they ate the Passover contrary to what was prescribed. But Hezekiah prayed for them, saying, "May the good Lord pardon all who set their hearts to seek God, the Lord the God of their ancestors, even though not in accordance with the sanctuary's rules of cleanness" (2 Chr. 30:18-19). Thus, there is unconditional evidence that there could be no talk of a total expulsion of the Israelite tribes to Assyria. There is no doubt that only a very small part of the Israelites was taken captive to Assyria, but the majority of them either remained in their homes or went to neighboring Judah for temporary or permanent residence. After the fall of Samaria, the Bible often mentions "the people of Israel and Judah who lived in the cities of Judah" as well as "Israelites who were present in Jerusalem during Passover" (2 Chr. 31:6; 35:18). As had happened repeatedly before during invasions, many residents of the Northern Kingdom found temporary refuge in the mountain ranges of Galilee and in the Judean mountains of the Southern Kingdom.

Thanks to Assyrian sources, another important fact became known: around 720 BCE, about a year and a half to two years after the fall of Samaria, its residents launched a new rebellion against the Assyrians. At that time, many Syrian, Phoenician, and Philistine cities rebelled against Assyrian rule, and Samaria joined them in the hope of liberation (*Ancient Near Eastern Texts*, p. 285). If all its Israelite inhabitants had been evicted from the city, who, in that case, would have revolted against the Assyrians? After all, the people from Syria and Mesopotamia had only just begun to arrive and, not having settled in their new home, were not yet capable of resistance.

20. Israelite deportees in a relief from the Palace at Nimrud. 730 BCE.

The Assyrians were so afraid of possible resistance from the Israelites that they settled them in three widely separated areas. The first group was settled in the city of Gozan, located on the river of the same name, a tributary of the Khabur River. Ironically, this place of exile for the Israelites was not far from Haran, the ancestral home of Abraham and his family. The other area where the residents of Samaria were taken was Halah. The exact location of the biblical Halah is still unknown, but it is suggested that it refers to the ancient Assyrian city of Halahu, which was located northeast of Nineveh. Finally, a third group of inhabitants of the Northern Kingdom was settled in the far east of the Assyrian Empire, in the cities of Media, which is in northwestern Iran.

What was the fate of the Israelites taken to Assyria? Neither biblical nor Assyrian sources report anything about it. However, some Assyrian documents contain the names of royal officials and military commanders whose Israelite origin is beyond doubt. It is also known that the Assyrian army had units composed entirely of Israelites, for example, chariot detachments. However, no information has survived about the fate of the tens of thousands of Israelites taken to Assyria. The Assyrian captivity of the Israelites did not end as quickly as the Babylonian one for the Judahites; the people from the Northern Kingdom also did not have a wall of monotheistic faith to separate them from the local pagan population. Therefore, over time, all three groups of Israelites mostly merged with the surrounding peoples. It is possible that some of them later managed to return to their homeland, secretly or openly, while the Assyrians were still in power.

3. The Babylonian Captivity of the Judahites: What Really Happened?

Narrating the fall of Judah and Jerusalem in 587–586 BCE, the biblical books make it clear that the country was destroyed and the vast majority of the Judahites were deported to Babylonia. The Book of Kings asserts that "Judah went into exile out of its land," and the Book of Chronicles adds that "[Nebuchadnezzar] took into exile in Babylon those who had escaped from the sword" (2 Kings 25:21; 2 Chr. 36:20). However, the available evidence does not support this myth, which has persisted for thousands of years.

First of all, the biblical books themselves contain information that suggests the opposite. For example, the prophet Jeremiah, an eyewitness to this tragedy, testifies that "Nebuzaradan the captain of the guard left in the land of Judah some of the poor people who owned nothing and gave them vineyards and fields at the same time" (Jer. 39:10). But these so-called "poor people" constituted the majority of the population of all ancient Near Eastern countries. The Book of Kings acknowledges the same fact and reports that the Babylonians left only "the poorest people of the land" in Judah. But the Book of Kings said the exact same thing after the first fall of Jerusalem in 597 BCE, when it reported that the Babylonian king "carried away all Jerusalem... and no one remained except the poorest people of the land" (2 Kings 24:14). But, as we already know, these "poorest people of the land," who remained in Jerusalem at that time included the royal court of Zedekiah, his army, wealthy citizens, and the entire mass of people whom Nebuzaradan took to Babylonia after the second siege of the capital.

It must not be forgotten that the very appointment of Gedaliah by the Babylonians as their governor in Judah already indicated that a significant portion of the people remained in the country. In ancient times, governors from the local population were not appointed over a deserted country. In the Book of Jeremiah, one interesting fact stands out: many Judahites fled to neighboring countries during the invasion of Nebuchadnezzar's army and then returned to Judah after the Babylonians had left. "When all the Judeans who were in Moab and among the Ammonites and in Edom and in other lands heard that the king of Babylon had left a remnant in Judah and had appointed Gedaliah son of Ahikam son of Shaphan as governor over them, then all the Judeans returned from all the places to which they had been scattered and came to the land of Judah, to Gedaliah at Mizpah, and they gathered wine and summer fruits in great abundance" (Jer. 40:11-12). Consequently, according to the same biblical data, only a part of the Judean people was taken into Babylonian captivity. But how significant was it? Fortunately, this can be calculated.

As is known, the Book of Kings speaks of 10,000 people who went into exile with the young King Jehoiachin after the first siege of Jerusalem in 597 BCE. It does not specify the number of captives after the second siege in 587–586 BCE. However, the missing information is in the book of the prophet Jeremiah: "This is the number of the people whom Nebuchadrezzar took into exile: in the seventh year [of his reign, that is, in 597 BCE] – three thousand twenty-three Judeans; in the eighteenth year of Nebuchadrezzar [that is, in 587–586 BCE] he took into exile from Jerusalem eight hundred thirty-two persons; in the twenty-third year of Nebuchadrezzar [that is, in 582 BCE], Nebuzaradan the captain of the guard took into exile of the Judeans seven hundred forty-five persons; all the persons were four thousand six hundred" (Jer. 52:28-30).

As can be seen, even the total number of all captives cited by Jeremiah is much lower than the number given by the Book of Kings for 597 BCE alone. One of the most likely explanations for this discrepancy is the assumption that Jeremiah did not include the seven thousand warriors in the number of captives from 597 BCE, perhaps because there were many foreign mercenaries among them. It is noteworthy that such a knowledgeable historian as Josephus also preferred not to include the mercenary warriors in the total number of those taken to Babylonia in 597 BCE and, like Jeremiah, limited himself to the figure of three thousand people. As for Jeremiah's data for 586 BCE, there is hardly any reason to doubt them, for who would know better than he? The prophet was initially in the crowd of captives and walked with them in chains from Jerusalem to Ramah, where he was released by the personal order of Nebuchadnezzar II.

But even if we assume that Jeremiah's data are somehow significantly understated, and that the number of those taken into Babylonian captivity in 586 BCE was no less than in 597 BCE, and that we include seven thousand soldiers in both of these figures, the total number of exiles would still not exceed 20,000 people. At the same time, according to the most modest estimates of archaeologists, the population of Judah at the end of the 7th and beginning of the 6th centuries BCE must have numbered no less than 75,000 people (Finkelstein I., *The Bible Unearthed*, p. 306). Consequently, approximately a quarter of the Judahites were taken into Babylonian captivity, or perhaps even significantly less, considering that we compared the maximum number of captives with the minimum population size.

If we make calculations based only on biblical data, the percentage of exiles becomes completely insignificant. For example, we can take the numbers of captives indicated by the prophet Jeremiah, whom we have no reason to distrust, and compare them with the results of the census of the population of Judah conducted by King Amaziah as far back as the 8th century BCE. As is known, at that time, 300,000 men over the age of twenty were counted. Even if we assume that Jeremiah also counted only adult men and did not consider women and children, the exiles to Babylonia would still have constituted a negligible percentage. Thus, a paradoxical situation arises: on the one hand, the myth of the total Babylonian captivity arose and continues to exist precisely because of the claims of biblical authors; on the other hand, the same biblical books contain information that actually denies it.

Today, we have irrefutable archaeological data according to which a number of cities north of Jerusalem were not affected by the war at all, and their population remained in place. We are talking about the cities in the land of the tribe of Benjamin that belonged to Judah, for example, Mizpah, Gibeon, and Gibeah (Mazar A., *Archaeology of the Land of the Bible,* p. 460). It is no coincidence that Mizpah became the residence of the Babylonian governor Gedaliah; it was practically untouched by Nebuchadnezzar's army. But the most surprising discovery was the finding of rich burials in the area of Jerusalem itself, dating back to the time of the Babylonian captivity (Ibid., p. 548).

Thus, the Babylonian captivity was not a catastrophe in a demographic sense, because the vast majority of the Judean people remained in their homes, and Judah was not depopulated, as one might think when reading the biblical books. Moreover, some of its cities, for example, in the north, were not even destroyed.

CHAPTER V.

The Revival of Judea

1. Judah within the Persian Empire

The Babylonian captivity lasted for about half a century and affected only a clear minority of Judah's population. However, the most literate, cultured, spiritually and economically advanced part of Judahite society was deported to Babylonia. The captives included the royal court, priests, the best part of the army, and the most skilled artisans. This explains the great significance of the Babylonian captivity in the life of Judah, as it was these people who typically shape a country's history. Just a few years later, another tragic, though less-known, event occurred: the murder of Gedaliah, the Babylonian governor in Judah, which led to the flight to Egypt of the remaining part of the army, officials, and wealthy people in general. Although the majority of the Judahite population remained in their homes, there was no one left to rebuild the destroyed and devastated country; Jerusalem and the Temple lay in ruins.

In Babylonia, the Judahite captives were not separated like the Israelites in Assyria; they were all settled together in the center of the country, between Babylon and Nippur. They were brought to a free settlement where they were exempt from all forced labor. However, they found themselves on land devastated by wars, where there was nothing but ruins and everything had to be rebuilt from scratch. The Babylonian exile was probably not difficult, and over the years in Babylonia, many Judahites prospered economically, while others achieved high positions in the army and at the royal court. The members of the Judahite royal family, including King Jehoiachin, were treated with honor and were supported by the Babylonians themselves. The forced stay in Babylonia had two important consequences: first, it unified the Judahites, and second, it strengthened Jewish monotheism. The Judahite prophet Ezekiel, who was in Babylonia at the time, played a major role in the spiritual and religious life of the captives. Thanks to him and the captured priests, Yahwism, which was dominant during the First Temple period, was transformed into a consistent Jewish monotheism. It was during the years of the Babylonian captivity that the remnants of Canaanite cults and rituals disappeared, the ritual of worship changed, and the main emphasis was placed on prayer and prayer meetings.

When the Persian king Cyrus, having defeated the Neo-Babylonian Empire in 539 BCE, allowed all the captive peoples to return home, the Judahites were the only ones to take advantage of this opportunity. However, not everyone returned; many of those who had prospered remained in Babylonia or returned later. The Persian king did not just let the Judahites go home; he ordered the Temple to be rebuilt at the expense of the royal treasury and commanded that all the gold and silver Temple utensils captured by the Babylonians in Jerusalem be returned (Ezra 1:7-11). The Persian king appointed Sheshbazzar, the son of the Judahite king Jehoiachin, as the first governor in Judah. Later, he was replaced in this position by another member of the Judahite royal family, Zerubbabel, the son of Shealtiel, and the high priest became Joshua, the son of Jozadak (Ezra 1:8; 2:65; Neh. 7:67).

The return of the former captives took place in at least two stages. The first group set out in 538 BCE and numbered nearly 50,000 people, including 7,000 slaves. This group included not only Judahites but also Moabites, as well as descendants of Canaanites, for example, from the city of Keilah, and southern Hivites from Gibeon, Kiriath-Jearim, Beeroth, and Kephirah. There were also "those who could not prove their ancestry or their descent, whether they were of Israel... a total of 652 people" (Ezra 2:59-60; Neh. 7:61-62). Among those returning to Judah were also priests who could not confirm their lineage. It is possible that their ancestors were priests of the pagan cults of the peoples of Canaan. Such people had to be temporarily removed from the priesthood (Neh. 7:63-65). Nehemiah provides data on the descendants of King Solomon's slaves and subjects who also returned to Judah. There were 392 of them (Neh. 7:57-60). The majority of them were non-Jews (originating from Philistines, Canaanite peoples, as well as people from the Aegean region and Asia Minor) but had adopted Jewish monotheism. They later settled in the Ophel quarter of Jerusalem (Neh. 11:21). Thus, the ethnic composition of the first group already represented evidence of how the Jewish people were formed, and the fact that it was a pan-Canaanite ethnic group, that is, the result of the merging of all the peoples of historical Canaan.

The former captives' top priority was the construction of a new Temple of Jerusalem on the site of the old one, which had been destroyed by the Babylonians. The foundation of the new, Second Temple was laid by Sheshbazzar, a direct heir of the Davidic dynasty and the son of the Judahite king Jehoiachin (Ezra 5:14). However, the construction was delayed and was completed in 516 BCE by another member of the royal family, Zerubbabel, who was also appointed by the Persians as governor of Judah. The delays in the Temple's construction arose from a conflict with the neighbors, the Samaritans. They considered themselves the heirs of the "House of Joseph" and wanted to participate equally in both the construction of the Temple and the worship there. In fact, it was about creating a new union between the descendants of the northern and southern Hebrew tribes, between the heirs of the main southern tribe of Judah and the claimants to the inheritance of the "House of Joseph." However, in the 6th–5th centuries BCE, the real balance of power between the two sides was completely different from what it was in the 11th–10th centuries BCE. The Samaritan "House of Joseph" no longer had the northern tribes behind it and controlled only the region of Samaria. And Samaritan Yahwism was very different from Judean monotheism: of the entire Tanakh (Old Testament), the Samaritans recognized only their version of the Pentateuch of Moses and the Book of

Joshua. The fact of the mixing of the descendants of the Ephraim tribe with the settlers from Syrian and Mesopotamian cities further weakened the position of the Samaritans. From then on, there could be no equality, and the spiritual leaders of the Judeans rejected the idea of a new union and did not recognize the Samaritans' right to be considered the heirs of the "House of Joseph." Subsequently, the Samaritans were not even allowed to pray in the Temple of Jerusalem due to doubts about the nature of their monotheism. Moreover, the Judean clergy contemptuously called them "Cuthites" (Cuthah being a city in Mesopotamia). The offended Samaritans flooded the court of the Persian king with their denunciations, which delayed the construction of the Second Temple for more than two decades.

Forced pauses in the construction of the Temple, the hostility of neighboring peoples, and the difficult economic conditions of life in Judah destroyed by the Babylonians – all this oppressed the former captives and deprived them of hope for the revival of Judah. In this difficult period of history, a special role in the spiritual life of the people fell to the last Judean prophets: Zechariah, Haggai, and Malachi. Zechariah, who himself had returned from the Babylonian captivity, comforted and encouraged his people the most. Zechariah prophesied: "Thus says the Lord: 'I have returned to Jerusalem with compassion; My house shall be built in it... and My cities shall again overflow with prosperity; the Lord will again comfort Zion and again choose Jerusalem" (Zech. 1:16-17). Haggai also prophesied about this, conveying the Lord's command to the people to build a Temple for Him (Hag. 1:4-15). Haggai urged them not to be afraid, for God was with His people (Hag. 2:4-9).

The second stage of the return from Babylonia to Judah took place 70–80 years later, already after the construction of the Second Jerusalem Temple, approximately in the mid-5th century BCE. This new wave of returnees no longer consisted of the Judean captives themselves, but of their descendants, and it was led by the teacher of the Law Ezra, who was destined to become the spiritual leader of his people. The Persian king Artaxerxes granted Ezra, a high-ranking official, full religious and judicial authority in Judah. Josephus called Ezra "a personal friend of King Xerxes" (*Antiquities of the Jews* 11.5.1). Interestingly, the caravan of thousands of people with valuable property and livestock returned to Judah along a far from safe route with no escort whatsoever. Ezra did not ask the Persian king for protection, believing that God protects those who are devoted to Him and punishes only those who forsake Him (Ezra 8:22).

In his book, Ezra reports the shock he experienced upon returning to Judah. This shock was related to the scale of the assimilation of the Judeans with the peoples of Canaan. "The officials approached me and said, "The people of Israel, the priests, and the Levites have not separated themselves from the peoples of the lands with their abominations, from the Canaanites, the Hittites, the Perizzites, the Jebusites, the Ammonites, the Moabites, the Egyptians, and the Amorites. For they have taken some of their daughters as wives for themselves and for their sons. Thus, the holy seed has mixed itself with the peoples of the lands, and in this faithlessness the officials and leaders have led the way" (Ezra 9:1-2). It turned out that not only the common people but also their spiritual leaders, the priests and Levites, had entered into marital relations with the surrounding peoples (Ezra 10:18-19). This mingling with pagans undermined the unique character of Jewish monotheism and introduced pagan customs and traditions into the life of the Judean people. The only way to erect a barrier against paganism was to prohibit marriages with other nations, which at that time were universally pagan and idolatrous. To preserve the idea of Moses' monotheism – an idea forged through 700 years of struggle – Ezra took a step unprecedented for that period: he forbade marriages with those of other faiths unless they accepted Jewish monotheism and renounced idolatry. From then on, assimilation with other peoples became possible only through their Judaization, that is, through their adoption of monotheism and rejection of paganism. Thus was born the ban on marriages with foreigners, which later came to be interpreted by the surrounding world as an attempt by the Jews to separate themselves from other nations.

Ezra's idea was shared by another spiritual leader of the Judean people, Nehemiah, who was then the governor of Judah. This is how he described his reaction to the same problem: "In those days also I saw Jews who had married women of Ashdod, Ammon, and Moab, and half of their children spoke the language of Ashdod, and they could not speak the language of Judah but spoke the language of various peoples. And I contended with them and cursed them and beat some of the men and pulled out their hair, and I made them take an oath in the name of God, saying, "You shall not give your daughters to their sons or take their daughters for your sons or for yourselves" (Neh. 13:23-25). The scale of the assimilation of the Jews with the peoples of historical Canaan was so significant that Ezra and Nehemiah even demanded the expulsion of wives taken from other nations. It is no coincidence that it was precisely in the days of Ezra and Nehemiah that a prohibition against marriages with Ammonites and Moabites was "suddenly" discovered in the Torah. Under the pressure of Ezra and Nehemiah, all heads of households undertook a commitment not to give their daughters to other nations, and not to take their daughters for their own sons (Neh. 10:31–32). Yet even this commitment could not halt the process of mixing between the Judeans and the peoples of Canaan. Only now assimilation proceeded through the Judaization of these peoples. However, the adoption of Jewish monotheism at that time was rather formal in character, especially for women. The scale of the mixing of the Judeans with the peoples of Canaan through their Judaization is indirectly attested by the prophecies of Zechariah, who returned in the first group of exiles from Babylonia. "Many peoples and strong nations shall come to seek the Lord of hosts in Jerusalem, and to entreat the favor of the Lord. Thus says the Lord of hosts: In those days ten men from the nations of every tongue shall take hold of the robe of a Jew, saying, 'Let us go with you, for we have heard that God is with you… And many nations shall join themselves to the Lord in that day, and shall be my people" (Zech. 8:22-23; 2:11).

Nehemiah arrived in Judah after the construction of the Second Temple of Jerusalem, so his task was to restore the walls of Jerusalem. These walls were to protect the capital of Judah from the attacks of unfriendly neighbors, although they were all part of the Persian Empire and had no right to wage wars on their own. The greatest hostility toward Judah was shown by the Ammonites and the Samaritans. Both of these peoples feared Judah's strengthening and its hegemony over the entire territory of historical Canaan. The Ammonites were afraid of the emergence of a new United Monarchy, where Judah would play the main role, as it was during the reigns of David and Solomon. As for the Samaritans, they were offended by the Judeans' refusal to allow them to participate in the construction of the Second Temple of Jerusalem and their non-recognition as the heirs of the "House of Joseph." Unfriendliness toward Judah was also shown by the people of Ashdod, residents of the former Philistine city located closest to Jerusalem, as well as the Nabataean Arabs who had come from Arabia and captured the lands of the Edomites and Moabites in southern Transjordan. Nehemiah names the head of the Samaritans, Sanballat, the Ammonite governor Tobiah, and the leader of the Arabs, Geshem, as the main enemies of Judah's revival and the restoration of Jerusalem (Neh. 2:10). It was they who wrote denunciations to the Persian king and tried to prevent the restoration of the walls of Jerusalem. Despite this, the city walls and fortifications of Jerusalem were eventually restored. In his book, Nehemiah recounts the difficult and dangerous conditions under which this took place. "From that day on, half of my servants worked on construction, and half held the spears, shields, bows, and body-armor, and the leaders posted themselves behind the whole house of Judah who were building the wall. The burden bearers carried their loads in such a way that each labored on the work with one hand and with the other held a weapon. And each of the builders had his sword strapped at his side while he built. The man who sounded the trumpet was beside me" (Neh. 4:16-18).

Not only the Judeans themselves took part in the construction of the fortress walls, but also people of Canaanite origin, for example, from the city of Keilah, which had once closed its gates to David's detachment (Neh. 3:17-18). The descendants of the southern Hivites from Gibeon and Mizpah, and the Moabites also helped to build (Neh. 3:7). Nehemiah particularly notes the participation of Pedaiah ben-Parosh, the son of the ruler of Moab, in the restoration of the walls (Nehemiah 3:25). Representatives of all these peoples had adopted Jewish monotheism; otherwise, they would not have been allowed to participate in the construction, as happened with the Samaritans. Thus, Nehemiah, albeit indirectly, actually confirms the fact of the Judaization of the Moabites, Hivites, and Canaanites. His testimony is of particular importance, as he held the post of Persian governor of Judah and, of course, must have known everything that was happening in the country entrusted to him.

21. A fourth-century BCE silver coin from the Persian province of Yehud

As Nehemiah testified, the Judeans in his time not only did not restrict themselves in choosing wives from the pagan peoples of Canaan but also did not observe the laws of the Sabbath: they both worked and traded on Saturdays (Neh. 13:15-18). And this happened in the mid-5th century BCE, that is, seven centuries after the proclamation of the Mosaic legislation, the most important part of which was the law of the Sabbath. Nehemiah was also concerned about the social tension in Judah, which was under his rule. Not only were the laws of the Sabbath not observed, but also those that protected the poor and needy. This is how he describes the situation at the time: "Now there was a great outcry of the people and of their wives against their Jewish kin. For there were those who said, "With our sons and our daughters, we are many; we must get grain, so that we may eat and stay alive." There were also those who said, "We are having to pledge our fields, our vineyards, and our houses in order to get grain during the famine." And there were those who said, "We are having to borrow money on our fields and vineyards to pay the king's tax. Now our flesh is the same as that of our kindred; our children are the same as their children; and yet we are forcing our sons and daughters to be slaves, and some of our daughters have been ravished; we are powerless, and our fields and vineyards now belong to others" (Neh. 5:1-5). Nehemiah used the power of his authority to enforce the laws of the Torah regarding both the Sabbath and the poor. "Then they said, "We will restore these and require nothing from them. We will do as you say." And I called the priests, and took an oath of them to do as they had promised" (Neh. 5:12).

Nehemiah and Ezra were by no means the only ones who were concerned about the non-observance of the laws of the Torah. The Judean prophet Haggai worried about the same thing, but he believed that the people did not observe the commandments because they did not know the Torah (Hag. 2:10-19). In order to familiarize the people with the Torah and its laws, Ezra, with the help of the Levites, convened a general assembly in Jerusalem at which he read the Torah and explained its laws. During this assembly and afterward, the Levites continued to explain the Mosaic law to the people. Later, Ezra gathered all the heads of the people and the elders to sign a covenant and take an oath of strict observance of all the laws of the Torah. From this time on, the tradition of teaching the Torah and interpreting its laws began to take shape. A new group of religious authorities appeared – scribes and scholars – who not only rewrote biblical books but also interpreted them for the people. It was probably at that time that the Oral Torah (Oral Law) also appeared, the dissemination of which was carried out by scribes and scholars, most of whom were Levites by origin. These were the ones who would later, during the Maccabean wars, be called "Hasideans" ("the righteous"). It was this group of religious authorities that replaced the prophetic movement, which ended in the 5th century BCE.

Ezra and Nehemiah set the norms for the religious and social life of Judah for at least the entire period of Persian rule, which lasted for two centuries. This was a rather dark period of Jewish history, about which much less is known than about the time of the existence of the Kingdoms of Israel and Judah. In the Persian Empire, Judah was known by the name of the province of Yehud and enjoyed a wide internal autonomy. Persian governors were appointed there, as a rule, from among the Jews themselves, and at first, from members of the Judean royal family. However, over time, the powers of the governor were transferred to the high priest, and he began to have not only religious but also administrative authority. The reasons for this are unknown, just as is the disappearance of any mention of the Davidic royal family, whose members enjoyed honor and respect at the courts of both the Neo-Babylonian and Persian kings. The dynasty of King David, which ruled Judah for more than 400 years, mysteriously disappears from the pages of both Jewish and world history. Most likely, the powers of the governor were transferred to the high priest as a result of constant conflicts between them. This confrontation between secular and religious authority, between the king and the high priest, is well known from the history of the Kingdom of Judah. Nehemiah, as he himself admits in his book, also did not avoid sharp clashes with the high priest (Neh. 13:4-9). Obviously, the Persian court considered it more reliable to entrust all power in Judah to a religious authority rather than to a secular ruler, especially one of royal origin.

2. In Ptolemaic Egypt

The conquest of the Southern Levant by the army of Alexander the Great in 332 BCE did not just mean a change of power – from Persian to Greco-Macedonian – but also significant shifts in the cultural and religious life of the region. The Greeks and Macedonians brought a completely new culture, Hellenism, which could be adopted in all countries except one: Judea, because this culture was pagan and incompatible with Jewish monotheism. Not only was Hellenism new to the Southern Levant, but so were its bearers – tens of thousands of Greeks and Macedonians who settled in the Mediterranean ports of Philistia and Phoenicia, as well as in former Israelite and Judahite cities.

Alexander the Great's unexpected death in 323 BCE led to a series of bloody wars among his generals for the division of his vast empire. In the end, all of Alexander the Great's possessions in the East were divided between two Hellenistic kingdoms: the Syrian Seleucids and the Egyptian Ptolemies, two dynasties founded by Alexander the Great's generals. Judea became a subject of dispute and the object of five wars between them. At first, the Ptolemies held this country, then it passed to the Seleucids. All this time, Judea represented a strategically important border territory for both Hellenistic kingdoms. In an attempt to strengthen their power there, the Ptolemies and Seleucids heavily settled the former Israelite and Judahite cities with their officials, soldiers, and colonists. Thus, starting from the 3rd century BCE, Hellenistic cities populated by descendants of Greeks and Macedonians, people from Asia Minor, as well as Syrians of Aramean origin, appeared on the territory of the former Israelite and Judahite kingdoms. Hellenization led to changes not only in the ethnic composition of the population of the Southern Levant, its culture, and religion, but even to changes in toponymy. The names of cities and countries were Hellenized, sometimes beyond recognition. For example, the Phoenician-Canaanite port city of Acre (Akko) became Ptolemais, the capital of Ammon – Rabbah – turned into Hellenistic Philadelphia, and the Israelite Beth-Shean became Hellenistic Scythopolis. The Hellenes began to call the territory of the former Israelite and Judahite kingdoms Coele-Syria, and southern Judah, where the Edomites had settled, Idumea.

The Ptolemaic period in the history of Judea lasted for at least a full century (302–201 BCE), but it is even less known to us than the Persian period. For two decades after Alexander the Great's death, during the wars for his inheritance among the Diadochi (Alexander's generals), Judea passed from hand to hand until it finally went to Ptolemy Lagus (Ptolemy I Soter), the founder of the ruling dynasty of Hellenistic Egypt, in 302 BCE. The history of Judea during this time is not reflected in any source, except for brief mentions. All the information known to us can be summarized as follows:

First, Judea suffered greatly from the wars of Alexander's Diadochi, which took place in its territory. Josephus mentions that because the Diadochi "began to quarrel among themselves, envying each other's power, a series of fierce and bloody wars ensued, from which cities especially suffered and a multitude of residents lost their lives" Ptolemy Lagus "captured Jerusalem by cunning and deception, namely, by entering the city on a Sabbath under the pretext of making a sacrifice, he did not meet with the slightest obstacle from the Judeans (they in no way assumed him to be an enemy)... he easily captured the city and began to rule over it with cruelty" (*Antiquities of the Jews,* 12.1.1).

Second, Ptolemy I (323–282 BCE), having taken tens of thousands of Judeans captive and forcibly relocated them to Egypt, thereby created a large Jewish community in this country. Josephus gives the total figure of 120,000 Judeans forcibly relocated from Judea to Egypt (*Antiquities of the Jews,* 12.2.1). If this data is correct, it indicates the large number of the Jewish population of Judea and the creation of a huge Jewish community for that time in the delta and valley of the Nile. The number of Judeans relocated to Egypt was many times greater than the number of those who were taken into Babylonian captivity. However, this time the elite of Judean society remained at home in Judea, and Jerusalem and the Temple were not harmed.

Third, the most favorable time for both Judea and the Egyptian Jews came during the reign of Ptolemy II Philadelphus, who ruled the country for 39 years (285–246 BCE). This king liberated the Jewish captives relocated from Judea and ordered the Tanakh (Old Testament) to be translated from Hebrew into Greek. The initiator of the translation was Demetrius of Phalerum, the founder and first head of the famous Library of Alexandria. He informed the king that "the Jews have many interesting works worthy of the royal library on the laws in force among the Jews, but that the translation of these books into Greek will present considerable difficulties due to the Hebrew script and language... The legislation set forth in them, as coming from God himself, testifies to the considerable wisdom and sublimity of the Judean teaching." The king wrote a letter to the Judean high priest Eleazar, in which he expressed a desire to implement Demetrius's plan (*Antiquities of the Jews,* 12.2.1, 4-5). The translation of the Old Testament into Greek, which later became known as the Septuagint, was carried out, according to the story cited by Josephus, by "seventy elders" sent by the Judean high priest to the king's palace (*Antiquities of the Jews,* XII, 2, 1-15). Most likely, only the Torah (the Pentateuch) was translated during the reign of Ptolemy Philadelphus, and the rest of the Old Testament was translated later. In any case, the appearance of the Septuagint was of great importance for both the Hellenistic world and the Hellenized Jews. The spoken language of the Jewish diaspora at that time became Koine, a dialect of the ancient Greek language prevalent in the Eastern Mediterranean. Unlike in Judea, the absolute majority of Jews in the Hellenistic kingdoms lost their knowledge of the Hebrew language and could get acquainted with the historical and religious heritage of their people only thanks to the Septuagint. In general, the entire reign of Ptolemy Philadelphus was favorable for both the Egyptian Jews and for Judea. It is clear that Josephus had reason to assert that the Judeans were "in extraordinary honor" with Ptolemy Philadelphus (*Antiquities of the Jews,* 12.3.1).

A completely different situation developed during the reign of Ptolemy IV Philopator (221–204 BCE). Under him, Judea suffered greatly from the next, fourth war between the Ptolemies and Seleucids, who were vying with each other for the right to possess Coele-Syria, that is, the territories of the former Hebrew kingdoms. In addition to this, the Egyptian Jews were subjected to persecutions, the true reasons for which remain unknown to this day. The Third Book of Maccabees is entirely dedicated to these persecutions. According to it, during a visit to Jerusalem and the Temple, Ptolemy IV Philopator was not allowed into the Holy of Holies, which only the high priest had the right to enter, and that only once a year, on Yom Kippur. The outraged king then decided to vent his anger on the Jews of Egypt, especially since envious courtiers had deliberately fanned Ptolemy Philopator's wrath against the Egyptian Jews loyal to him. The book's plot is very similar to the Megillat Esther, which forms the basis for the Jewish holiday of Purim, only the place of action was not the Persian Empire but Ptolemaic Egypt. Unfortunately, there is no historical document that could confirm these persecutions. On the other hand, knowing the vicissitudes of the history of the Jews in the Hellenistic world, one can hardly doubt that similar events could have actually taken place.

The Third Book of Maccabees was written in the second or first century BCE and is a non-canonical Old Testament book. It has been preserved in the Alexandrian Codex of the Septuagint but is absent from the Tanakh. The Third Book of Maccabees notes the large number of Egyptian Jews and the fact that they enjoyed all civil rights in Ptolemaic Egypt. It testifies that the Jews had a very great influence on the royal court and played an important role in the army and economy of Egypt at that time. At the same time, the book acknowledges that the Judeans, both in their faith and lifestyle, were very different from the rest of the population, and this caused misunderstanding and animosity from some Egyptians. The Third Book of Maccabees confirms the existence of antisemitism, when as early as the end of the 3rd century BCE, the

Jews faced a hostile attitude towards them in the Hellenistic countries. Neither the Greeks and Romans, nor the Syrians and Egyptians, understood the fundamental refusal of the Jews to worship pagan gods and deify local rulers. In fact, even then, a clash between Jewish monotheism and Hellenistic paganism was taking place. The Egyptians and Greeks did not understand either the laws of Sabbath observance or the prohibitions on food (kashrut).

It is quite possible that the persecution suffered by the Jews during the reign of Ptolemy Philopator was the main reason they welcomed the arrival of the army of Antiochus the Great in Judea and helped the Seleucids conquer the entire Southern Levant from the Egyptian Ptolemies.

3. Under the Seleucid Empire

The transition of Judea from Ptolemaic Egypt to the Seleucid kingdom occurred as a result of the fifth war (202–200 BCE) between them. The war was fought throughout Coele-Syria, including Judea, and caused great damage to the population. This is how Josephus described these calamities: "During the reign of Antiochus the Great over Asia, the Judeans had to endure great calamities not only in their own country but also in Coele-Syria. The fact is that during the war waged between Antiochus and Ptolemy Philopator, together with his son Ptolemy Epiphanes, the Jews had to suffer equally in cases of his victory and in cases of his defeat. They were then completely like a ship during a storm, when it suffers from waves on both sides: they were, so to speak, in the middle between the successes and failures of Antiochus. Meanwhile, victory went to Antiochus, and he annexed Judea to himself. When Philopator died, his son sent a huge army against the inhabitants of Coele-Syria under the command of General Scopas, who managed to occupy many Syrian cities and also capture our country, which lay on his way and resisted him. A little later, however, Antiochus defeated Scopas in a battle at the sources of the Jordan and at the same time destroyed a significant part of his army. When Antiochus then took possession of the cities of Coele-Syria... the Judeans submitted to him voluntarily, accepted him into their city, provided his entire army and his elephants with abundant supplies, and willingly helped him in the siege of the garrison left by Scopas in the Jerusalem fortress. Finding it appropriate to reward the Judeans for the zeal and favor they showed him, Antiochus then sent messages to his commanders and confidents in which he testified to how well the Judeans treated him, and also indicated what rewards he had decided to give the Judeans for this" (*Antiquities of the Jews*, 12.3.3).

In gratitude for the help and warm welcome, Antiochus the Great (223–187 BCE) freed the Jerusalem Temple and its clergy from all taxes forever, and the residents of Jerusalem for three years. But most importantly, Judea received broad autonomy within the vast Seleucid empire. Moreover, Antiochus III the Great himself began to provide support and patronage to all Jewish communities of his empire, which stretched from the borders of Greece to India. It seemed that Judea and the Jewish diaspora had found a worthy place in the Hellenistic world of the Seleucids. However, the power and prosperity of the Seleucids turned out to be short-lived. The main threat no longer came from Ptolemaic Egypt, but from the increasingly powerful Roman Republic, from its attempts to seize the Balkans and Asia Minor.

22. The Seleucid King Antiochus III the Great

The intrigues of the Romans in Asia Minor forced Antiochus the Great to hurry there. In 195 BCE, while in Ephesus, he met with Hannibal, who had fled from Carthage. Hannibal tried to convince Antiochus of the inevitability of war with Rome and suggested attacking the Romans in Italy itself without wasting time. But the Seleucid king chose to negotiate, hoping to still reach an agreement with the Romans on the division of spheres of influence. The negotiations dragged on for three years and ended without result. In 192 BCE, having failed to reach an agreement, Antiochus attacked the Romans. The so-called Syrian War began, the outcome of which was determined by the decisive battle at Magnesia (in Greece) in 190 BCE. Antiochus's army suffered a crushing defeat there, as a result of which the Seleucid king was forced to conclude the extremely difficult Treaty of Apamea with the Romans in 188 BCE. According to it, the Seleucid kingdom lost all its European territories in the Balkans, as well as its Asia Minor lands west of the Taurus mountains. But worst of all was something else: The Treaty of Apamea obliged the Seleucids to pay the Romans a fabulously large contribution of 15,000 talents, plus another 500 talents to Pergamon, an ally of Rome. It was this treaty that undermined the power and well-being of the Seleucid empire, from which Parthia and Bactria immediately fell away. The heaviest financial obligations forced Antiochus the Great to fundamentally reconsider his fiscal policy and look for money wherever he could. In 187 BCE, he and a small detachment attacked the temple of Bel in Elymais (Elam, southern Iran), which was famous for its riches, but was surrounded by local residents and killed. The Seleucid throne and the obligation to pay a huge tribute to the Romans were inherited by his son, Seleucus IV (187–175 BCE).

The Treaty of Apamea, which bankrupted the Seleucid empire, could not but affect Judea, because the Seleucid kings began to look for money where there was always a lot of it – in temples. From then on, the position of the high priest, who was also the royal governor in Judea, began to be put up for sale. The desperate need for money for the Seleucids intensified the struggle for power within the priestly class and, most importantly, gave rise to corruption among the clergy of the Jerusalem Temple. Now, it was not the most noble and worthy religious authority who became high priest, but the one who could offer the most money to the Seleucid king. However, even the sale of the highest positions was not able to cover the need for funds to pay the tribute to the Romans, so Seleucus IV began to look at the treasures of the temples. The struggle for the position of high priest in Judea drew the attention of the Seleucid king to the possibility of replenishing his treasury at the expense of the funds of the Jerusalem Temple. This is how the Second Book of Maccabees describes the events of that time: "But a man named Simon, of the tribe of Balgea, who had been made captain of the temple, had a disagreement with the high priest about the administration of the city market. Since he could not prevail over Onias, he went to Apollonius of Tarsus, who at that time was governor of Coelesyria and Phoenicia, and reported to him that the treasury in Jerusalem was full of untold sums of money, so that the amount of the funds could not be reckoned, and that they did not belong to the account of the sacrifices but that it was possible for them to fall under the control of the king. When Apollonius met the king, he told him of the money about which he had been informed. The king chose Heliodorus, who was in charge of his affairs, and sent him with commands to effect the removal of the reported wealth" (2 Macc. 3:4-8).

Heliodorus, a close courtier of Seleucus IV, arrived in Jerusalem with a detachment of soldiers and demanded that the treasures of the Temple be handed over to him for transfer to the royal treasury. The high priest tried to explain to the royal official that the Temple's money was the personal savings of the inhabitants of Judea, given for temporary storage. "And he said that it was utterly impossible that wrong should be done to those people who had trusted in the holiness of the place and in the sanctity and inviolability of the temple that is honored throughout the whole world" (2 Macc. 3:10-12). However, Heliodorus insisted on fulfilling the king's order and entered the Temple with his men to confiscate the valuables. The further course of events is described by the

Second Book of Maccabees as the intervention of the Lord, which ended with the punishment of the courtier and the salvation of the Temple's property. Having returned, Heliodorus, when asked by the king whom he should send to Jerusalem in the future, answered as follows: "If you have any enemy or plotter against your government, send him there, for you will get him back thoroughly flogged, if he survives at all, for there is certainly some power of God about the place" (2 Macc. 3:38).

Later, the informer Simon, trying to explain the failure of Heliodorus's mission, claimed that the high priest Onias had simply intimidated him (2 Macc. 4:1). However, a much more likely reason for Heliodorus's failure was his own fear of repeating the fate of Antiochus the Great in Elymais, especially since, as the Second Book of Maccabees admits, the whole of Jerusalem rose up and "people also hurried out of their houses in crowds to make a general supplication because the holy place was about to be brought into dishonor" (2 Macc. 3:18). It is possible that the high priest, in order to avoid conflict with the king, generously rewarded his close associate for the stress he had endured. Be that as it may, Seleucus IV abandoned his intention to lay hands on the treasures of the Jerusalem Temple, especially since his father, Antiochus the Great, had forever freed only this temple and its clergy from all taxes and duties.

In 175 BCE, Seleucus IV was treacherously killed by Heliodorus, and Mithridates, the king's younger brother, was hastily placed on the Seleucid throne, taking a new name for himself – Antiochus IV Epiphanes (175–164 BCE). His coronation was essentially a thinly veiled usurpation of power, as the true heir was Seleucus's son, Demetrius. However, Demetrius was in Rome as a hostage for the fulfillment of the Treaty of Apamea, and it was none other than his own father, Seleucus IV, who had sent him there to free his younger brother Mithridates, who had been given as a hostage by Antiochus the Great. In turn, Antiochus IV Epiphanes not only did not rescue his savior's son from captivity but also stole the royal throne from him. The rule of the usurper gave rise to internal strife among the Seleucids and brought untold troubles for

Judea. Antiochus IV Epiphanes became famous for being the only ruler in the entire history of the Hellenistic world who tried to forbid Judaism and force the Jews to accept Hellenistic paganism. He was known for his greed, robbery of temples, vanity, and extravagant actions. Being an ardent admirer of Hellenism, he wanted to unite his multiethnic empire on the basis of a single Hellenistic culture and religion for everyone. "Then the king wrote to his whole kingdom that all should be one people" (1 Macc. 1:41). He considered Jewish monotheism as the main obstacle to the implementation of his plans, and its spiritual superiority over Hellenistic paganism deeply offended him.

In 174 BCE, he took advantage of a conflict among the clergy of the Jerusalem Temple to replace the high priest Onias III with his brother Jason (Joshua). If Onias was a supporter of preserving traditions and fundamentally rejected everything that was associated with Hellenistic paganism, then Jason showed himself to be an outspoken Hellenizer. It is very likely that the influential clan of the Tobiads, Judean aristocrats who had huge land holdings in northern Transjordan, stood behind Jason's candidacy. According to Josephus, the Tobiad family was in conflict with the high priest Onias III and tried to replace him. "Jason the brother of Onias obtained the high priesthood by corruption," offering the king an incomparably larger sum of money for it (2 Macc. 4:7). The Second Book of Maccabees reports that "there was such an extreme of Hellenization and increase in the adoption of foreign ways because of the surpassing wickedness of Jason, who was ungodly and no true high priest, that the priests were no longer intent upon their service at the altar. Despising the sanctuary and neglecting the sacrifices, they hurried to take part in the unlawful proceedings in the wrestling arena after the signal for the discus throwing, disdaining the honors prized by their ancestors and putting the highest value upon Greek forms of prestige" (2 Macc. 4:13-15).

Three years later, Antiochus IV sold the position of high priest for an even greater sum to a certain Menelaus, the brother of the informer Simon, an outright intriguer and Hellenizer. As the Second Book of

Maccabees notes, Menelaus possessed "no qualification for the high priesthood but having the hot temper of a cruel tyrant and the rage of a savage wild beast. So, Jason, who after supplanting his own brother was supplanted by another man, was driven as a fugitive into the land of Ammon" (2 Macc. 4:25-26). First of all, Menelaus hurried to deal with Onias, bribing a close associate of the Seleucid king for this purpose. To pay for the purchased position, Menelaus, with the help of his brother Lysimachus, began to secretly sell the gold vessels from the treasury of the Jerusalem Temple, thereby causing the indignation of the priests and an open rebellion of the city's residents. The enraged Jerusalemites dealt with Lysimachus right at the Temple treasury, and the Council of Elders of Judea appealed to the Seleucid king. However, with bribery and rich gifts, Menelaus managed to hush up this crime and deal with the complainants.

It must be admitted that Hellenistic culture was brought into Judea not by the high priests-Hellenizers such as Jason or Menelaus. Greek culture had entered Judea long before, ever since the Hellenes took control of the Southern Levant, and its spread within Judean society, though slow, was steady. Hellenistic culture was adopted primarily – and most readily – by the Judean aristocracy, and later by all the more or less affluent strata of society. There was no alternative to this process, because Judea was under the rule of the Hellenistic kingdoms and was surrounded by Hellenized peoples. The Hellenes – their culture, language, and religion – dominated the entire Eastern Mediterranean. The Jews could not live and prosper in the Hellenistic world without knowing its culture and language.

Hellenization began with the Jewish diaspora of the Eastern Mediterranean, and first of all with the largest Judean community in Egypt. As early as the 3rd century BCE, it had virtually switched to the Greek colloquial language of the time, Koine. It is no coincidence that it was during this period that the Septuagint – the Greek translation of the Tanakh – appeared, since the Judeans of the Hellenistic diaspora could no longer read the Bible in their native language. With the Greek language, the Jews also acquired a second set of names, Greek names, and an interest in Greek literature, philosophy, and theater emerged. Having received the same civil rights as the Hellenes, the Jews of the Hellenistic countries could not refuse to participate in sports competitions, to study in gymnasiums, and to be members of ephebia. The Jews of the diaspora very quickly discovered that living according to the norms of Greek culture was incomparably easier and more pleasant than according to the laws of Judaism. The life of a Hellene was not burdened by the laws of the Sabbath and kashrut; on the contrary, it was full of pleasures and entertainments unthinkable for Judaism. If the culture of the Hellenes called for the enjoyment of life, for physical perfection and beauty, then Judaism required righteousness and spiritual perfection, which are so difficult for a person to achieve. For the Jews, Hellenism was a great temptation, and the richer a person was, the more pleasures he could afford, leading a Hellenic lifestyle. The Judean way of life was much more righteous, but also incomparably more difficult. For believing Judeans, Hellenism also had an extremely unpleasant side: Greek culture was deeply pagan and glorified pagan gods. Pagan religious ceremonies were an indispensable attribute of any holiday, sports competition, or theatrical performance. Sculptures of Greek gods stood not only in temples but also in all public buildings, and most importantly, they demanded worship and reverence, obliged people to make sacrifices and participate in religious processions and ceremonies. The provision of equal civil rights in any Hellenistic city required the Jews to necessarily recognize local deities, which was impossible for monotheistic Judeans. Jewish monotheism could not coexist peacefully with Hellenistic paganism, which was an integral part of Greek culture. All attempts to combine them ended unsuccessfully, both in the Jewish diaspora and in Judea itself, because neither the Judeans nor the Hellenes were satisfied with half-measures. In the diaspora, the conflict between Judaism and Hellenism led to the emergence of ancient antisemitism, and in Judea itself, it gave rise to the Maccabean Wars.

A direct confrontation with Judaism and the Jews occurred with Antiochus IV much later, in 169 BCE. At that time, he was completing a successful war with Ptolemaic Egypt and had only one city left to capture – Alexandria. Unexpectedly, ambassadors from Rome arrived, who, threatening war, demanded that he leave the almost conquered country. Humiliated and insulted, deprived of all the results of his victory, Antiochus IV was forced to return home. At this time, a rumor spread in Jerusalem that the Seleucid king had died in Egypt, and Jason, the former high priest who had been replaced by Menelaus, decided to take revenge. This is how the most informed and closest to these events, the Second Book of Maccabees, tells the story: "When a false rumor arose that Antiochus was dead, Jason took no fewer than a thousand men and suddenly made an assault on the city. When the troops on the wall had been forced back and at last the city was being taken, Menelaus took refuge in the citadel. But Jason kept relentlessly slaughtering his compatriots, not realizing that success at the cost of one's kindred is the greatest misfortune but imagining that he was setting up trophies of victory over enemies and not over compatriots. He did not, however, gain control of the government; in the end, he got only disgrace from his conspiracy and fled again into the country of the Ammonites" (2 Macc. 5:5-7). Antiochus IV, learning about the attack in Jerusalem on his protege Menelaus, decided to take out all the bitterness of his humiliation and disgrace from the Romans on the Judeans. "When news of what had happened reached the king, he took it to mean that Judea was in revolt. So, raging inwardly, he left Egypt and took the city by storm. He commanded his soldiers to cut down relentlessly everyone they met and to kill those who went into their houses. Then there was massacre of young and old, destruction of boys, women, and children, and slaughter of young girls and infants. Within the total of three days eighty thousand were destroyed, forty thousand in hand-to-hand fighting, and as many were sold into slavery as were killed. Not content with this, Antiochus dared to enter the most holy temple in all the world, guided by Menelaus, who had become a traitor both to the laws and to his country… So, Antiochus carried off eighteen hundred talents from the temple and hurried away to Antioch, thinking in his arrogance that he could sail on the land and walk on the sea, because his mind was elated" (2 Macc. 5:11-15, 21).

However, no matter how greedy Antiochus IV was, the robbery of the Jerusalem Temple was not his main goal. He decided to carry out his long-standing intention: to forbid Judean monotheism and force the Jews to accept Hellenistic paganism. This was intended not against the Jews as a people, but against their monotheistic religion, against monotheism as a religious and philosophical idea. The tragedy was that the Seleucid king was not able to understand that Judean monotheism had by then become inseparable from the Jewish people, had become the essence of their existence, the form and content of their life. Therefore, any attempts to eradicate Judean monotheism inevitably turned into a policy of exterminating the Jewish people themselves.

23. A coin depicting Antiochus IV Epiphanes

Antiochus IV Epiphanes did not just desecrate the Jerusalem Temple; he turned it into a pagan temple of Zeus Olympius and forbade, under penalty of death, the performance of all laws, rituals, and rites of Judaism. He decreed death as the penalty even for reading or keeping scrolls of the Old Testament (Tanakh). "The books of the law that they found they tore to pieces and burned with fire. Anyone found possessing the book of the covenant or anyone who adhered to the law was condemned to death by decree of the king" (1 Macc. 1:56-57). The Samaritans also suffered: their temple on Mount Gerizim was also desecrated and turned into a temple of Zeus Xenios. The fact that their monotheistic faith, albeit archaic, was also banned testifies to the attempt of the militant pagan to eradicate the very idea of monotheism from people's consciousness. The Second Book of Maccabees describes the forced Hellenization in Judea as follows: "For the temple was filled with debauchery and reveling by the nations, who dallied with prostitutes and had intercourse with women within the sacred precincts and besides brought in things for sacrifice that were unfit. The altar was covered with abominable offerings that were forbidden by the laws. People could neither keep the Sabbath nor observe the festivals of their ancestors nor so much as confess themselves to be Jews. On the monthly celebration of the king's birthday, the Jews were taken, under bitter constraint, to partake of the sacrifices, and when a festival of Dionysus was celebrated, they were compelled to wear wreaths of ivy and to walk in the procession in honor of Dionysus" (2 Macc. 6:4-7).

The situation of the Jews was no better in the so-called Hellenistic cities created on the lands of the former Hebrew kingdoms: "At the suggestion of the people of Ptolemais, a decree was issued to the neighboring Greek cities that they should adopt the same policy toward the Jews and make them partake of the sacrifices and should kill those who did not choose to change over to Greek customs. One could see, therefore, the misery that had come upon them. For example, two women were brought in for having circumcised their children. They publicly paraded them around the city with their babies hanging at their breasts and then hurled them down headlong from the wall. Others who had assembled in the caves nearby in order to observe the seventh day secretly were betrayed to Philip and were all burned together, because their piety kept them from defending themselves, in view of their regard for that most holy day" (2 Macc. 6:8-11).

4. The Maccabean Wars

The intention of Antiochus IV Epiphanes to make Hellenistic culture the sole and mandatory way of life for all the peoples of his vast empire was a completely unrealistic undertaking, which he himself soon abandoned. Even more delusional was his plan to convert the Jews into pagans. Unlike the highly Hellenized Jewish diaspora in the Greco-Roman world, Hellenization in Judea itself had been shallow, affecting only the upper strata of Jewish society – its aristocracy and, somewhat paradoxically, a part of the temple priesthood. Josephus admitted that even in his time, that is, in the first century CE, it was difficult to find a Jew in Judea who knew Greek. The overwhelming majority of the Judean populace clung steadfastly to the monotheistic traditions of their forefathers and looked with scorn and horror upon the pagan "abominations" and idol worship imposed by foreign powers and their local collaborators. The Seleucid Hellenizers understood this all too well. To maintain order, they constructed a formidable fortress in Jerusalem near the Temple, known as the Acra (from the Greek *akropolis*, "citadel"), and stationed a large garrison there. It was a constant threat, meant to dissuade the people from open revolt – though none among the hereditary priests or aristocrats would have dared or been able to lead such a rebellion. The leadership of the resistance came from elsewhere: from provincial priests and *scribes* – interpreters of the Law.

In 167 BCE, a series of wars broke out that would last for years – wars for freedom and faith, later known as the Maccabean Revolt. The uprising was led by a rural priest named Mattathias the Hasmonean, from the town of Modiin. With his five sons, he fled into the Judean wilderness to organize resistance against the tyranny of the pagans. The First Book of Maccabees tells us: "At that time many who were seeking righteousness and justice went down to the wilderness to live there, they, their sons, their wives, and their livestock, because troubles pressed heavily upon them" (1 Macc. 2:29–30). But it was not the Jews who fired the first shot – it was the Seleucid punitive forces who launched an attack deliberately on a Saturday, a day of rest and prayer when the Law forbade Jews from taking up arms. The slaughter of a thousand innocent men, women, and children – who refused to defend themselves on the holy day – forced the resistance to reevaluate the Sabbath laws: "So they made this decision that day: "Let us fight against anyone who comes to attack us on the Sabbath day; let us not all die as our kindred died in their hiding places" (1 Macc. 2:41).

The earliest core of the resistance was made up of the so-called Hasideans ("pious") (1 Macc. 2:42) – a distinct class within Judean society, composed of scribes and scholars of the Law, men who copied and interpreted both the Written and the Oral Torah. This social class of Torah experts had emerged after the return from the Babylonian exile, under the leadership of Ezra and Nehemiah, who strove to reintroduce the people to the laws of Moses. The Hasideans likely came from the Levites – traditionally associated with worship but later marginalized by the temple priesthood, the Sadducees. It is possible that the Hasideans were the original creators of what would become the Oral Torah, later preserved in the Mishnah. They were also the ideological forebears of both the Pharisaic and Essenic movements in Judaism.

Though the revolt was initiated by the priest Mattathias Hasmonean, leadership passed, the very next year after his death, to his son Judah, known by the name Maccabee ("The Hammer"). Judah soon proved to be a gifted organizer and a brilliant military commander. His nickname, Maccabee, became a title for all his brothers and comrades-in-arms – they became known collectively as the Maccabees. The first enemy Judah faced was Apollonius, a commander of mercenaries from Mysia (in Asia Minor), who held military authority in nearby Samaria. In a swift and decisive battle, Apollonius's forces were completely routed, and he himself was slain. "Judas took the sword of Apollonius, and used it in battle the rest of his life" (1 Macc. 3:10–12).

Apollonius's defeat prompted Seron, the military commander of all Coele-Syria, to march personally against the Jewish rebels with a substantial force. The vast difference in numbers between the Seleucid army and Judah's ragtag fighters initially caused dismay in the ranks of the latter: "They said to Judah, "How can we, few as we are, fight against so great and so strong a multitude? And we are faint, for we have eaten nothing today." Judah replied, "It is easy for many to be hemmed in by few, for in the sight of heaven there is no difference between saving by many or by few. It is not on the size of the army that victory in battle depends, but strength comes from heaven. They come against us in great insolence and lawlessness to destroy us and our wives and our children and to despoil us, but we fight for our lives and our laws. He himself will crush them before us; as for you, do not be afraid of them." When he finished speaking, he rushed suddenly against Seron and his army, and they were crushed before him. They pursued them down the descent of Beth-horon to the plain; eight hundred of them fell, and the rest fled into the land of the Philistines. Then Judah and his brothers began to be feared, and terror fell on the nations all around them" (1 Macc. 3:17–25).

The second crushing defeat of the Seleucid army left a heavy mark upon the royal court in the capital at Antioch. The situation was worsened by reports of unrest and turmoil not only in Judea, but also in the East – in Persia. King Antiochus IV gathered military forces from every corner of his realm, but soon found himself confronted with a dire shortage of funds: the royal treasury was nearly empty. Hoping to replenish it with overdue tribute from Persia, he divided his forces in two: with one half he set out eastward himself, while the other he entrusted to his official Lysias, with orders to suppress the uprising in Judea. Lysias was not just a trusted minister and "friend of the king." He was also the guardian of Antiochus's young son, the heir to the throne. All territories of the Seleucid kingdom located between Egypt and the Euphrates River were transferred to the control of Lysias. Wasting no time, Lysias dispatched an army of forty thousand infantry and seven thousand cavalry to subdue Judea, reinforced by detachments from Syria and the Hellenistic cities of the Southern Levant. The Seleucid garrison stationed in Jerusalem, along with segments of the Hellenized Jewish aristocracy who had entered the king's service, also promised their aid (1 Macc. 3:38–41).

Meanwhile, the Jewish rebels prepared for a decisive confrontation. They gathered at Mizpah, an ancient city that had once been a religious center of the Hebrew tribes. "They fasted that day, put on sackcloth, and sprinkled ashes on their heads, and tore their clothes… And Judas said, "Arm yourselves and be courageous. Be ready early in the morning to fight with these nations who have assembled against us to destroy us and our sanctuary. It is better for us to die in battle than to see the misfortunes of our nation and of the sanctuary. But as his will in heaven may be, so shall he do" (1 Macc. 3:47, 58–60). The main battle was fought near the Judean town of Emmaus. A reinforced Seleucid force attempted a surprise night assault on the rebels' camp. Yet Judah anticipated their design: he abandoned his encampment in time and struck first at the enemy. Shattering the main body of the Greco-Syrian army, he then awaited the return of those who had gone out to ambush him in the night – and crushed them as well. The remnants of the Seleucid host fled southward into Idumea and the Hellenistic cities of Philistia – Ashdod and Yavneh.

The unexpected defeat at Emmaus provoked the wrath of Antiochus IV and placed Lysias in a difficult position. Yet he was not prepared to yield. The very next year he mustered a fresh army against the Jewish rebels: sixty thousand picked infantry and five thousand cavalry. This time Lysias himself took command, advancing from the south out of Idumea and encamping near the fortress of Beth-Zur (1 Macc. 4:28–29). The First Book of Maccabees recounts the clash between Judah's forces and those of Lysias: "Then both sides attacked, and there fell of the army of Lysias five thousand men; they fell before them. When Lysias saw the rout of his troops and observed the boldness that inspired those of Judas and how ready they were either to live or to die nobly, he withdrew to Antioch and enlisted mercenaries in order to invade Judea again with an even larger army" (1 Macc. 4:34–35).

This victory proved decisive. It opened the way for the liberation of Jerusalem and all Judea from Seleucid rule. In 164 BCE the Jewish insurgents entered the city and first of all purified the Temple from its pagan defilement. Judah Maccabee "chose blameless priests, devoted to the Law," who re-consecrated the sanctuary and renewed the worship of Israel's God. The Greco-Syrian garrison in Jerusalem was defeated; its survivors, along with the Hellenized Jews, withdrew into the Acra, the powerful fortress the Seleucids had built after their conquest of the city.

With Judea free, Judah's army turned against the surrounding peoples who had aided Antiochus IV and sought to besiege the Jews. Their first campaign struck southward against the Idumeans, who had actively supported the Seleucid army; then north-eastward into Gilead (northern Transjordan), to defend Jewish communities from attacks by the Ammonites. Finally, their march carried them west to the Mediterranean seaports – Ashdod, Ashkelon, Yavneh, Jaffa, and Gaza – cities that had once been Philistine strongholds but had since become Hellenistic towns with mixed populations. Large Jewish communities had long lived in these cities, but under Antiochus's decrees they had been harshly persecuted. Of all the neighboring peoples, only the Samaritans maintained neutrality, neither aiding the blockade of Judea nor participating in hostilities. This was in part because the Samaritans themselves, with their monotheism, had suffered under the militant paganism of the Seleucid king. As for the Moabites, by the mid-second century BCE they had so thoroughly merged with the Jews and partly with the Nabataeans that they vanish altogether from the historical record.

The campaigns of Judah Maccabee reveal an important phenomenon: the high population density of Judea had given rise to waves of migration into surrounding regions – Galilee, the Golan, Gilead (north Transjordan), as well as the Mediterranean port cities stretching from Gaza to Akko (Ptolemais). The inhabitants of these areas were a mixed population – descendants of the Hebrew tribes, together with remnants of Canaanites and Amorites. Rapidly growing Judean communities there preserved their separateness, refusing to intermarry even with descendants of the northern Hebrew tribes, whom they regarded, like the Samaritans, as "pagans." Judah's expeditions were aimed at defending Jewish communities throughout Coele-Syria. Yet in cases where their safety could not be guaranteed, the rebels gathered up their kinsmen and brought them back to Judea (1 Macc. 5:23, 45). The laws of Ezra and Nehemiah, which forbade intermarriage with pagans, were the primary cause of the communities' closed nature. Kinship was possible only through conversion – by abandoning paganism and embracing Jewish monotheism. Large-scale Judaization, however, would come later, once Judea extended its power across nearly the whole of historical Canaan.

The military successes of the Jewish insurgents stood in sharp contrast to the failures that dogged Antiochus IV Epiphanes in Persia. Unable to extract sufficient tribute from the rebellious population, he attempted to plunder the temple of the Akkadian goddess Nanai in Elam (whom the Greeks identified with Artemis). There he met a shameful end – trapped and beheaded by enraged priests. Another, more "respectable" version tells that, disheartened by defeat and by his failed attempt at temple robbery, he died of a grievous and painful illness. Before his death in 164 BCE, Antiochus revoked his decree banning Judaism and named as his heir his underage son, who would be known as Antiochus V Eupator. As regent he appointed his confidant and minister Philip, who had accompanied him throughout the Persian campaign (1 Macc. 6:8–17). Thus, in effect, the prohibition of Jewish monotheism had lasted scarcely three years.

Meanwhile, Judah Maccabee's army laid siege to the last Seleucid stronghold in Judea – the fortress of the Acra in Jerusalem, where the remnants of the Greco-Syrian garrison and their local collaborators had taken refuge. Yet the rebels had no time to capture it. Antiochus V Eupator gathered the full might of the empire to subdue Judea: "one hundred thousand foot soldiers, twenty thousand horsemen, and thirty-two elephants accustomed to war" (1 Macc. 6:30). This vast host, commanded by Antiochus V himself together with his minister Lysias, advanced north from Idumea into Judea. Judah, abandoning the siege of the Acra, marched his army south to meet them.

The decisive encounter took place at the Judean village of Beth-Zechariah, south of Jerusalem. The rebels succeeded in routing the Seleucid vanguard, but their advance was checked by the war elephants. Then

Eleazar, Judah's brother, hurled himself upon the largest beast, armored and richly adorned, believing the king himself sat upon its back. "Now Eleazar, called Avaran, saw that one of the animals was equipped with royal armor. It was taller than all the others, and he supposed that the king was on it. So, he gave his life to save his people and to win for himself an everlasting name. He courageously ran into the midst of the phalanx to reach it; he killed men right and left, and they parted before him on both sides. He got under the elephant, stabbed it from beneath, and killed it, but it fell to the ground upon him and he died" (1 Macc. 6:43–46). The battle raged with uncertain outcome until nightfall, when Judah withdrew with his most loyal followers into Jerusalem, taking refuge behind the walls of the Temple sanctuary. The Seleucid army then commenced a prolonged siege of the fortified Temple complex. The year was 163 BCE.

It is hard to say how or when the siege of the Temple might have ended, had not dramatic events in Antioch altered the course of war. Philip, the courtier whom Antiochus IV had named regent of the empire and guardian of his son, returned from Persia with the royal army and seized power in the capital. News of this alarmed the young king and Lysias so much that they abandoned the siege, hastily concluded peace with Judah Maccabee, and marched their forces back to Antioch.

The treaty between Antiochus V Eupator and Judah Maccabee repealed all prohibitions on Judaism, restored the Temple's former privileges, granted Judea internal autonomy, and recognized Judah as governor of the land. All Jews held in captivity were to be freed, and the rebels were granted amnesty. Only full sovereignty and independence from the Seleucid kingdom remained beyond their grasp. Thus ended the first stage (167–163 BCE) of the Maccabean wars for faith and freedom. Antiochus V, however, appointed his own candidate to the high priesthood: Alcimus (Joakim), a man of priestly descent from Aaron and Zadok, yet outside the line of Onias, the hereditary high priests. Alcimus represented the interests of that faction of Jewish aristocrats and Hellenized priests allied with the Seleucids and hostile to the Maccabees and the Hasideans.

The treaty granting Judea religious freedom and autonomy provoked open resentment in the Hellenistic cities of Coele-Syria. Most opposed of all were the inhabitants of Ptolemais (Akko), long-standing adversaries of Judea and the Jews. Lysias was compelled to exert considerable effort to pacify the discontent of Hellenistic Ptolemais (2 Macc. 13:25–26).

Although the courtier Philip had fled Antioch before the new king's return to the capital, the reign of Antiochus V Eupator and his minister Lysias proved short – no more than two years. Yet even this brief rule aroused dissatisfaction among both the army and the royal court. Seeking to avoid another war with Rome, Antiochus V made serious concessions, drastically reducing his army and fleet in accordance with Roman demands. The professional mercenaries, deprived of their livelihood, provoked unrest and disorder throughout Syria. When Demetrius, son of Seleucus IV, who had long been held in Rome as a hostage, learned of these events, he escaped and in 162 BCE landed on the Syrian coast. The army at once went over to his side. Entering Antioch in triumph, he seized the Seleucid throne under the name Demetrius I Soter (162–150 BCE). Antiochus V Eupator and Lysias were immediately executed.

Demetrius I refused to honor the treaty concluded by Antiochus V with Judah Maccabee. True, he had no intention of prohibiting Judaism, as Antiochus IV had done, but neither was he willing to grant Judea autonomy or confirm Judah Maccabee as governor. He confirmed only Alcimus as high priest, since Alcimus represented the Hellenized Jewish aristocracy that had supported Seleucid authority. Judah, on the other hand, he regarded as a dangerous rebel striving to sever Judea from the empire. To secure his rule, Demetrius sent Alcimus back to Judea accompanied by a powerful army under one of his ablest generals, Bacchides. On arriving, Bacchides dispatched envoys to Judah, summoning him to talk. But Judah, discerning the trap, refused to enter the Seleucid camp. This refusal provoked dissension within the Maccabean ranks. Many of the Hasideans argued that the original aims of the revolt had been achieved: the ban on Judaism had been revoked, the sanctity of the Temple restored. Since independence had never been their declared goal, why not now make peace with the king's representatives? The First Book of Maccabees relates: "Then a group of scribes appeared in a body before Alcimus and Bacchides to ask for just terms. The Hasideans were first among the Israelites to seek peace from them, for they said, "A priest of the line of Aaron has come with the army, and he will not harm us." Alcimus spoke peaceable words to them and swore this oath to them, "We will not seek to injure you or your friends." So, they trusted him, but he seized sixty of them and killed them in one day, in accordance with the word that was written, "The flesh of your faithful ones and their blood they poured out all around Jerusalem, and there was no one to bury them." Then the fear and dread of them fell on all the people, for they said, "There is no truth or justice in them, for they have violated the agreement and the oath that they swore" (1 Macc. 7:12–18). From that time the Maccabean war for the faith of the fathers became a war for the freedom of Judea.

The arrival of Alcimus with the Greco-Syrian army thus unleashed not one, but two wars: first, the struggle for Judea's freedom from Seleucid rule; and second, a civil war between Hellenized Jews and traditionalists. Bacchides, confronted with a protracted guerrilla struggle, left Alcimus with a strong garrison and returned to Antioch. From the account in First Maccabees, it is clear that Judea was plunged into a serious civil war in 162–160 BCE: "Alcimus struggled to maintain his high priesthood, and all who were troubling their people joined him. They gained control of the land of Judah and did great damage in Israel. And Judas saw all the wrongs that Alcimus and those with him had done among the Israelites; it was more than the nations had done. So Judas went out into all the surrounding parts of Judea, taking vengeance on those who had deserted and preventing those in the city from going out into the country. When Alcimus saw that Judas and those with him had grown strong and realized that he could not withstand them, he returned to the king and brought malicious charges against them" (1

Macc. 7:21–25). Evidently Alcimus, despite the support of the Seleucid garrison, lost the civil war and was forced to request a full-scale intervention by the imperial army.

What sort of army was it that the Maccabees so often had to face? Above all, the Seleucid army was a professional force of mercenaries, men who devoted their entire youth and maturity to the art of war. In skill and experience, they generally outmatched any militia drawn from common citizens. Yet their great weakness lay in loyalty: mercenary warriors served those who paid better. They could easily change sides or even countries, depending on who proved more generous and reliable in rewarding their dangerous trade. The Seleucid host was as multiethnic as the empire itself. The entire command staff, like the ruling elite, consisted of descendants of those Greeks and Macedonians who came to the East with the army of Alexander the Great. Second place after them was shared by people from Asia Minor (for example, Mysia, Galatia, Caria, Cilicia, etc.) and natives of the Aegean islands, Crete and Cyprus, most of whom were also Greeks. And finally, the last part of the army consisted of Syrians of Aramean origin. Towards the end of the Seleucid Empire, the local, Syrian component began to predominate in its army. Hellenistic authors called the Seleucid army variously: Macedonian, Greek, Syrian. But most accurately it should be called Greco-Syrian.

In 160 BCE Demetrius I Soter dispatched Nicanor, one of his distinguished generals, with a great army to Judea as governor. Mindful of the failures of his predecessors, Nicanor at first sought to establish peace with the Maccabees. For a time he succeeded, and Judea enjoyed a fragile peace, though at the price of dual authority: Nicanor and Judah effectively shared power in the land. Alcimus, however, was sidelined, contrary to his ambitions. He complained to Demetrius I of Nicanor's betrayal and his pact with Judah. "The king became excited and, provoked by the false accusations of that depraved man, wrote to Nicanor, stating that he was displeased with the covenant and commanding him to send Maccabeus to Antioch as a prisoner without delay" (2 Macc. 14:26–27). Thus ended the brief peace and dual rule in Judea. At first

Nicanor resorted to threats, vowing to burn the Temple and slaughter the priests if the Maccabees did not surrender. When intimidation failed, he turned to arms. Marching out of Jerusalem, Nicanor encamped at Beth-Horon, where reinforcements from Syria joined him. There, a decisive battle was fought with Judah's rebels. In the fierce clash, the Greco-Syrian army was utterly defeated, and Nicanor himself was slain. The victors "cut off Nicanor's head and the right hand that he had so arrogantly stretched out and brought them and displayed them just outside Jerusalem" (1 Macc. 7:39–47). Judea became free again, and Alcimus and the Hellenizers fled to Antioch to Demetrius I.

Judah and his brothers, the Maccabees, understood perfectly well that the Seleucid Empire would not accept its defeat and would try many more times to subjugate Judea. To defend its freedom against such a formidable foe, Judea required a strong ally. Ptolemaic Egypt no longer possessed sufficient military power to oppose the Seleucids; moreover, the Ptolemies, as immediate neighbors, themselves laid claim to Coele-Syria, including Judea. The Maccabees therefore sought allies among the Seleucids' principal enemies and fixed their choice upon Rome. The Roman Republic already stood unmatched in strength, waging wars against the Seleucids for Asia Minor and Anatolia, yet it was still too distant geographically to threaten Judea itself. To establish ties of alliance, Judah dispatched an embassy to Rome, led by the Jewish historian Eupolemus. The Judean envoys were successful and managed to conclude an alliance treaty between the Roman Republic and Judea. The Romans found this treaty attractive. It provided them with legitimate pretext to intervene in the affairs of the Seleucid Empire, which they subsequently took advantage of.

The destruction of Nicanor's army forced Demetrius I Soter to regard the situation in Judea with far greater seriousness. This time he again entrusted command to Bacchides – his most capable general – and gave him the best units of his army, preferring quality to quantity. Bacchides acted with great swiftness: he descended upon Judea so rapidly that he took Judah by surprise. With no time to muster his forces, Judah was compelled to battle. The First Book of Maccabees recounts that Judah was troubled in his heart, for he had no time to gather his warriors. "He was crushed in spirit, for he had no time to assemble them. He became faint, but he said to those who were left, "Let us get up and go against our enemies. We may have the strength to fight them." But they tried to dissuade him, saying, "We do not have the strength. Let us rather save our own lives now, and let us come back with our kindred and fight them, for we are too few." But Judas said, "Far be it from me to do such a thing as to flee from them. If our time has come, let us die bravely for our kindred and leave no cause to question our honor" (1 Macc. 9:6–10). On the eve of the battle, Bacchides' army numbered 22,000 elite warriors, while Judah had only 800 men. Yet despite the immense disparity, the struggle raged the entire day: "The earth was shaken by the noise of the armies, and the battle raged from morning until evening. Judas saw that Bacchides and the strength of his army were on the right; then all the courageous men went with him, and they crushed the right wing, and he pursued them as far as Mount Azotus. When those on the left wing saw that the right wing was crushed, they turned and followed close behind Judas and his men. The battle became desperate, and many on both sides were wounded and fell. Judas also fell, and the rest fled. Then Jonathan and Simon took their brother Judas and buried him in the tomb of their ancestors at Modein and wept for him. All Israel made great lamentation for him; they mourned many days…" (1 Macc. 9:13–20).

The defeat of the Jewish rebels and the death of their leader, Judah Maccabee, marked the end of the second phase (163-160 BCE) of the Maccabean Wars. While the first phase, from 167-164 BCE, was won by Jewish patriots and traditionalists, the second phase was won by Hellenizers and Seleucid collaborators. The chronicler writes: "After the death of Judas, the renegades emerged in all parts of Israel; all the wrongdoers reappeared. In those days, a very great famine occurred, and the country went over to their side. Bacchides chose the godless and put them in charge of the country. They made inquiry and searched for the friends of Judas and brought them to Bacchides, who took vengeance on them and made sport of them. So, there was great distress in Israel such as had not been since the time a prophet had last appeared among them" (1 Macc. 9:23–27). Yet neither the Seleucid authorities nor their Jewish collaborators now dared lay hands upon the Jewish faith or the Temple, though no autonomy was granted to Judea.

The victory of Bacchides and the famine in the land could not long sustain the Hellenistic order. The executions of Maccabean supporters merely rekindled civil strife. Leadership now passed to Jonathan, another of the Maccabee brothers. Though the Hasideans had been greatly reduced, their ranks were replenished with fresh adherents. As the famine receded, popular support grew. Alarmed by the revival of Maccabean strength, Bacchides sought to deliver a preemptive blow. His first clash with Jonathan occurred near the place where the Jordan River flows into the Dead Sea. Choosing to attack on the Sabbath, Bacchides nevertheless met stiff resistance and lost over a thousand men without result. Jonathan, wishing to preserve his army for future battles, under cover of darkness ferried it across to the east bank of the Jordan and left Bacchides. Unable to destroy the rebels, Bacchides turned to fortifying strongholds and seizing hostages. He took the sons of Judea's most notable families and confined them in the citadel of Acra at Jerusalem. Around this time Alcimus, the high priest, died suddenly while undertaking alterations to the Temple. Soon after, Demetrius I recalled Bacchides to Antioch for two years. Jonathan and his followers seized the opportunity to restore their authority in Judea.

But complaints from the Hellenizers against the growing power of the Maccabees compelled Demetrius to send Bacchides once more with his army to pacify the land. Jonathan, avoiding open battle, withdrew into the fortified town of Beth-Basi on the edge of the Judean wilderness. Bacchides besieged the place, launching repeated assaults, but without success. Meanwhile, Jonathan, leaving his brother Simon to hold the town, broke out with a chosen band and sought allies among the neighboring population. These were likely not Nabataeans or Arabs at large, but the Maonites – descendants of an Edomite tribe that had joined Hebrews during the conquest of Canaan. This was the same rugged wilderness where David had once hidden from the army of King Saul. At the outbreak of the Maccabean Revolt, the Maonites, like their kinsmen the Idumeans, had supported the Seleucids. But Jonathan persuaded them to aid the Maccabees, reminding them of the choice made by their forefathers – an argument that proved decisive. With a large levy of local people, Jonathan fell upon Bacchides, while "Simon and his men sallied out from the town and set fire to the engines of war. They fought with Bacchides, and he was crushed by them. They pressed him very hard, for his plan and his expedition had been in vain. So he was very angry at the renegades who had counseled him to come into the country, and he killed many of them. Then he decided to go back to his own land" (1 Macc. 9:65–69).

To the dismay of the local Hellenizers, Bacchides resolved suddenly to abandon Judea and return with all his remaining forces to Antioch. Moreover, to the astonishment of all, he concluded peace with the Maccabees, as once Nicanor had done, and he returned all the prisoners to them. After the withdrawal of the Greco-Syrian army, Jonathan exacted retribution upon the local Hellenizers and began to govern from the town of Michmas, where once another Jonathan – the son of King Saul – had gained a brilliant victory over the Philistines.

The hasty retreat of Bacchides from Judea and his peace with Jonathan were explained by dramatic turns of fortune within and around the Seleucid realm. In 152 BCE, there appeared at Smyrna in Asia Minor a new pretender to the Seleucid throne – Alexander Balas – who claimed to be the son of Antiochus IV Epiphanes and the brother of Antiochus V Eupator. It is quite possible he was indeed the son of a Seleucid king by one of his concubines. The pretensions of Alexander Balas were soon supported by the kings of Pergamum and Cappadocia, then by Ptolemy VI Philometor of Egypt, and finally, his rights to the throne were recognized by the Roman Senate. With such powerful patronage, Balas landed with his adherents at Ptolemais (Akko), where the garrison and the citizens at once proclaimed him king. Demetrius I Soter, alarmed, began feverishly to assemble an army against the "usurper." These events were the true reason for Bacchides' recall from Judea. At that moment, the Maccabees and their forces were the strongest military power not only in Judea but in all Coele-Syria. Needing their support, Demetrius concluded peace with Jonathan and conferred upon him full authority in Judea. "So, Demetrius gave him authority to recruit troops, to equip them with arms, and to become his ally, and he commanded that the hostages in the citadel [Acra at Jerusalem] should be released to him" (1 Macc. 10:3–6). Jonathan thus began to rule from Jerusalem as the legitimate and recognized governor of all Judea.

Yet the rise of Jonathan and of the Maccabees did not end there. Alexander Balas, embroiled in his contest with Demetrius, required their support even more urgently and therefore surpassed his rival in generosity. Learning of the privileges bestowed by Demetrius, Alexander confirmed them and added greater honors still: he appointed Jonathan as high priest, bestowed upon him the title "Friend of the King," and sent him the purple robe and the golden wreath. But the contest of gifts did not cease: Demetrius, striving to win the Jews to his side, went yet further. He exempted Judea from many taxes and imposts, declared Jerusalem sacred and free from all tribute, granted the citadel of Acra to Jonathan, ordered the release of all captive and enslaved Jews in all corners of his kingdom free of charge, and also the exemption of them from taxes. Demetrius made all Jewish holidays days of privilege and freedom for all the Jews of the Seleucid Empire and forbade anyone to bother them or exact anything from them on these days. Moreover, he gave the city of Ptolemais as a gift to the Jerusalem Temple - for the expenses necessary for the Sanctuary and promised that all funds for the rebuilding of the walls of Jerusalem and the renovation of the Temple will also be provided at the king's expense (1 Macc. 10:26–45).

However, the Maccabees did not trust Demetrius, who had caused them so much harm, and preferred Alexander Balas. The war of the two kings lasted a year and a half and ended in 150 BCE with the death of Demetrius. Thus concluded the third stage of the Maccabean Wars (160–150 BCE), in which Judea gained her freedom and Jonathan became both ruler and high priest. From that time all military, civil, and religious authority was gathered in his hands, while dependence upon the Seleucid kingdom became purely nominal.

The accession of Alexander Balas (150–145 BCE) led to a temporary alliance with Ptolemy VI Philometor of Egypt. To strengthen it, Ptolemy gave his daughter, Cleopatra Thea, in marriage to Alexander, thereby affirming anew the legitimacy of his reign. Both monarchs – the Seleucid and the Egyptian – invited Jonathan to Ptolemais, where the marriage was celebrated. There Jonathan was solemnly "robed in purple," which signified the official confirmation of all his rights and positions (1 Macc. 10:59-66). From now on, Jonathan was no longer the leader of the Jewish rebels, but the officially recognized ruler and high priest of the entire Judean people.

Meanwhile, the struggle for power in the Seleucid kingdom continued. The son of the slain king Demetrius I, Demetrius II Nicator, recruited a mercenary army in Crete and landed with it in Cilicia. He managed to win over Apollonius Taos, the commander of Coele-Syria, as well as the inhabitants of several Hellenistic port cities. The only military force in the Southern Levant loyal to Alexander remained the Judean army of Jonathan. Apollonius, having gathered a large army, challenged Jonathan to battle. Possessing a marked superiority in cavalry, he endeavored to draw the Judean army into the coastal plain, where he might impose battle upon them. He succeeded – but despite his advantage, his army was utterly routed, and its remnants fled into their ally Ashdod (Azotus). Jonathan stormed the city at once, captured it, and burned it to the ground. "When King Alexander heard of these things, he honored Jonathan still more, and he sent to him a golden buckle, such as it is the custom to give to the King's Kinsmen. He also gave him Ekron and all its environs as his possession" (1 Macc. 10:88–89).

Historians differ sharply concerning the loyalty of Apollonius. The First Book of Maccabees declares that he was appointed governor of

Coele-Syria by Demetrius II and acted on his orders. Josephus, however, charges Alexander Balas with duplicity, maintaining that Apollonius was his own trusted general (*Antiquities of the Jews,* 13.4.4). Be that as it may, the independent conduct of Jonathan and the growing power of Judea aroused the anxieties of both contenders for the Seleucid throne. Just as the Seleucids had once exploited Judea's civil war between Hellenizers and traditionalists, so now the Maccabees turned the dynastic struggle of the Seleucids to the advantage of their nation's independence.

The rivalry between Alexander Balas and Demetrius II grew even more entangled when Egypt's Ptolemy VI Philometor entered the struggle. Earlier, when Alexander sought Egyptian support, he had promised to cede to him the coastal cities of Coele-Syria – territories which once had belonged to the Ptolemaic kingdom. Under the pretext of aiding his son-in-law in the war against Demetrius II, and hoping to receive the pledged reward, Ptolemy VI advanced with his army along the Mediterranean seaboard of Coele-Syria, leaving Egyptian garrisons in every port he passed. The inhabitants of defeated Ashdod lodged complaints against Jonathan, yet the Egyptian king dared not provoke a clash with the Maccabees; on the contrary, when he met Jonathan, "he bestowed upon him costly gifts and showed him every mark of honor" (*Antiquities of the Jews* 13.4.5). In Ptolemais, however, Ptolemy narrowly escaped death, for one of Alexander's intimates attempted an assassination and then fled. When Ptolemy demanded the culprit's surrender, Alexander refused outright. Having gained the throne he desired, Alexander Balas had no wish to honor his debt of the coastal cities, and instead resolved to rid himself of his father-in-law. Enraged, Ptolemy severed the alliance: "he broke all ties of kinship with Alexander and took his daughter from him. Then he immediately dispatched envoys to Demetrius, proposing a treaty of friendship, promising to give him his daughter in marriage and to restore him to his father's kingdom. Demetrius welcomed the offer, concluded the alliance at once, and married her" (*Antiquities of the Jews,* 13.4.7).

While Alexander was occupied suppressing revolts in Cilicia, the Egyptian army captured his capital Antioch. Thus, Ptolemy VI realized the long-cherished dream of his ancestors – to place the Seleucid kingdom under Egyptian sway. Only fear of Roman intervention restrained him from formally assuming a second crown. Meanwhile Alexander returned from Cilicia with his forces and gave battle to Ptolemy near Antioch. The encounter ended grimly for both sides. Alexander was defeated and fled to the Arab tribes of the Syrian desert. As for Ptolemy, he fell from his horse and suffered grievous wounds. His guards rescued him from the enemy, but he "was in such a desperate state that for four days he could neither speak nor regain consciousness. Then the Arab ruler Zabdiel sent Ptolemy the head of Alexander, so that when the king recovered on the fifth day, he was met with the most welcome of sights – the news of Alexander's death and the severed head as proof. Overcome with joy at this, Ptolemy himself soon thereafter died" (*Antiquities of the Jews,* 13.4.8).

Once Demetrius ascended the Seleucid throne as Demetrius II Nicator (145–138; 129–125 BCE), he hastened to rid himself of the Egyptian troops. As Josephus records, "Demetrius began most disgracefully to slaughter the army of Ptolemy, entirely forgetting both his alliance with the Egyptian king and the fact that Ptolemy was his father-in-law through marriage to his daughter Cleopatra. The Egyptians fled from his outrages back to Alexandria, while Demetrius seized all the war elephants of Ptolemy" (*Antiquities of the Jews,* 13.4.9).

While the Seleucids struggled among themselves and with Egypt, Jonathan – now high priest and sole ruler of Judea – laid siege to the Acra, the last bastion of Greco-Syrian power in Jerusalem. Within its strong walls were stationed a formidable Greco-Macedonian garrison and those Jews who opposed the Maccabees. Having lost the civil war, the local Hellenizers and collaborators of the Seleucids made their final stand there. The fortress was so strong that the siege dragged on. When Demetrius II learned of the assault on this key stronghold of Seleucid authority, he advanced his army against Jonathan. Yet the king's advisors, mindful of past defeats, counseled him not to fight the Maccabees but to negotiate. Their meeting took place in Ptolemais, where a compromise was reached. Jonathan pledged loyalty to the Seleucid crown, and Demetrius confirmed his authority as governor and high priest of Judea. Moreover, Demetrius agreed to reduce Judea's tax burden and to grant it three districts of Coele-Syria which formerly belonged to Samaria. At the close of the meeting, "the king treated him as his predecessors had treated him; he exalted him in the presence of all his Friends. He confirmed him in the high priesthood and in as many other honors as he had formerly had and caused him to be reckoned among his First Friends" (1 Macc. 11:26–27). In essence, the treaty left the status quo unchanged: Judea remained nominally dependent on the Seleucid realm, while the Maccabees retained full civil, military, and religious authority at home. Yet even this minimal dependence left Judea entangled in the turbulence of Seleucid affairs, above all the fierce contests for the throne.

The accord with Jonathan spared Demetrius II from war in Judea. His large army, gathered for the campaign, was no longer needed, and the king, eager to refill his depleted treasury, repeated the fatal mistake of Antiochus V: he disbanded most of his troops without paying them. "Thus, he brought upon himself the resentment and even the hatred of his soldiers… for his royal predecessors had paid them alike in war and in peace, thereby securing their goodwill and their loyalty" (*Antiquities of the Jews* 13.4.9). The discontent of the army was seized upon by a certain Diodotus, later known as Tryphon. Once a trusted general of Alexander Balas, he knew that before his death Alexander had hidden his young son Antiochus with an Arab sheikh. Persuading the Arabs to surrender the child, Diodotus in 144 BCE proclaimed this four-year-old heir as the rightful Seleucid king, Antiochus VI Dionysus. Diodotus himself assumed the regency, becoming master of the realm in all but name.

Almost at the same time as the appearance of the child-king Antiochus VI, Demetrius II Nicator faced a rebellion among the citizens of Antioch, who threatened to take his life. Bereft of the loyalty of most of his army, he could not quell the uprising and begged Jonathan to hasten to his aid. In gratitude, Demetrius promised to grant whatever Jonathan desired – above all, the fortresses of the Acra in Jerusalem and Beth-Zur. Jonathan dispatched three thousand of his finest warriors, who in fact rescued the king from his enemies. Yet Demetrius failed to fulfill even a single promise, and this faithlessness bred estrangement, even hostility, between the Maccabees and the Seleucid monarch. When Antiochus VI and his regent Diodotus commenced hostilities against Demetrius, they at once took advantage of this rift. Their first act was to confirm all the offices and honors already bestowed upon Jonathan, and beyond this they appointed his brother Simon governor of all Coele-Syria. "Then the young Antiochus wrote to Jonathan, saying, "I confirm you in the high priesthood and set you over the four districts and make you one of the king's Friends." He also sent him gold plates and a table service and granted him the right to drink from gold cups and dress in purple and wear a gold buckle. He appointed Jonathan's brother Simon governor from the Ladder of Tyre to the borders of Egypt" (1 Macc. 11:52–59).

The forces that deserted to Antiochus VI and Diodotus soon defeated the remnants still loyal to Demetrius and seized Antioch itself. Demetrius fled to Phoenicia, where he found support among the port cities. Thus, the Seleucid kingdom was effectively divided: the capital and the vast northeastern provinces fell under the rule of Antiochus VI and Diodotus, while the Phoenician coast and central Syria remained in the hands of Demetrius II. The fate of Coele-Syria now depended on Jonathan, who chose to support the son of Alexander. The Judean army set out along the Mediterranean coast. Ascalon (Ashkelon) submitted without resistance, but Gaza was taken by storm. Joppa (Jaffa) was captured by Jonathan's brother Simon, who stationed a Judean garrison there lest the city revert to Demetrius. Meanwhile Jonathan was forced to march swiftly northward, for Demetrius' troops had suddenly appeared in Galilee. After several brief but fierce engagements, the remnants of Demetrius' army fled back toward Syria, pursued by Jonathan as far as Damascus. Having become master of almost all of Coele-Syria, Jonathan, without the Seleucids' knowledge, began fortifying the cities and fortresses of Judea, while his brother Simon managed to capture the strategically important fortress of Beth Zur and expel its Greco-Syrian garrison. The Maccabees intended to once and for all end all dependence on the Seleucid kingdom, where the struggle for power had already descended into civil war.

Demetrius II, trying to recapture Mesopotamia, unexpectedly encountered the Parthian army and was captured by them for a long time. Learning that his chief rival was now a prisoner, Diodotus refused any longer to play the part of Regent. In 142 BCE he murdered the young Antiochus VI and proclaimed himself king of the Seleucid Empire under the name of Diodotus Tryphon (142–138 BCE). He did not even hide the fact that he was an outright usurper and had no relation to the Seleucid dynasty. At this perilous moment for the royal house, Demetrius' wife Cleopatra Thea appealed to the king's brother, later known as Antiochus VII Sidetes (138–129 BCE). Thus, a new phase of civil war broke out within the Seleucid kingdom – between the usurper and the brother of the lawful, though captive, king.

While Antiochus VII was still gathering forces to confront Tryphon, it was Jonathan's Judean army that became the usurper's foremost adversary. Mustering all his troops, Tryphon advanced into Judea. Jonathan, in turn, marched out with forty thousand warriors. The First Book of Maccabees describes their meeting at Beth-Shean (Scythopolis): "When Trypho saw that he had come with a large army, he was afraid to raise his hand against him. So, he received him with honor and commended him to all his Friends, and he gave him gifts and commanded his Friends and his troops to obey him as they would himself. Then he said to Jonathan, "Why have you put all these people to so much trouble when we are not at war? Dismiss them now to their homes and choose for yourself a few men to stay with you and come with me to Ptolemais. I will hand it over to you, as well as the other strongholds and the remaining troops and all the officials, and will turn around and go home. For that is why I am here" (1 Macc. 12:42–45). Tryphon succeeded in dispelling Jonathan's doubts and convincing him of his goodwill. He lavished costly gifts upon him and solemnly proclaimed that the cities and fortresses once promised by Demetrius should now pass to Judea. Trusting him, Jonathan dismissed his army and went with only a small company to Ptolemais, there to take possession of that vital port. Yet as soon as he entered the city, his men were cut down, and Jonathan himself was seized – caught in the snare of the treacherous usurper.

Intending to take the Jews by surprise, Tryphon immediately set out from Ptolemais with a large army toward Jerusalem. However, Judea was not left leaderless: Jonathan's brother Simon took his place. The Judean army blocked the usurper's path. All of Tryphon's attempts to break into Judea from various directions and by roundabout routes proved unsuccessful: each time, Simon's warriors stood in his way. Tryphon even failed to bring relief to the besieged garrison in the Acra. Mindful of the fate of his predecessors, Tryphon feared to engage in a decisive battle with Simon's army and was forced to turn back to Antioch. On his return journey, near Gilead, Tryphon killed the captive Jonathan, despite receiving hostages and a huge ransom for his release.

Tryphon's treachery and open conflict with him forced Simon to seek reconciliation with the legitimate king of the Seleucid Empire, Demetrius II. The king in turn desired alliance with powerful Judea in his struggle against the usurper. In 142 BCE formal peace was concluded: Demetrius renounced all claims to tribute or taxation from Judea, recognizing its independence and sovereignty. Shortly thereafter this independence was also confirmed by Antiochus VII Sidetes, who, during Demetrius' Parthian captivity, ascended the Seleucid throne and led the war against Tryphon (1 Macc. 15:1–9). Thus ended the last, fourth phase of the Maccabean wars, which had endured for a quarter of a century (167–142 BCE).

The recognition of Judea's independence and peace with the Seleucid Empire deprived the besieged garrison of Acre in Jerusalem of any hope of salvation. Faced with starvation, the garrison surrendered to the mercy of Simon and his warriors. By Simon's order, the fortress of Acre and the hill on which it stood were razed to the ground. In 141 BCE, Simon convened the "Great Council" in Jerusalem, where he was proclaimed ruler, high priest, and military commander of Judea.

CHAPTER VI.

Ethnic Changes in the Southern Levant (6th Century BCE – 2nd Century CE)

From the beginning of the 6th century BCE, the entire Southern Levant came under the rule of the Neo-Babylonian Empire. During the reign of King Nebuchadnezzar II, the Babylonians conquered Judah – the most powerful kingdom in the region – in 586 BCE. A few years later, in 582 BCE, they subjugated the three smaller Transjordanian kingdoms of Ammon, Moab, and Edom. The Mesopotamian conquerors also destroyed nearly all the Philistine cities and several Phoenician cities along the Mediterranean coast. In southern and central Syria, major urban centers such as Damascus, Hamath, and Arpad were likewise devastated. Not stopping there, the Babylonians advanced south into Midian, burning tribal encampments, seizing large numbers of captives, and confiscating all the Midianites' livestock.

The Babylonians did not merely ravage the Southern Levant; they also deported parts of the populations of the most defiant nations to Mesopotamia – including the Judahites, Moabites, Ammonites, Philistines, Phoenicians, and Syrian Arameans. Nebuchadnezzar II ordered the destruction of Jerusalem, the capital of Judah, and the deportation of its inhabitants to Babylonia. The Philistine cities were leveled, their populations exiled, and the same fate befell the Phoenician cities of Sidon and Tyre, as well as the Syrian cities of Damascus and Hamath.

Roughly half a century later, the Persian king Cyrus the Great defeated the Neo-Babylonian Empire and permitted the exiled peoples to return to their ancestral lands. By then, however, the Southern Levant lay in ruins – an opening quickly exploited by new arrivals from the Arabian Peninsula, the Nabataean tribes.

1. The Arrival of the Nabataeans

In the 6th century BCE, a new nomadic people calling themselves "Nabatu" began to infiltrate southeastern Transjordan, into the lands of Edom. Gradually, over one or two centuries, the Nabataean tribes took control of the entire territory of the Edomites (Idumaeans), forcing most of them to resettle farther west, in southern Judea. Not satisfied with Edom, the Nabataeans moved north and subjugated another Transjordanian people, the Moabites. But before occupying the territories of Edom and Moab, the Nabataeans had seized Midian in northwestern Arabia, subduing the local Midianite nomads. The Amalekites, who roamed the deserts of the Negev and Sinai, were next.

Later, the Nabataeans established their own Nabataean Kingdom in the conquered territories and began to wage wars against much more powerful adversaries – Hasmonean Judea and the Syrian Seleucids. So, who were the Nabataeans and where did they come from? Unfortunately, those who called themselves the "Nabatu" people left behind no written records other than numerous short inscriptions in Aramaic, the *lingua franca* of the Levant at the time. Like almost all peoples of that era, the Nabataeans had no authors of their own, let alone their own writing system, to tell their story. However, Greek, Roman, and Judean historians have left us a good deal of information about them. Many ancient authors mentioned the Nabataeans, but the most comprehensive information was left by three of them: Diodorus Siculus, Strabo, and Josephus. They all call the Nabataeans Arabs and their homeland

Arabia. Most modern historians agree with this, but hold different opinions on which part of the vast Arabian Peninsula the Nabataeans might have come from. Some believe the country of origin was Yemen, others place the Nabataeans' homeland in the Hejaz, and a third group suggests the nomadic Arabs could have come from northeastern Arabia, bordering Southern Mesopotamia.

On the other hand, the Book of Genesis recalls that Nebayoth was the eldest son of Ishmael, the firstborn of the patriarch Abraham and the Egyptian Hagar, and was considered the progenitor of the eponymous tribe that roamed in Sinai and Midian. However, today's historians are skeptical of the biblical version of the Nabataeans' origin and are convinced that this people were unrelated to the biblical family and that their original homeland should be sought deep within Arabia.

Assyrian and then Neo-Babylonian written records from the 8th to 7th centuries BCE report on military campaigns by Mesopotamian kings against plundering Arab tribes. Among the names of these tribes is a name very similar to "Nabatu." It is impossible to say whether this refers to the Nabataeans, or whether it is merely a coincidence of names. Unlike the Assyrians and Babylonians, the Persians, who established their rule over the Levant from the 6th to 4th centuries BCE, had little interest in the desert regions of Midian and southeastern Transjordan, so they did not conduct any military campaigns there. This circumstance significantly helped the Nabataeans consolidate their power and establish an extraordinarily profitable trade in frankincense, myrrh, and spices, which they transported from southern Arabia.

It is commonly believed that in the first centuries of their penetration into southern Transjordan (6th to 5th centuries BCE), the Nabataeans had good relations with the Judeans. However, this is far from the truth. Nehemiah, the Jewish governor of Judea during Persian rule and the author of the biblical book of the same name, unambiguously testifies that the Arab Geshem was an enemy of the Judeans and, together with the Samaritans and Ammonites, tried to hinder the construction of the walls around Jerusalem (Neh. 2:10). In the mid-5th century BCE, when the Judeans who had returned from Babylonian captivity were rebuilding the walls of Jerusalem, the term "Arabs" typically referred to the Nabataeans; other Arab tribes, such as the Qedarites, appeared in Transjordan much later. Even then the Nabataeans feared the strengthening of Judea, their northwestern neighbor.

The first truly reliable information about the Nabataeans can only be found in the ancient Greek historian Diodorus Siculus (1st century BCE), who extensively quotes another, earlier historian, Hieronymus of Cardia, who lived three centuries before him. Hieronymus of Cardia was a participant in Alexander the Great's campaign against the Persians and a witness to the great general's funeral. During the struggle for Alexander's inheritance, he served his famous diadochus, Antigonus Monophthalmus. Antigonus tasked Hieronymus with organizing the extraction of asphalt from the Dead Sea, which was highly valued in the ancient world. However, this could not be done due to Nabataean bandit raids.

As Hieronymus reports, in 312–311 BCE, Antigonus commissioned one of his courtiers, a certain Athenaeus, to conduct a punitive expedition to Petra, the principal city of the Nabataeans, to punish them and seize all their spoils. Taking advantage of the temporary absence of the main Nabataean forces, Athenaeus made a three-day forced march to Petra, where he easily captured both the city and a large amount of plunder. However, the Greek and Macedonian soldiers were so exhausted from the desert journey and the heavy load that they set up a night camp without even going far from Petra. Worse still, confident that the Nabataeans were still far away and unaware of the defeat of their city, Athenaeus made a fatal mistake by not securing his camp. That night, the Nabataeans suddenly descended and slaughtered the entire Greco-Macedonian detachment; only a few dozen horsemen managed to escape.

Upon learning of the deaths of Athenaeus and his soldiers, Antigonus sent a new, twice-as-large force to Petra, commanded by his son Demetrius. Demetrius managed to take Petra again, but he did not achieve a victory: the main Nabataean forces had retreated beforehand, avoiding a disadvantageous battle. In the end, Demetrius was forced to return, settling for a modest ransom from the Nabataeans (Diodorus Siculus, *Bib. hist,* 19. 95-100). However, even after the military expeditions of Athenaeus and Demetrius, the Nabataean attacks on the asphalt miners at the Dead Sea did not cease, so all work there was shut down.

According to Hieronymus of Cardia, "many Arab tribes pasture livestock in the deserts, but the Nabataeans surpass all of them in wealth, even though they number no more than ten thousand." Hieronymus considered their main source of wealth to be the incense trade, which they had an exclusive monopoly on. However, they were not above banditry and piracy in the coastal waters of the Red Sea. Diodorus Siculus accused the Nabataeans of attacking the ships of the Egyptian Ptolemies. He claimed that their piracy became so widespread that the Ptolemies even organized a military expedition against them, although he did not report how it ended (Diodorus Siculus, *Bib. hist,* 19. 95-100). Quoting Hieronymus, Diodorus considered the Nabataeans' main advantage to be their ability to find and preserve water in the desert. Incidentally, other hereditary nomads, the Amalekites, who must have been under Nabataean rule at the time, were always distinguished by this skill. In this context, it is appropriate to recall the opinion of the Israeli archaeologist Avraham Negev that the very name "Nabatu" in early Arabic meant "a person who digs for water." But the Nabataeans left no written records in their own language, only in Aramaic, so it is not possible to refute or confirm this assumption.

Hieronymus, and following him Diodorus, claimed that the Nabataeans highly valued their freedom. If a dangerous enemy approached them, they would hide in the desert as if it were their fortress. They knew perfectly well where to find water in the waterless desert but skillfully concealed this knowledge from strangers. Ancient Greek historians noted that the Nabataeans, being nomads, did not build houses, sow grain, plant crops or trees, or drink wine (Diodorus Siculus, *Bib. hist,* 19. 94.2-95.2). In this respect, they were similar to the biblical Rechabites, about whom the Jewish prophet Jeremiah wrote. Unlike the Rechabites, however, the Nabataeans made their main occupation not pastoral livestock herding but the trade in incense and spices. In contrast to the righteous Rechabites, the Nabataeans periodically staged bandit raids and ambushes and engaged in piracy in the coastal waters of the Red Sea. And finally, if the Rechabites firmly adhered to Jewish monotheism, the Nabataeans were overt pagans.

The periodic wars between the Egyptian Ptolemies and the Syrian Seleucids, as well as the power struggles within these Hellenistic kingdoms, helped the Nabataeans maintain their independence and monopoly on the caravan trade of incense. The expansion of Rome into Asia Minor further weakened the Seleucid Empire and made the creation of the Nabataean Kingdom possible, whose power extended over all of Midian, eastern Transjordan, the Negev, and southeastern Sinai. Most likely, the Nabataean Kingdom arose in the middle of the 2nd century BCE, and its first king was the Nabataean tribal chief Harithat, who became better known in the Hellenized form as Aretas I.

From its very beginning, the Nabataean Kingdom was a multiethnic state. The Nabataean Arabs themselves constituted only the dominant minority that maintained its nomadic or semi-nomadic character. Hieronymus of Cardia noted the small numbers of the Nabataeans for good reason. The majority of the population consisted of dependent and controlled peoples: Midianites, Amalekites, Idumaeans, Moabites, and later, after the conquest of northern Transjordan and southern Syria, they were joined by the Ammonites and Syrians (Arameans of Syria). While the Midianites and Amalekites, like the Nabataeans, maintained their nomadic way of life, the other peoples were unambiguously sedentary, and it was they who made up the urban and agricultural population in the Nabataean Kingdom. For example, the semi-desert Negev was inhabited mainly by Idumaeans, who also predominated in the now-excavated Nabataean settlements of Avdat, Mamshit, Shivta, and Haluza. Consequently, the achievements of the Nabataean Kingdom in agriculture and their original methods of water conservation belong not so much to the nomadic Nabataeans or Bedouins in the modern sense of the word, but rather to the Idumaean farmers who turned the semi-desert into flourishing oases. These same Idumaeans also constituted the majority of Petra's population. Even before this city became Nabataean, it belonged to the Idumaeans, and was originally founded by the Midianite ruler Rekem (Raqmu), whose name it bore for a long time. The Nabataeans, however, remained nomads and their main occupation was caravan trade, not agriculture and craftsmanship. Diodorus Siculus pointed out that the Nabataeans held tenaciously to their nomadic way of life and punished anyone who tried to change it with death (Diodorus Siculus, *Bib. hist*, 19. 94.2-95.2). Some Nabataeans were merchants and trade intermediaries, others were soldiers and caravan guides, and a third group supplied camels, and serviced and guarded caravan routes and stops in the desert. The trade in frankincense and spices brought the Nabataeans fabulous incomes, which tempted first the Ptolemies and Seleucids, and later Rome. However, their nomadic way of life and knowledge of the secrets of the waterless deserts repeatedly saved the Nabataeans from their more powerful enemies. It is noteworthy that a thousand years before the appearance of the Nabataeans, the biblical Ishmaelites (descendants of Nebayoth) were also exclusively engaged in caravan trade and also considered the desert their best fortress.

The greatest prosperity and power of the Nabataean Kingdom occurred in the 1st century BCE and the 1st century CE. During this time, the Nabataeans captured eastern Transjordan and part of southern Syria. For several years, they even managed to seize Damascus. Here the Nabataeans clashed with the Syrian Seleucids and Hasmonean Judea. While the Seleucids were trying to preserve their kingdom, which was shrinking like a piece of shagreen leather, the Hasmoneans were fighting for the return of the lands of the Hebrew tribes that had previously belonged to the Kingdoms of Israel and Judah. The Nabataean conquests in the Negev and then in Transjordan made them immediate neighbors of the Judeans.

The first reliable information about contacts between them is provided by the Second Book of Maccabees. It reports that the high priest Jason (Joshua), known for his Hellenizing activities, sought refuge with the Nabataean ruler Aretas I in 168 BCE, but did not receive it (2 Macc. 5:5-8). Relations between the two peoples developed with difficulty. At first, friendly relations predominated: both the Judeans and the Nabataeans suffered from the expansion of the Seleucid Empire, so they tried to support each other during periods of confrontation with it. For example, during the Maccabean wars, the Nabataeans adopted a friendly stance toward the Jewish rebels. But as the Seleucid kingdom retreated and weakened, the Judeans and Nabataeans began to compete with each other for lands in Transjordan.

During the reign of the Judean king Alexander Jannaeus, a series of wars began between Hasmonean Judea and the Nabataean Kingdom. The Judeans won most of the battles, and Alexander Jannaeus managed to recover Gilead and Perea – the territories of the Transjordanian Israelite tribes. Moreover, he succeeded in recapturing almost all the areas of the Decapolis, which had belonged to the Kingdom of Israel in the past. It seemed that in a little more time all of Transjordan would fall under the rule of the Judeans. However, in 93 BCE, the Nabataean king Obodas I defeated Jannaeus, and the eastern part of Transjordan remained in the hands of the Nabataeans. The Nabataeans were much more successful in fighting the Seleucid kingdom. In 84 BCE, Obodas won an important victory over Antiochus XII, and his son Aretas III was able to capture Damascus.

A new clash between the Nabataeans and the Judeans occurred in 65 BCE, during the civil war in Judea between the sons of Alexander Jannaeus – Hyrcanus II and Aristobulus II. The Nabataean king Aretas III decided to support the legitimate heir Hyrcanus, who, in exchange for help, promised to return everything Alexander Jannaeus had taken from the Nabataeans. The Roman-Jewish historian Flavius Josephus describes these events as follows: "Prompted by such [attractive] promises, Aretas at the head of a fifty-thousand-strong army, partly cavalry and partly infantry, marched against Aristobulus and defeated him in battle. Since many soldiers defected to Hyrcanus after this victory, Aristobulus found himself abandoned and fled to Jerusalem" (*Antiquities of the Jews,* 14.2.1). Aretas III, together with Hyrcanus, besieged Jerusalem. However, events then took a completely unexpected turn. Aristobulus bribed the Roman general Scaurus, who had recently, on the orders of Pompey, captured Damascus. Scaurus, threatening war, demanded that Aretas and Hyrcanus immediately lift the siege of Jerusalem. Josephus reports that "the frightened Aretas hurried from Judea to Philadelphia (Rabbath-Ammon), and Scaurus returned to Damascus. Aristobulus, however, was not satisfied with just being saved from the impending captivity. He pursued the enemy, overtook him at the place called Papyron and gave him battle there, in which he killed more than six thousand men..." (*Jewish War,* 1.6.2-3).

24. Petra's theater, built by local red stone under Roman rule.

The defeat of Aretas III's army at Papyron served as a stern warning to both the Nabataeans and the Judeans and showed that a new power, Rome, had become the master of the Southern Levant. At first, however, the Romans repeated the mistakes made by the Macedonians and Greeks: in 62 BCE, Scaurus was in a hurry to march on Petra, but failing to win a victory over the main Nabataean forces, he was forced to settle for a ransom from them. Later, in 60, 58, and 55 BCE, the Romans organized new campaigns against the Nabataean Kingdom and eventually forced it to acknowledge its dependence on Rome.

The civil war in the Roman Republic (44–41 BCE) and then the Parthian capture of Syria (40–38 BCE) helped the Nabataeans get rid of their humiliating dependence on Rome, but not for long. For supporting the Parthians, the Nabataeans were punished with an increased tribute. The Roman general Mark Antony entrusted the collection of it to the Judean king Herod the Great – a trusted person and a friend of the entire Roman triumvirate of that time. Herod's mother, Cyprus, came from a noble Nabataean family, but this circumstance did not help Herod's relations with the Nabataeans. Despite Nabataean resistance, Herod successfully extracted tribute for the Romans and inflicted several painful defeats on the Nabataeans. During the new civil war in Rome, this time between the triumvirs Octavian and Antony, the Nabataeans again chose the "wrong" side, supporting Antony. This cost them dearly: Emperor Octavian Augustus imposed an even greater tribute on them and for a time wanted to give the entire Nabataean Kingdom to his friend, the Judean king Herod the Great.

After Herod's death, relations between the Nabataeans and Judeans improved, so much so that the royal dynasties of both peoples intermarried. The Nabataean king Aretas IV Philopatris (9 BCE – 40 CE) married his daughter to Herod Antipas, the son of Herod the Great, whom the Romans had appointed as tetrarch of Galilee and Perea. However, this dynastic union was short-lived. Herod Antipas divorced Aretas IV's daughter to marry Herodias, the former wife of his half-brother Philip. This act was contrary to the laws of Judaism and was severely condemned by John the Baptist. But the matter did not end there. The offended Aretas decided to punish Antipas and, gathering his troops, marched on the former son-in-law's possessions. Only Roman intervention put an end to the military confrontation between their vassals. A new outbreak of tension in Judean-Nabataean relations occurred during the Great Jewish Revolt against Rome (66–73 CE). The Nabataean king

Malichus II (40–70 CE) sent his army to Judea to assist Vespasian and Titus. However, the Nabataean Arabs became infamous for such a cruel and barbaric attitude toward the Jewish population that it even drew sharp condemnation from the Roman commander Titus.

25. Petras famous Khazneh - the tomb for Nabatean king Aretas IV (9 BCE- 40 CE).

The Nabataean Kingdom ceased to exist in 106 CE, when the Roman emperor Trajan incorporated its territory into the new Roman province of Arabia, with its capital at Bostra. From this time on, Petra gradually began to lose its significance as the main Nabataean city. The transformation of the Nabataean Kingdom into a regular Roman province gave rise to an accelerated cultural and religious Hellenization of the Nabataeans. Thus, the main Nabataean deity, Dushara, acquired the features of Zeus and Dionysus, and the mother of the gods, Allat, became the equivalent of

Athena and Aphrodite. In the third century CE, the Nabataeans stopped using the Aramaic alphabet and switched entirely to Greek. By the beginning of the 5th century, the Nabataeans painlessly and rapidly adopted Christianity. In the 6th century, exactly one thousand years after their appearance on the land of Edom, the Nabataeans disappeared from the pages of history as a people. Petra became so deserted that it turned into a ghost city. New Arab tribes from distant Yemen – the Qahtani, Ghassanids, Himyarites, and Kindites – came to the empty lands of the Nabataeans. All of them became vassals of a new empire – Byzantium.

Where and why did the Nabataeans disappear? This question troubles historians and archaeologists. Some of them see the primary cause of the depopulation in the powerful earthquakes that destroyed Petra in 363 and 551 CE, while others suspect terrible epidemics. Another possibility is that the disappearance of the Nabataeans is connected with the shift of caravan routes to the northeast toward Syria and Mesopotamia, as the entire life of this nomadic people was linked to the caravan trade. Along with it, the Nabataeans also left. In the 7th century, the Nabataeans must have gone through a wave of Islamization, which erased their ethnic identity, turning them into Arabs and Muslims, or more precisely, into Bedouin-Muslims.

As for the other peoples in this multiethnic state, their fates were different. The Midianites and Amalekites, who roamed in Sinai, the Negev, and Midian under Nabataean rule, underwent Arabization and, having converted to Islam, became the same Bedouin-Muslims as the Nabataeans themselves. The Idumaeans and Moabites mostly accepted Jewish monotheism and were absorbed into the Jewish people. The Ammonites and Arameans of northern Transjordan retained their identity the longest, but they eventually succumbed to Islamization and Arabization.

2. The Migration of the Idumaeans

The fall of Judah and the destruction of Jerusalem by the Babylonians in 586 BCE allowed the Edomites to take revenge on their younger brother and even seize the southern part of Judah up to Hebron. But this was short-lived. A new invasion by Nebuchadnezzar II in 582 BCE led to the complete defeat of Edom, and the situation of its inhabitants was no better than that of their Judahite brethren. The biblical prophet Obadiah described this situation as follows: "But you should not have gloated over your brother on the day of his misfortune; you should not have rejoiced over the people of Judah on the day of their ruin; you should not have boasted on the day of distress. You should not have entered the gate of my people on the day of their calamity; you should not have joined in the gloating over Judah's disaster on the day of his calamity; you should not have stolen his goods on the day of his calamity... As you have done, it shall be done to you; your deeds shall return on your own head" (Obad. 1:12-13, 15). The subsequent fate of Edom became intertwined with the history of Judea. Both countries successfully survived Persian rule and became part of the Hellenistic kingdoms, first the Egyptian Ptolemies and then the Syrian Seleucids. Starting with the arrival of the Hellenes in the Near East (332 BCE), the name of Edom was also Hellenized. From this time on, it began to be called Idumaea, and the Edomites became known as Idumaeans.

Beginning in the 6th century BCE, from the time of the fall of Judah and the Transjordanian kingdoms of Edom and Moab, the semi-nomadic Arab tribes of the Nabataeans began to penetrate the Southern Levant. Their advance was slow, taking more than a century, but it was relentless. The Midianite nomads were the first to suffer from them. While the Midianites submitted, the Edomites preferred to move west, into southern Judea, especially since after the fall of Jerusalem and the captivity of the royal court and the army, this country was left defenseless. Southern Judea had attracted the Edomites before, as many of their fellow tribesmen already lived there, such as the Kenizzites and the Maonites, whose ancestors had joined the Hebrews on their way to conquer Canaan. Thus, southern Judea became the new homeland of the Edomites. Within one or two centuries, the Nabataeans completely displaced the Idumaeans from their homeland into southern Judea. From this time, the territory of Edom was seized by the Arabs and turned into Nabataea, and the Idumaeans were forced to migrate to southern Judea, which as a result became more widely known as Idumaea.

A new round of confrontation between the Idumaeans and the Judeans occurred during the Maccabean wars (167–142 BCE). During the rebellion of Judah Maccabee against the religious persecutions of the Seleucid king Antiochus IV Epiphanes, the Idumaeans sided with the strong – the Seleucids. Therefore, after liberating Jerusalem and purifying the Temple of pagans, Judah was also forced to fortify the fortress of Beth Zur, "so that the people might have a stronghold that faced Idumea" (1 Macc. 4:61). The First Book of Maccabees reports an interesting fact: the Idumaeans, having moved to southern Judea, did not displace the Judeans from there but came to live as neighbors. However, the Jewish rebellion against Seleucid rule inevitably led to clashes with the Idumaeans, who supported the Seleucid king. In addition, the Seleucids, knowing the old enmity between the two closely related peoples, tried to pit the elder brother against the younger. "When the nations all around heard that the altar had been rebuilt and the sanctuary dedicated as it was before, they became very angry, and they determined to destroy the descendants of Jacob who lived among them. So, they began to kill and destroy among the people. But Judas made war on the descendants of Esau in Idumea, at Akrabattene, because they kept lying in wait for Israel. He dealt them a heavy blow and humbled them and despoiled them" (1 Macc. 5:1-3).

However, this was far from the only campaign against the Idumeans. Later Judah Maccabee was forced to undertake a new campaign, this time against Hebron, which had fallen into Idumaean hands. The dominance of the Edomite tribe of the Kenizzites in Hebron greatly facilitated the peaceful transition of this important city to the Idumaeans. As is known, Hebron was given to the Kenizzites in gratitude for their help to the Hebrew tribes during the conquest of southern Canaan. The Kenizzites united with the tribe of Judah, and the Kenizzite nobility, such as Caleb and his son Othniel, even led this Hebrew tribe. "Then

Judas and his brothers went out and fought the descendants of Esau in the land to the south. He struck Hebron and its villages and tore down its strongholds and burned its towers on all sides. Then he marched off to go into the land of the Philistines and passed through Marisa" (1 Macc. 5:65-66). The ancient Canaanite, and then Judahite, city of Mareshah was located southwest of Hebron, on the way to Gaza, which was where Judah Maccabee was heading. Mareshah was then inhabited mostly by the same Idumaeans, only Hellenized. Therefore, the conquest of this city was a continuation of the campaign against the Idumaeans.

At the end of the 2nd century BCE, Johanan Hyrcanus, the ruler of Hasmonean Judea, conquered Idumea and presented its people with a choice: either accept Jewish monotheism or leave southern Judea. Up to this time, the Idumaeans had remained pagans and for the most part worshiped the main Edomite god, Qaus. However, according to ancient Egyptian sources, among the Edomite tribes, whom they called "Shasu," there were also those who worshiped Yahweh, for example, the Kenizzites. This is also indirectly confirmed by the earliest biblical texts, which attributed Mount Seir and the region of Teman in Edom to the domain of the God of Israel (Judges 5:4-5). However, the Edomites, unlike the Judeans, remained pagans until the end of the second century BCE. It is noteworthy that despite the very difficult relations between the pagan Edomites and the monotheistic Judeans, the Book of Deuteronomy constantly reminded the Jews of their kinship with their closest neighbors: "You shall not abhor any of the Edomites, for they are your kin" (Deut. 23:7).

Johanan Hyrcanus's ultimatum forced the Idumaeans to choose Jewish monotheism. From this time on, the Idumaeans became Judeans; the elder brother was again reunited with the younger. However, later the elder brother again made his presence known: Herod the Great, who ruled the Judean kingdom from 37 to 4 BCE, came from a noble Idumaean family. This great and terrible ruler destroyed the entire Hasmonean dynasty, and his son, Herod Antipas, executed John the Baptist and interrogated Christ. The last mention of the Idumaeans was by Josephus. In his book on the Jewish War (66–73 CE), he specifically mentioned the Idumaean detachments that came to defend Jerusalem from the Romans. Since then, the name of the Idumaeans (Edomites) no longer appeared in the pages of history. They completely merged with the Judeans and shared their fate.

3. The Separation of the Samaritans

After the fall of the Kingdom of Israel in 722 BCE, Assyrian conquerors deported some of the Israelites to Assyria and brought in new settlers from Syria and Mesopotamia. The Bible provides the names of the places from which the new settlers came: three of them – Hamath, Avva, and Sepharvaim – were in western Syria, and two – Babylon and Cuthah – were in central Mesopotamia. The inhabitants of all these cities, like the Israelites, had also been expelled from their homelands for repeated rebellions against Assyria.

These forced migrants were ethnically very similar to the people of the Northern Kingdom. For example, the Syrian cities of Hamath, Sepharvaim, and Avva were originally settled by Canaanites, then conquered by Amorites, and finally by Arameans. Over time, these three related ethnic groups thoroughly intermingled and formed a single West Semitic people who spoke Aramaic but culturally absorbed much of the heritage of the Canaanites and Amorites. The people from Babylon and Cuthah did not differ much from the inhabitants of central Syria: they were also predominantly Amorite and Aramean. Babylon was originally founded and settled by Amorites, a group that included the famous Babylonian king Hammurabi II. Later, Chaldeans, which was a name for one of the Aramean tribal groups, settled in this area of Mesopotamia and gradually took over Babylon, Cuthah, and neighboring cities. However, in place of the Canaanite element present in the settlers from central Syria, the settlers from Babylon and Cuthah had a mix of Akkadian (East Semitic) and Sumerian blood. This was perhaps one of the few things that ethnically distinguished them from the Israelites.

The Assyrians settled the inhabitants of the Mesopotamian and Syrian cities not only in Samaria itself but throughout the region of the tribes of Ephraim and part of Manasseh. Thus, the term Samaria came to denote not only the capital of the former Kingdom of Israel but also the territory of these two tribes, which was transformed into a separate Assyrian province called "Samerina." The new settlers brought with them the pagan cults they had worshiped in their former homelands. For the most part, they were variations of Canaanite and Amorite deities, which were also known in the territory of the Israelite tribes. However, some pagan beliefs were unique to Mesopotamia, such as the cult of the god of death Nergal, whose center of worship was the Mesopotamian city of Cuthah.

Very quickly, under the influence of the Israelites who remained in Samaria, the newcomers began to adopt Yahwism. This process accelerated when the Assyrians allowed Israelite priests to return to the religious center in Beth-El. The Book of Kings explains this by stating that the new settlers "did not worship the Lord; therefore, the Lord sent lions among them that killed some of them. So, the king of Assyria was told, "The nations that you have carried away and placed in the cities of Samaria do not know the law of the god of the land; therefore, he has sent lions among them; they are killing them because they do not know the law of the god of the land." Then the king of Assyria commanded, "Send there one of the priests whom you carried away from there; let him go and live there and teach them the law of the god of the land." So, one of the priests whom they had carried away from Samaria came and lived in Bethel; he taught them how they should worship the Lord" (2 Kings 17:25-28).

Regardless of the reasons or pretexts used for the return of the Israelite priests, this biblical episode confirms a very important circumstance: the activity of the Yahwist center in Beth-El was fully restored, and the new settlers began to practice Yahwism alongside the worship of their own gods. The biblical text testifies to this polytheism as follows: "So these nations worshiped the Lord but also served their carved images"

(2 Kings 17:41). Subsequently, the Aaronites from the Kingdom of Judah repeatedly used the polytheism of the inhabitants of Samaria and the fact of the Israelites' intermingling with the new settlers to deny them the right to be considered heirs of the "House of Joseph" and, therefore, to claim leadership among the descendants of the Hebrew tribes. Be that as it may, after the fall of the Kingdom of Israel, the Samaritans – the descendants of the tribes of Ephraim and Manasseh who had mixed with the settlers from Syrian and Mesopotamian cities – became the sole continuators of the history of the "House of Joseph."

The attitude of the Judeans toward the Samaritans changed many times over the centuries. The Judahite king Hezekiah, who witnessed the fall of the Israelite capital, Samaria, tried to attract the Israelites to Judah, repeatedly inviting them to celebrate Jewish holidays and pray in the Temple in Jerusalem. Unable to militarily annex the lands of the former Kingdom of Israel, which were then under Assyrian rule, Hezekiah tried to extend the religious influence of the Jerusalem Temple over them. This was only partially successful. The Judahite king Josiah pursued a completely different policy. Taking advantage of the weakening and subsequent defeat of Assyria in 612 BCE, he forcibly extended Judahite rule over part of the territory of the former Kingdom of Israel. He likewise forcibly eliminated all pagan cults there and coercively introduced Jewish monotheism. However, Judahite rule in Samaria did not last long, as the entire Levant fell under the rule of a new predator – the Neo-Babylonian Empire.

The stay of part of Judahites in Babylonian captivity led to the strengthening of Jewish monotheism and its final crystallization. Therefore, the return of the Jews from Babylonian captivity was also a return of Judah to the consistent monotheism of Moses. However, the uncompromising demands of the spiritual leaders – Ezra and Nehemiah – for the observance of all commandments and their claim to a monopoly on religious and spiritual life threatened to undermine good relations with neighboring peoples, especially with the Samaritans. The idea of rebuilding the Jerusalem Temple captivated the Samaritans, who for the most part adhered to monotheism and revered the Pentateuch of Moses, just like the Judeans. Moreover, many noble Samaritan and Judean families were linked by kinship ties. For example, one of the grandsons of the Judean high priest Eliashib was the son-in-law of the Samaritan leader Sanballat (Neh. 13:28).

However, the Samaritans' desire to build the new Second Temple together with the Judeans was met with a categorical refusal from the Judean spiritual leaders of the time. The lawgiver Ezra describes the beginning of the conflict with the Samaritans as follows: "They [Samaritans] approached Zerubbabel and the heads of families and said to them, "Let us build with you, for we worship your God as you do, and we have been sacrificing to him ever since the days of King Esar-haddon of Assyria, who brought us here." But Zerubbabel, Jeshua, and the rest of the heads of families in Israel said to them, "You shall have no part with us in building a house for our God, but we alone will build for the Lord, the God of Israel, as King Cyrus of Persia has commanded us" (Ezra 4:2-3). Offended by the refusal, the Samaritans turned from potential allies into overt enemies of the Judeans. "Then the people of the land discouraged the people of Judah and made them afraid to build, and they bribed officials to frustrate their plan throughout the reign of King Cyrus of Persia and until the reign of King Darius of Persia" (Ezra 4:4-5). Thus began a centuries-long conflict between two parts of the same people. With their complaints and denunciations to the Persian king, the Samaritans managed to temporarily stop the construction of the Temple and then the walls of Jerusalem, but not for long. The Judeans managed to allay the Persians' fears and finish the construction (Ezra 4:24).

The conflict between the Judeans and the Samaritans was in fact a continuation of the schism between the southern and northern Hebrew tribes, between the main southern tribe of Judah and the core of the northerners – the "House of Joseph." This was a rivalry for the right to unite under their rule not only the Hebrew tribes but the entire territory of historical Canaan. This rivalry tore apart the United Monarchy in 931-928 BCE, and the fact that during two centuries of separate existence, Judah and Israel were never able to reunite speaks to the non-random nature of this schism. In reality, the Judahites and Israelites came from related but different tribal groups that had different histories. The only thing they had in common was their stay in Egypt and the need to reconquer their lands in Canaan. But they went to Egypt at different times, held different positions there, and returned to Canaan in different centuries. Their historical narratives and genealogies were skillfully woven together by the Levites and Aaronites during the period of the United Monarchy, but this was not enough to make one people out of two. Subsequently, the mixing of the descendants of the "House of Joseph" with people from Syrian and Mesopotamian cities only exacerbated the differences between the Judeans and Samaritans. Both peoples adhered to monotheism, but in different forms. The Samaritan version of the Torah (Pentateuch) differed from the Judean one. But most importantly, besides the Book of Joshua, the Samaritans did not recognize any other prophetic and historical biblical literature. They honored only Moses as a prophet. As a result, Judean monotheism was much deeper and more consistent than the Samaritan version. The refusal to admit the Samaritans to the Jerusalem Temple led them to view Mount Gerizim in the area of Shechem as the true Mount Moriah, where the biblical patriarch Abraham tried to sacrifice his son Isaac to the Lord. In the mid-5th century BCE, they built their own temple there (also dedicated to Yahweh) to rival the one in Jerusalem. From this time on, the Samaritans gradually separated from the Judeans into a distinct ethno-religious group, and relations between them became hostile. The deepening of the schism between the two peoples was also aided by the decision of the lawgiver Ezra to convert the Hebrew language to the Aramean square script so that even in writing the Judeans would differ from the Samaritans, who retained the early biblical alphabet from the time of David and Solomon.

The arrival of Alexander the Great's army in the Southern Levant in 332 BCE gave the Samaritans an excuse to break away from the

Persian king Darius. Their ruler even expressed his readiness to support Alexander and appeared before him with 8,000 warriors. However, the Samaritans later revolted and killed the Macedonian governor. In retaliation, the Macedonians destroyed Samaria and founded a Hellenistic city in its place (Curtius Rufus, Quintus. *History of Alexander,* 4.8.9-11). From this time on, the Samaritans made the neighboring Shechem their center.

For the first century of Hellenistic rule, the entire region of Samaria, like Judea, was under the authority of the Egyptian Ptolemies. However, as during the time of Persian rule, the hostility between the Samaritans and Judeans did not subside. It spread to the territory of Egypt itself, where Samaritan and Judean diasporas lived. Josephus noted that even in Egypt "...the Jews had a quarrel with the Samaritans, because the former wanted to preserve the customs established in ancient times. They began to fight each other because the people of Jerusalem considered only their temple sacred and demanded that sacrifices be sent there. The Samaritans, however, insisted on the requirement to send these offerings to Mount Gerizim" (*Antiquities of the Jews,* 12.1.1).

Ironically, at the end of the 4th century BCE, the high priest of the Samaritan temple on Mount Gerizim turned out to be the brother of the high priest of Judea. He was married to the daughter of the ruler of Samaria (*Antiquities of the Jews,* 11.7.4). That is, just as in the time of Ezra and Nehemiah, a hundred years later, the Judean and Samaritan aristocracy were still related to each other. According to Josephus, "such marriages were concluded among a significant number of priests and [other] Israelites, and this caused no small confusion for the people of Jerusalem" (*Antiquities of the Jews,* 11.8.2). Thus, rivalry in the religious and political spheres did not prevent the two peoples from intermarrying. Josephus, a Jewish aristocrat and historian, had an interesting view on the relations between the Judeans and Samaritans. "The Samaritans," he wrote, "have such a habit: when misfortune befalls the Jews, they renounce kinship with them and in such a case tell the truth; but when good fortune befalls the Jews, they are immediately ready to join them, claiming their right and tracing their origin to the descendants of Joseph – Ephraim and Manasseh" (*Antiquities of the Jews,* 11.8.6).

According to Josephus, the Samaritans asked Alexander the Great to exempt them from paying taxes every seventh year, when, in accordance with the commandments of the Torah, they did not sow or harvest crops. The king asked them who they were to make such requests to him. When they answered that they were Jews and inhabitants of Shechem, the king asked them again if they were Judeans. Having received a negative answer, he said: "I granted this privilege to the Judeans, therefore only after learning more about you will I give you an answer" (*Antiquities of the Jews,* 11.8.6). Josephus had a clear bias against the Samaritans and believed that their main city, Shechem, which lay at the foot of Mount Gerizim, was built by "apostates of the Jewish people." He claimed that "everyone among the people of Jerusalem who was accused of violating the prescriptions regarding food, or of desecrating the Sabbath, or of any other violation of this kind, fled to Shechem and insisted that he had been exiled without guilt" (*Antiquities of the Jews,* 11.8.7).

Beginning in the second century BCE, the Samaritans, like the Judeans, became part of the Seleucid Empire. In 167 BCE, they also experienced persecution of their monotheistic faith by the Seleucid king Antiochus IV Epiphanes. This king was hostile not only to Judean monotheism but also to Samaritan monotheism. Antiochus hated the very idea of monotheism, which he regarded as incompatible with Hellenistic paganism. While he intended to dedicate the Jerusalem Temple to Zeus Olympios, he planned to dedicate the Samaritan temple to Zeus Xenios (2 Macc. 6:1–2). However, unlike the Judeans, the Samaritans did not rebel; they did not support Judah Maccabee; moreover, during the Maccabean wars, they showed loyalty to the Seleucids. It is not surprising that after the victory of the Maccabees, the Judean ruler Johanan Hyrcanus captured the entire region of Samaria and in 110 BCE, destroyed the Samaritan temple on Mount Gerizim to its foundations. This put an end to the rivalry between the Samaritans and the Judeans for the right to unite under their hegemony not only the descendants of the Hebrew tribes but all the peoples of historical Canaan. This rivalry, which began with the confrontation between the Israelite king Saul and the Judahite military leader David, lasted for almost 900 years and ended with the complete victory of Hasmonean Judea over Samaritan Israel. From then until the arrival of the Romans in 63 BCE, the Samaritans were under the rule of the Judeans. The Romans, wanting to weaken the Judeans, granted the Samaritans some autonomy within the Judean kingdom, but with the rise of Herod the Great (37–4 BCE), this autonomy was eliminated. It is noteworthy that two of Herod the Great's main heirs, namely Ethnarch Archelaus and Tetrarch Antipas, were the sons of a Samaritan woman named Malthace. However, Archelaus's unsuccessful ten-year reign led to Samaria, like Judea itself, becoming part of the Roman province of Syria in 6 CE.

The cruelty, lawlessness, and corruption of the Roman administration were felt by both the Judeans and the Samaritans. However, among all the Roman prefects and procurators, Pontius Pilate (26–36 CE) – the killer of Christ – proved to be the most merciless toward the Samaritans. Thousands of Samaritans who had gathered on their sacred Mount Gerizim without the procurator's knowledge to unearth vessels allegedly hidden by Moses fell victim to Pilate. The Samaritans' complaint about the mass murder of innocent people was supported by the Roman governor in Syria, Vitellius. Pontius Pilate was summoned to trial in Rome, where, accused of unlawful killings and embezzlement, he was sentenced to death.

The New Testament contains two significant episodes about the Samaritans at the beginning of the Common Era. From them, it follows that the relations between the two peoples were so hostile that the Judeans who lived in Galilee preferred to bypass Samaria during their pilgrimage to Jerusalem. The disciples of Christ considered the Samaritans to be almost pagans, and Jesus himself avoided preaching among them or sending his disciples into their midst. According to the Gospel of Luke, the Samaritans did not allow Jesus to even stay for the night in their village (Luke 9:53). Despite this, Christ condemned the hostility toward the Samaritans and believed that their moral qualities should not be judged on the basis of their teachings. However, despite all this, when addressing a Samaritan woman, he emphasized: "You worship what you do not know; we worship what we do know, for salvation is from the Jews" (John 4:22). He thereby made it clear what a great difference existed between the teachings of the Samaritans and the Judeans.

In 52 CE, a real massacre occurred between the Samaritans and Judean pilgrims traveling to Jerusalem, leading to the death of people. The conflict was so serious that the Roman emperor Tiberius was forced to intervene. As a result, he blamed the Samaritans for everything and replaced Procurator Cumanus (48–52 CE) with Felix (52–60 CE) (Tacitus, *Annales*, 12.54).

As during the Maccabean wars, the Samaritans took no part in the Great Jewish Revolt against Rome (66–73 CE). However, in July 67 CE, a large number of Samaritans gathered on Mount Gerizim. The Roman general Vespasian, who had already arrived in Judea with troops, sent an entire legion with infantry and cavalry to Samaria. But the Samaritans refused to disperse and offered resistance (*Jewish War* 3.5.34). The reasons for the clash with the Romans remain unknown. But this was the only episode when the Samaritans showed themselves during the Jewish War against the Romans. Likewise, we know nothing about the participation of the Samaritans in the Bar Kokhba revolt (132–135 CE). Obviously, the hostile relations between the two peoples did not allow the Samaritans to support the Jewish rebels, although what they were fighting for should have been close to the Samaritans themselves.

The catastrophic consequences of the three Jewish revolts against Rome completely changed the demographic picture throughout Judea. The Roman-Jewish Wars, especially the last Bar Kokhba revolt, led to a serious depopulation of the country. However, these events, so tragic for the Judeans, did not affect the Samaritans at all. After the Roman army left Judea, the Samaritans became the main ethnic group of the country, which the Romans ordered to be called by a new name – "Palestine." The Samaritans settled in the deserted Judean cities and villages, and the next two centuries, the 3rd and 4th centuries, proved to be their "golden age." They received broad autonomy from the Roman authorities, and the number of Samaritans increased to at least a million people. Thanks to the Samaritan factor, Judea in these centuries did not yet become Palestine; rather, it probably became Israel again, for the Samaritans always called themselves by that name. The name of Baba Rabba (288–362 CE) – the high priest and leader of the Samaritan community, a religious reformer, and the author of most of the Samaritan liturgy – is associated with these years of flourishing. At the same time, the religious schism between the Samaritans and the Jews continued to deepen. To the Samaritans' rejection of the prophetic and historical books of the Tanakh (Old Testament) was added a categorical refusal to recognize the Mishnah and Gemara (Talmud), created in the 2nd–4th centuries. However, this was to be expected, since the Samaritans never recognized the Oral Torah (Oral Law).

The golden age of Samaritan Israel was followed by a period (5th–6th centuries) of persecution of the Samaritans and their faith. Such a sharp change in the fate of this people was connected with the adoption of Christianity as the official religion of the Roman Empire. Beginning in the 5th century, the emperors of the Eastern Roman Empire (Byzantium) began to pursue a policy of forced Christianization of the population. The Samaritans were equated with pagans and forbidden to practice their monotheistic religion under penalty of death (Abulfati, *Annales Samaritani,* 170). The religious persecutions of the Samaritans, heavy tax burdens, and unlawful confiscations of their property caused a series of Samaritan revolts. The most significant of them were two: the revolt of Justa in 484 and the revolt of Tzabar in 529.

The first Samaritan uprising occurred during the reign of Emperor Zeno (474–491 CE). A barbarian from the Isaurian tribe who had usurped the Byzantine throne and was notorious for his moral corruption, Zeno displayed particular zeal in the forced Christianization of the Samaritans. In response to the violence and oppression of the Byzantine authorities, a Samaritan revolt broke out in 484. Its center was Mount

Gerizim, and its leader was Justa (Justus), who was later proclaimed king by the Samaritans. The rebels defeated the Byzantine garrisons and captured Neapolis (Shechem) and Caesarea, cities with predominantly Samaritan populations. Within two years, they succeeded in liberating most of Palestine from Byzantine control. The insurgents burned churches that had been built on the sites of former Samaritan synagogues and killed priests who, under threat of death, had forced them to convert to Christianity. In 486, Zeno suppressed the rebellion with extraordinary cruelty, exterminating tens of thousands of people. To humiliate the Samaritans and insult their religious feelings, he ordered the construction of a Church of the Holy Virgin Mary on the summit of their sacred Mount Gerizim (John Malalas, *Excerpta historica: De insidiis,* 44; Procopius, *Aedificiis,* 5.7.7).

The second major revolt was caused by the same reasons as the first. It occurred during the reign of Emperor Justinian in 529 and was led by Julian Tzabar, who also became king of Samaritan Israel and proclaimed independence from Byzantium. As before, the rebels captured Shechem (Neapolis), Scythopolis, and the main city of the province – Caesarea. They dealt with those who robbed them and forbade them to practice their religion. The Byzantine historians Procopius of Caesarea (*History of the Wars*) and John Malalas (*Chronographia*) left us a lot of information about the Samaritan revolts, but unfortunately, their works are difficult to use due to the extreme bias in their presentation of facts and their overt hostility toward the Samaritans.

Tzabar's rebel army consisted of peasants untrained in military affairs, so it was doomed to defeat in a war against the numerically superior and experienced mercenary soldiers. Tzabar's position was further complicated by the fact that the Ghassanid Arabs came to the aid of the Byzantines. Like the previous one, this revolt was drowned in blood. According to Procopius of Caesarea, about a hundred thousand Samaritans died, and tens of thousands of young men and women were sold into slavery outside of Palestine; even more Samaritans fled the country. The Byzantine historian laments that "the land was deprived of its peasants" (*History of the Wars*, 1:11). Subsequently, the deserted cities and villages of the Samaritans were occupied by Christian Syrians (Arameans of Syria).

The revolts of the 5th and 6th centuries against Byzantium had consequences for the Samaritans as devastating as those the Roman–Jewish Wars of the 1st and 2nd centuries had for the Jews. Using modern terminology, one could say that if pagan Rome committed genocide against the Jewish people, Christian Byzantium is guilty of genocide against the Samaritans. Until the end of the 5th century, the Samaritans, together with the Jews, constituted the absolute majority of the population of Palestine. However, by the beginning of the 7th century, when Byzantine rule ended and Muslim Arabs arrived in the country, the number of Samaritans had fallen to 350,000 people. This was not so much the result of forced conversion to Christianity as it was of the Byzantine policy of exterminating the Samaritans. It is noteworthy that just as the Samaritans did not support the Jews during their wars against Rome, the Jews were almost not involved in the Samaritan revolts against Byzantium. This was despite the fact that they shared a common enemy.

4. The "Disappearance" of the Moabites and Philistines

Of all the Transjordanian peoples, the Judahites had the best relations with the Moabites. During times of drought and war, Judahites often found refuge in Moab, and Moabites in Judah. The lands of both peoples were separated by the Dead Sea, a circumstance that prevented them from having disputed territories. Based on the descriptions of the prophet Jeremiah, this Transjordanian kingdom was subjected to a total defeat and devastation, no less than that of Judah. To make matters worse, the Moabites suffered the exact same Babylonian captivity as the Judahites. "Woe to you, O Moab! The people of Chemosh have perished, for your sons have been taken captive and your daughters into captivity… Chemosh shall go out into exile, with his priests and his attendants. The destroyer shall come upon every town, and no town shall escape; the valley shall perish, and the plain shall be destroyed, as the Lord has spoken. Set aside salt for Moab, for she will surely fall; her towns shall become a desolation, with no inhabitant in them" (Jer. 48:46, 7-9). The Babylonian captivity of the Moabites lasted for almost half a century, the same length as the Babylonian captivity of the Judeans. Only the Persian king Cyrus, after defeating the Neo-Babylonian Empire (539 BCE), released both peoples to return to their homeland.

While in Babylonian captivity, the Moabites grew closer to the Judeans, and many of them adopted Jewish monotheism. Nehemiah, who served as the Persian governor in Judea for 12 years, reports that a portion of the Moabites, along with descendants of the ruler of Moab (from the sons of Jeshua and Joab), returned from Babylonia with the Judeans. But they returned not to Moab, but to Judea. Nehemiah states that in the first wave of those who rushed to return to Judea, there were 2,818 Moabites (Neh. 7:11). In the second wave of Judeans from Babylonia, with whom the scribe Ezra returned, there was another group of Moabites – "of the descendants of Pahath-moab, Eliehoenai son of Zerahiah, and with him two hundred males" (Ezra 8:4). Ezra and Nehemiah counted only the men as heads of households, but each of these men was usually followed by a large family. In addition, many exiles returned gradually, not only in the first two groups.

Listing the leaders of the Judeans, Nehemiah first names a certain Parosh, the ruler of Moab, and Pahath-Moab (Neh. 10:14-15). Furthermore, both spiritual leaders, Ezra and Nehemiah, mention another noble Moabite from the royal family, a certain Hasshub, son of Pahath-Moab, who lived in Jerusalem and helped to restore the walls around the city (Ezra 2:6; Nehemiah 3:11). It is noteworthy that the writing of the Book of Ruth also dates to this period. The very appearance of such a work and the mention that the Moabite Ruth was the great-grandmother of King David were intended to justify the merging of Judeans with Moabites, despite the Torah's prohibition against intermarrying with them as a people who had committed incest and refused to allow the Hebrew tribes returning from Egypt to pass through their lands.

As for the Moabites who escaped the Babylonian captivity and remained in their land, they, like the Edomites, had to either assimilate with the Nabataeans or move to the territory of Judea and, again, accept Jewish monotheism. This process was facilitated by the fact that the relations between the Judeans and the Moabites were almost always much better than with their other neighbors. It is noteworthy that Ezra and Nehemiah, when listing both the enemies and the neighbors of the Judeans, say nothing about the Moabites, and if they do mention them, it is only as part of their own Judean people. The First and Second Books of Maccabees do the same: while recounting the peoples neighboring the Judeans, they say nothing about the Moabites. Moreover, they do not even mention their existence. And this is about the closest neighboring people geographically! It is obvious that by the time of the Maccabean wars, the Moabites had already completely merged with the Judeans, and the territory of Moab had passed to the Nabataeans, just as it had happened with the lands of Edom.

The Moabites were not the only people who disappeared from the map of the Southern Levant. The same fate befell the Philistines, who at one time claimed dominance over all of Canaan. These formidable newcomers from the Aegean Sea region were very quickly Canaanized, intermingling with the local Canaanites and Rephaim. As early as the 9th-8th centuries BCE, this originally Indo-European people had become, in terms of language and culture, typical Western Semites. However, the most terrible blow to the remnants of Philistine identity was dealt by the deportations of the inhabitants of Philistine cities, practiced by the Assyrians and then the Babylonians in the 8th-6th centuries BCE. The Assyrians and Babylonians deported the population of most Philistine cities that resisted them to Mesopotamia. Unlike the Judeans, the inhabitants of the Philistine cities did not return from Assyrian and Babylonian captivity but completely dissolved among the local population. For example, in 604 BCE, the Babylonian king Nebuchadnezzar

II stormed the cities of Ashkelon and Ashdod, destroyed them to their foundations, and drove all their inhabitants into captivity in Mesopotamia. The cities lay in ruins for more than 70 years, but the people of Ashkelon and Ashdod never returned home. The cities were rebuilt and resettled by others – Phoenicians, whom the Persian king Cambyses settled there. The total devastation experienced by the Philistine cities at that time was very figuratively conveyed by the Judean prophet of the 6th-5th centuries BCE, Zechariah: "Ashkelon shall see it and be afraid; Gaza, too, and shall writhe in anguish; Ekron also, because its hopes are withered. The king shall perish from Gaza; Ashkelon shall be uninhabited; a mongrel people shall settle in Ashdod, and I will make an end of the pride of Philistia" (Zech. 9:5-6).

It is not surprising that the new population of Philistia no longer identified themselves as Philistines, although the names of the cities remained the same. The new settlers in the former Philistine cities began to consider themselves "Ashdodites," "Ashkelonites," or residents of Yavneh and Jaffa, but not Philistines or Canaanites. With the arrival of Alexander the Great's army, the former Philistine city-states became definitively Hellenistic. The population of those cities that resisted the Macedonian army were subjected to new total deportations. Thus, the city of Gaza, which did not surrender to Alexander the Great's army, was destroyed, and its inhabitants were taken to other Hellenistic cities. These deportations finally changed the ethnic and cultural appearance of the former Philistine cities; many Greeks and Macedonians appeared in them, but most of all Syrians of Aramean origin. At the same time, many descendants of the Philistines and Canaanites were resettled in the Hellenistic cities of the Decapolis and Idumaea. As a result of all these sweeping migrations, the former Philistine cities became completely Hellenistic and at the same time completely disunited. They showed loyalty to the Egyptian Ptolemies and the Syrian Seleucids, but not to each other, and even less so to the surrounding Judean population.

The books of Ezra and Nehemiah, dating to the 5th century BCE, no longer mention the Philistines or Philistia, who were the main enemies of the Israelites and Judahites. At the same time, Nehemiah mentions the "Ashdodites," firstly as ill-wishers of Judea, and secondly, as merely inhabitants of a city with whom many Judeans had family ties. According to Nehemiah's complaints, the children from these mixed families spoke more in the language of Ashdod (Neh. 4:1-2; 13:23-25). The Book of Nehemiah testifies not only to the disappearance of the Philistines as a people but also to instances of assimilation between the Judeans and the inhabitants of the former Philistine cities. The First and Second Books of Maccabees, created in the 2nd-1st centuries BCE, confirm the complete absence of Philistines and speak of the presence of significant Jewish communities in the former Philistine cities. The Books of Maccabees state that the Maccabean army repeatedly stormed Gaza, Ashdod, Ashkelon, Yavneh, and Jaffa, defending their co-religionists in those cities. By this time, the former Philistine cities had become the bulwark of Hellenism in the Southern Levant.

The Syrian Seleucids, unable to defeat the rebels of Judah Maccabee in open battles, tried to pit the former Philistine cities, which were part of their empire, against him. The first clash between them took place near the coastal city of Yavneh (Jamnia) and ended unsuccessfully for the detachment of Jewish rebels. At that time, Judah Maccabee himself and the main forces of his army were fighting the Ammonites and Syrians in northern Transjordan, in Gilead. Upon returning victorious, Judah went to conquer the Idumaeans, and from there he moved directly to the Philistine city of Ashdod. After taking Ashdod, "he tore down their altars, and the carved images of their gods he burned with fire; he plundered the towns and returned to the land of Judah" (1 Macc. 5:68).

During the Maccabean wars, the Seleucid king Alexander Balas, who needed the help of the Judeans, gave the former Philistine city of Ekron to Jonathan Maccabee along with the surrounding area. Hasmonean Judea had always claimed ownership of all these Mediterranean ports. This was fully achieved only by the Judean king Alexander Jannaeus; he annexed all the former Philistine cities to Judea. The only exception was Ashkelon, which partially retained self-government because it voluntarily surrendered to the Judean army.

The Romans, who arrived in the Southern Levant in the 60s BCE, took all the coastal cities of former Philistia away from the Judean kingdom and restored their Hellenistic character. They gave them the same autonomy as the Decapolis and annexed them to the Roman province of Syria. These cities, like the Decapolis, became the stronghold of Roman rule in the region and a potential threat to Judea should it attempt to gain independence from Rome. However, one of the former Philistine cities, Jaffa, was nevertheless returned to Judea by Julius Caesar. Another, formerly Philistine city, Yavneh, became a Jewish religious center after the destruction of Jerusalem and the Temple in 70 CE.

It seemed that everyone, even in the former Philistine cities, had forgotten about the Philistines and Philistia. But this turned out not to be the case. They were remembered, or rather, made to be remembered, after the Bar Kokhba revolt (132-135 CE). The Roman Emperor Hadrian, enraged by the third Jewish revolt against Rome, decided not only to expel the Jews from Judea but also to force the whole world to forget the name of their homeland. Among the new names suggested to him by historians, the emperor deliberately chose the name of a long-defunct people — the Philistines, who could not in any way challenge the Romans for this country. Hadrian was also impressed by the fact that the Philistines came from the Greek islands and had no relation to the local peoples of the Levant. And the name Philistia was once in use among the ancient Greeks, who traded with the cities of southwestern Canaan. Thus, Judea turned into Palestine. This name immortalized the name of a people who had long since disappeared from the pages of history.

5. The Ammonites in the Service of the Seleucids

The Babylonian captivity of the Ammonites brought them closer to those Jews who had been taken there a few years earlier. There is indirect evidence that during the nearly half-century of their joint stay in Babylonia, some of the Ammonites adopted Jewish monotheism and intermarried with the Jews. This was a natural process, considering that the Hebrews and the Ammonites had originally been one and the same people. Like the Jews, the Ammonites were able to return to their homeland only after the Persians destroyed the Neo-Babylonian Empire in 539 BCE.

The rapprochement between the Ammonites and the Judeans occurred not only in Babylonia but also in Ammon itself, where many refugees from Judah had fled. As the Book of Nehemiah shows, after the destruction of Jerusalem, quite a few Jews found themselves in Ammon, and even the Ammonite governor Tobiah was connected to the Judeans by family ties: his wife and his son's wife came from noble Judean families. As Nehemiah himself admitted, "in those days the nobles of Judah sent many letters to Tobiah, and Tobiah's letters came to them. For many in Judah were bound by oath to him..." (Neh. 6:17–18).

It is noteworthy that even such a staunch opponent of the Ammonites as Nehemiah acknowledged the presence of a "good part of the sons of Ammon," by which he meant those who had become Judaized during or after the Babylonian captivity. In those times, many Jews, including members of the nobility, intermarried with the Ammonites. Even the Judean high priest Eliashib was related by marriage to Tobiah. Moreover, he provided the Ammonite governor with one of the finest chambers in the Jerusalem Temple, which provoked Nehemiah's fierce indignation (Neh. 13:4–9).

To halt the growing wave of marriages between Jews and Ammonites, Nehemiah and Ezra were forced constantly to remind their people of the Torah's prohibition against intermixing with Ammonites (Neh. 13:1–3). However, relations between Jews and Ammonites began to deteriorate for another reason. The Ammonites were alarmed by the strengthening of Judea, the construction of the new Second Temple, and even more so by the restoration of Jerusalem's defensive walls. Although in the 5th–4th centuries BCE both Judea and Ammon were equally subject to the

Persian Empire, the memory of the Ammonites' former dependence on the Jews and the rapid revival of Judea filled them with anxiety.

Nehemiah reports that when Tobiah learned that the rebuilding of Jerusalem's walls had begun, he was very angry, and that the Ammonites conspired with the Samaritans, the Ashdodites, and the Arabs "to come and fight against Jerusalem" (Neh. 4:3-8). From that time onward, the Ammonites became one of Judea's principal enemies.

The two centuries of Persian rule over the Levant (539–332 BCE) left us almost no mention of Ammon. Slightly more information is provided by the Hellenistic era, which began with the arrival of Alexander the Great's army in the East (332 BCE). After prolonged wars between Alexander's generals – Ptolemy and Seleucus – the Ammonites came under the rule of the Seleucids. To please the Hellenes, the capital of Ammon – Rabbah or Rabbath-Ammon – was renamed. From the mid-3rd century BCE, it was known as Philadelphia.

Unlike their southern neighbors, the Idumeans and Moabites, who were forced to cede their lands to the Nabataean tribes, the Ammonites withstood the onslaught of the newcomers from Arabia and preserved the territory of historical Ammon. True, they managed to do this only with the help of the Seleucid kingdom, of which Ammon became a part. The military might of the Seleucids served the Ammonites as a bulwark against which all waves of the advancing Nabataean tribes broke. Had the Seleucid state arisen two centuries earlier, it is quite possible that both the Idumeans and the Moabites might also have preserved their lands in southern Transjordan.

It is therefore hardly surprising that during the Maccabean wars for Judea's freedom (167–142 BCE), the Ammonites took the side of the enemies of the Jews – the Syrian Seleucids. The leader of the Jewish rebels, Judah Maccabee, was then compelled to conduct several campaigns into Transjordan to protect the Jewish inhabitants of those regions from Ammonite attacks.

According to the First Book of Maccabees, the Ammonites at that time were "a warlike and numerous people," commanded by a certain

Timothy. Whether this Timothy was a Hellenized Ammonite ruler appointed by the Seleucids, or a military commander sent from Syrian Antioch, is unknown. The book merely states that Judah Maccabee "engaged in many battles with them, and they were crushed before him; he struck them down. He also took Jazer and its villages; then he returned to Judea" (1 Macc. 5:6–8).

However, the war with the Ammonites did not end there. The next confrontation took place farther north, in Gilead, which the Ammonites had claimed since the days of their king Nahash. The Jewish inhabitants of this region again called for help: "The nations around us have gathered together to destroy us. They are preparing to come and capture the stronghold to which we have fled, and Timothy is leading their forces. Now then, come and rescue us from their hands, for many of us have fallen…" (1 Macc. 5:9–12).

Judah's new campaign proved even more successful. He defeated Timothy's army and subdued all the cities and fortresses of Gilead. Yet later, fighting with the Ammonites and their ruler Timothy flared up again in Gilead with renewed force. As the First Book of Maccabees reports, "Timothy gathered another army and encamped opposite Raphon, on the other side of the stream. Judas sent men to spy out the camp, and they reported to him, "All the nations around us have gathered to him; it is a very large force. They also have hired Arabs to help them, and they are encamped across the stream ready to come and fight against you." And Judas went to meet them… When Judas approached the stream of water, he stationed the officers of the army at the stream and gave them this command, "Permit no one to encamp, but make them all enter the battle." Then he crossed over against them first, and the whole army followed him. All the nations were defeated before him, and they threw away their arms and fled into the sacred precincts at Carnaim. But he took the town and burned the sacred precincts with fire, together with all who were in them. Thus, Carnaim was conquered; they could stand before Judas no longer" (1 Macc. 5:37–44). In truth, the Ammonites did not fight of their own will; they were directed and incited against the Judeans by the Syrian Seleucids, while Ammon was merely a province within their vast empire.

The last mention of the Ammonites dates to the 2nd century CE, when the early Christian theologian Justin (Justin Martyr, 100–165 CE) noted in his "Dialogue with Trypho" that this people was still present in Transjordan in considerable numbers (*Dialogue with Trypho*, 119). Apparently, those Ammonites who had not assimilated with the Jews formed a significant part of the Hellenized population in the cities of the Decapolis in Transjordan.

6. Hellenistic Cities

Alexander the Great's campaign to the East brought tens of thousands of Macedonians and Greeks into the region. The overwhelming majority of them never returned to their homeland, but remained permanently in the Hellenistic kingdoms of the Ptolemies and the Seleucids. Natives of Macedonia and Greece, as well as their descendants, became the ruling elite and the main support of these two kingdoms founded by Alexander's generals. It was precisely these Macedonians and Greeks who became the founders and the initial population of the Hellenistic cities in the Southern Levant, where the border between the territories of the Seleucids and the Ptolemies ran. The strategic importance of the Southern Levant, for control over which these two kingdoms repeatedly fought, compelled the Ptolemies and later the Seleucids to actively establish their fortified cities with a reliable and loyal population. Thus, in the territories that had previously belonged to the kingdoms of Israel and Judah, roughly three dozen fortified cities with foreign Greco-Macedonian populations appeared. These cities are customarily called Hellenistic because Greek culture and religion dominated there, and in their structure they were typical Greek poleis – independent communities with their own governing councils (boule). All city affairs were administered by officials elected by the citizens themselves. These Greek cities possessed such extensive autonomy that they could even mint their own coinage. All of them were surrounded by strong walls and military fortifications. Each such city owned a large territory of its own and controlled the settlements located on it.

The Hellenistic cities of the Southern Levant were divided into two main groups: 1) Mediterranean ports and 2) the cities of the Decapolis ("the Ten Cities"). The first group consisted of former Philistine-Canaanite and Phoenician cities on the Mediterranean coast, namely Raphia, Gaza, Ashkelon (Ascalon), Ashdod, Yavne (Jamnia), Jaffa (Joppa), Dor, Akko (Ptolemais), and Tyre. Later, the Ptolemaic and Seleucid kings added new port cities to them: Anthedon, Apollonia, and Straton's Tower (the future Caesarea). Some of these cities suffered heavily at the hands of Alexander the Great's army; for example, Gaza and Tyre were completely destroyed, and their populations were either killed or expelled. It was Greek and Macedonian settlers who gave these coastal cities their new Hellenistic character, forming the initial core of their inhabitants. However, in several Mediterranean ports Greeks had lived even before the arrival of Alexander the Great. For instance, in Akko there had long been a permanent colony of merchants and traders from Athens. Over time, all these port cities underwent substantial Semitization. The majority of their inhabitants came to be townspeople of local West Semitic origin, while the descendants of Greeks and Macedonians remained only a privileged minority. Still, the two ethnic groups were united by their belonging to Hellenistic culture and way of life.

The second part of Hellenistic cities, the Decapolis, was located in the northern and central Transjordan on lands of both the former Kingdom of Israel and Ammon. It received its name, "the Ten Cities," after the arrival of the Romans, when in the time of Pompey this group included Damascus and comprised exactly ten cities: Philadelphia, Raphana, Scythopolis, Gadara, Hippos, Dion, Pella, Gerasa, and Kanatha. All these Hellenistic cities were founded not on empty ground, but on the ruins of well-known Israelite settlements. Greek and Macedonian colonists changed or simply Hellenized the West Semitic names of the ancient cities. For example, Sussita came to be called Hippos, though both names – West-Semitic and Greek – meant one and the same thing: "horse." The Canaanite Pehal, mentioned already in the inscriptions of Egyptian pharaohs in the second millennium BCE, became Pella. This happened to be the name of Alexander the Great's native city, so Macedonian colonists replaced the foreign Semitic name with one that was familiar and dear to them from their former homeland. The Israelite Beth Shean began to be called Scythopolis, and the former capital of the Ammonites, Rabbah, was renamed Philadelphia. The city of Dion received its name from the city of the same name in distant Macedonia. In general, the cities of Dion, Pella, and Gerasa were initially only settlements of Macedonian soldier-veterans, while in Gadara Greeks from Attica predominated. As for the southernmost city of the Decapolis, Philadelphia, it was settled by Hellenized inhabitants from Phoenician Tyre, which had been completely destroyed and depopulated. Over time, the number of cities in the Decapolis changed, and by the second century CE there were already eighteen of them. Among others, such well-known cities as Abila, Edrei, and Gedor were added.

The cities of the Decapolis occupied the best lands of Transjordan, and therefore, unlike the Hellenistic cities of the Mediterranean coast, their population was engaged primarily in agriculture and in trade involving agricultural products. The main trade routes to Syria, Arabia, and Mesopotamia passed through the territory of the Ten Cities, which contributed to the development and prosperity of these urban centers.

In addition to the two main groups of Hellenistic cities – the ones on the Mediterranean coast and those of the Decapolis – there were also several separate and isolated cities in Galilee, Samaria, and Idumea that undoubtedly belonged to the Hellenistic category. In Upper Galilee, such a city was Paneas (Banias). Although it owed its name to the Greek god Pan, it had once again been built on the site of the Israelite city of Dan, which earlier still had been the Canaanite city of Laish (Leshem). Paneas is known for having been rebuilt and adorned – out of regard for the Romans – by Philip, one of the sons of Herod the Great, who ruled in Upper Galilee and southern Syria. The second such Hellenistic city, this time in Lower Galilee near Nazareth, was Sepphoris. It, too, owed its origin to the arrival of the Hellenes in the East. But unlike other Hellenistic cities, it always had a more than substantial Jewish population and even a second, exclusively Hebrew name – Tzippori. It is possible that Sepphoris was a city of Hellenized Jews who preferred the Greek way of life to the Jewish one. It owed its flourishing to another son of Herod the Great – Antipas, who received Galilee and Perea (central Transjordan) as his domain. After the Jewish-Roman War (66–73 CE) and the destruction and losses associated with it, Sepphoris became, in effect, the capital of Jewish Galilee.

Two more Hellenistic cities – Mareshah (Marissa) and Adoraim (Adora) – were located in Idumea. In the past, these had been Canaanite-Judahite cities, but the Egyptian Ptolemies altered their character by settling their soldier-veterans and officials there. In addition, many Hellenized inhabitants from the Phoenician port of Sidon were forcibly resettled in Mareshah. Subsequently, the populations of Mareshah and Adoraim were supplemented by residents of Idumean origin.

Finally, another Hellenistic city was built on the ruins of the capital of the Kingdom of Israel – Samaria. This site was allotted for the settlement of Macedonian soldiers. Yet the Hellenistic Samaria did not last long; it was destroyed by Johanan Hyrcanus, ruler of Hasmonean Judea. However, the Roman generals Pompey and Gabinius restored it, and Herod the Great rebuilt it anew and renamed it Sebaste in honor of his friend and patron, the Roman emperor Augustus. Not content with that, Herod dedicated yet another city to Augustus – Straton's Tower, renaming it Caesarea. Both names – Sebaste and Caesarea – mean the same thing, only the former in Greek and the latter in Latin. But Caesarea fared far better; it grew rapidly and became the residence of the Roman procurator of Judea.

The creation of Hellenistic cities in the territory of the former Hebrew kingdoms posed a twofold danger for the Jews. First, these cities served as centers of paganism and idolatry, thereby challenging Jewish monotheism, painfully forged by the Judeans over the course of many centuries. Second, the Hellenistic cities, in which the majority consisted of an alien population, became a support for foreign rule and an obstacle to Judea's striving for independence. Indeed, it was precisely for this purpose that they had been built by the Ptolemies and the Seleucids. These cities – especially those with a significant Jewish population – often generated serious conflicts and tensions in relations between Jewish monotheists and foreign pagans.

The expansion of the Hellenistic cities in the Southern Levant was halted as a result of the Maccabean wars (167–142 BCE), which restored the independence and sovereignty of Judea. Subsequently, the rulers of Hasmonean Judea gradually regained control over most of the lands that had previously belonged to the Hebrew kingdoms. Simon, the first ruler of independent Judea, succeeded in retaking only Jaffa and Gezer. When the Seleucid king Antiochus VII Sidetes began threatening him with war and demanded that these cities be returned, "Simon said to him in reply: "We have neither taken foreign land nor seized foreign property, but only the inheritance of our ancestors, which at one time had been unjustly taken by our enemies. Now that we have the opportunity, we are firmly holding the inheritance of our ancestors" (1 Macc. 15:33–34).

Simon's son, Johanan Hyrcanus, achieved far more: he retook Sebaste in Samaria, Scythopolis in Galilee, as well as Mareshah and Adoraim in Idumea. All the rest – the Decapolis and the cities of the Mediterranean coast – fell to the Judean king Alexander Jannaeus. It was he who brought under his authority almost all the Hellenistic cities of the Southern Levant, with the exception of two of them – Ptolemais (Akko) and Ascalon (Ashkelon). As a rule, he was prepared to spare each Hellenistic city and its inhabitants if they would renounce idolatry and accept monotheism. Some agreed to this; others, such as Pella and Gadara, could not abandon their pagan cults. Although Gadara was a strong and well-fortified citadel, the Judean army took it by storm after a ten-month siege. The same unhappy fate befell Macedonian Pella, which clung stubbornly to Hellenistic paganism. Ironically, a century later Pella did in fact accept monotheism – brought there by Jewish Christians fleeing from Jerusalem before the advancing Romans.

However, the Decapolis, like the other Hellenistic cities, did not remain in ruin and desolation for long. In 63 BCE, as Judea was being torn apart by civil war, the Roman legions of Gabinius and Pompey entered the land. The Romans took the Hellenistic cities away from Judea, rebuilt them, restored their autonomy, and attached them to their province of Syria. Like the Ptolemies and Seleucids before them, the Romans regarded these cities as strongholds of their rule in Judea. And indeed, the Hellenistic cities became bases for the Roman army during the Jewish revolts against Rome. In the years of the Jewish War, Mediterranean Caesarea and Ptolemais played this role, while during the Bar Kokhba revolt it was Gerasa in the Decapolis, from which Emperor Hadrian advanced against Judea. In effect, both groups of Hellenistic cities – the Mediterranean ports and the Decapolis – formed a vise tightening Judea from west and east; therefore, the rulers of Hasmonean Judea viewed them as a potential danger to their independence and sovereignty.

Still, in relation to Judean kings loyal to them, the Romans were prepared to loosen their suffocating "embrace." For example, Herod the Great received Gadara and Hippos from his Roman friends – though only for the duration of his reign. Under the same conditions, his great-grandson Agrippa II gained control of Kanatha and Raphana in the Decapolis. Later, in 106 CE, the Romans incorporated the entire Decapolis into the new province of Arabia.

If the original inhabitants of the Decapolis were, for the most part, Greeks and Macedonians, the population of the Mediterranean Hellenistic cities was from the outset considered mixed. Greeks and Macedonians formed a minority there. Most of the residents of the port cities came from the local peoples. Later, they were joined by migrants from the peoples of Asia Minor and, in even greater numbers, by Arameans from Syria, who served as soldiers, officials, and merchants in the kingdoms of the Ptolemies and the Seleucids. Later still, colonies of Jews appeared there. The latter served in great numbers in the army of the Egyptian Ptolemies. If the Greeks, Macedonians, and natives of Asia Minor belonged to the Indo-European peoples, then the Canaanites (Phoenicians), the Arameans of Syria, and the Jews were West Semitic peoples – and it was they who predominated in the ports of the Southern Levant. Almost all of these peoples were united by Hellenistic culture and way of life. Their primary occupations were trade, crafts, military or administrative service. The West Semitic religious cults blended with the Greek ones, all the more so because Hellenism – as a pagan culture and religion – was always ready to accept into its pantheon the gods of any nation whatsoever. In this it differed fundamentally from Jewish monotheism. Thus, the West Semitic goddess Asherah (Ashtoret) blended harmoniously with the Greek Aphrodite, Tyrian Melqart with Heracles, and Resheph of Gaza with Apollo. All the local Semitic gods remained intact but received parallel Greek names.

Hellenization influenced the peoples of the Southern Levant in different ways. In the former Philistine and Phoenician (Canaanite) Mediterranean port cities, it erased ethnic identity, turning their inhabitants essentially into Hellenes; but "in the hinterland," far from the sea and the trade routes, Hellenistic culture and religion never played a major role. Thus, whereas the Arameans of Syria and the Phoenicians (Canaanites) dissolved into the Hellenistic population of the coastal cities, the Idumeans, Ammonites, and Nabataeans fully preserved their ethnic identity, adopting Hellenism only superficially. As for the Jews, they turned out to be the only people of the ancient world who not only did not accept it, but fought against it – and defeated it.

Over time, the population of the Decapolis became just as mixed as that of the Hellenistic ports of the Southern Levant. In the Ten Cities as well, the descendants of Greeks and Macedonians became a clear minority, while the majority came to be the local West Semitic peoples. Yet, unlike the port cities, in the Decapolis the Hellenized Semites were predominantly Ammonites and Arameans from Syria. Almost every Hellenistic city, both on the Mediterranean coast and in the Ten Cities, had

Jewish communities – sometimes quite sizable ones. Relations between Jews and pagans there depended directly on the situation in Judea itself. During the Jewish revolts against the Seleucids and the Romans, the Hellenistic pagans usually attacked the Jews, and Jewish rebels had to make raids into these cities to save their fellow believers.

The First Book of Maccabees reports that because of attacks on the Jews, Judah Maccabee's army was forced to undertake a campaign against Mareshah in Idumea and Ashdod on the Mediterranean coast. Judah passed through Mareshah and then turned aside to Ashdod, the land of foreigners, destroyed their altars, burned the statues of their gods, seized booty in the cities, and returned to Judea (1 Macc. 5:66, 68).

The Second Book of Maccabees recounts a crime committed by the inhabitants of Hellenistic Jaffa (Joppa) against the Jews of that city: "And the people of Joppa did so ungodly a deed as this: they invited the Jews who lived among them to embark, with their wives and children, on boats that they had provided, as though there were no ill will to the Jews, and this was done by public vote of the city. When they accepted, because they wished to live peaceably and suspected nothing, the people of Joppa took them out to sea and drowned them, at least two hundred. When Judas heard of the cruelty visited on his compatriots, he gave orders to his men and, calling upon God, the righteous judge, attacked the murderers of his kindred. He set fire to the harbor by night, burned the boats, and massacred those who had taken refuge there. Then, because the city's gates were closed, he withdrew, intending to come again and root out the whole community of Joppa. But learning that the people in Jamnia meant in the same way to wipe out the Jews who were living among them, he attacked the Jamnites by night and set fire to the harbor and the fleet, so that the glow of the light was seen in Jerusalem, thirty miles distant" (2 Macc. 12:3–9).

Flavius Josephus, in his "Antiquities of the Jews," asserts that not only Judah but also his successor, his brother Jonathan, was likewise forced to storm the Hellenistic cities on the Mediterranean, in particular Ashdod, Gaza, and Jaffa. Concerning Ashdod, Josephus writes that "Jonathan took the city at the first assault and burned it and the neighboring villages. He also did not spare the temple of Dagon, but consigned both the temple and those who had taken refuge in it to the flames… Having thus prevailed over such a great host, Jonathan marched from Ashdod to Ashkelon and encamped before that city; there the Ashkelonites came out to meet him with gifts and in every way expressed their respect for him. Accepting their voluntary submission, he returned to Jerusalem with the rich booty that his victory over the enemies had brought him" (*Antiquities of the Jews,* 13.4.4).

Rescuing Jews was also necessary in the neighboring Decapolis. The Second Book of Maccabees names the Hellenistic cities of Carnaim and Atargatis, against which Judah the Maccabee marched. "After the rout and destruction of these, he marched also against Ephron, a fortified town where Lysias lived with multitudes of people of all nationalities. Stalwart young men took their stand before the walls and made a vigorous defense, and great stores of war engines and missiles were there. But the Jews called upon the Sovereign who with power shatters the might of his enemies, and they got the town into their hands… Setting out from there, they hastened to Scythopolis, which is seventy-five miles from Jerusalem. But when the Jews who lived there bore witness to the goodwill that the people of Scythopolis had shown them and their kind treatment of them in times of misfortune, they thanked them and exhorted them to be well disposed to their race in the future also. Then they went up to Jerusalem, as the Festival of Weeks was close at hand" (2 Macc. 12:26–31).

The hostility of the Hellenistic cities toward the Jews manifested itself most of all in Ptolemais (Akko). Together with Trypho – usurper of the Seleucid throne – the elders of that city conspired against Jonathan, who had taken command of the Maccabean uprising after the death of his brother Judah. They invited Jonathan to Ptolemais and promised to make him their ruler. "But when Jonathan entered Ptolemais, the people of Ptolemais closed the gates and seized him, and they killed with the sword all who had entered with him" (1 Macc. 12:48). It was from

Hellenistic Ptolemais that Trypho set out with his army against Judea. Another detail is noteworthy. Hellenistic Philadelphia in the Decapolis became a refuge for Ptolemy, who murdered the last of the Maccabean brothers, Simon, and attempted to seize power in Judea.

Time failed to soften the animosity between the pagan population of the Hellenistic cities and the Jews. This hostility was sharply felt even two centuries after the Maccabean wars, and the best example of this is the attitude of the Hellenistic pagans toward the reign of the Judean king Agrippa I (37–44 CE). This king, raised from childhood in the imperial palace in Rome together with the son of Emperor Tiberius, was a refined Roman and a Greek at once. After receiving power in Judea, he spared neither effort nor expense to improve the Hellenistic cities in his kingdom. He did far more for them than the Ptolemies and Seleucids, who had founded those cities. Not a single Judean city received from him as much attention and care as his beloved Caesarea. And what happened? When the inhabitants of Hellenistic Caesarea learned of Agrippa's death, they held a noisy celebration in the city, and their joy knew no bounds.

The estrangement between the Jews and the population of the Hellenistic cities was far from accidental. In the Southern Levant, a cultural and religious war was underway between the two main West Semitic peoples – the monotheistic Jews and the pagan Arameans. This war was the continuation of the old conflict between Israel and Aram. But with the coming of the Greeks, the form of confrontation changed from territorial to cultural-religious. Pagan Aram readily accepted Hellenistic culture and religion, becoming a conduit for the interests of the Ptolemies and Seleucids in the Southern Levant. Monotheistic Judea could in no way do the same and was doomed to confrontation with Hellenistic paganism. The Hellenistic cities ended up at the very center of this confrontation, so the entire struggle between the two opposing cultures and religions unfolded primarily through them. The Greek-Macedonian elite, both in Ptolemaic Egypt and in Seleucid Syria, naturally took the side of the Hellenized Arameans and attempted by every means to facilitate the Hellenization of Judea itself. This inevitably led to conflict between Judea and the Seleucid royal court, which from the 2nd century BCE onward ruled the Southern Levant. The conflict flared up during the reign of Antiochus IV Epiphanes, who resolved to force the Jews by brute strength to accept paganism. But the result turned out to be the exact opposite: the Jews revolted and achieved complete independence from the Seleucids.

The very existence of Hellenistic cities on the territory of Judea and along its borders posed a constant threat to the Jewish people, and the Great Revolt of the Jews against Rome in 66–73 CE reminded everyone of this once again. Taking advantage of the outbreak of war between the Jews and the Romans, the inhabitants of the Hellenistic cities – for the most part Syrians of Aramean origin – rushed to destroy the Jews. As Josephus testifies, "the inhabitants of Caesarea killed all the Jews in the city; in a single hour more than twenty thousand were slain, so that not a single Jewish soul remained in the entire city..." In Hellenistic Scythopolis more than thirteen thousand Jews perished, and "they were attacked at night, when, suspecting nothing, they lay asleep in peaceful slumber... and afterwards all their property was plundered." The massacre in Scythopolis was followed by killings in other Hellenistic cities. Two thousand five hundred people were killed in Ascalon, and two thousand in Ptolemais (*Jewish War,* 2.18.1–5). The city rabble set upon the Jews almost everywhere in the cities of the Decapolis. Only Gerasa rose to defend its Jewish inhabitants. It is noteworthy that the initiators and perpetrators of this slaughter were not the Romans at all, but the Arameans of Syria – then everywhere simply called "Syrians" – who by that time formed the majority of the population of the Hellenistic cities. In this regard, the words of the commander of the Roman army and future emperor Titus Flavius are of interest. Addressing the Nabataean Arabs and the Syrians, he said the following: "And you, in a war that does not concern you, first of all seek to satisfy your beastly instincts, and then to make the Romans responsible for your savage bloodthirstiness and your hatred of the Jews" (*Jewish War,* 5.13.5).

7. The Beginning of the Jewish Diaspora

The Jewish diaspora began very early, with the forced resettlement of the Israelite and Judahite populations to Mesopotamia. Assyrian and Babylonian conquerors widely practiced the deportation of populations from cities that offered them the most stubborn resistance. The first to suffer were the residents of Israelite Galilee in the mid-8th century BCE, who were deported to Assyria as punishment for their heroic resistance to the Assyrian invasion. In 722 BCE, the same fate befell the inhabitants of Samaria, the main city of the Kingdom of Israel. In 701-700 BCE, the Assyrian army descended on another Hebrew kingdom, Judah, but was met with fierce resistance at the Judahite cities of Lachish and Azekah in the Shephelah region. After suffering heavy losses, the Assyrians retaliated by deporting the residents of these cities to Mesopotamia.

A century later, the Neo-Babylonian kingdom replaced the defeated Assyrian empire, but the Babylonians continued the policy of forced resettlement for those who resisted their rule the most. In 595 BCE, after a long and fierce siege of Jerusalem, the Babylonians deported part of the city's population, including the Judahite king Jehoiachin, to Babylonia. A new siege of the Judahite capital in 586 BCE ended far worse. The city and the Temple were completely destroyed, and even more residents were taken into Babylonian captivity. A few years later, in 582 BCE, after a failed revolt and the assassination of Gedaliah, the Babylonian governor of Judah, many Judahite warriors and their families fled to neighboring Egypt. They were joined by many remaining residents of Judah who feared repression from the advancing Babylonian army. This is confirmed by the biblical prophet Jeremiah, who was also forcibly taken to Egypt by the fleeing warriors.

Thus, by the early 6th century BCE, many Israelites and Judahites, who had arrived at different times and usually not by choice, were in Mesopotamia and Egypt. The Babylonian captivity of the Judahites lasted for about half a century until the Neo-Babylonian kingdom was defeated by the Persians. However, no more than half of the captives returned to their homeland in Judah. Many Jews who had succeeded economically chose to stay in Babylonia. This is how the Jewish diaspora in Mesopotamia began, lasting for about two and a half millennia. The Jewish community in Egypt was just as old. Judahites and Israelites made up a significant portion of the mercenary soldiers in the Egyptian army, and the protection of Egypt's southern borders (including the island of Elephantine on the Nile) was entirely entrusted to Jewish soldiers. The Jewish community grew even more during the Hellenistic period when Judea was under the rule of the Egyptian Ptolemies. The founder of this dynasty, Ptolemy I Soter, forcibly resettled 30,000 Jews to Alexandria to expedite the city's development and prosperity. Josephus reports on this: "Ptolemy, taking captive a multitude of people from the mountainous part of Judea, from the vicinity of Jerusalem, from Samaria, and from Mount Gerizim, led them all to Egypt and settled them there. When he learned that the Jerusalemites were especially trustworthy in keeping their oaths and promises... he placed many of them in garrisons and made them equal in rights with the Macedonian citizens of Alexandria, taking an oath from them that they would remain loyal to his descendants as well. A considerable number of other Jews also voluntarily moved to Egypt, partly attracted by the excellent quality of the soil there and partly by Ptolemy's generosity" (*Antiquities of the Jews* 12.1.1). By the 3rd century BCE, there were far more Jews living in Egypt than at the time of the Exodus from Egypt led by Moses.

The Jewish diaspora was not limited to communities in Egypt and Babylonia. During the period when Judea was part of the Hellenistic kingdoms of the Ptolemies and Seleucids, Jewish communities began to appear in Syria, Asia Minor, Greece, Cyprus, the Aegean islands, and Italy – throughout the Hellenistic world. In some cases, Hellenistic rulers, such as Ptolemy I Soter, resettled Jews there, while in others, they were welcomed to settle new areas and develop crafts, trade, and agriculture. A prime example of how Jewish communities appeared in Asia Minor is the order from the Seleucid king Antiochus the Great to his commander Zeuxis: "Having learned that there are disturbances in Lydia and Phrygia, I have concluded that I should pay special attention to this. When I consulted with my friends, we decided to resettle two thousand Jewish families from Mesopotamia and Babylonia to the fortresses and most dangerous places, providing them with everything they need. I am convinced that these people, because of their piety, will be loyal guards for us, especially since, as I know, my ancestors attested to their loyalty and readiness to provide support where it is required of them. Therefore, despite the difficulty of this matter, I would like to resettle them there with permission to live according to their own laws... Assign each of them a plot for building a house, as well as a plot for agriculture and viticulture, and exempt them from all taxes on their fields for a ten-year period" (*Antiquities of the Jews* 12.3.4).

Josephus revealed one of the reasons why Jews were highly respected by many rulers of the Hellenistic kingdoms: they served in their armies and actively participated in their campaigns. It was for this reason that Seleucus Nicator, Alexander the Great's general and the founder of the Seleucid kingdom, "granted them citizenship and made them equal in rights with the Macedonians and Greeks in all the cities he founded in Asia and Syria, as well as in the capital itself, Antioch" (*Antiquities of the Jews*, 12.3.1). In Ptolemaic Egypt, the participation of Jews in the army was even more significant; they served in all military fortresses and garrisons, even the most remote ones. In the first century BCE, the role of Jews in the Egyptian army grew so much that they became the main support of the royal court. The Egyptian queen Cleopatra III was forced to abandon a war with the Judean king Alexander Jannaeus simply because she feared losing the support of her Jewish soldiers.

The attitude of Hellenistic rulers toward Jews varied even within the same countries and dynasties. While Ptolemy II Philadelphus held the Jews in "unusual honor" in Egypt, they were at one time out of favor with Ptolemy IV Philopator (*Antiquities of the Jews*, 12.3.1; 3 Macc.). In the Seleucid kingdom, while Antiochus III the Great treated the Jews with great respect and favor, his son Antiochus IV Epiphanes went so far as to forbid the practice of Judaism and fought against the Jews. A similar situation existed in the Roman Republic and later the Empire. While Julius

Caesar and Mark Antony were sympathetic and favorable to the Jews, Crassus and Pompey showed them ill will. Almost all representatives of the first Roman imperial dynasty of the Julio-Claudians, and above all Octavian Augustus himself, supported the Jews and encouraged them with various preferences. However, Caligula and Nero from the same dynasty, suffering from megalomania, conflicted with the Jews, and the latter even provoked a war with them.

By the beginning of the Common Era, approximately 3 million Jews lived outside of Judea. With this in mind, Philo of Alexandria wrote: "The Jewish people are so numerous that one land cannot contain them. Therefore, Jews are found in many prosperous lands – European and Asian, insular and continental, considering the Holy City, where the supreme temple of the Most High is erected, their original homeland; however, they consider as their own country either the lands in which they were born and raised, inheriting them from their fathers, grandfathers, great-grandfathers, and more distant ancestors, or those regions where they settled during their development and were welcomed by the founders" (Philo, *Against Flaccus*, 7.2-3). The words of Philo of Alexandria are also confirmed by the author of the Sibylline Oracles (c. 140 CE), according to whom "every land and sea is full of Jews" (*Or. Sib.*, 3.271). However, having a large diaspora was characteristic not only of the Jews but also of their relatives, the Phoenicians, as well as the Greeks.

The Greco-Roman historian and geographer Strabo, in one of his historical works, quotes the words of Lucius Cornelius Sulla, a Roman military leader and dictator, spoken by him to the consul Lucullus. The latter was sent to Cyrene (modern Libya) to suppress a rebellion by local Jews. The discussion was about the Jews and their place in the Ancient World. According to Strabo, Sulla said the following: "In the city [of the region] of Cyrene, all residents are divided into four groups: citizens, peasants, colonists, and Jews. The latter have already settled in all cities, and it is difficult to find a place on earth where this people do not live. Cyrene and Egypt are under the rule of the same rulers. While these rulers are indifferent to all others, they accept the Jews most willingly and in large numbers. Following the Jewish laws, they prosper with them. In Egypt itself, the Jews have both residential and civic rights, and in Alexandria, a significant part of the city belongs to this people. There they even have their own ruler (ethnarch), who governs his people, resolves their disputes, and ratifies their transactions and decisions. Moreover, this is done by virtue of being a representative of a sovereign and independent people. In Egypt, the Jewish people achieved such power because the Egyptians and Jews are of the same origin and also because Judea is located near Egypt and was formerly part of it, and Cyrene, like Judea, borders on Egypt" (*Antiquities of the Jews,* 14.7.2). This excerpt from Strabo is interesting not only because it presents Sulla's opinion but also because it is one of the few surviving quotes from his lost work.

The Jewish dispersion was divided into two parts: the diaspora in the Hellenistic, Greco-Roman world, whose spoken language was Greek (Koine), and the Babylonian, or Parthian, diaspora, which used the Aramaic language. The largest Jewish community outside of Judea was in Hellenistic Egypt. Philo of Alexandria claimed that "no less than a million Jews live in Alexandria and throughout the country from the Libyan desert to the borders of Ethiopia" (*Against Flaccus,* 6.12). The vast majority of Egyptian Jews lived in Alexandria itself, the largest center of the Hellenistic world, where they made up almost half of all the city's residents. Philo of Alexandria wrote: "Alexandria is divided into five quarters, named after the first letters of the alphabet; two of them are called 'Jewish,' for most of the Jews live in them, although there are many of them scattered in the other quarters" (*Against Flaccus,* 8.7).

By the beginning of the Common Era, the Jewish community of Egypt had become so numerous and influential that it could quite justifiably be called an "Egyptian Judea." It was the most educated, cultured, and wealthy Jewish community in the ancient world. At the same time, it was also the most Hellenized Jewish community in the Greco-Roman world.

In the mid-second century BCE, during the reign of Ptolemy VI Philometor, a temple to the God of Israel was erected in the city of Leontopolis in the Nile Delta at the initiative of Onias IV (the son of the high priest Onias III). It was almost a complete copy of the First Temple in Jerusalem. Moreover, the priestly service in this temple was permanently headed by the descendants of Onias – the most renowned and aristocratic high priest of the Jerusalem Temple before the outbreak of the Maccabean wars. No Jewish community in the ancient world would have dared to build a temple that rivaled the one in Jerusalem, but the Jews of Egypt were able to afford such a thing. This temple became known as the Temple of Onias and existed until the year 73 CE (three years longer than the one in Jerusalem), when it was destroyed by order of the Roman emperor Vespasian.

In terms of Jewish population, Mesopotamia, Syria and Asia Minor ranked second. We do not possess any precise data for these regions, but Philo of Alexandria notes that in every city of Syria and Asia Minor lived "very many" Jews (*On the Embassy to Gaius*, 33.3).

The third most significant centers of Jewish settlement were the Jewish communities in mainland Greece and Italy. In the imperial capital itself, Rome, already at the beginning of the first century CE there lived between 30,000 and 50,000 Jews. According to Philo of Alexandria, "the greater part of Rome beyond the Tiber is inhabited by Jews. They were Roman citizens, most of them freedmen; they had arrived in Italy as captives, their masters granted them freedom, and [no one] forced them to violate even a single ancestral custom" (*On the Embassy to Gaius*, 23.7–8).

In this regard, notable is the letter of the Judean king Agrippa I addressed to the emperor Gaius Caligula: "... Jewish settlers, have established themselves both in the neighboring lands – Egypt, Phoenicia, and Syria – and in distant ones – Pamphylia, Cilicia, and Asia as far as Bithynia and the most remote bays of Pontus; likewise in Europe – in Thessaly, Boeotia, Macedonia, Aetolia, Attica, Argos, Corinth, and in most of the finest regions of the Peloponnese. Nor only the continents: the most renowned islands (Euboea, Cyprus, Crete) are full of Jewish settlements. I say nothing of the lands beyond the Euphrates, for with few exceptions everywhere – in Babylon and in other regions where the soil is fertile – Jews live" (Philo of Alexandria, *On the Embassy to Gaius*, 36.10–12).

The sheer numbers and strength of the Jewish people were among the factors that stopped Petronius, the Roman governor of Syria, from installing a statue of Gaius Caligula in the Jerusalem Temple. "Petronius began to reflect upon this people: they are very numerous, but not having received for their possession a land within which they might be confined like any other nation, they are compelled to maintain their unity, one might say, throughout the whole world. For this nation is scattered across all continents and islands, so that they seem not much inferior in numbers to the native inhabitants. Would it not then be the height of recklessness to turn such multitudes of enemies against oneself? ... Yet even the inhabitants of Judea alone are numberless, strong of body and courageous of soul, ready to give their lives for their ancient laws... Petronius was also alarmed by the thought of the army stationed beyond the Euphrates, for he knew – not only from reports but from experience – that in Babylon and many other regions there were countless Jews..." (*On the Embassy to Gaius*, 31.12–14).

At the same time, the Jews of the diaspora, especially in the Greco-Roman world, faced a serious problem related to the unique nature of Jewish monotheism. While the local population was willing to accept the one God of the Jews into their pantheon of gods, the Jews could not worship any of the pagans' deities. Moreover, in their monotheism and rejection of idolatry, the Jews saw a spiritual and intellectual superiority over pagan peoples. And although the Jews, in order not to offend the feelings of the locals, tried not to flaunt their aversion to idols, the Greeks and Romans did not forgive the Jews for their rejection of Hellenistic gods and traditions. For example, the Greeks of Ionia put the question as follows: "If the Jews actually belong to our community, then let them worship the same gods that we do" (Tcherikover, V., *Hellenistic Civilization and the Jews*). The Alexandrian historian Apion, known for his slanderous writings about the Jews, also reproached the Jews for not worshiping local gods: "If the Jews (says he) be citizens of Alexandria, why do they not worship the same gods with the Alexandrians?" (Josephus, *Against Apion*, 2.65).

However, the rejection of pagan gods and the associated Hellenistic customs and traditions was not the only "guilt" of the Jews before the Greco-Roman world. Another problem was the success of the Jews in almost everything: agriculture, crafts, trade, finance, science, and medicine. The only exception was the field of art, and even that was because Judaism forbade any images of living beings (for fear that they could be turned into pagan idols). The Jews were not just outsiders who considered their monotheism superior to Hellenistic paganism; they were too successful outsiders to be tolerated. The animosity toward the Jews resulted in the first pogrom in Egyptian Alexandria in 38 CE because the local Jews refused to worship the statue of the Roman emperor Gaius Caligula.

The problems of the Jewish diaspora in Hellenistic Egypt are the subject of the Third Book of Maccabees. It notes that the Jews were numerous and lived throughout the entire territory of Egypt, but most of all in Alexandria. This book testifies that the Jews enjoyed full civil rights in Egypt, played an important role in the economy and the Egyptian army, and were highly influential at the royal court. At the same time, the book acknowledges that the Jews differed from the rest of Egypt's population both in their faith and in their way of life, and that this fact caused misunderstanding and irritation, and consequently, hostility on the part of some Egyptians.

The Third Book of Maccabees also recounts a failed attempt at persecuting the Jews and their faith during the reign of Ptolemy IV Philopator (221–205 BCE). In this respect, the idea of the book echoes the earlier biblical book *Megillat Esther* (the Book of Esther), on which the festival of Purim was established. In essence, both works – the apocryphal Third Book of Maccabees and the canonical *Megillat Esther* – speak of the same thing: the problems and threats facing the Jewish diaspora.

Only the first concerns the Jewish diaspora in the western, Hellenistic world, whereas the second concerns the eastern, Babylonian-Parthian one. Both works also have a real historical parallel: in 167 BCE, the Seleucid king Antiochus IV Epiphanes forbade the practice of Judaism, thereby provoking an entire series of Maccabean wars of liberation.

The Greco-Roman world saw in Judaism a religious and philosophical system alien to it, and felt before it a certain sense of "inferiority." It was unpleasant for Hellenistic authors to acknowledge that there existed another culture, far more ancient and universal than Hellenism, which was founded on paganism. Unable to defeat Judaism on the ideological plane, many Greco-Roman writers resorted to another method of combating it – distorting the principles of the Jewish religion and openly slandering it.

The rejection of Hellenistic paganism, a forced separation from the customs and traditions of idolaters, and finally, the material success of the Jews drew upon them the hostility of Greco-Roman society and gave rise to the phenomenon of ancient antisemitism. It emerged simultaneously with the Jewish diaspora and long before the appearance of accusations concerning the crucifixion of Christ.

8. The Itureans

The Itureans were a semi-nomadic, West Semitic people of Aramean origin. They lived in the Beqaa Valley and the surrounding mountain ranges of Lebanon and Anti-Lebanon. Today, this entire territory lies within the borders of modern Lebanon and the northern part of the Israeli Golan Heights. The Mount Hermon region also belonged to the Itureans. The ethnonym of this people almost completely coincided with the name Yetur, one of the sons of Ishmael, the firstborn of the biblical patriarch Abraham from his concubine Hagar (Gen. 25:13-15). Since Ishmael was considered the ancestor of all Arabs, many historians believed the Itureans to be one of the Arab nomadic peoples or even a part of the Nabataean Arabs. However, as with the origin of the

Nabataeans, the coincidence of names seems to have been accidental. The situation was further complicated by the fact that Hellenistic historians called any nomads who engaged in banditry "Arabs," and plunder was a common practice for the Itureans. However, Strabo, and later the medieval Arab historian Ibn Khaldun, clearly distinguished between the Itureans and Arabs, although they acknowledged that both engaged in banditry (Strabo, *Geography,* XVI. 2. 18-20; Ibn Khaldun, *Muqaddimah,* 5).

The area where the Itureans lived is known for the fact that around the 23rd century BCE, nomadic Amorite tribes arrived there from the northeast. It is likely that the Beqaa Valley and the mountainous part of southern Lebanon were occupied by the Amorite tribes of the Hivites, the same ones who, according to the Book of Genesis, also inhabited Galilee and Samaria and were close allies of the "House of Joseph." For a whole millennium, the Iturean territory was part of the land of Amurru, that is, the "land of the Amorites." Later, in the 12th century BCE, new West Semitic nomadic tribes, the Arameans, arrived in these areas. The Beqaa Valley and the mountain ranges of Lebanon and Anti-Lebanon became the border of the Arameans' maximum advance. West and south of them, Canaanites and peoples of Amorite origin continued to dominate. In the 11th-10th centuries BCE, the lands of the Itureans were divided among small Aramean kingdoms: Maacah, Beth-Rehob, Zobah, and Damascus. The ancestors of the Itureans are mentioned in the Bible as "Maachatites," residents of the kingdom of Maacah, and also as "Arameans" of Beth-Rehob, Zobah, and Damascus. According to the Book of Samuel, in the first half of the 10th century BCE, David, the king of the United Monarchy, conquered all these Aramean kingdoms of Syria (2 Sam. 8:3-13). The father of church history, Eusebius of Caesarea, also mentions David's war with the Itureans, citing the earlier Jewish author Eupolemus (Eusebius, *Praeparatio Evangelica,* IX. 30). Unfortunately, Eupolemus's works have not survived; we know about them only from citations by other historians. However, Eupolemus himself lived eight hundred years after the events described, and his source of information raises many questions. It is quite possible that it was the same Book of Samuel.

After the split of the United Monarchy, the lands of the Itureans fell under the rule of Aram-Damascus. In the 9th-8th centuries BCE, the southernmost part of the Iturean territory (the former kingdom of Maacah) became a bone of contention between Israel and Aram-Damascus. During the reign of the king Hazael, all Iturean regions were seized by Aram-Damascus, and during the reign of the Israelite king Jeroboam II, not only Iturea but all of Syria came under the control of Israel. From the end of the 8th century until the end of the 6th century BCE, the southern Levant was under the rule of first Assyria and then the Neo-Babylonian kingdom. Then for another two hundred years, the Persians ruled there, and from the end of the 4th century BCE, the Hellenes became the rulers of the Levant. Until the arrival of the Romans, the territory of the Itureans was mostly under the rule of the Seleucid Empire. As a small semi-nomadic people, the Itureans showed no political, military, or economic activity, and therefore did not receive attention from historians throughout all these centuries. They began to attract the interest of Hellenistic authors only when their history intertwined with that of Judea and the Jews.

This time came at the end of the 2nd century BCE, when Aristobulus, the son of the Judean ruler Johanan Hyrcanus, recaptured Upper Galilee and the southern slopes of Mount Hermon – the historical lot of the Hebrew tribe of Dan. Having reclaimed the land belonging to the Kingdom of Israel, the Jews found newcomers there – the nomadic Itureans. Aristobulus, who became both the Judean king and high priest in 104-103 BCE, gave the Itureans an ultimatum: if they wanted to remain in Judea, they had to give up idolatry and accept Jewish monotheism; otherwise, they had to leave Judea. The Itureans abandoned paganism and became a part of the Jewish people and their history. These events are described in detail by Josephus and mentioned by Strabo. However, it is important to remember that this concerned only a small portion of the Itureans, those who roamed only in Upper Galilee and the northern part of the Golan Heights. The vast majority of the Itureans who lived in the mountain ranges of Lebanon and Anti-Lebanon, as well as in the Beqaa Valley, remained pagans and did not change their way of life, traditions, or faith.

The weakening of the Seleucid kingdom allowed a certain Ptolemy, son of Mennaeus, to become an independent or semi-independent ruler of Chalcis and Abilene – areas where the main mass of Itureans lived at the time. It is unknown whether this Ptolemy was a descendant of the Greco-Macedonian elite who came to the East with Alexander the Great or a representative of the Hellenized Iturean nobility. Over time, Ptolemy managed to strengthen himself militarily to the point that he even tried to capture Damascus. However, the Judean queen Salome Alexandra (76-67 BCE) did not allow him to do so, sending her army to help Damascus, which in turn caused tension between them. Ptolemy ruled for a very long time, 45 years (85-40 BCE), surviving both the fall of the Seleucid kingdom and the arrival of Roman legions in Syria in 66 BCE. However, he had to pay a heavy price for the right to remain ruler: he handed over 1,000 talents personally to the Roman general Pompey.

The history of Iturea then intersected with Judea again. Ptolemy married the daughter of the Judean king Aristobulus II, and, most importantly, provided refuge to her persecuted brother Antigonus II, who would also become a future Judean king (Josephus, *The Jewish War* 1.12.2). It should be noted that Josephus speaks very unfavorably of Ptolemy, the son of Mennaeus, calling him a "vile man" who escaped punishment only because of the large sum of money paid to Pompey (*Antiquities of the Jews,* 14.3.2). However, Josephus never explains the reason for his low opinion of him. It may be related to the fact that Ptolemy Mennaeus killed his son Philippion to marry his wife, Alexandra, with whom he had fallen madly in love (*Antiquities of the Jews,* 14.7.4).

The year 40 BCE was a time of serious change and troubles for the entire Levant. Taking advantage of the civil war in the Roman Republic, the Parthians attacked the Roman legions stationed on the Euphrates River, inflicting heavy losses on them and forcing them to hastily retreat from Mesopotamia and Syria. In this year, Ptolemy dies, and his son Lysanias, with the support of the Parthians, becomes the sovereign ruler of Iturea. The Roman historian Dio Cassius confirms that Lysanias (40-36 BCE) became king of Chalcis and Abilene, with his residence in the city of Chalcis. At the same time, Antigonus II returns to Judea, to Jerusalem, where he is proclaimed Judean king, while his enemies – Tetrarch Herod and his supporters – urgently seek refuge. However, the triumph of the opponents of Rome did not last long; already in 37 BCE, the Roman legions returned as the victors over the Parthians, and Antigonus II, and then Lysanias, lost their kingdoms. The entire Levant passed into the hands of the Roman triumvir Mark Antony. While Antigonus's death was at Herod's hands, the execution of Lysanias in 36 BCE was on the conscience of the Egyptian queen Cleopatra, who had taken a liking to the lands of the Itureans. Cleopatra persuaded her lover-husband Antony to give her Chalcis and Abilene and to execute Lysanias for his connection with the Parthians. Cleopatra leased her new acquisition to a certain Zenodorus. Whether he had any relation to Ptolemy and Lysanias, or was their relative, remains unknown.

A new civil war between the Roman triumvirs ends with the death of Antony and Cleopatra. Iturea becomes the property of the victor, Octavian Augustus, who allows Zenodorus to continue leasing Chalcis and Abilene but significantly increases the rent. Perhaps the rent for economically poor Iturea was too high, or perhaps greed overcame Zenodorus, but he entered into an agreement with bandit clans and began to encourage the plundering raids of the Itureans on the neighboring regions of Byblos, Beirut, and Damascus. As expected, the complaints of the robbed reached the governor of the Roman province of Syria and were sent to the emperor in Rome. In 23 BCE, Augustus decided to transfer the greater part of Iturea – Chalcis – to his friend and protege, the Judean king Herod, and in 20 BCE, when Zenodorus died, the remaining part – Abilene. Herod restored order in Iturea, brutally cracking down on all who engaged in banditry, and the complaints ceased.

Starting with Herod the Great, Iturea remained in the hands of Judean rulers and kings for a long time. After Herod's death (4 BCE), Iturea went to his son, the tetrarch Philip, who also owned the Golan Heights and all of southern Syria. The fact that Iturea was inherited by Herod's son, Tetrarch Philip, is also confirmed by the Gospel of Luke (Luke 3:1). After Philip, Iturea passed to the Judean king Agrippa I, and after his death, it again passed to his son, the Judean king Agrippa II. However, the smaller part of Iturea – Abilene – was for some time transferred by Emperor Gaius Caligula to a certain Sohemus, after whose death it again passed to Agrippa II. It is noteworthy that, unlike the Judean kings of the Hasmonean dynasty, who fought against the paganism of their new subjects, the Judean kings of the Herodian dynasty never demanded the adoption of Jewish monotheism. The Herodian rulers not only did not interfere in the religious life of non-Jews but, moreover, encouraged their Hellenistic traditions and customs, financing their temples, festivals, and sporting events. In this sense, Iturea was no exception. Excavations in Heliopolis (modern Baalbek) showed that this city was the main cultic center of the Itureans in both the Hellenistic and Roman periods. They worshiped both local and Hellenistic cults, which had in fact merged, forming the most important triad for the Itureans: the Syrian Hadad united with the Greek Dionysus, the West Semitic goddess Atargatis with the Roman Venus, and the Semitic Baal with the Hellenistic Jupiter-Zeus. Thus, Judaization affected only a small part of the Itureans who found themselves in Upper Galilee and on the southern slopes of Mount Hermon during the Hasmonean rule.

Characterizing the Itureans as a whole, almost all ancient authors agreed on the following:

1. They were a semi-nomadic people of Semitic origin. While some authors considered them Arabs descended from the biblical Ishmaelites, others classified them as Arameans. It is noteworthy that in the surviving Latin inscriptions, the Itureans have typically Syrian (Aramean) names (*HJP, First Div., II, p. 326*).

2. They were bandits. Strabo believed that robbery was a characteristic occupation for them (*Strabo,*XVI.*2.10*). The Romans considered the Itureans predatory and treacherous people who could not be trusted (Cicero, *Philipp. II. 112*).
3. They were skilled archers. The Romans were so impressed by their archery skills that they formed several cohorts of Iturean archers for their army, typically for auxiliary units (Caesar, *Bell. Afr. 20*).

Today, we can define the Itureans as Aramean nomads who mixed with Amorite nomads, known in the 2nd millennium BCE as "Sutu." Both were Western Semites, spoke related languages, and had the same way of life. Moreover, the Amorite Sutu, like the Itureans, were constantly accused of a tendency toward banditry. Both roamed in the mountains of Lebanon and were known as skilled archers. Life under the rule of Judean kings and rulers did not make them Jews, although for a time they had to abandon banditry. After the death of the childless Agrippa II, all the lands of the Itureans were included in the Roman province of Syria, and ancient authors lost interest in them (Tacitus, *Annals, XII. 23*). It can be assumed that the Itureans, like other peoples, underwent Christianization when they came under the rule of the Byzantine Empire. In the 7th century, Arabs arrived, and with them, forced Islamization and Arabization, and as a result, a complete loss of Iturean identity.

CHAPTER VII.

Judea – the Heir of the Peoples of Canaan

1. The Unification of the Land of Israel under the Hasmoneans (2nd-1st Centuries BCE)

The recognition by the Seleucids of the independence and sovereignty of Judea did not mean that they abandoned their intention to subjugate it again. Unlike the times of the Hebrew kingdoms, when the Southern Kingdom gave way to the Northern, Judea in the 2nd century BCE was the most developed and most populated part of the Southern Levant. Of all the regions of Coele-Syria, it provided the Seleucids with the greatest income, so it was difficult for them to give it up. But while the Seleucid king Demetrius II Nicator was in Parthian captivity, and his brother Antiochus VII Sidetes fought for power with the usurper Diodotus Tryphon, no one tried to challenge the sovereignty of Judea. Antiochus VII tried to maintain the best relations with militarily strong Judea. For his part, the Maccabean ruler Simon openly supported Antiochus in his confrontation with Tryphon, sending him select soldiers and equipment to help. However, after Antiochus VII defeated the usurper Tryphon in 139-138 BCE, he demanded that Judea return the Hellenistic cities of Gezer and Jaffa to the Seleucids, as well as the fortress of Acre in Jerusalem, threatening war otherwise. To which Simon replied that "we have neither taken foreign land nor seized foreign property, but only the inheritance of our ancestors, which at one time had been unjustly taken by our enemies. Now that we have the opportunity, we are firmly holding the inheritance of our ancestors" (1 Macc. 15:33-34). As is known, the Canaanite city of Gezer was given to King Solomon by the Egyptian pharaoh as a dowry for his daughter, whom he married to the Israelite-Judahite king. From then on, Gezer became part of Judah; it was converted into a Hellenistic city almost seven hundred years later by the Macedonians and Greeks. As for Jaffa, this originally Canaanite and then Philistine city was conquered by the Kingdom of Israel, and after its fall it passed to Judah.

Having dealt with Tryphon, Antiochus VII sent his troops under the command of the military leader Kendebey against Judea. In order to wear out Simon's army, Kendebey chose the tactics of predatory raids on the territory of Judea. Having fortified the ancient Judahite town of Kidron, not far from Gezer, he began to organize cavalry raids from there into the depths of Judea, and then hide behind the walls of Kidron. At first, this tactic was successful, but Kendebey still could not avoid a decisive battle: he was defeated, and the remnants of his army fled to Kidron and Ashdod. Thus, Gezer and Jaffa remained in the hands of Judea. Josephus claims that Simon also captured the port city of Yavne, but the Maccabean books are silent about this (*Jewish War* 1. 2. 2). In any case, under Simon, Judea regained access to the Mediterranean Sea, which was of great economic and strategic importance. Perhaps Simon could have conquered other Mediterranean cities, but he avoided exacerbating relations with the Seleucid kingdom. Despite the constant struggle for power, it was still quite strong, owning all of Syria, Mesopotamia and part of Coele-Syria. Trying to enlist the support of potential allies and friends, Simon renewed treaties with the Romans and Spartans. The Romans were the most serious opponents of the Seleucids, and Simon attached great importance to an alliance with them.

Having failed to force Simon to retreat by military means, Antiochus VII decided to act differently: he found supporters among the Jewish aristocrats, dissatisfied with the fact that the Hasmoneans, being far from the most noble family, seized all power in Judea. He involved

Ptolemy, Simon's son-in-law, in his conspiracy, promising to make him the ruler of the country and to provide him with military assistance to seize power. Ptolemy, having invited Simon, his wife and their two sons to his castle-fortress near Jericho, first killed the ruler himself, and then his sons and their mother. At the same time, he sent assassins to Gezer, where the third son, Johanan Hyrcanus, was then located. However, the latter was warned in time and dealt with Ptolemy's people himself. Then Johanan hurried to Jerusalem, where he was immediately proclaimed the new ruler and high priest of Judea. Ptolemy was besieged in his fortress near Jericho, but, taking advantage of religious holidays, managed to escape to Hellenistic Philadelphia (former Rabat Ammon).

Despite the failure of the conspiracy, Antiochus VII Sidetes invaded Judea with his entire army, plundered the country and besieged Johanan in Jerusalem. He was going to take revenge on the Hasmoneans for all the defeats suffered by the Seleucids and again subjugate Judea to his kingdom. Johanan Hyrcanus found himself in a very difficult situation: he did not have time to strengthen his power, nor to gather an army and prepare for the defense of Jerusalem. However, the siege of the Judean capital, contrary to Antiochus's calculations, dragged on for a long time. According to Josephus, this happened "both because of the height of the walls and the valor of the besieged, despite their extreme lack of water" (*Antiquities of the Jews,* 10.8.2). Meanwhile, the Parthians attacked the eastern borders of the Seleucid Empire, and the Romans, reminding Antiochus of their alliance with Judea, threatened war. Both sides, each for their own reasons, were in dire need of a truce. The Jewish holiday of Sukkot served as a pretext for starting the negotiations. On the occasion of the holiday, Antiochus "sent precious sacrificial offerings to the city, namely bulls with gilded horns, as well as silver and gold bowls full of fragrant incense" (Ibid.). Moreover, the Seleucid king also arranged a feast for his army in honor of the Jewish holiday. The besieged Jews, touched by the kindness and piety of the king, sent an embassy to him for peace negotiations. Antiochus, constrained by circumstances, was forced to limit himself to minimal demands: the right to collect tribute from the Hellenistic cities under the rule of Judea, a contribution of 500 talents, and the issuance of hostages as a guarantee of the fulfillment of the peace treaty. Thus, despite significant financial losses, Judea retained its independence and sovereignty.

In order to find the required sum of money as quickly as possible, "Johanan Hyrcanus ordered the tomb of King David, who was the richest king, to be opened and 3,000 talents taken from there. With a gift of 300 talents, he persuaded Antiochus to immediately lift the siege and leave. He used the rest of the sum to recruit foreign mercenary soldiers" (*Jewish War* 1.2.5). Johanan Hyrcanus became the first ruler from the Hasmonean dynasty who, following the example of the Hellenistic kings, began to hire foreign soldiers into his army.

The peace treaty with Antiochus VII subsequently led to the conclusion of a short-term military alliance with him. Josephus claims that the relations between them became so friendly that "Johanan Hyrcanus received him into his city and in abundance and with pleasure supplied his army with everything necessary. Then Hyrcanus participated with him in the campaign against the Parthians" (*Antiquities of the Jews,* 13.8.4). This joint campaign turned out to be very successful: the allies managed to defeat the Parthian army and return Mesopotamia to the Seleucids. However, the alliance of Johanan with Antiochus did not last long; in 129 BCE Antiochus VII undertook a new campaign against the Parthians, but without Johanan. This time he was defeated and killed. The unexpected death of Antiochus VII Sidetes freed Johanan Hyrcanus from all obligations to him and, taking advantage of the confusion and struggle for power in the Seleucid kingdom, in the same year of 129 BCE he began to recapture the lands that had previously belonged to the Kingdom of Israel. First of all, he occupied the area of Medava and Samega in southern Transjordan, which had previously belonged to the Hebrew tribe of Reuben. Then his attention turned to Samaria, the historical territory of the "House of Joseph" and the most important northern Hebrew tribe of Ephraim. In a short time, he captured the entire territory of Samaria, including the city of Shechem. Here, on Mount

Gerizim, he destroyed the Samaritan temple, which had challenged the Jerusalem Temple since the 5th century BCE. Without staying long in Samaria, Johanan moved his army south to Idumea, or more precisely to the southern Judean regions, where the Idumeans had resettled in the 6th century BCE, driven out of their homeland by the Nabataean Arabs. Despite the fact that the Idumeans (Edomites) were the closest relatives of the Hebrews, their relations throughout the first millennium BCE remained hostile. But the most serious resistance to the Judean army was offered by two Hellenistic cities in Idumea: Maresha (Marisa) and Adoraim (Adora). These originally Judahite-Canaanite cities were turned by the Greeks and Macedonians into bastions of Hellenism in southern Judea and were heavily fortified. At first they served the Egyptian Ptolemies, and then they just as loyally defended the interests of the Syrian Seleucids. As Josephus reports, "Hyrcanus took the Idumean cities of Adoraim and Maresha and, having subjugated all the Idumeans to his power, allowed them to remain in the country, but only on the condition that they accept circumcision and begin to live according to the Jewish laws. The Idumeans, indeed, out of love for their fatherland, accepted the rite of circumcision and generally built their entire life on the Jewish model. From that very time, they became completely Jews" (*Antiquities of the Jews*, 3.9.1). Johanan completed his military campaigns by recapturing the Mediterranean cities of Ashdod, Yavne and Apollonia. Apart from Apollonia, which was founded by the Phoenicians during the Persian period, these originally Canaanite cities changed hands constantly throughout their history. First they were captured by the Philistines (12th-11th centuries BCE), then they passed to the Kingdom of Israel (9th-8th centuries BCE), and then to Judah (7th-6th centuries BCE). For exactly two centuries they belonged to the Persian Empire, and after its defeat, the Macedonians and Greeks Hellenized these cities. Johanan Hyrcanus's last acquisition was the ancient Canaanite-Israelite city of Beth-Shean in the Jordan Valley. The Greeks and Macedonians Hellenized it and renamed it Scythopolis. At that time, it was considered the largest of the Decapolis cities.

All the cities and territories conquered by Johanan Hyrcanus belonged to the Seleucid kingdom, which, after the death of Antiochus VII Sidetes, was experiencing a new round of struggle for power. In 129 BCE, the brother of the deceased Antiochus, Demetrius II Nicator (129-126 BCE), returned to the Seleucid throne from Parthian captivity. Josephus wrote that "King Demetrius very much wanted to go on a campaign against Hyrcanus, but he did not succeed, both due to lack of time and lack of funds, because the Syrians, and the troops, hated him for his difficult character" (*Antiquities of the Jews,* 13.9.3). In reality, the situation of Demetrius II was even worse. A new impostor, Alexander II Zabina, appeared in Egypt, posing as the son of the deceased Antiochus VII Sidetes. The Egyptian ruler Ptolemy VIII Physcon gave him an army to seize the Seleucid throne. Demetrius tried to defend his throne, but was defeated and fled to his wife Cleopatra Thea in Ptolemais. But she not only refused to help him, but did not even accept him under the protection of her walls. Demetrius fled to Tyre, where he was captured and died under the torture of his enemies. However, the impostor was not destined to rule for long. A few years later, he was defeated by the son of the tortured Demetrius, Antiochus VIII Grypus, and died himself. However, the struggle for power between the Seleucids did not end there. Josephus reports that "having seized the Syrian throne, Antiochus immediately prepared to go to war against Judea. But when he heard that his half-brother (Antiochus IX of Cyzicus) was recruiting an army in Cyzicus to undertake a campaign against him, he decided to remain in Syria for now and prepare to repel his brother" (*Antiquities of the Jews,* 13.10.1). From this time on, the Seleucid kingdom was effectively divided into two parts: the descendants of Antiochus VII Sidetes began to rule in Cilicia and northern Syria, and the children of his brother Demetrius II Nicator began to rule in the rest of Syria and Phoenicia.

The struggle for power and civil wars transformed the great Seleucid empire into a medium-sized Hellenistic kingdom, consisting only of the territories of Syria and Phoenicia. While the Seleucids were fighting each other and the impostors, Johanan Hyrcanus, according to

Josephus, "enjoyed complete peace. Ever since the death of Antiochus, he had completely withdrawn from the Macedonians and did not provide them with anything either as a subject or as an ally... The civil war between the two brothers gave Hyrcanus the full opportunity to calmly enjoy the fruits of his land, so that during this period he managed to accumulate significant wealth" (*Antiquities of the Jews,* 13.10.1).

Taking advantage of the strife in the Seleucid kingdom, Johanan Hyrcanus began to conquer the entire territory of Samaria, which then belonged to the Seleucids. However, the Seleucids made attempts to prevent the conquest of Samaria. Its siege was entrusted to Johanan's sons - Aristobulus and Antigonus. They, according to Josephus, "brought the Samaritans to such a desperate situation that they began to eat all kinds of abominations out of hunger and eventually turned to Antiochus of Cyzicus for help. The latter immediately responded to this call, but was defeated by the troops of Aristobulus, and then fled, pursued all the way to Scythopolis by both brothers" (*Antiquities of the Jews,* 13.10.2). Then the Samaritans turned to [another] Antiochus (Grypus). He also tried to help, but was ambushed, lost part of his army and was forced to leave.

Like his father, Johanan Hyrcanus renewed the alliance with the Roman Republic, the main enemy of the Seleucids in the West. At the same time, we are not aware of any contacts with Parthia, the main enemy of the Seleucid kingdom in the East. Perhaps Johanan Hyrcanus viewed the Parthians as a potential threat not only to the Seleucids, but also to Judea, especially since he fought against them together with Antiochus VII Sidetes.

Johanan Hyrcanus's successful reign was marred by a conflict with the Pharisees, who were the ideological heirs of the Hasideans. The Hasideans, who had great influence on the Jewish people, actively helped the Hasmoneans during the Maccabean wars. The Pharisees also supported Simon, and then his son Johanan, especially since the latter initially belonged to their followers. However, over time, Johanan became close to representatives of another movement in Judaism - the Sadducees, which included the priests of the Jerusalem Temple. The main reason for the disagreement was the attitude towards the Oral Torah (Oral Law). The Pharisees claimed that in addition to the Written Torah (Pentateuch), Moses passed on to the Jewish people a set of oral laws - the Oral Torah, which is just as important as the Written Torah. The priests of the Jerusalem Temple (Sadducees) never recognized the Oral Torah and considered it the fruit of the creativity of the Pharisees themselves. At the end of his reign, Johanan Hyrcanus sided with the Sadducees and forbade the people to follow the Oral Law of the Pharisees. However, the Pharisees had enormous influence on the people and the conflict with them threatened the country with civil war, which happened later under one of Johanan Hyrcanus' sons. The transition of the Hasmoneans from the Pharisees to the Sadducees was not accidental: it reflected the change in the social base of this dynasty. From now on, its support was the Jewish aristocracy, the priests of the Temple and the wealthiest and most Hellenized strata of the population. As Josephus testifies, "on the side of the Sadducees stood only the wealthy class, and not the common people" (*Antiquities of the Jews*, 13.10.6).

Johanan Hyrcanus died in 104 BCE after 30 years of successful rule and many military victories. However, the succession to the throne did not happen at all as he wanted. He bequeathed the rule of the country to his wife, and the post of high priest to his eldest son Aristobulus. However, Aristobulus, who was entrusted with the command of the army, decided otherwise: he seized power and became the first of the Hasmoneans to declare himself king. His mother and three brothers were thrown into prison, and later his beloved brother Antigonus (who went down in history as Antigonus I) was also killed, suspected of plotting against the king. Aristobulus I (104-103 BCE) ruled for only one year and died of an unknown disease or poisoning. Despite the short term of his reign, he managed to recapture Galilee, an important region of the former Kingdom of Israel, where the lands of five Israelite tribes were located: Issachar, Zebulun, Naphtali, Dan and Asher. The Judean army, then commanded by Aristobulus I's brother Antigonus, reached the southern slopes of Mount Hermon, where it subdued the Itureans, semi-nomads of Aramean origin.

Josephus severely condemned the cruelty of Aristobulus I toward his family and relatives. However, as a statesman, he evaluated him positively: "He showed himself to be a friend of the Greeks and rendered great services to his country by waging war against Iturea. He annexed a significant part of this country to Judea, forcing those Itureans who wanted to remain in their region to accept circumcision and live according to Jewish laws" (*Antiquities of the Jews,* 13.11.3).

Also of interest are Josephus's quotes from the works of the Alexandrian historian Timagenes and the geographer Strabo (their writings have not been preserved). Both of these Hellenistic authors wrote the following about the Judean king Aristobulus I: "This man was gentle and brought great benefit to the Jews because he expanded the Judean territory and settled a part of the Itureans among his people, compelling them to undergo circumcision. By nature, he was a gentle and very modest person" (*Antiquities of the Jews,* 13.11.3). It can be assumed that Aristobulus I earned such a complimentary assessment from Greco-Roman authors primarily because he was the first of the Hasmoneans to present himself as a "friend of the Greeks."

After Aristobulus I's death, his widow, Salome Alexandra, released his three brothers from prison and made one of them, Alexander Jannaeus, king, entering into a levirate marriage with him in accordance with ancient Jewish tradition. However, Alexander Jannaeus's ascent to the throne was not entirely smooth; according to Josephus, it cost the life of another brother who had also sought the throne (*Jewish War,* 1.4.1).

Alexander's entire 27-year reign (103–76 BCE) was spent in almost continuous wars, both to reclaim the lands of the former Israelite kingdom and against internal opponents of his rule. First, Alexander reconquered the coastal port cities for Judea that had previously belonged to the Hebrew kingdoms. He managed to return almost the entire Mediterranean coast to Judea, from Sinai in the south to Mount Carmel in the north, including cities such as Raphia, Gaza, Anthedon, Ashdod,

26. Judean Kingdom in the time of Alexander Jannaeus, Salome Alexandra, and Aristobulus II. 103-63 BCE.

Yavneh, Jaffa, Apollonia, Strato's Tower, and Dor. Some of these had been conquered by his father and grandfather. Only Ashkelon (Ascalon) maintained its independence, becoming an ally of Judea. Ptolemais (Akko) became a stumbling block for Alexander, as it was the most powerful fortress-port on the entire coast of Coele-Syria at the time. Jannaeus besieged Ptolemais several times, but each time the rulers of the

Hellenistic kingdoms – either the Ptolemies or the Seleucids and their allies – came to its aid.

Another direction of his campaigns was the Hellenistic cities of the Decapolis, located on the territory of the former Israelite kingdom, on the lands of the Hebrew tribes of Gad and Manasseh. Alexander Jannaeus was far from the only one interested in the Golan Heights, as well as northern and central Transjordan. In these areas, the interests of three kingdoms clashed: Judean, Seleucid, and Nabataean. Although military actions in Transjordan had mixed success, Jannaeus managed to conquer almost the entire Decapolis. Moreover, he also succeeded in reclaiming a part of Moab's territory, which the Nabataeans had seized.

By the end of his reign, Alexander Jannaeus had recovered most of the lands of the former Hebrew kingdoms. The territory of Hasmonean Judea stretched from Sinai in the south to Mount Hermon in the north, and from the Mediterranean coast in the west to the border of the Syrian Desert in the east. To reach the borders of historical Canaan, he only had to conquer the eastern part of Transjordan – the regions belonging to Ammon, Moab, and Edom – relatives of the Hebrews and traditional tributaries of the Hebrew kingdoms. However, Alexander Jannaeus was not destined to do so; all his plans for conquest were disrupted by a conflict with the Pharisees, which later escalated into a bloody civil war. The confrontation between the Hasmonean dynasty and the Pharisees, which began at the end of Johanan Hyrcanus's reign, reached its peak during the reign of his son, Alexander Jannaeus. When the king forbade the observance of the Oral Law, the Pharisees responded by refusing to recognize the Hasmoneans' right both to the royal throne and to the high priesthood. The leaders of the Pharisees accused the Hasmonean rulers of violating three major Jewish traditions. First, the right to the kingship belonged only to the descendants of the Davidic dynasty, to whom the Hasmoneans were not related. Second, high priests could only be chosen from the direct descendants of the first high priest, Zadok – that is, from the Sadducees, to whom the Hasmoneans also did not belong. Finally, and third, Judean kings were not supposed to take on the functions of the high priest. From the perspective of Jewish tradition, the most the Hasmoneans could claim was the position of ruler of the people – an ethnarch. A part of the Jewish aristocracy, who considered the Hasmoneans "upstarts" without rights to kingship and the high priesthood, joined the dissatisfied Pharisees. Gradually, the clashes between supporters and opponents of the Hasmoneans escalated into a fierce civil war that lasted for about six years (94–88 BCE). According to Josephus, during this fratricidal war, no less than 50,000 Jews died, and even more fled to neighboring countries.

After being defeated, the Pharisees and their allies called upon the enemies of Judea, and especially the Seleucid king Demetrius III Eucaerus, for help. He hastened to Judea with his entire army, where tens of thousands of Jews who opposed Alexander joined him. United, the Greco-Syrians and Jews routed Jannaeus's army near the city of Shechem, but their interests diverged, and the allies began to fight each other. The strife between the Greco-Syrians and the Jews saved Alexander and allowed him to assemble a new army. At the same time, Demetrius was forced to leave Judea immediately because his brother Philip was trying to seize the Seleucid throne. Left without the support of the Greco-Syrians, Alexander's opponents were defeated: some of them died, while others fled beyond the borders of Judea and remained in exile until the end of Jannaeus's life (*Antiquities of the Jews,* 13.14.2).

The end of the civil war allowed Alexander to resume his offensive in Transjordan against the Syrian Seleucids and the Nabataean kingdom. But in his final years, Alexander suffered from fever and became very weak. Death overtook him during one of his military campaigns. Shortly before his death, he tried to reconcile with the Pharisees, understanding what great influence they held among the people. Moreover, he bequeathed the royal throne not to his sons but to his wife, Salome Alexandra, who was known to the people for her closeness to the Pharisees and her disapproval of her husband's cruelty. He hoped that Salome's reign would bring peace to the country and end the confrontation between the Hasmoneans and the Pharisees. He was not mistaken.

As Josephus testified, "his hope did not deceive him. The reputation for piety that this woman enjoyed secured her dominance. She strictly observed the ancient national customs and removed violators of the sacred laws from office... The Pharisees took the closest part in the rule under her. The devout Alexandra was very devoted to them; and they, taking advantage of her simplicity and gradually winning her trust, soon became the de facto rulers..." (*Jewish War,* 1.5.1–2).

Her brother, Shimon ben-Shetach, played a major role in the reign of Salome Alexandra. He was a well-known Pharisee and, possibly, the head of the Sanhedrin, the supreme religious court. While the Sadducees set the tone in religious life during the reign of Alexander Jannaeus, the Pharisees did so during the reign of Salome Alexandra. This was explained not only by the queen's worldview and her ties with the Pharisees but also by the expansion of the latter's social base. The Pharisees now represented not only the lower classes but also the wealthy segments of the population. While the Sadducees were generally Jewish aristocrats and Temple priests, the Pharisees had the support of both the poor and the rich; the absolute majority of the people followed them. The favorable attitude towards the Pharisees was by no means a whim of the queen but a well-thought-out policy that fully justified itself. Salome Alexandra managed to win the favor of the people primarily through her good relations with the Pharisees. In addition, as a woman, the queen could not be the high priest, so she appointed her eldest son, Hyrcanus (known as Hyrcanus II), to this post, thereby returning to the former tradition of separating religious and civil power, which the Pharisees had demanded.

Despite her concessions to the Pharisees, Salome Alexandra was not a weak-willed queen. As Josephus admitted, "she, despite her gender, was in no way inferior to a man in the strength of her character... In the most serious situations in life, she proved in practice how firm her will was and how unreasonable men are when they fail in state affairs" (*Antiquities of the Jews* 13.16. 6). Salome ruled for only nine years (76–67 BCE), but these years were the most peaceful and tranquil in the history of Hasmonean Judea. Despite her peace-loving foreign policy, Salome increased the size of her mercenary army so much that she instilled fear in her neighbors. The strength and power of the Judean army were the main reasons why the Armenian king Tigranes II, after defeating Seleucid Syria and seizing Damascus in 70 BCE, did not dare to advance further into Judea.

Salome Alexandra bequeathed the royal throne to her elder son Hyrcanus and the high priesthood to her younger son Aristobulus. However, as Josephus states, "of these sons, Hyrcanus was unfit for state affairs and preferred peace and a tranquil lifestyle above all, whereas the younger, Aristobulus, was more energetic and enterprising" (*Antiquities of the Jews,* 13.16.1). Although Josephus believed that "the superiority of strength and intellect was on Aristobulus's side," he also acknowledged that "Hyrcanus was by nature an honest man and, due to his integrity, was not easily swayed by slander" (*Jewish War,* 1.6.1; *Antiquities of the Jews,* 14.1.3). Aristobulus openly sided with the Sadducees and enjoyed their full support, while Hyrcanus, like his mother, favored the Pharisees.

Shortly before the queen's death, Aristobulus secured the support of the army, and this circumstance decided the outcome of the struggle for the succession. In the very first battle near Jericho, the army defected to Aristobulus, and Hyrcanus was forced to cede supreme power to his younger brother, settling for the high priesthood himself. Thus, contrary to the will of Salome Alexandra, Aristobulus II (67–63 BCE) became the Judean king, not Hyrcanus II.

Probably, considering Hyrcanus's "inactivity and intellectual sluggishness" (as defined by Josephus), peace and tranquility would have reigned in the country if it had not been for an Idumean aristocrat named Antipater, Hyrcanus' closest friend and advisor. Because of his closeness to Hyrcanus, he was in an openly hostile relationship with Aristobulus, and after the latter's accession, he became greatly concerned about his fate. Antipater came from one of Idumea's wealthiest and most prominent families. His family, like all Idumeans, had adopted Jewish monotheism. Alexander Jannaeus had appointed Antipater's father as the governor of Idumea. It was Antipater who persuaded, or rather, forced the indecisive Hyrcanus to flee to the Nabataean king Aretas III and ask for help in restoring his rights to the kingdom. Aretas agreed without hesitation, as Hyrcanus promised to return all the Transjordanian territories that Alexander Jannaeus had won from the Nabataeans. Aretas fielded a 50,000-man army, which was joined by thousands of Hyrcanus's supporters in Judea. This combined Nabataean-Judean army defeated Aristobulus II's followers and besieged them in Jerusalem. Only the Sadducees remained on Aristobulus's side. Most likely, Hyrcanus and Aretas would have achieved a complete victory if not for the intervention of the Romans.

While the struggle for power in Judea escalated into a new civil war, Roman legions seized Damascus, ending the existence of the Seleucid kingdom. At the same time, the Roman general Pompey completed the conquest of Armenia, having defeated King Tigranes II. The Roman army stopped at the borders of Judea, awaiting Pompey's orders. To assess the situation, he sent his aide, Scaurus, to Judea. Aristobulus managed to offer Scaurus a much larger sum of money than Hyrcanus, and the Roman sided with him. On behalf of the Romans and Pompey, he demanded the immediate lifting of the siege of Jerusalem and ordered the Nabataean Arabs to withdraw from Judea. Humiliated and frightened, Aretas hastened back to Petra. However, Aristobulus's triumph was premature. Pompey, who arrived in Damascus in 63 BCE, decided to make Hyrcanus, not him, the ruler of Judea. Aristobulus II tried to resist, but Pompey deceived him and, luring him into a trap, sent him to Rome as a prisoner. Aristobulus's supporters took refuge on the Temple Mount, but the Romans, along with Hyrcanus's followers, quickly dealt with them.

Pompey was afraid of leaving Judea as a large and powerful kingdom as it had been under Alexander Jannaeus, Salome Alexandra, and Aristobulus II. To weaken it as much as possible and tie it to Roman rule, he took away all the former Hellenistic cities on the Mediterranean coast, in the Decapolis, Idumea, and Galilee. However, he did not dare to turn Judea into a Roman province, as he had done with Seleucid Syria, and left the Jews broad internal autonomy. Pompey appointed Hyrcanus, who had helped him take control of the entire country, as the ruler and high priest of Judea, but he did not give him the coveted royal title.

Josephus believed that the struggle for power between Aristobulus and Hyrcanus was the main reason for the Roman conquest of Judea. "Hyrcanus and Aristobulus, who quarreled with each other, were the culprits of this disaster that befell Jerusalem. Now we have lost our freedom and have become subject to the Romans; now we have been forced to give up to the Syrians the regions we regained by force of our arms..." (*Antiquities of the Jews,* 14.4.5). However, the supporters of Aristobulus II resisted the Romans for a long time and quite successfully. Alexander, Aristobulus's eldest son, managed to escape from Roman captivity and, upon returning to Judea, led an anti-Roman uprising there. Already in 57 BCE, Jewish rebels led by Alexander managed to defeat the Roman garrisons in the country and liberate almost all of Judea. To cope with the uprising, the Romans were forced to send troops to Judea under the command of Mark Antony, who for a time managed to "pacify" the country. However, two years later, in 55 BCE, Alexander raised a new rebellion and again established his power over most of Judea. To save their governor Hyrcanus, the Romans had to urgently summon legions from Egypt and Syria. A few years later, in 47-46 BCE, another anti-Roman uprising, this time a popular one, broke out in Galilee under the leadership of a local Galilean leader, Hezekiah.

Each time, Hyrcanus proved to be too weak a ruler, constantly dependent on Roman help. This is precisely why he was chosen by Pompey, who was wary of the independent and decisive Aristobulus. Over time, against the backdrop of the listless and spineless Hyrcanus, his closest advisor and friend Antipater, along with his son Herod, began to stand out. Both of them showed the qualities that Hyrcanus lacked. The Romans noticed this and began to rely more and more on this Idumean aristocrat and his family. For example, when Julius Caesar needed help in Egypt, Antipater was the first to come to his rescue with a Judean army. A grateful Caesar did not remain in his debt: while confirming Hyrcanus's authority as ruler and high priest of Judea, he created a new post specifically for Antipater – "Roman governor in Judea." Gradually, Antipater became so entrenched that he became Hyrcanus's de facto co-ruler and, most importantly, the true arbiter of all state affairs. He put his elder son, Phasael, in charge of Jerusalem and its garrison, and sent his second son, Herod, to govern the north of the country – Galilee. When Hezekiah's uprising broke out there, Herod independently and with extreme cruelty dealt with all its participants. Even the Jewish aristocrats could not fail to notice and condemn this. Appearing before Hyrcanus, they tried to draw his attention to the de facto seizure of power by Antipater's family: "Don't you see that Antipater and his sons have divided all power among themselves... Don't deceive yourself that Antipater and his sons are still your helpers but pay attention to the fact that they are already openly recognized as full-fledged rulers!" (*Antiquities of the Jews,* 14.9.3). Hyrcanus tried to limit Antipater's power and Herod's willfulness, but it was already too late. These Idumean aristocrats had become trusted people of the Romans, and they would not allow them to be touched. The Roman governor in Syria stood up for Herod and, moreover, threatened Hyrcanus with punishment if he tried to harm Antipater's son in any way. Thus began Herod's rapid rise to power.

The civil wars in the Roman Republic did not prevent Herod's rise; he knew how to find a common language with Caesar, with his assassin Cassius, with the triumvir Mark Antony, and with his conqueror Octavian Augustus. Hyrcanus was left with only the high priesthood, while real power in Judea passed to Herod and his brother Phasael. All attempts to stop this Idumean family, even after their father Antipater was poisoned, were unsuccessful. The Romans, extremely pleased with Herod, promised him the royal title. Only the unexpected offensive of the Parthians in Mesopotamia and Syria in 40 BCE postponed Herod's triumph. The Parthian army quickly drove the Roman legions out of Syria, Phoenicia, and Judea. Taking advantage of the Romans' departure and having made an agreement with the Parthians, power in Judea was seized by Antigonus, the younger son of Aristobulus II. Supported by his people and the Parthians, he besieged Herod, his brother Phasael, and the high priest Hyrcanus in Jerusalem. Herod managed to escape from the city, Phasael committed suicide so as not to be subjected to the ridicule of his enemies, and Hyrcanus was taken to Parthia as an honorary prisoner. Antigonus was proclaimed the new Judean king in Jerusalem and went down in history as Antigonus II (40–37 BCE).

Meanwhile, Herod hastened to Rome to his friends and patrons, who had not forgotten the services of Herod and his father Antipater to the Roman Republic. The triumvirs of that time, Mark Antony and Octavian, persuaded the Senate to proclaim Herod king of Judea and Antigonus II a rebel. However, Herod had to wait three years to take the royal throne of Judea. It was not until 37 BCE that the Romans managed to capture Judea and Jerusalem. The assault on Jerusalem involved eleven Roman legions and dozens of auxiliary detachments from Syria and Phoenicia. Abandoned by their Parthian allies, Antigonus II and his warriors withstood the onslaught of the Roman army for almost six months. But the enormous difference in forces between the city's defenders and their besiegers made the fall of Jerusalem inevitable. Antigonus was taken prisoner by the Romans and, at Herod's insistence, was executed. He became the last Judean king of the Hasmonean dynasty. Josephus gave the following assessment of this dynasty: "This family was distinguished by brilliance and glory, not only by originating from a noble family and possessing the high priesthood, but also by the heroic deeds performed by their ancestors for the benefit of the people. But the Hasmoneans lost power due to their constant feuds, and this power passed to the son of Antipater, Herod..." (*Antiquities of the Jews,* 14.16. 4).

2. The Judean Kingdom of Herod the Great (37–4 BCE)

Herod's ascension to the Judean throne brought an end to the Hasmonean dynasty. At the same time, to appear as a legitimate heir to this heroic Jewish dynasty, Herod married Mariamne the Hasmonean, the granddaughter of Hyrcanus II. However, to ensure the Hasmoneans could never again claim royal power, Herod sought to physically eliminate all members of the dynasty who could pose a threat to him. As his morbid suspiciousness grew, he began to execute even members of his own family who had Hasmonean ties. Thus, he took the lives of his beautiful wife Mariamne, their two sons, her brother, her mother, and even her grandfather, Hyrcanus II, who had returned from Parthian captivity.

Unlike the Hasmoneans, he never tried to also occupy the post of high priest, but gave it only to Sadducees loyal to him, such as Simon, son of Boethus, the father of one of his wives. However, this did not save him from constant accusations by the Jewish aristocracy that, as an Idumean, he had no right to occupy the royal throne of Judea. Particularly telling is Antigonus II's appeal to the Romans, in which he claimed "that they would violate all justice if they handed over the royal power to Herod, who is a mere private person and an Idumean, that is, a half-Jew, whereas, according to justice and the customs [of the country], this power should belong only to native-born Jews. If, he continued, the Jews are now unhappy that he (Antigonus) gained royal power with the help of the Parthians and have decided to take it away from him, there are still many members of his family who have caused no harm to the Romans and are also priests. They are being treated unjustly by being deprived of this power" (*Antiquities of the Jews,* 14.15.2).

While accusing the Romans of injustice and violating the customs of the country by giving the Judean throne to Herod, Antigonus concealed the fact that the Hasmoneans themselves had no right to royal power, as they were also not descendants of the Davidic dynasty. As for being "native-born Jews," the Idumeans were ethnically as Jewish as the Judeans. Before the departure to Egypt, the Judeans and Idumeans were one people: elder and younger brothers with a common ancestry. The stay in Egypt alienated the younger brother – the Judeans – from the elder – the Idumeans – who remained in Canaan. Thereafter, only religion separated them: the Judeans embraced monotheism, while the Idumeans remained pagans. But since the time of Johanan Hyrcanus, the Idumeans had adopted Jewish monotheism and become "perfect Jews."

Moreover, the Torah repeatedly reminded the Judeans: "You shall not abhor any of the Edomites, for they are your kin" (Deut. 23:7).

Why couldn't the Judean nobility forgive Herod for his Idumean roots, yet paid no attention to the Moabite ancestors of King David? The reason is obviously in the history of relations between these peoples. While the Judeans were good neighbors with the Moabites, they were often at odds with the Edomites. As for his origin, Herod's family was one of the most prominent and wealthy in his Idumea. This was a line of Idumean rulers that had close ties with their neighbors, the Nabataeans. Herod's mother, Cypros, came from a noble Nabataean family. In short, he was neither a foreigner, a commoner, nor an infidel, as the Talmud and some authors claim.

The problem with Herod, as with his father Antipater, was that they belonged to neither the hereditary Judean aristocracy nor the priestly Aaronites and therefore were never "their own." Another "flaw" of Herod was considered to be his deep and sincere loyalty to the Romans, which is what they valued him for. If to his own people he was a servant of pagans, to the Romans he was a reliable and loyal friend. He enjoyed special favor and trust from both Emperor Octavian Augustus and the Roman Senate. His policy of an honest and unconditional alliance with Rome was fully justified. In the thirty-three years of his reign, Judea transformed into a large and strong state, almost independent from Rome. If Simon, Johanan Hyrcanus, Aristobulus I, and Alexander Jannaeus spent all the years of their rule in military campaigns to reclaim the lands of the Hebrew kingdoms, Herod only had to fight for the Judean throne. Having achieved royal power, he achieved even more peacefully through his diplomacy than all the Hasmonean rulers did through war.

The kingdom of Judea during Herod's reign included the territory of all of historical Canaan. To the west of the Jordan River, he owned all the lands of Judea, Idumea, northern Negev, Samaria, and Galilee, as well as most of the Hellenistic cities on the Mediterranean coast. To the east of the Jordan River, Herod's kingdom included the regions of Gilead and Perea, as well as most of the Hellenistic cities of the Decapolis.

To the northeast, he owned not only Golan and Iturea, but also the vast territories of Batanea, Trachonitis, and Hauran (Auranitis) in Southern Syria. Emperor Octavian Augustus gave his friend and protégé Herod almost all the Hellenistic cities of the Decapolis and the Mediterranean coast that Pompey had taken from Judea. The few Hellenistic cities that were never returned to Herod were more than compensated for with lands in Southern Syria. During the reign of Herod, his sons, grandsons, and great-grandsons, they owned not only Southern Syria but also almost the entire territory of modern Lebanon. He achieved all of this not through military campaigns, as the Hasmoneans did, but peacefully, through a trusting relationship with Rome, and especially with Emperor Augustus. Moreover, Augustus was ready to give the Judean king the entire territory of the Nabataean kingdom as well, if Herod had not been of advanced age and had not had problems with choosing his heir. In general, Emperor Augustus did not hide that "Herod's country is too small for his generosity and that he is worthy of being king of all Syria and Egypt" (*Antiquities of the Jews,* 16.5.1). For Herod himself, his relationship with Emperor Augustus was paramount. Josephus noted the following about this: "What was most important for Herod was that he could consider himself Augustus's first favorite after Agrippa (a Roman friend of Augustus) and Agrippa's favorite after Augustus" (*Jewish War,* 1.20.4).

Herod's true fame and reputation came from his city-building, for which he earned the name the Great. The main project and achievement of his life was the construction of the new Jerusalem Temple, built directly over the old one. This magnificent Temple became one of the best architectural structures of the ancient world. But the Judean capital did not only receive a new Temple; Herod also built a royal palace, a large amphitheater, a hippodrome, and the powerful Antonia Fortress (in honor of Mark Antony). According to the Roman historian Pliny the Elder, "Jerusalem has become one of the most famous cities of the East" (*Natural History*, 5. 70).

27. Model of Herod's Temple by Israeli archaeologist M. Avi-Yonah.

Herod's equally large-scale projects were the cities of Caesarea and Sebaste, which were named in honor of the Roman Emperor Augustus (the first in Latin, the second in Greek). The first was built on the site of the Mediterranean town of Strato's Tower, and the second – on the ruins of the capital of the Israelite kingdom – Samaria. In addition to the Antonia Fortress in Jerusalem, Herod built or restored dozens of other fortresses throughout Judea. The most famous of these were Herodium, where the king himself is buried, Cypros (in memory of Cypros, the king's mother), a powerful fortress that towered over Jericho, the famous Masada in the Judean Desert, Machaerus, where John the Baptist was beheaded, as well as Alexandrion and Hyrcania. For his parents and deceased brothers, he erected magnificent tombs and monuments and immortalized their names by naming fortresses and public buildings after them.

Herod the Great's building activity was not limited to Judea alone. He paid for the construction of public buildings, most often gymnasiums, amphitheaters, and aqueducts, in many Hellenistic cities in Syria, Asia Minor, and on the islands of the Aegean Sea. Thus, in Tripolis, Damascus, and Ptolemais, he built gymnasiums; in Byblos, he restored the city walls; in Beirut and Tyre – colonnades, galleries, temples, and markets; in Sidon and Damascus – theaters; in Laodicea – an aqueduct; in Ascalon – colonnades, baths, and wells. He gave money to the inhabitants of the island of Rhodes for the construction of a fleet. He rebuilt the burned Temple of Apollo Pythios in Delphi (Greece) with his own money. Josephus claimed that "Athens, Lacedaemon, and Pergamon are filled with Herod's gifts" (*Jewish War,* 1.21.11). He donated considerable funds to organize the Olympic Games and even helped Hellenistic cities mired in debt. For example, he paid the debts of the inhabitants of the Greek island of Chios and thereby saved them from being sold into slavery. He became famous for his generosity and magnanimity in all the Hellenistic countries of the Eastern Mediterranean. It was there that he became known as Herod the Great. However, he could sometimes show generosity to his own people as well. In lean years, the king reduced, or even completely exempted, his subjects from paying taxes and duties. When Judea and the neighboring regions were struck by drought and famine, Herod the Great sold the valuables from his palace in order to purchase grain in Egypt with the proceeds. He distributed this bread, as well as warm clothes in winter, to all those in need for free. He provided the exact same help to neighboring Syria.

The kingdom of Herod the Great was significantly different from Hasmonean Judea. While the Hasmoneans were independent and sovereign rulers, Herod and his heirs were direct appointees of the Romans. While the Hasmoneans were Jewish patriots, Herod and his descendants – the Herodians – were Hellenistic rulers who violated the laws of Judaism. Herod became the first of the Judean kings who openly disregarded the traditions and customs of Judaism. Josephus wrote about this: "Herod increasingly departed from the observance of ancient laws and customs, and through the introduction of foreign practices he gradually undermined the long-established and seemingly unshakable order of life." The "Hellenistic entertainments" caused particular outrage among the Jews, when "wild animals were released to fight both among themselves and with people sentenced to death." If this gave the Hellenes pleasure, then "the Jews considered it obvious impiety to provide people to wild beasts for the pleasure of other people" (*Antiquities of the Jews,* 15.8.1).

As in Hasmonean Judea, the majority of the population in Herod's kingdom was Jewish. However, unlike the Hasmonean state, there were significantly more non-Jews in Herod's kingdom. This was because Herod's power extended to all of Southern Syria and Iturea in Lebanon, where many non-Jews lived. Herod's kingdom was a country where Hellenism and Judaism were bizarrely combined. The Jewish nobility led a Hellenistic way of life, while the people adhered to Jewish laws and customs. Such a rift between the aristocracy and the general populace did not exist during the Hasmonean rule. While the Hasmonean rulers Simon, Johanan Hyrcanus, and Salome Alexandra enjoyed the support of the Pharisees, and Aristobulus I, Alexander Jannaeus, and Aristobulus II relied on the Sadducees, behind Herod stood foreign mercenaries, and most importantly – the Romans.

Not trusting the people of Judea, Herod enlisted Jews from the diaspora, and especially from Babylonia, into his service. He also preferred to hire mercenary soldiers not from Asia Minor, as the Hasmoneans did, but from Idumea – his own tribesmen – as well as from Europe – Germans, Gauls, and Thracians. As governors in all regions of the Judean kingdom, Herod generally appointed only his relatives. Unlike the Hasmoneans, who preferred to make appointments based on political and ideological proximity, Herod trusted only his own family. The Hellenistic world called Herod the Great and had every right to do so, but the Jewish people considered the king a foreign appointee and hated him for his extreme cruelty and loyalty to the "Roman pagans," so they met his death with relief.

3. The Herodians – Judean Rulers of the Southern Levant (4 BCE – 100 CE)

Herod the Great made and changed his will many times because he could not choose his heir. The choice was difficult; he had 15 children from ten legal wives. However, he had already executed his eldest, most noble and beloved sons on suspicion of trying to seize his power. From the remaining sons, he chose three: Archelaus, Antipas, and Philip. He made Archelaus his primary heir, bequeathing to him the royal throne and the main regions of the country: Judea, Idumea, and Samaria. The other two sons were to become tetrarchs (rulers of a fourth part) and were bequeathed more modest territories. Antipas received Galilee and Perea, while Philip received Upper Galilee, southern Syria (Golan, Batanea, Trachonitis, Hauran) and Iturea (from Mount Lebanon and the Beqaa Valley to the Anti-Lebanon Mountains in Syria).

Emperor Augustus approved Herod the Great's will but, out of respect for his family's requests, did not give Archelaus the royal title. Instead, he appointed him only an ethnarch (a ruler of the people). He promised to grant Archelaus the royal throne later if he proved to be a worthy ruler. Thus, Herod the Great's kingdom of Judea was divided into three parts among his sons. This arrangement suited the Romans best, as they were wary of leaving Judea too large and powerful. In addition, the Romans took some Hellenistic cities, specifically Gaza, Gadara, and Hippos, from Herod's heirs and re-annexed them to the province of Syria.

Subsequently, seven more grandsons and great-grandsons of Herod the Great were added to the three Herodian rulers, and they also became rulers and kings in the Southern Levant. Considering the significance of each, they should be listed in the following order: Agrippa I and Agrippa II, grandson and great-grandson of Herod the Great through his son Aristobulus; Herod II, brother of Agrippa I; Aristobulus V, son of Herod II; then Tigranes V and Tigranes VI, grandson and great-grandson of Herod the Great through his son Alexander; and finally, Alexander, son of Tigranes VI. All ten of the Herodian rulers were united not only by their belonging to Herod's dynasty and their Jewish origin but also by the Hellenistic nature of their education, upbringing, and most importantly, their rule. All of them became rulers and kings by the will of the Romans and were representatives of their interests in the Southern Levant. However, some of them, such as Agrippa I, Agrippa II, and Philip, tried to find a reasonable compromise between Judaism and Hellenism, adhered to Jewish monotheism, and observed the traditions and customs of the Jewish people. Hellenistic historians spoke highly of them as statesmen and gave a high assessment of their human qualities. Others, such as Antipas, evoked mixed opinions. However, the one who drew the greatest condemnation was Herod's principal heir, Herod Archelaus, who proved to be as cruel a tyrant as his father.

The Herodian dynasty was more numerous and, above all, produced far more kings and rulers of the southern Levant than the Hasmonean dynasty. Yet in Jewish and world history its place is incomparable to that of the Hasmoneans. This is largely because the former were Roman protégés, whereas the latter were sovereign rulers and national patriots.

Archelaus, Ethnarch (4 BCE - 6 CE)

Four days before his death, Herod the Great changed his will and made Archelaus his main heir. He was to receive the most important part of the Judean kingdom – Judea proper, along with Samaria and Idumea. These territories were considered the wealthiest and generated three times more revenue than all the other parts of the Judean kingdom combined. The royal family strongly opposed his new choice, for, knowing the cruelty and unpredictability of Herod Archelaus, they feared falling under the authority of a new tyrant. In an effort to dissuade Augustus from confirming Archelaus as king, the entire family of Herod the Great traveled to Rome. Delegates of the Jewish people also arrived there to support the family's petition. However, Augustus did not dare to violate the last will of his closest friend and protégé, so he approved Herod's testament.

The fact of Archelaus's cruelty and his penchant for tyranny is indirectly confirmed by the Gospel of Matthew. Narrating the return of Joseph with the child and his mother from Egypt to the land of Israel, it states: "But when he heard that Archelaus was ruling Judea in place of his father Herod, he was afraid to go there. And after being warned in a dream, he went away to the district of Galilee" (Matthew 2:22).

Archelaus was the son of Herod the Great by his wife Malthace, a Samaritan by origin. Together with his full brother Antipas and his half-brother Philip, he spent his childhood and youth in Rome, studied alongside the offspring of Roman aristocrats, and received the best Hellenistic education and upbringing of the time. His personal life was not simple. His marriage to Glaphyra, the daughter of the king of Cappadocia, caused a lot of controversy and criticism. Glaphyra was the widow of his half-brother Alexander, whom Herod had executed on suspicion of trying to seize his power. She then married the Libyan king Juba II, and some time later became the wife of Archelaus. Jewish tradition did not approve of such marriages. However, Archelaus did not accept the reproaches of the traditionalists; moreover, he changed the high priests three times when they did not please him.

From the very beginning, his rule was marred by a bloody massacre of his own people who had come to the Jerusalem Temple to celebrate Passover (Pesach). Then, immediately after his father's death, the people demanded the release of those languishing in prison and the punishment of Herod's executioners. Unable to reach an agreement with the "rebels," Archelaus unleashed his soldiers upon them, turning peaceful protests into a mass slaughter. As his family had feared, Archelaus proved to be as cruel a ruler as his father. But unlike Herod the Great, he did not possess his diplomatic skill; he was unable to negotiate and reach compromises with his opponents. Trying to imitate his father, he built a royal palace in Jericho, planted the local valley with date palms, and created a skillful irrigation system there. He also built a Hellenistic town there, naming it Archelais, after himself. However, his city-building ended there due to lack of funds.

The population of Archelaus's ethnarchy was quite homogeneous and consisted exclusively of Jews. The absolute majority of them were Judeans (Judea and Idumea). Samaritans were in a dual position: they were considered Jews but not Judeans, lived mostly in the territory of Samaria, and were significantly outnumbered by the Judeans. The Hellenistic population was concentrated in the three cities of the ethnarchy: Caesarea, Jaffa, and Sebaste.

Archelaus turned out to be an unsuccessful ruler; he ruled for only ten years but managed to cause widespread discontent among both the Judeans and the Samaritans. In 6 CE, the Judeans and Samaritans, without consulting each other, sent delegations to Emperor Augustus with complaints about Archelaus's tyranny. The emperor summoned Archelaus to Rome and, after listening to the arguments of each side, deprived Archelaus of his power and exiled him to Gallic Vienne (now the city of Vienne in southern France). Archelaus's ethnarchy was annexed to the Roman province of Syria and, with the exception of the years 41–44, was governed by Roman prefects and procurators.

Antipas, Tetrarch (4 BCE – 39 CE)

This tetrarch became the most famous among the descendants of Herod the Great. He was mentioned not only by Hellenistic authors but also in the New Testament. He is perhaps the only one of the Herodians who is mentioned repeatedly in the Gospels and the Acts of the Apostles. The New Testament refers to him not so much as Antipas, but simply as "Herod." The special attention given to him was due to several reasons. First, he was considered the principal heir of Herod the Great in all his wills until the king changed it to Archelaus four days before his death. All of Herod's relatives unequivocally defended Antipas's candidacy for the throne of Judea before Emperor Augustus in Rome. Antipas was considered intelligent, rather mild, and, most importantly, a calm and balanced person who was not susceptible to his father's cruelty and impulsiveness. His rival, Archelaus, was his full brother from the

Samaritan woman Malthace, with whom he spent his childhood and youth in Rome. Like Archelaus, Antipas received a good Hellenistic, and later a Jewish religious education. From his father, Herod the Great, he inherited the second most important part of the Judean kingdom: Galilee in the north of the country and Perea in central Transjordan. Although these regions were not contiguous and were quite far from each other, the absolute majority of their population was Jewish.

The first scandal associated with Antipas's name arose because of his niece, Herodias. She was married to his half-brother Philip, whose mother was the daughter of the high priest Simon Boethus. Philip (Boethus) himself did not receive any territorial allotment from his father, so he moved to Rome to live on the funds Herod left him. When Antipas arrived in Rome on business, he considered it his duty to visit his brother. Upon seeing the beautiful Herodias, he immediately fell in love with her and proposed that she leave his brother and marry him. Herodias, whether out of great love for Antipas or motivated by greed and vanity, preferred the powerful tetrarch's palace in Galilee to her modest dwelling in Rome. However, both of them forgot a very important circumstance: what is not forbidden to pagans is forbidden to Jews. Jewish laws allowed a man to marry his brother's wife only if she remained a childless widow. But Philip, Antipas's brother, was alive and had a daughter with her, Salome. By taking his brother's wife, Antipas violated the biblical commandment: "You shall not uncover the nakedness of your brother's wife; it is your brother's nakedness" (Leviticus 18:16).

Antipas's unworthy act became widely known in Judea and provoked a furious condemnation from John the Baptist. In response, Antipas imprisoned and then executed the most famous Jewish preacher of the time. However, the Gospel of Mark places all the blame for John the Baptist's death solely on the vengeful Herodias, and by no means on Antipas. Here is how the Gospel of Mark tells this story, referring to Antipas simply as "Herod": "For Herod himself had sent men who arrested John, bound him, and put him in prison on account of Herodias, his brother Philip's wife, because Herod had married her. For John had been telling

Herod, "It is not lawful for you to have your brother's wife." And Herodias had a grudge against him and wanted to kill him. But she could not, for Herod feared John, knowing that he was a righteous and holy man, and he protected him. When he heard him, he was greatly perplexed, and yet he liked to listen to him. But an opportunity came when Herod on his birthday gave a banquet for his courtiers and officers and for the leaders of Galilee. When his daughter Herodias came in and danced, she pleased Herod and his guests, and the king said to the girl, "Ask me for whatever you wish, and I will give it." And he swore to her, "Whatever you ask me, I will give you, even half of my kingdom." She went out and said to her mother, "What should I ask for?" She replied, "The head of John the baptizer." Immediately she rushed back to the king and requested, "I want you to give me at once the head of John the Baptist on a platter." The king was deeply grieved, yet out of regard for his oaths and for the guests, he did not want to refuse her. Immediately the king sent a soldier of the guard with orders to bring John's head. He went and beheaded him in the prison, brought his head on a platter, and gave it to the girl. Then the girl gave it to her mother" (Mark 6:17-28).

While the New Testament blames Herodias for John's death, Flavius Josephus points to the tetrarch Antipas himself as the sole culprit of this tragedy. According to his version, "since many flocked to the preacher, whose doctrine exalted their souls, Herod began to fear that his enormous influence over the masses (who were completely submissive to him) would not lead to any complications. Therefore, the tetrarch preferred to preempt this by seizing John and executing him before it would be too late to repent. Thanks to such suspicion on Herod's part, John was sent in chains to the fortress of Machaerus and was executed there" (*Antiquities of the Jews,* 18.5.2). Josephus's version is supported to some extent by the Gospel of Matthew, according to which Antipas himself wanted to deal with John, but "he feared the crowd, because they regarded him as a prophet" (Matthew 14:5). There is, however, a serious reason to believe that Antipas dealt with John at the insistence of Pontius Pilate, the Roman procurator of Judea. Pilate was very worried about the Jewish preachers in whom the people wanted to see the long-awaited Savior.

To officially marry Herodias, Antipas had to get rid of his first wife, the daughter of the Nabataean king Aretas IV. The Jewish ruler's break with her was received very painfully by the Arabs and led to a war with the Nabataean kingdom. The military actions that took place in Transjordan ended unsuccessfully for Antipas: his army was defeated. However, Antipas's tetrarchy was in fact part of the Roman Empire, and an attack on it was an act of aggression against the empire itself. When Antipas informed Emperor Tiberius about this, "he was enraged at the actions of Aretas, sent a command to Vitellius (the Roman governor in Syria) to declare war on him and to bring Aretas either alive in chains or his head... Some Jews, however, saw in the destruction of Herod Antipas's army a completely just punishment from the God for the killing of John" (*Antiquities of the Jews,* 18.5.1–2).

Like all Herodian rulers, Antipas was fond of city-building. His main project was the city of Tiberias on the western shore of Lake Kinneret. The city was named in honor of Emperor Tiberius, with whom Antipas had a good relationship. This city became the capital of both Galilee and Antipas's entire tetrarchy. A luxurious tetrarch's palace, an amphitheater, and gymnasiums were built there, and the city itself was surrounded by a powerful wall. The city was originally conceived as a Hellenistic-Jewish one, so there were both Hellenistic temples and a large synagogue. The value of the city was also increased by its springs with healing waters. But Tiberias was built on the site of an ancient settlement, and the builders had to erect new buildings on the remains of ancient structures and even tombs. This circumstance caused the Jews to consider the city's territory "unclean" and to avoid settling there at first.

Antipas was the only Herodian who interacted with Christ. According to the Gospel of Luke, when Pontius Pilate learned that Jesus was from Galilee, he sent Christ to Antipas, the ruler of that region, who was in Jerusalem at the time. However, Antipas refused not only to execute but even to judge Christ and sent him back to Pilate. The Gospel of Luke states: "When Herod saw Jesus, he was very glad, for he had been wanting to see him for a long time because he had heard about him and was hoping to see him perform some sign. He questioned him at some length, but Jesus gave him no answer." Then a disappointed Antipas "put an elegant robe on him and sent him back to Pilate. That same day Herod and Pilate became friends with each other; before this they had been enemies" (Luke 23:8-9, 11-12). The New Testament also preserved for posterity Jesus's own opinion of the cunning Antipas. Christ called him a "fox" (Luke 13:32). Antipas, who was not without religious beliefs, was haunted throughout his life by pangs of conscience for the execution of the innocent John. When Jesus began his preaching among the people after John, Antipas was seized with a superstitious fear: "John, whom I beheaded, has been raised" (Mark 6:16). According to the Gospel of Mark, Antipas was convinced that "John the baptizer has been raised from the dead, and for this reason these powers are at work in him." (Mark 6:14). If Herod Antipas believed in the resurrection of the dead, this suggests that he was close to the Pharisees or shared many of their views. This would explain the presence of numerous Pharisees at his court, even though most Judean aristocrats – and especially the Herodians – were generally regarded as committed Sadducees.

In the Gospel of Luke, there are vague hints of Antipas's attempt to seize Jesus: "At that very hour some Pharisees came and said to him, "Get away from here, for Herod wants to kill you" (Luke 13:31). However, Antipas never dared to lay a hand on Jesus, neither at that time nor later, despite Pilate's request.

The prosperous reign of the tetrarch Antipas ended quite unexpectedly, and all because of the vanity of his wife Herodias. In 37 CE, Antipas's nephew, Agrippa I, received the title of Judean king and the tetrarchy of his deceased uncle Philip in Southern Syria and the mountains of Lebanon from the Roman Emperor Caligula. This was the same Agrippa who, just a few years earlier, had lived with his uncle Antipas as a poor relative and had nothing but huge debts. Herodias was Agrippa

I's sister, but even this circumstance did not help the impoverished nephew remain on the payroll of his powerful uncle. The fantastic rise of Agrippa I's career took away the peace of his sister Herodias. From this time on, she began to persuade her husband Antipas to immediately go to Rome and ask the Roman emperor for the same – a royal title and new lands. Antipas, being a very intelligent man by nature, expected nothing good from an audience with the unbalanced and mentally ill Caligula. However, Herodias would not stop: "Be ashamed to be inferior to those who lived off your compassion just yesterday and the day before!" Antipas, being a gentle man, "did not know how to refuse her anything and submitted to her decisions" (*Antiquities of the Jews* 18.7.2). Antipas's bad feelings did not deceive him. In Rome, Caligula accused Antipas of an anti-Roman conspiracy with the Parthians and sentenced him to exile in Gaul, where he died very soon. Galilee and Perea, which constituted Antipas's tetrarchy, were transferred to the Judean king Agrippa I in 39 CE. Emperor Caligula also handed over all of Antipas's property to Agrippa I.

Philip II, Tetrarch (4 BCE – 34 CE)

Philip II was the son of Herod the Great by his fifth wife, Cleopatra from Jerusalem. Like his half-brothers, Archelaus and Antipas, he spent his childhood and youth in Rome, at the emperor's court. According to his father's will, he received the northernmost part of the Judean kingdom – Southern Syria, which included Golan, Batanea, Trachonitis, and Hauran (Auranitis), and later also the mountains of Lebanon (Iturea). He was married to Salome, the same daughter of Herodias who, according to the Gospels of Mark and Matthew, enchanted the tetrarch Antipas with her dance and, at her mother's instigation, asked for the head of John the Baptist. Tetrarch Philip is often confused with Philip Boethus, another son of Herod the Great who had the same name. But Philip Boethus was the son of another wife of Herod and did not receive any land grant in his father's will. However, Philip Boethus was the father of Salome, who became the wife of his half-brother Philip the tetrarch, and was also famous for being the first husband of the famous Herodias, whom his other half-brother Antipas took from him.

Philip's tetrarchy consisted of vast but sparsely populated areas of Southern Syria and the mountains of Lebanon. The population of the tetrarchy consisted mainly of Itureans (in the north) and Syrians of Aramean origin (in the east). Jews constituted an absolute majority of the population only in the Golan Heights and in Upper Galilee, while in the other areas of his tetrarchy they remained a minority. Thus, unlike his brothers – Archelaus and Antipas – he ruled mainly non-Jews. In addition, Philip's tetrarchy was far inferior to the regions of Archelaus and Antipas in terms of economic development and profitability. However, Philip, as a person and a ruler, turned out to be incomparably more worthy and better than his other brother-rulers. As Josephus wrote about him, "his rule was distinguished by its mildness and tranquility. He spent his whole life within the confines of the region subject to him. When he happened to travel, he did so in the company of a few chosen people. At the same time, his chair was always carried behind him, and he would sit on it to administer justice. If anyone came to him with a complaint along the way, he, without hesitation, would immediately set down the chair, sit on it, and listen to the accuser. He would immediately punish the guilty and immediately release those who had been unjustly accused" (*Antiquities of the Jews* 18.4.6).

Philip ruled for a long time, almost 38 years. He made Paneas, located at the very sources of the Jordan River in Upper Galilee, the main city of his tetrarchy. He rebuilt, improved, and decorated this city, making it a mixed Jewish-Hellenistic one. He named it Julia in honor of Emperor Augustus's wife, but in history, it is better known as Caesarea Philippi (in contrast to Herod the Great's Caesarea on the Mediterranean coast). His second creation was Bethsaida on the northern shore of Lake Kinneret. He also turned it into a Jewish-Hellenistic city.

Philip died in Julia in 34 CE and was buried there in a mausoleum that he had built for himself in advance. Since he had no children, his tetrarchy was first annexed to the Roman province of Syria, and in 37 CE, it was transferred to the Judean king Agrippa I.

Agrippa I, Judean King (37–44 CE)

Among all the grandsons and great-grandsons of Herod the Great, Agrippa I holds the most significant place. He became the Judean king and fully restored the Herodian Kingdom of Judea to its borders. Agrippa was Herod's grandson through his son Aristobulus, whom he had executed. Given that Aristobulus's mother was Mariamne the Hasmonean, Agrippa was effectively the heir of two dynasties at once: the Hasmoneans and the Herodians. He spent his childhood, adolescence, and youth in Rome, where he was raised at the imperial court alongside Drusus, the son of Emperor Tiberius. After the death of his close friend Drusus, he returned to his homeland, Judea, and lived for a time with his uncle, Tetrarch Antipas. However, not wanting to be dependent on his whims, Agrippa returned to Emperor Tiberius's palace, who at the time was living on the island of Capri. There, Agrippa so pleased the Roman emperor that he entrusted him with the upbringing of his grandson.

Later, Agrippa moved to Rome, into the circle of his eminent friends, Roman aristocrats and senators. There, he became particularly close to Gaius Julius Germanicus, nicknamed Caligula ("little boot"), the great-nephew of Emperor Tiberius. They became so friendly that Agrippa almost ruined himself by wishing for Gaius to become emperor as soon as possible. Tiberius, upon learning of this, ordered Agrippa to be imprisoned and put in chains. However, six months later, Tiberius unexpectedly died, and Gaius Caligula became the Roman emperor. The new emperor immediately freed Agrippa, giving him a golden chain equal in weight to the iron one his friend had to carry in prison. In that same year, 37 CE, Caligula granted Agrippa the title of Judean king and gave him the tetrarchy of his uncle Philip (Southern Syria and the mountains of Lebanon), who had died three years earlier. At the same time, Herod Agrippa I received another tetrarchy, Abilene, which had previously belonged to the tetrarch Lysanias. Two years later, in 39 CE, Agrippa added a third tetrarchy to his possessions – Galilee and Perea – which had belonged to his uncle, Herod Antipas. Yet even this did not mark the end of the expansion of Agrippa's kingdom. In 41 CE, when Gaius Caligula was the victim of a conspiracy by his Praetorian Guard, Agrippa was in Rome and played an important role in the negotiations between the Praetorians, who put forward Claudius as the new emperor, and the senators, who wanted to return to a republican form of government. The Roman army was divided between supporters of the former and the latter, which threatened a new civil war. Agrippa used all his connections among the Roman aristocracy to persuade the senators to accept Claudius as the new emperor, and he negotiated concessions for the senators with Claudius. A grateful Claudius not only confirmed Agrippa's royal title and his right to the previously acquired territories but also annexed Judea, Idumea, and Samaria to his kingdom, revoking direct Roman rule there. Thus, Agrippa I managed to restore the Judean kingdom as it was under Herod the Great. Furthermore, at Agrippa's request, Emperor Claudius granted his brother Herod II the neighboring kingdom of Chalcis, which occupied parts of Western Syria and Lebanon. In this way, the entire Southern Levant came under the rule of Judean kings.

As his life showed, Agrippa I successfully combined the extraordinary diplomatic skills of his grandfather, Herod the Great, on the one hand, with the patriotism of the Hasmoneans, inherited from his grandmother Mariamne, on the other. However, unlike his grandfather, Herod the Great, Agrippa did not eliminate his opponents but negotiated with them. Contemporaries described him as a gentle, kind, and magnanimous person. Josephus characterized him as follows: "This king was by nature very generous with gifts and loved to bestow them upon his subjects. Often spending significant sums on this, he earned a reputation, finding pleasure in his generosity; he believed that his life was only enhanced by it. In this, he was completely unlike his predecessor Herod [the Great]. The latter was characterized by passionate vindictiveness and an unrestrained hatred for all his opponents, while at the same time he openly admitted that his sympathies were more on the side of the Greeks than the Jews... Agrippa, on the contrary, was of a gentle character and equally generous to all. With foreigners, he was attentive and loved to bestow gifts upon them, but he also showed himself to be no less generous to his own countrymen and even tried to show them special sympathy and favor. He loved to live for long periods in Jerusalem and always carried out the prescriptions of the laws precisely. In everything, he tried to strictly observe the requirements of the ritual, and not a day passed that he did not perform the sacrifice prescribed by law" (*Antiquities of the Jews,* 19.7.3). The fact that Agrippa I meticulously observed Jewish laws and traditions is also confirmed by the Talmud, which considers him a righteous Jewish king (Mishnah, Sota, 7. 8; Bikkurim, 3. 4).

At the same time, unlike the Hasmoneans, Agrippa never forced his Hellenistic subjects to abandon paganism and adopt Jewish monotheism. Under Agrippa I, Hellenistic cities of the Judean kingdom – such as Caesarea Maritima, Jaffa, and Sebastia – regularly hosted athletic competitions and theatrical performances. New Hellenistic temples and gymnasia were constructed, while older ones continued to function. Although Agrippa himself was a convinced Jewish monotheist, he showed religious tolerance for the pagan traditions in the Hellenistic cities of his kingdom. His flexibility in matters of faith is best seen in his coinage. While in the Hellenistic cities of Judea coins were minted with portraits of the Roman emperor and the Judean king, coins from Jerusalem had no human images.

The New Testament book "Acts of the Apostles" attributes the execution of James, son of Zebedee, and the imprisonment of the Apostle Peter to Agrippa (Acts 12:1-18). However, firstly, Agrippa died in 44 CE, before the execution of James. Secondly, this contradicted Agrippa's liberal and religiously tolerant policy. Thirdly, the very nature of the execution – "killed James, the brother of John, with the sword" – indicates its non-Jewish execution. The Jews executed their heretics by stoning, while the Romans "killed with the sword" or crucified. If the execution was Roman, it occurred after Agrippa's death, when Judea once again became a Roman province. The same applies to Peter's arrest. It is therefore possible that the idea of attributing the death and imprisonment of the Christian apostles to the Jewish king Agrippa did not originate with Luke, the traditional author of *Acts,* but rather with second-century copyists who introduced anti-Jewish "revisions" and "additions" into New Testament writings that had not yet been canonized.

Unlike his grandfather, Herod the Great, Agrippa I was willing to sacrifice his well-being for the good of the Jewish people more than once. Risking his position, he was not afraid to confront Caligula and supported his people's request not to place a statue of the emperor in the Jerusalem Temple. He helped the Jews of Alexandria restore their rights, which the Hellenistic pagans had deprived them of for refusing to worship the emperor's statues. It was thanks to Agrippa's efforts that Emperor Claudius issued an edict on privileges for the Jews of Alexandria.

None of the Herodian rulers maintained such close ties with the imperial court and the Roman Senate as Herod Agrippa I. These connections placed the Jewish king in a privileged position among all of Rome's allies and client rulers in the East. The Roman governor in Syria, Gaius Vibius Mars, saw Agrippa as a dangerous rival and tried in every way to discredit him in the eyes of the emperor. For example, when Agrippa began strengthening the walls of Jerusalem, Mars sent a denunciation to the emperor, accusing him of intending to secede from Rome. Claudius regarded these works as an unnecessary "innovation" and ordered that the fortification of the walls be halted.

In 44 CE, Agrippa I organized games in Caesarea in honor of Emperor Claudius. On the second day of the festival, at a formal dinner, he felt severe stomach pains and died in terrible agony five days later. Contemporaries speculated that Agrippa, who had not been seriously ill before, was poisoned on the orders of the Roman governor Mars.

Despite his short reign (7 years), Agrippa I left a legacy as an outstanding king of Judea. During his reign, all the lands of the Southern Levant, including all the areas of historical Canaan, became part of Judea. The king himself was a brilliantly educated man for his time, who received the best Hellenistic education at the Roman imperial court and a Jewish religious one at home. According to the memoirs of his contemporaries, Agrippa could be a refined Roman among Latins, a hundred percent Hellene among Greeks, and a knowledgeable Judean in the Scriptures among his fellow Jews. He strictly observed Jewish laws and traditions and at the same time showed rare religious tolerance towards his pagan subjects in the Hellenistic cities, not limiting their Greek way of life in any way. He was a king who managed to find a reasonable compromise between two antagonists, two cultural and religious worlds: Judaism and Hellenism. He achieved what Herod the Great failed to do. Unlike the cruel violence of his grandfather, he used the power of persuasion. The Jewish people hated Herod, but they loved Agrippa. And if a premature death had not ended his reign, he would have gone down in history as the Judean king "Agrippa I the Great."

Agrippa II, Judean King (48–100 CE)

Agrippa II was the son of Agrippa I, so Emperor Claudius initially intended to transfer his father's Judean kingdom to him. However, the emperor's inner circle dissuaded him from this step, reminding him that the young Agrippa II was not yet 17 years old, "and that it would be risky to entrust a young man, barely out of childhood, with the rule of such a vast kingdom, with which it would be impossible for him to cope and which would present significant difficulties even for an adult" (*Antiquities of the Jews,* 19.9.2). Thus, Marcus Julius Agrippa II remained in the imperial palace in Rome, and direct rule by Roman procurators was introduced in the territory of the Judean kingdom.

In 48–49 CE, Agrippa II received the kingdom of Chalcis, which his uncle Herod II had ruled until his death. This was a relatively small region in southwestern Syria and Lebanon, populated mainly by Itureans and Aramaic-speaking Syrians. In addition, he was granted the royal title. So that he would not feel cut off from his native Judea, he was given the right to supervise the Jerusalem Temple and to appoint high priests. Having become convinced of his ability to successfully rule Chalcis, Emperor Claudius in 53 CE replaced the modest Chalcis (which he handed over to his cousin Aristobulus) with two large tetrarchies that had previously belonged to Lysanias and Philip. Thus, the power of Agrippa II extended to all of southwestern Syria and Lebanon, where the non-Jewish population predominated: Itureans, Phoenicians (Canaanites), and Syrians (Aramaeans). However, Agrippa made his main residence Caesarea Philippi in Upper Galilee, where the majority of the inhabitants were Jews. In 54 CE, when Emperor Nero came to power, Agrippa II received new territories: part of the former tetrarchy of Antipas, consisting of Galilee and Perea. These were purely Jewish regions, which strengthened Agrippa's image as a Jewish king. However, the main territories of the Judean kingdom: Judea, Idumea, and Samaria remained under the direct rule of Roman procurators.

Agrippa II is mentioned in the New Testament work "Acts of the Apostles," where he, while in Caesarea with the procurator of Judea Festus, spoke in defense of the Apostle Paul. Agrippa found him absolutely innocent and worthy of immediate release: "This man is doing nothing to deserve death or imprisonment." Agrippa said to Festus, "This man could have been set free if he had not appealed to the emperor" (Acts 26:31-32).

Agrippa II, like his father, was a Judean-Hellenistic king who, in the interests of his Jewish and non-Jewish subjects, constantly sought a compromise between Judaism and Hellenism. But unlike his father's vast kingdom, where Jews constituted an absolute majority, Agrippa II's possessions were much more modest, and most importantly, their population was predominantly non-Jewish. This forced the king to lean more towards Hellenism than Judaism. For example, Agrippa expanded and improved Caesarea Philippi as a Hellenistic city; he even renamed it in honor of Emperor Nero. In Berytus (Beirut), he erected a luxurious theater and paid for all the performances there at his own expense. He decorated this entire city with statues and works by ancient masters. According to Josephus, "he transferred all the splendor of his court to this very city... He spent huge sums on this. At the same time, he distributed bread and oil to the people" (*Antiquities of the Jews,* 19.9.4). As a result, his Jewish subjects were not very fond of their king, as he took all the funds from them that went to decorate a foreign Hellenistic city.

Despite this, Agrippa was considered a successful and fair ruler. However, his success and good fortune gave rise to many envious and ill-wishers among both Jews and Romans. Malicious tongues spread a rumor about his intimate relationship with his sister Berenice. This Judean princess, the daughter of Agrippa I, was of rare beauty and attracted the attention of Jewish and Roman aristocrats. At one time, the Roman emperor Titus wanted to marry her. Although the rumors of incest were not confirmed, they severely damaged Agrippa II's reputation and prevented Emperor Titus's marriage. According to contemporaries, the entire story of "incest" was invented only to prevent Titus's marriage to Berenice and to discredit Agrippa. It is possible that the fabrications about "incest" were spread by the temple priests, with whom Agrippa II constantly conflicted. The priests accused Agrippa of abusing his right to dismiss and appoint high priests of the Jerusalem Temple.

Although Agrippa was often accused of neglecting Jewish laws and traditions, as a true Jew, he demanded that the non-Jewish fiancés of his beautiful sisters Berenice and Drusilla abandon paganism and adopt Jewish monotheism. And both of them, the Pontic king Polemon II and the king of Emesa (Homs in Syria) Aziz, converted to Judaism.

The Great Jewish Revolt against Rome in 66-73 CE was a great trial for Agrippa II. Agrippa, more than anyone else, understood what calamities a war with the invincible Roman Empire would bring to the Jewish people at that time, and he did everything to avoid it. Risking his life, he rushed to Jerusalem with a small detachment of soldiers and personally addressed his angry people. However, he failed to prevent the catastrophe. Unlike his father, he did not rule over Judea and Jerusalem; all power there belonged to the Roman procurator Florus, who, trying to hide his crimes, deliberately provoked the Jews into a war with Rome. As a king dependent on Rome, Agrippa II was obliged to participate in the war against his own people. He did so formally, but he minimized his participation. To encourage his Jewish ally, Emperor Vespasian confirmed his royal title and expanded his possessions in Syria and Lebanon, but left Judea, Samaria, and Idumea under direct Roman administration.

Agrippa II reigned for a very long time, more than half a century. He died around 100 CE without children, so all his possessions were transferred to the Roman province of Syria.

Herod II, Judean King of Chalcis (41–48 CE)

Herod II was the brother of the Judean king Agrippa I and the grandson of Herod the Great, after whom he was named Herod. In 41 CE, Emperor Claudius granted him the region of Chalcis and the royal title. This was done at the request of Agrippa I, who had considerable influence on the Roman emperor. After the unexpected death of Agrippa I, his authority to supervise the Jerusalem Temple and the right to appoint high priests were transferred to his brother, Herod II.

Chalcis was a relatively small region in southwestern Syria and Lebanon, where the non-Jewish population – Itureans and Syrians – predominated. Chalcis got its name from the city of Chalcis, which was located in the Beqaa Valley, between Beirut (Berytus) and Damascus. Herod II ruled there until his death in 48 CE. After him, Chalcis was given to Agrippa II. In 57 CE, this territory was transferred to yet another Judean king, Aristobulus V, the son of Herod II. In total, Chalcis was under the rule of Jewish kings for over a century, considering that Herod the Great had also owned it. The connection of Chalcis to Jewish history began during the reign of David and Solomon (10th century BCE), when this region was part of the United Monarchy, and later, during the reign of the Israelite king Jeroboam II (8th century BCE), it became part of the Northern Kingdom.

Aristobulus V, Judean King of Chalcis and Lesser Armenia (57–92 CE)

Aristobulus V was the eldest son of Herod II, king of Chalcis. Despite this, he could not immediately inherit Chalcis after his father's death in 48 CE. First, his cousin Agrippa II ruled there, and only later, in 57 CE, did Emperor Nero return his father's kingdom to him. The wife of Aristobulus V was the famous Salome, the same one who, at the instigation of her mother Herodias, demanded the head of John the Baptist for her dance. She married Aristobulus only after the death of her first husband, Tetrarch Philip.

It is possible that Aristobulus V was not only the ruler of Chalcis but also ruled for a time (55–72 CE) in the so-called Lesser Armenia. There is historical evidence that Emperor Nero, during the Roman-Parthian war, sent Aristobulus of Chalcis to rule a part of the territory of Armenia. If it was indeed Aristobulus V, then he was only able to return to Chalcis in 72 CE and ruled it until his death in 92 CE. Although Aristobulus V left heirs, they did not receive their father's possessions, as Chalcis became part of the Roman province of Syria.

Tigranes V, Judean King of Armenia (6–12 CE)

Tigranes V was the grandson of Herod the Great through his son Alexander. He was born in 16 BCE in Jerusalem, when his powerful grandfather was still in full power. He received his Armenian name, unusual for a Jew, thanks to his mother, Glaphyra, the daughter of the king of Cappadocia. Glaphyra's mother was Armenian, in whose memory Glaphyra named her Jewish son. Perhaps this name and the Armenian origin of his grandmother played a major role in Emperor Augustus's decision to send the grandson of Herod the Great to rule in Armenia, which was a

Roman vassal state. The Jewish king began to rule in Armenia in 6 CE under the name Tigranes V. The very next year, he married Erato, the widow of the former Armenian king Tigranes IV. Erato helped the Jewish king to adapt to the foreign environment and to find common ground with the Armenian nobility. However, the reign of Tigranes V did not last long: in 12 CE, he was replaced by another Roman appointee. For several years in a row, he tried to regain the Armenian throne, but without success. Later, he returned to his native Judea and married a relative of Herod the Great, thereby proving that he had not abandoned Judaism and had not become a pagan. However, the end of Tigranes turned out to be sad: in 36 CE, he fell into disfavor with Emperor Tiberius and was executed.

Tigranes VI, Judean King of Armenia (58–63 CE)

Tigranes VI was the nephew of Tigranes V on his father's side and the great-grandson of Herod the Great. He received the name Tigranes in honor of his distinguished uncle. However, unlike his uncle, he grew up not in Judea but in Rome, in a Hellenized environment, and was known by the Roman name Gaius Julius Tigranes. His wife also came from a noble Hellenized Jewish family, originally from Phrygia (Asia Minor).

The fact that his uncle, Tigranes V, was king in Armenia influenced the fate of the young Tigranes. The Roman imperial court repeatedly sent him to that country on various missions until, finally, in 58 CE, Emperor Nero decided to grant him the royal title and send him to Armenia. However, the rule of Tigranes VI in Armenia was short-lived and ended due to an unsuccessful war with Adiabene, a small kingdom in northern Mesopotamia that was an ally of the Parthians. Tigranes VI, counting on easy prey, was the first to attack Adiabene but was repulsed and defeated. Ironically, the kings of Adiabene were as Jewish as Tigranes VI himself. The entire royal family of Adiabene had converted to Judaism and maintained close ties with Judea and Jerusalem. The war between Tigranes and Adiabene led to the intervention of Parthia:

the Parthians quickly captured Armenia and installed their own king there. This, in turn, provoked a new Roman-Parthian war and ruined the career of the Roman-Jewish king. Later, Emperor Nero intended to restore the rule of Tigranes VI, but his plans were not realized. There is no reliable information about Tigranes's subsequent fate.

Gaius Julius Alexander II, Judean King of part of Cilicia

Gaius Julius Alexander II was the son of Tigranes VI and the great-great-grandson of Herod the Great. The date of his birth is unknown. Like many Herodians, he was raised in Rome in a Hellenized environment. He married Iotape, the daughter of the Commagenian king Antiochus. The Roman emperor Vespasian granted him the royal title and the region of Cetis in Cilicia (in southern Asia Minor). The years of Alexander's reign in Cilicia are unknown. It is only known that he lost his kingdom at the end of Emperor Domitian's reign. At one time, Alexander was a Roman senator. He died in 108 or 109 CE and was probably one of the last Herodians to rule or reign in the Levant after his great-great-grandfather. Alexander was also the last of his line who considered himself a Jew or felt a connection to Judaism. Josephus wrote about this: "All the offspring of Alexander immediately upon birth abandoned their ancient Jewish customs and lived according to the model of the Greeks" (*Jewish War,* 18.5.4).

The Herodian Women: A Legacy of Fame

Although none of the women of the Herodian dynasty became queens or rulers in the Southern Levant, the names of some of them nevertheless entered world history. The most famous of them all was **Herodias**, the granddaughter of Herod the Great and the full sister of the Judean king Agrippa I. Perhaps her worldwide fame is due to the fact that she is mentioned in three Gospels at once: Mark, Matthew, and Luke. Herodias was married to her uncle Philip (Boethus) and had a daughter,

Salome, with him. This very attractive woman was at the center of three scandals. Firstly, she left her husband and married his brother, which was severely condemned by Jewish morality. Secondly, the Gospel of Mark considered her the main culprit in the execution of John the Baptist, who most of all denounced her and her new husband, Tetrarch Antipas, for violating Jewish law. And, finally, thirdly, her vanity ruined Antipas himself when she forced him to ask for a royal title and new possessions from Emperor Caligula. However, although the emperor exempted her from sharing her husband's fate, she still followed him, not considering herself entitled to abandon him when his fate changed.

28. Herodias, 1843, by Paul Delaroche.

Thanks to Herodias, her daughter **Salome** also gained worldwide fame, who with her dance so enchanted Tetrarch Antipas and his guests that he promised to fulfill her every wish. But even after that, Salome did not disappear from the stage of history. First, she married her father's namesake and brother, Tetrarch Philip, and after his death, she became the wife of another of her Herodian relatives, Aristobulus V, the Judean king of Chalcis.

No less impressive is the story of another beauty, **Berenice**, the great-granddaughter of Herod the Great, who was the daughter of the Judean king Agrippa I. Many Hellenistic authors wrote about her: Flavius Josephus, Tacitus, Juvenal, Suetonius, Dio Cassius, and Aurelius Victor. The New Testament also mentions Berenice. Her contemporaries regarded her as an exceptionally beautiful woman and, moreover, as the co-ruler of her brother, the Judean king Herod Agrippa II. Berenice captivated the Roman emperor Vespasian, and his son, the future emperor Titus, wanted to marry her. Roman aristocrats, tired of the love stories of Caesar and Antony with the Egyptian queen Cleopatra, did not want a repeat of the same with Berenice, so they gladly seized upon the malicious fabrication about her love affair with her brother Agrippa II.

Berenice was married to her uncle Herod II, the king of Chalcis. In her marriage to him, she had two sons. Upon becoming a widow, she found refuge in the palace of her brother Agrippa II. Later, she married the Pontic king Polemon II. He converted to Judaism for Berenice's sake, but this marriage also did not last long. She became a true queen only in Titus's palace in Rome. According to Roman historian Dio Cassius, "Berenice was then in her prime, and she appeared in Rome with her brother Agrippa: he was honored with the rank of praetor, and she settled on the Palatine and became intimate with Titus, with the intention of marrying him, and therefore she behaved as if she had indeed become the emperor's wife" (*Roman History*, 66.15. 3-5). But under pressure from the Roman aristocrats, Emperor Titus sent Berenice out of Rome. According to Roman historian Gaius Suetonius Tranquillus, "he did this against her and his own will" (*The Twelve Caesars. The Divine Titus*, 7). Berenice returned to her homeland in Judea, where no information about her later life has survived.

Another great-granddaughter of Herod the Great, **Drusilla**, was no less beautiful than her older sister Berenice. When their father, the king Agrippa I, died unexpectedly, Drusilla was only six years old, so their older brother, Agrippa II, took on the role of her father. It was he who found her a fiancé, Aziz, the king of Emesa (Homs). Aziz's possessions directly adjoined Agrippa II's kingdom in Syria, and Aziz, struck by Drusilla's beauty, converted to Judaism to marry her. However, their marriage lasted until the Roman procurator of Judea, Antonius Felix (52-58 CE), saw Drusilla. Captivated, like Aziz, by her extraordinary beauty, Felix did everything possible to persuade Drusilla to divorce Aziz and marry him. Drusilla agreed, which was met with condemnation in Judea. The New Testament mentions Drusilla as the wife of Felix and a witness to the speeches of the Apostle Paul before the procurator of Judea: "Some days later when Felix came with his wife Drusilla, who was Jewish, he sent for Paul and heard him speak concerning faith in Christ Jesus" (Acts 24:24). Drusilla's children settled in Italy, and one of them, Marcus Agrippa, died in Pompeii during the eruption of Vesuvius in 79 CE. It cannot be ruled out that Drusilla, who was with her son, shared his fate.

In Jewish history, the significance of the dynasty of Herod the Great has always been downplayed, and its Jewish character has been questioned, and its Idumean origin has been exaggerated. However, this contradicts historical truth. Despite the strong Hellenization and dependence on Rome, the Herodian dynasty in its spirit and character remained predominantly Jewish. The fact that the Herodians did not fight against Rome but served it does not diminish the role of this dynasty in Jewish history. Tetrarch Philip and King Agrippa I proved that, even by serving Rome, one can help one's people. The members of the dynasty of Herod the Great ruled in the Southern Levant for about 130 years, significantly longer than the Hasmoneans. Of this time, for almost half a century they ruled over the entire Southern Levant, which included historical Canaan. Their names entered Hellenistic history and left a deep mark on world culture. It should not be forgotten that the dynasty of Herod the Great represented only the core of a much more numerous group of the Jewish nobility, who are commonly called the "Herodians." These Hellenized Jewish aristocrats sought, through an honest alliance with Rome, to preserve Jewish autonomy to some extent within this vast empire. The Herodians, more than anyone else, understood that a confrontation with the then-invincible Roman Empire could lead to a national catastrophe, so they made any compromises with the Romans. As history has shown, the collaborationism of the Herodians was more beneficial to the Jewish people than the heroism of the Zealots.

4. The Merging of the Peoples of Canaan into One – the Jewish People

The Jews were the only people in the Southern Levant who managed to break free from the Seleucid Empire and, with weapons in hand, defend their freedom and independence. This fact indirectly confirmed the testimonies of Hellenistic authors about the numerousness and military strength of the Jewish people. The Maccabean wars also showed something else: by the middle of the 2nd century BCE, the Jews had become the main people of historical Canaan. Many peoples of pre-Israelite Canaan, such as the Hittites, Jebusites, Perizzites, Canaanites, Kenizzites, Kenites, southern Hivites, and Rephaim, had already merged with the southern Hebrew tribe of Judah before the Babylonian captivity and ceased to exist as separate ethnic groups. The same thing happened with the Hebrew tribes of Simeon and Benjamin, whom history brought together in the Southern – Judahite kingdom. After the fall of the Northern – Israelite kingdom in 722 BCE, almost all the Levites and many people from the northern Hebrew tribes moved to Judah.

As a result of the intermingling of all these ancient ethnic groups and tribes of Canaan, a new and numerous people emerged. This people inherited its ethnonym from the Hebrew tribe of Judah and its history and genealogy from the Hebrew tribes that conquered Canaan in the twelfth century BCE. In reality, however, the history of the autochthonous Canaanite populations that became part of the Judeans is far older than the biblical narrative and goes back to the first Neolithic cities of Canaan, which appeared eight to ten thousand years BCE.

By the beginning of the period of the Second Temple (late sixth century BCE), the Judeans consisted not so much of the direct descendants of the Hebrew tribes as of a mixed population – an amalgam of all the ethnic groups and tribes of Canaan, among whom the original Hebrews occupied only a modest place. The largest southern Hebrew tribe, Judah, became the nucleus that drew to itself the peoples and tribes of southern Canaan, even as it gradually merged with them. Thus, the Judeans evolved into a pan-Canaanite people – the legitimate heirs of all the ethnic groups and tribes that had ever lived in Canaan.

However, the ethnogenesis of the Jewish people did not end there. The Babylonian captivity and the return from it ended with the merger with yet another people – the Moabites. This Transjordanian people, a part of whom ended up in Babylonian captivity along with the Jews, was literally driven out of their land by the Nabataean tribes advancing from the south. The majority of the Moabites went to neighboring Judea, where, having accepted Jewish monotheism, they mixed with the Jews. Another Transjordanian people, the Ammonites, managed to hold on to their territory, but a part of them, having converted to Judaism, also merged with the Jews.

At that time, Judea, as Hellenistic historians like Philo and Josephus testified, was very densely populated, possibly even much more than it is today. It is no coincidence that the Macedonian general Ptolemy I Soter, who founded his dynasty in Egypt, found it possible to resettle over a hundred thousand Jews to Alexandria and the Nile Valley. The high population density and land shortage in Judea itself led to both the migration of Jews to Galilee and Transjordan (Gilead and Perea) and the Jewish diaspora in the Hellenistic world. The fact of the mass migration of Jews to Galilee, Gilead, and the port cities of the Southern Levant is indirectly confirmed by the First and Second Books of Maccabees. The military campaigns of Judah Maccabee there were caused by the need to protect his tribesmen and co-religionists from pagan attacks. It is quite possible that by "pagans," the authors of the Maccabean books meant not only foreigners but also the descendants of the northern Hebrew tribes.

There has long been a debate in the academic world about the origin of the Jewish population north of Judea – in Galilee and in Transjordan (Gilead and Perea), that is, in the territory of the former Kingdom of Israel. According to one point of view, the Jewish population of these regions was formed as a result of the mixture of the descendants of the Hebrew tribes with the remnants of the local Canaanites and Amorites. Another point of view is that the territories of Galilee and northern Transjordan were completely devastated as a result of the Assyrian invasions in the second half of the 8th century BCE, and the Hebrew population of these places was partially taken to Assyria and partially fled south to Judea. This second version is based on the complete depopulation of all the regions of the Kingdom of Israel and actually supports the myth of the disappearance of the ten Israelite tribes. Supporters of this concept believe that the Jewish population of Galilee, the Golan, and Transjordan was formed only due to the mass migration of the population of Judea to the devastated territories of the former Kingdom of Israel.

Perhaps only the fact of the mass migration of the population of Judea to the areas of the former Kingdom of Israel is indisputable. This happened over several centuries, both BCE and CE, albeit for different reasons. Confirmation of this can even be found in the New Testament. Jesus's parents, Mary and Joseph, who settled in Galilean Nazareth, were Jewish migrants from Bethlehem in Judea. Their status as Jewish migrants in Galilee is confirmed by the Gospel of Luke. According to the census rules established by Quirinius, the Roman governor in Syria, every person had to return to the city of their birth: "In those days a decree went out from Caesar Augustus that all the world should be registered. This was the first registration and was taken while Quirinius was governor of Syria. All went to their own towns to be registered. Joseph also went from the town of Nazareth in Galilee to Judea, to the city of David called Bethlehem, because he was descended from the house and family of David. He went to be registered with Mary, to whom he was engaged and who was expecting a child" (Luke 2:1-5).

While the migration of Judeans to the territory of the former Kingdom of Israel cannot be doubted, the claim of the complete depopulation of Galilee and northern Transjordan does not hold up to any criticism. This also contradicts Assyrian written sources. While the Assyrian king Tiglath-Pileser III reported the deportation of 13,500 people from Galilee and Gilead, and his successor, Sargon II, deported another 27,290 residents of Samaria to Assyria, all these losses combined do not exceed 5%, or at most 10%, of the total population of the Kingdom of Israel at that time. Archaeological excavations do not and cannot confirm the version of the total depopulation of all of Galilee and northern Transjordan. The destruction of many Israelite cities by the Assyrians did not mean the physical extermination of their inhabitants, especially since the Assyrians were interested not in extermination but in robbing the population. The fact that the majority of the inhabitants of the Kingdom of Israel remained in their places is also confirmed by the Old Testament, which states that the Judahite king Hezekiah invited all of them to Jerusalem and accepted some of them there to celebrate Passover together. And this was after all the Assyrian deportations! From this whole version of depopulation, one can only accept that there was enough free land on the territory of the former Kingdom of Israel to attract migrants from overpopulated Judea. Moreover, after the fall of the Northern Kingdom, which was hostile to Judea, no one else prevented them from doing so. Thus, migrants from Judea, like Joseph and Mary from Nazareth, represented only a part of the population of Galilee, the Golan, and Transjordan; the rest of the inhabitants of these regions were descendants of the northern Hebrew tribes, as well as Canaanites and Amorites. In Upper Galilee and the Golan, there was also another ethnic group – Arameans.

The difficulties with the merger of Jews and non-Jews began around the 5th century BCE, when Judaism became a truly monotheistic religion, and Judea became the only country in the ancient world where monotheism reigned supreme. The laws of Ezra and Nehemiah, adopted in the mid-5th century BCE, forbade Jews from marrying pagans. Marriages were only possible with those who renounced their paganism and accepted Jewish monotheism. From this time on, Jewish migrants could mix with the inhabitants of the former Kingdom of Israel only through their Judaization. The archaic monotheism of the Samaritans and the descendants of the northern Hebrew tribes was clearly insufficient for the Judeans, who were consistent monotheists, and was considered by them as a variant of paganism. This is what Josephus meant when he emphasized that although the Samaritans were Jews, they were not Judeans. To protect the Judeans from "pagans," the Maccabean army carried out military campaigns in Galilee and Gilead, and if the threat to the lives of the Jews persisted, they took them back to Judea. Obviously, despite the migration of Jews there, the process of Judaization of the former Israelites was slow, and even in the middle of the 2nd century BCE, when the Maccabean wars took place, it was far from complete.

The situation changed radically after Judea gained independence from the Seleucid kingdom and began to conquer the territories of the former Kingdom of Israel. The Hasmonean rulers demanded the same thing from the population of all newly acquired regions: either renounce paganism and accept Jewish monotheism, or leave the lands of monotheistic Judea. The Hasmonean kings, being simultaneously high priests, did not allow any idolatry in their country. Any manifestations of sorcery or black magic, so characteristic of pagans, were punished by death. It was during the reign of the Hasmoneans (142–37 BCE) that the final Judaization of Galilee, Idumea, Gilead, the Golan, and Perea took place. Thus, the population of the former Kingdom of Israel became Judeans. Concessions were made only for the Samaritans, but even their temple on Mount Gerizim was destroyed as "pagan." The inhabitants of not only the southern part of the country, Judea and

Idumea, but also its north – Galilee and the Golan – as well as Gilead and Perea (Transjordan) began to identify themselves as Judeans. The term "Judean" came to serve both as an ethnic and a religious designation. From then on, all who professed monotheism – including the former Israelites – regarded themselves as Judeans. The ethnonym *ivri* (Hebrew) became synonymous with the name *yehudi* (Judean), which in turn signified faith in the one Lord and absolute rejection of idolatry. Thus, the name of one of the Hebrew tribes (Judah) became the name not only of an entire people (Judeans) and their land (Judea), but also of the only monotheistic religion of that time – Judaism.

The situation changed with the beginning of the Herodian rule. Neither Herod the Great (37–4 BCE), nor his son Archelaus (4 BCE–6 CE), nor his grandson, the Judean king Agrippa I (37–44 CE), nor even his great-grandson, the Judean king Agrippa II (48–100 CE), demanded that their subjects renounce paganism and compulsorily accept Jewish monotheism. Other Herodians – the tetrarchs (rulers of a quarter) Antipas and Philip – also did not demand this. Under their rule were not only areas inhabited by Jews but also all of Southern Syria and the mountains of Lebanon, where many non-Jews lived, for example, Itureans and Aramaic-speaking Syrians. However, unlike the Hasmoneans, the Herodians did not force anyone to renounce their pagan cults and accept monotheism. This dynasty was a carrier of predominantly Greco-Roman culture, and its rule expressed the interests of the Roman Empire. Unlike the Hasmoneans, the Herodians were never high priests and did not even claim this post.

Although the process of Judaization slowed down under the Herodians, it still did not stop even during their reign. The best example of this is the complete Judaization of the Golan region during the reign of Herod the Great. Knowing his people's hostility toward him, Herod did not trust the Jews of Judea and tried to rely on the Jews of the diaspora, who were incomparably more loyal to him. Based on this, he invited many thousand Jewish families from Babylonia and settled them on the free lands of the Golan and Southern Syria – in Batanea, Trachonitis, and Hauran, which also belonged to the Judean kingdom at that time. These settlers were used by him in two ways: as skilled farmers and as a reliable reserve for his army. Perhaps the Golan has never flourished as much in its history as it did during the reign of Herod the Great. It was during his reign that the complete Judaization of the Golan and partly of all of Southern Syria took place, although no one, unlike in the time of the Hasmoneans, forced the local population to accept Jewish monotheism. Perhaps the very fact of the presence of Jewish rule for many years played a role in the Judaization of the population of these territories. After all, Southern Syria and the mountains of Lebanon, not to mention the Golan proper, were transferred by Rome to the rule of only the descendants of Herod the Great – Philip, Herod II, the Judean kings Agrippa I and Agrippa II, and also Aristobulus V. The Jewish character of the Golan territory and its population was once again confirmed during the First Jewish-Roman War (66–73 CE) – the Great Jewish Revolt against Roman rule in Judea. The Golan, like neighboring Galilee, put up stubborn resistance to the Roman army, then led by Vespasian Flavius, the future emperor of the Roman Empire. The Jews from the city of Gamla in the Golan fought especially fiercely. As Josephus, a direct participant in this war, testified, in the battle with them, the Roman legionaries suffered heavy losses, and moreover, Vespasian himself miraculously survived. Subsequently, the Jewish defenders of Gamla, surrounded by forces of the Romans that were many times superior, chose to commit suicide rather than surrender to the enemies.

The Judaization of the population in the territories of the former Kingdom of Israel occurred quickly enough only if the majority of the inhabitants were descendants of the Hebrew tribes or related West Semitic peoples – Canaanites, Amorites, or Arameans. A completely different picture was observed in the Hellenistic cities of the Decapolis in Transjordan and the Mediterranean ports of Coele-Syria. There, the tone was set by the Greco-Macedonian elite and by numerous settlers from Asia Minor, Cyprus, Crete, and the Aegean islands. Although the Judean king Alexander Jannaeus conquered all the cities of the

Decapolis, most of their inhabitants did not accept Jewish monotheism and remained pagans. The same can be said about the Mediterranean cities of former Philistia. They were conquered even earlier by the Judean rulers Simon and his son Johanan Hyrcanus, but even after coming under the rule of Judea, they remained Hellenistic. And this was despite the presence of large Jewish communities in these cities. In general, the more significant the Greco-Macedonian elite was in a given Hellenistic city, the more stubbornly it resisted Judaization. In this regard, of all the Mediterranean ports, Ptolemais (Akko) turned out to be the most hostile city for the Jews. Alexander Jannaeus besieged it several times, but was unable to take it. The Hasmoneans failed to subdue it by force, and the Herodians were likewise unable to obtain it from the Romans through diplomacy.

Samaria, which represented the central part of Western Canaan, also avoided Judaization. This region, which was the historical center of the "House of Joseph" and the tribal territory of the main northern tribe of Ephraim, became home to a new people – the Samaritans, who considered themselves descendants of the Israelites. The Samaritans originally adhered to Jewish monotheism, which, however, was significantly different from the Judean one, which was much more advanced and consistent. Be that as it may, the Hasmoneans did not pursue a policy of Judaization there, limiting themselves only to the destruction of the Samaritan temple on Mount Gerizim, a rival to the Jerusalem Temple.

Hasmonean Judea considered itself the legitimate heir to both Hebrew kingdoms – Israel and Judah – so its rulers considered it their duty to reconquer all the territories that in the past belonged to these kingdoms and were inhabited by the descendants of the Hebrew tribes. By the end of the reign of the Judean king Alexander Jannaeus, most of the regions of historical Canaan were under the rule of Hasmonean Judea. Only the eastern part of Transjordan remained unconquered, in the north of which was Ammon, subject to the Seleucids, and in the south – the lands of Edom, captured by the Nabataeans. Ammon was a traditional tributary of the Kingdom of Israel, and Edom – of Judah.

Both of these West Semitic peoples were the closest relatives of the Hebrews and came to Canaan with them as part of the tribal group of the biblical patriarch Abraham. The heirs of Alexander Jannaeus would have completed the conquest of historical Canaan if not for the arrival of the Romans in Syria and Judea. The Romans stopped the territorial expansion of Judea, and moreover, they tore away the Hellenistic cities of the Decapolis and the Mediterranean coast from it. However, they could not stop the process of the Judaization of historical Canaan. The migration of the Jewish population to all regions of Canaan continued until the beginning of the Great Revolt against Rome in 66 CE. The process of the formation of the Jewish people as a pan-Canaanite nation, which actively began after the Maccabean wars, continued for about two centuries and was interrupted only because of the Jewish-Roman wars.

Whereas the United Monarchy of David and Solomon's time represented a multi-ethnic, pan-Canaanite power, Hasmonean Judea, which dominated most of historical Canaan, was already a mono-ethnic state of the Judeans. However, the Judean people of the Hasmonean kingdom in the 2nd-1st centuries BCE were already fundamentally different from the Hebrew tribes who conquered Canaan in the 12th century BCE, because they had incorporated all the peoples of that land and become their legitimate successor. The merging of all the peoples of historical Canaan into a single nation – the Jewish people – took place over the course of the first millennium BCE. The Hebrew tribe of Judah became the core of this pan-Canaanite people, and Jewish monotheism served as the centripetal force.

Another center of ethnogenesis – the "House of Joseph" – was more numerous and stronger than the tribe of Judah, but it was weakened and ultimately deprived of a future by its adherence to polytheism. How can one not remember the biblical prophet Hosea, who said: "When Ephraim spoke, there was trembling; he was exalted in Israel, but he incurred guilt through Baal and died" (Hosea 13:1). Judean monotheism became the decisive force that revived Judea after the Babylonian conquest and exile, whereas the polytheism of the Northern Kingdom failed to enable the "House of Joseph" to withstand the Assyrian invasion and the ensuing deportations. The superiority of Judean monotheism over the more archaic Samaritan faith once again proved to be a key factor in the Judeans' triumph over the Samaritans in the struggle to unify historical Canaan. Following the reforms of Ezra and Nehemiah, Judean monotheism forbade intermarriage with pagans – thus preventing the Jews from dissolving among other nations – yet it remained open to all who were willing to renounce idolatry. It became a kind of iron curtain: impenetrable from within, but open to anyone ready to abandon paganism. Samaritan monotheism, by contrast, possessed no such power. Judean monotheism, instead, became a gravitational center that, while holding its own people firmly within, continuously drew others toward itself.

The descendants of the northern Hebrew tribes were the first and fastest to undergo Judaization. Despite the enduring myth of their total deportation to Assyria, most of them in fact remained in Galilee and Transjordan (Gilead and Perea). They were followed by related West Semitic peoples of Canaanite and Amorite origin. Despite the contradictory statements of the biblical books regarding the "extermination" or "expulsion" of these populations, all of them not only remained in their lands but eventually became an integral part of the Jewish people. The Samaritans were an exception – but only because they were not permitted to merge with the Judean population. This exclusion was purely political: the Samaritans regarded themselves as the heirs of the "House of Joseph," the same lineage that had long challenged the leadership of the tribe of Judah. Owing to their enduring conflict with Jerusalem, the Samaritans, though Jews by origin, never became Judeans.

Hellenistic authors offered varying estimates of the size of the Jewish population, but the figures they cited generally ranged between five and eleven million. Most modern historians agree that on the eve of the Jewish War – the first revolt of the Jews against Rome (66–73 CE) – there were approximately eight million Jews throughout the ancient world, about five million of whom lived in Judea itself. By the beginning of the

Great Revolt, the Jewish people effectively dominated most of the territory of historical Canaan, both west and east of the Jordan River. Yet by the dawn of the Common Era, they were no longer merely the heirs of the biblical Hebrews – from Abraham to Moses. Over time, they had absorbed nearly all the ethnic groups and tribes that had once inhabited ancient Canaan and had become their sole legitimate successor – a truly pan-Canaanite people.

CHAPTER VIII.

Wars with the Roman Empire and Their Demographic Consequences

1. The Great Jewish Revolt (66–73 CE)

After the unexpected death of Judean King Agrippa I in 44 CE, his vast kingdom was transformed into a Roman province, governed by procurators appointed by Rome. This position was sold to the highest bidder. A candidate would pay a substantial sum for the coveted post, and after purchasing it, would rush to not only recoup their expenses but also profit as much as possible. However, during the reigns of Emperors Claudius (41–54 CE) and Nero (54–68 CE), the terms of service for procurators in Judea were significantly shortened. This made each new Roman official who bought the post eager to get rich as quickly as possible, by any means necessary.

The procurators' immense greed and corruption fostered an atmosphere of lawlessness and arbitrariness. The worst offenders were Lucceius Albinus (62–64 CE) and Gessius Florus (64–66 CE). As their contemporary and a witness to their crimes, the Roman-Jewish historian Flavius Josephus writes: "There was no wickedness that Albinus did not commit. He not only stole public funds and confiscated the property of many private citizens, but he also burdened the entire populace with unbearable taxes. Furthermore, he would release criminals from prison for a fee... Only those who couldn't pay remained incarcerated... But Albinus was a model of virtue compared to his successor, Gessius Florus. While the former committed his crimes mostly in secret and with caution, Gessius flaunted his crimes openly to the entire nation. He engaged in all sorts of robberies and acts of violence, behaving as if he had been sent as an executioner for the condemned. In his cruelty, he was ruthless; in his audacity, shameless. No one before him was so skilled at cloaking truth with falsehood or inventing such convoluted paths to achieve his treacherous goals. Enriching himself at the expense of individuals seemed too petty; he plundered entire cities and utterly ruined whole communities. It was as if he was on the verge of proclaiming throughout the land: 'Anyone can rob wherever they please, as long as they share the spoils with me.' Entire districts were depopulated because of his greed; many abandoned their ancestral homes and fled to other provinces" (*Jewish War*, 2.14.1-2).

Complaints about Florus to the Roman governor of Syria, Cestius Gallus, greatly alarmed the procurator. To save himself from inevitable retribution, he did everything he could to provoke the Jewish people into rebellion against Rome. "In a war with the Jews," Josephus wrote, "he saw the only means of concealing his lawlessness. For as long as there was peace, he would always have to be ready for the Jews to complain about him to the emperor. But if he could instigate an open rebellion, he could hope that a greater evil would distract them from exposing a lesser on" (*Jewish War*, 2.14.3). As a direct witness and participant in these events, Josephus believed that "Florus was the one who compelled us to go to war with the Romans" (*Antiquities of the Jews* 20.11.1). Notably, even the Roman historian Tacitus was forced to admit that "still the Jews' patience lasted until Gessius Florus became procurator: in his time war began" (*Histories*, 5.10.1).

Another chronic problem during the 40s to 60s CE were the constant clashes between Jews and Syrians in the Hellenistic cities of Judea. The non-native, pagan population refused to respect the unique aspects of Jewish monotheism and, enjoying the support of the

Roman garrison (which was mostly recruited from the same Syrians of Caesarea and Sebaste), behaved provocatively towards the Judeans, who were the original inhabitants of the country. Conflicts between the Jews and Hellenized Syrians most often occurred in Caesarea, a Mediterranean city that served as the residence of the Roman procurator. The composition of the Roman garrisons in Judea also deepened the conflict between Jews and pagans. As a rule, the legionaries for these garrisons were not recruited from distant Italy, but from local Hellenized Syrians who did not have Roman citizenship. Being Aramaeans by origin, that is, Western Semites, they spoke practically the same language as the Jews and did not differ from them in appearance. However, despite their ethnic and linguistic closeness, the two peoples were divided by a long-standing feud. And the reason for this was not rooted in religion, although the Syrians were pagans and the Jews were monotheists, but in history. The conflict was tied to a centuries-old struggle between Israel and Aram-Damascus. These same Syrians also formed the bulk of the Seleucid armies that attacked Judea during the Maccabean wars. Josephus emphasized that even Alexander Jannaeus, a Judean king who created a large army of foreign mercenaries, "never employed Syrians due to their innate national animosity toward the Jews" (*Jewish War,* 1.4.3). Even Herod the Great, known for his reliance on foreigners, also never recruited Syrians. Yet it was these very Syrians who constituted the overwhelming majority of soldiers in the Roman garrisons of Judea. Taking advantage of their status as Roman legionaries, the Syrians often deliberately provoked the Jewish people into conflicts, especially during holidays when pilgrims flocked to Jerusalem from all over the country. The situation was further complicated by the fact that a significant portion of the inhabitants of the so-called Hellenistic cities in Judea, such as Caesarea, were also Syrians. When clashes occurred in Caesarea between the Jewish and Hellenistic populations, as Josephus testifies, although "in wealth and brave strength the Jews surpassed their enemies, the Hellenes had the advantage that the soldiers were on their side, since most of the Roman garrison stationed in the city consisted of Syrians, who were always ready to help their fellow countrymen" (*Jewish War*, 2.13.7).

In 66 CE, the Hellenistic residents of Caesarea managed to get an edict from Emperor Nero who effectively declared them the owners of the city. This fatal decision by Nero emboldened the Caesarean pagans to provoke the Jews: they defiantly offered sacrifices to their idols right in front of the synagogue door. The Roman procurator Florus, an Asia Minor Greek from the city of Clazomenae, ignored the Jews' outrage and openly supported the Hellenistic population, which was close to him in spirit and culture. On the pretext that the emperor needed money, he ordered seventeen talents of silver to be taken from the treasury of the Jerusalem Temple. As it turned out later, he simply appropriated the money for himself. To intimidate the protesting Jerusalemites, he ordered his soldiers to plunder several quarters of the city and slaughter all their inhabitants, sparing neither women nor children (*Jewish War*, 2.14.9). Thus, Jerusalem was on the brink of an anti-Roman revolt.

At this moment, the Judean King Agrippa II rushed to the city. Unlike his father, Agrippa I, he had no authority over Jerusalem or Judea, but he understood the terrible consequences that a war with Rome could bring. He tried to persuade the people not to take up arms against this invincible empire. "At a time when almost all peoples under the sun bow before the arms of the Romans, you alone want to wage war with them... Countless nations, inspired by an even greater desire for freedom, submit; only you consider it a shame to be subject to the one at whose feet the whole world lies..." He warned the Jerusalemites that "it is not worth hoping that when the Romans conquer you, they will rule over you mercifully. No, to intimidate other peoples they will reduce the holy city to ashes and wipe your entire race off the face of the earth; for even he who escapes will find no refuge, since all peoples are either subject to the Romans or fear falling under their dominion" (*Jewish War*, 2.16.4). However, when the king began to urge the Jerusalemites to obey Florus until the emperor sent a successor to replace him, this angered the people again. Led by radicals (Zealots and Sicarii), the rebels refused to listen to the king, massacred the Roman garrison, burned the palaces of the Jerusalem nobility and the debt archives, and then found and killed the high priest. Thus began the Great Revolt of the Jews against the Roman Empire, or as the Romans called it, the Jewish War.

The main Roman army forces in the East were then stationed on the western bank of the Euphrates and were intended for military operations against the Parthian Empire. News of the uprising in Judea forced the Roman governor of Syria, Cestius Gallus, to turn all these legions against the Jewish rebels. On his way to Judea, he added detachments from numerous vassals to his army, including soldiers of Agrippa II. However, despite such an impressive force, the assault on Jerusalem in 66 CE ended in failure. Cestius Gallus decided to lift the siege of the city and temporarily retreat to the friendly Hellenistic city of Caesarea. The Jewish rebels followed on the heels of the retreating Roman army, engaging in fierce battles with the legionaries and their allies every day. Finally, a decisive battle took place in the Beth Horon gorge, as a result of which the "invincible" Roman legions were utterly defeated by the Jewish rebels. Liberated Judea regained its sovereignty and became independent.

In early 67 CE, Emperor Nero entrusted the empire's best general, Vespasian Flavius, with the task of suppressing the revolt and restoring Roman rule in Judea. Having received unlimited authority from the emperor, Vespasian selected 60,000 of the most experienced soldiers from the most combat-ready Roman legions and with this elite army, he crossed over to Hellenistic Ptolemais (Acre). The armies of Rome's Asia Minor, Syrian, and Nabatean vassals also came to his aid. "In addition, a strong auxiliary corps was also formed from the kings: Antiochus, Agrippa, and Sohem each provided 2,000 foot archers and 1,000 horsemen; the Arabian Malchus sent 1,000 horsemen and 5,000 infantrymen – mostly archers... This did not include the colossal supply train that followed" (*Jewish War,* 3.4.2). Ptolemais, known for its hostility to the Jews, became the main stronghold and base for the Romans' offensive on Galilee and Golan.

However, it took Vespasian almost the entire year of 67 CE to capture the northern part of the country. Due to the strong resistance of the Jewish population, the Romans had to storm almost every city. Particularly fierce battles took place at the cities of Jotapata (Yodfat), Tarichaea (Magdala), Gischala (Gush Halav), and Gamla. At Gamla, Vespasian himself nearly died, so fiercely did its defenders fight. Moreover, "Vespasian was very depressed by the losses the army had suffered: such misfortune had never befallen it anywhere else" (*Jewish War,* 4.1.6). When the residents of Gamla realized they could not hold their city, they committed suicide rather than surrender to the enemy, throwing themselves into a ravine. "Many, in despair, embracing their wives and children, threw themselves with them into the bottomless abyss yawning beneath the fortress... No one was left alive except two women... They saved themselves by hiding from the fury of the Romans, for the latter did not even spare infants: they seized many such babies and threw them down from the height of the fortress" (*Jewish War,* 4.1.10).

The fact that the Romans had to spend a whole year to take control of the northern part of the country attested to both the large Jewish population of Galilee and Golan and the serious nature of their resistance to the Romans. Irritated by the Jews' stubborn resistance, "the Romans, without rest day or night, devastated the fields, plundered the property of the peasants, killed those capable of bearing arms, and sold the weaker ones into slavery" (*Jewish War,* 3.4.1). The defense of the city of Jotapata was then led by the commander of the Galilean rebels, Yoseph ben-Matityahu. Taken prisoner by the Romans, he was pardoned and later became close to the imperial Flavian family. Even later, he became known as the Roman-Jewish historian Flavius Josephus. The world owes its knowledge of the Jewish War and Judea of that time to his works.

At the beginning of the next year, 68 CE, Vespasian intended to march on the Judean capital. However, fierce clashes between radical and moderate rebel groups in Jerusalem, between the Zealots on one side and the aristocrats on the other, led him to decide to wait with the offensive to allow the rebels to weaken each other as much as possible.

"All the Roman commanders saw in the dissension of the enemy an unexpected stroke of luck for themselves and wanted to immediately attack the city. They also urged this upon Vespasian, for whom, they thought, almost everything was already won." However, Vespasian objected: "If you now descend on the city, you will thereby cause a reconciliation among the enemies and turn their still unbroken force against us; but if you wait, the number of enemies will decrease, as they will be devoured by internal war... While the enemy weakens itself, my army will rest from military labors and become even stronger" (*Jewish War*, 4.6.2).

Meanwhile, Idumean detachments came to Jerusalem to help the Zealots, and together they overcame the moderates, killing the Jerusalem nobility led by Hanan ben-Hanan. "12,000 men of noble birth" were killed by the Zealots during their clashes with the moderates in Jerusalem (*Jewish War*, 4.5.3). Power in the city passed to the Zealot leaders: John of Gischala and Simon bar-Giora. An even more radical part of the rebels, the Sicarii, led by Menahem, the son of Judas the Galilean, and his relative Eleazar ben-Yair, tried to seize power in Jerusalem at the very beginning of the revolt, but were defeated and took refuge in the fortress of Masada. While the rebels fought among themselves in Jerusalem, Vespasian sent his legions to "pacify" Transjordan, Idumea, and the cities of the Mediterranean coast. In essence, the war with the Romans was happening at the same time as a civil war among the Jews themselves. This is how Josephus, a direct witness and participant in this war, described the situation at the time: "In every city, unrest and civil strife began. As soon as these people breathed freely from the Roman yoke, they already took up arms against each other. Those who craved war fought fiercely with the friends of peace. At first, the struggle flared up between families that had long been at odds; but soon, friendly families also fell apart; everyone joined their like-minded supporters, and in a short time, they stood against each other in huge parties. Thus, civil strife was in full swing everywhere" (*Jewish War*, 4.3.2).

In the summer of 68 CE, military operations in Judea unexpectedly came to a halt: news arrived from Rome about the death of Emperor

Nero and a struggle for power among the contenders for the imperial throne. Vespasian, having his own claims to the throne, decided to save his strength and postponed the siege of Jerusalem. After the deaths of three contenders for the throne, Vespasian, taking advantage of the fact that he had the best forces of the Roman army at his disposal, proclaimed himself emperor in June 69 CE. All the Roman legions in the East immediately supported their general; later, support was also received from the rest of the army. Having become emperor, Vespasian immediately went to Rome and appointed his son Titus Flavius to command the Roman army in Judea, sending him four more legions for support.

In the spring of 70 CE, Roman troops began the siege of Jerusalem. The huge Roman army and its allies were opposed by about twenty thousand Zealots, among whom there was still no unity. "Even when the Romans were already encamped under the walls of Jerusalem, the civil war did not cease" (*Jewish War,* 5.6.1). The supporters of John of Gischala were openly at odds with the followers of Simon bar-Giora. While the former fought only for the freedom of Judea, the latter also put forward social demands, which brought them closer to the even greater radicals, the Sicarii. As Josephus, a participant in this siege, testified, "the Romans possessed power along with experience; on the side of the Jews was a boldness strengthened by despair and their inherent endurance in misfortune... Neither side knew fatigue; attacks, skirmishes near the walls, sorties in small groups took place continuously throughout the day, and no form of combat remained untried... Both sides spent the nights under arms, and with the first gleam of morning light, they already stood against each other ready for battle. The Jews always vied with each other for the right to be the first to rush into danger... The Jews did not mourn the losses they incurred in the least. All their thoughts and efforts were directed at inflicting losses on their part. Death seemed to them a trifle if they could, while dying, also kill an enemy" (*Jewish War,* 5.7.3). To intimidate the Jews and "compel them to submit," the Romans executed everyone they captured, crucifying them on crosses in full view of the city. "The number of the crucified so increased that there was no room for the crosses and no crosses for the bodies" (*Jewish War*, 5.11.1).

The Roman historian Cassius Dio testified to the huge losses of the Roman army near Jerusalem and that "Titus himself was struck by a stone in his left shoulder, so that his left arm was weaker ever since... Meanwhile, some other Romans, exhausted, as happens during a long siege, and moreover, suspecting that the talk about the inaccessibility of the city was true, themselves defected to the enemy, and the Jews, although constrained by a lack of provisions, welcomed them, so as to show that people were fleeing to them as well" (*Roman History*, 66.5.4).

Unable to take the city by storm, the Romans decided to first starve it into submission. This was not difficult, since a great number of pilgrims had gathered in Jerusalem. According to Josephus, "most of them were not originally from Jerusalem; for people from all over the country flocked to the capital for the Feast of Unleavened Bread (Passover) and were unexpectedly overtaken by the war, so that the density of the population first gave rise to a plague, and soon after, a famine... Every day, the famine, growing ever stronger, claimed whole houses and families from the people. The rooftops were covered with emaciated women and children, and the streets with dead old men. Boys and youths, sickly swollen, wandered like ghosts through the city squares and fell to the ground where they were overtaken by death from starvation" (*Jewish War*, 5.12.3). Defectors from the "upper class" estimated the number of poor people who had died at 600,000, while the number of "other" victims of the famine remained unknown (*Jewish War*, 5.13.7; 6.9.3). Those who managed to escape the city became victims of the barbarism and greed of the auxiliary troops – Arabs and Syrians – who, in the hope of finding gold, cut open the bellies of the fugitives. These crimes became so widely known that even Titus himself, the commander of the Roman army and future emperor, accused the Arabs and Syrians of "unparalleled bloodlust and hatred for the Jews" (*Jewish War*, 5.13.4-5).

Josephus noted an interesting detail: "The misfortunes of the besieged Jews led to a greater loss of spirit among the Romans than among the inhabitants of the city themselves. For the latter, despite their most terrible hardships, did not lose their resilience in the least and each time thwarted the hopes of the enemy, successfully opposing the erected ramparts with cunning, the battering rams with strong walls, and in hand-to-hand combat, with frantic courage. Seeing this strength of spirit that the Jews possessed and which elevated them above internal strife, famine, war, and other misfortunes, the Romans began to consider their thirst for battle as insurmountable and their courage in enduring misfortune as inexhaustible" (*Jewish War*, 6.1.2).

The defense of Jerusalem held out for five months. Almost all the defenders of the city died in battle, refusing to surrender. Cassius Dio, always on the side of the Romans, described the end of the assault as follows: "And even though there were not so many Jews and they fought against a many times superior enemy force, they could not be overcome until the Temple itself caught fire. Then they sought death, some throwing themselves on Roman swords, others taking their own lives or throwing themselves into the fire. Everyone thought that to perish with the Temple was not death, but victory, salvation, and happiness" (*Roman History*, 66. 6. 2-3).

The Romans captured only civilians, mostly women and children, and sold them into slavery. "Titus ordered the entire city and the Temple to be razed to the ground... The destroyers so leveled it with the surface of the earth that a traveler could hardly recognize that these places were once inhabited. Such was the end of this magnificent, world-famous city... The sight of the entire land was sorrowful. The country that had previously prided itself on its tree plantations and parks was now everywhere devastated and deforested. Of the foreigners who knew the former Judea and the magnificent suburbs of Jerusalem, none could hold back their tears at the sight of the desolation at that time and from expressing grief over this terrible change" (*Jewish War*, 7.1.1; 6.1.1).

29. Roman warriors carry the Menorah from Jerusalem Temple.
The Arch of Titus in Rome.

In 71 CE, a triumphal procession was held in Rome in honor of Vespasian and Titus, during which captured Jews were paraded through the city and sacred utensils from the Jerusalem Temple, including a huge golden menorah (seven-branched candelabrum), were carried. Later, Roman masters immortalized this procession with the menorah from the Temple on the Arch of Titus, which has survived to this day in Rome.

The Jewish War did not end with the destruction of Jerusalem and the Temple in 70 CE. Jewish rebels continued to hold some of the most important fortresses in the country, and above all, Masada, Herodium, and Machaerus. Masada held out the longest, its defense lasting until 73 CE. Thanks to the works of Josephus, we know the fate of Masada, which was defended by the Sicarii of Eleazar ben Yair. When, after a long siege, the fall of the fortress became inevitable, Eleazar ben Yair called on his warriors and their families to prefer death to slavery. "Let our wives die undefiled, and our children – who have not yet known slavery… then our preserved freedom will be our honorable shroud… Let us die without experiencing the slavery of our enemies, as free men, together with our wives and children, let us part with life… The Romans cherish the sweet dream of taking us captive, but we will make them shudder at the picture of our death and be astonished at our courage" (*Jewish War,* 7.8.7). The rebels first took the lives of their wives and children, and then committed suicide. When the Romans broke into the fortress, they found only 960 dead bodies. Later, they found two women and five children who had hidden in an underground aqueduct. It was they who told the Romans what had happened.

The reasons for the rebels' defeat were no secret. The Judean King Agrippa II had warned them from the very beginning, reminding everyone of the enormous military might of the Roman Empire, which no people of the ancient world could resist at that time. Worse, the Jews had to fight not only the Romans and their local vassals but also each other, as shown by the strife among the rebels in Jerusalem. And finally, as the commander of the Roman army Titus Flavius noted, "although the Jews are extremely brave and despise death, they are devoid of any military organization and inexperienced in battles" (*Jewish War,* 3.10.2).

The Great Revolt, or as it is also called, the Jewish War, caused by the crimes of the Roman administration in Judea, became the greatest tragedy in the history of the Jewish people. It began with the victory of the Jewish rebels over the Roman legions and ended with the devastation of the country and the destruction of Jerusalem and the Temple. Josephus, an eyewitness and active participant in this war, testified that as a result of the siege of Jerusalem alone, "the number of the fallen was one million one hundred thousand, and 97 thousand were taken captive" (*Jewish War* 6.9.3). However, the total number of victims of this war was immeasurably greater. The Romans killed not only those who resisted them but also the residents of towns and villages who had not participated in the revolt at all. A typical example in this regard is the Galilean town of Gabara. Despite the loyalty of its inhabitants to the Romans, Vespasian, "upon entering the city, ordered all the young men to be killed; the Romans, in their hatred for the Jews and out of revenge for the cruel treatment of Cestius, did not spare people of any age. After that, he (Vespasian) ordered not only the city itself but also all the villages in its vicinity to be burned;... the remaining inhabitants here and there were sold into slavery" (*Jewish War,* 3.7.1).

As for the residents of the cities who genuinely resisted the Roman invasion, their fate was no less sad. Thus, forty thousand residents died during the defense of the city of Jotapata in Galilee. Moreover, "Vespasian ordered the city to be razed to the ground and all its fortifications burned" (*Jewish War,* 3.7.36). During the battle for the city of Tarichaea (Magdala), located on the shore of Lake Kinneret, 6,500 people died. Vespasian deceitfully promised refugees from many cities in Galilee and Golan freedom, provided that they gathered in Tiberias, but he betrayed them: "here he ordered the killing of 1,200 of the old and weak; from the young, he chose 6,000 of the strongest to be sent to Nero on the Isthmus. The rest of the mass, about 30,400 people, he sold, except for those he gave to Agrippa" (*Jewish War,* 3.10.9-10). The Romans killed six thousand peaceful refugees from the Galilean city of Gischala (Gush Halav) right on the road (*Jewish War,* 4.2.4). There would have been even more victims if the Judean King Agrippa II had not interceded for the residents of Tiberias, thereby saving the city from destruction and its inhabitants from death and slavery (*Jewish War,* 3.9.7-8).

30. This coin depicts Judea as mourning woman and bound male captive. Minted during reign of Emperor Vespasian to commemorate the fall of Jerusalem in 70 CE.

The Romans did not only brutalize the north of the country; the situation in the south, in Judea and Perea, was no better. The Romans plundered all the settlements in Judea and killed 15,000 peaceful refugees from Perea who were trying to cross the Jordan to find refuge behind the fortress walls of Jericho. "The entire area through which they (the refugees) fled was full of blood, and not only was the Jordan choked with bodies, but the Lake Asphaltites (Dead Sea) was full of corpses carried there in masses by the river's current" (*Jewish War,* 4.7.5-6). Idumea also did not escape devastation. In the central part of this region alone, Vespasian ordered the killing of more than ten thousand inhabitants. He "left a significant part of the army on the spot, which devastated the entire mountainous country around" (*Jewish War* 4.8.1). The area of Gilead in central Transjordan was also devastated. The Romans stormed the city of Gerasa, "killed thousands of young men who did not escape, turned their families into prisoners of war, and the property of the inhabitants was given to the soldiers as spoil. After that, they set fire to the houses and devastated the neighboring settlements. Whoever could, fled; the weaker ones perished, and the settlements themselves were destroyed by fire" (*Jewish War,* 4.9.1).

However, all these descriptions of the horrors of war pale in comparison to the massacre the Romans carried out in Jerusalem: "while the Temple was burning, the soldiers plundered everything that came into their hands and killed the Jews in countless masses on their way. There was no mercy for age, no respect for rank: children and elders, laymen and priests were equally slaughtered" (*Jewish War,* 6.5.1). It is likely that the total number of dead and those who died from starvation was close to one and a half million people, and several hundred thousand more Jews were taken captive by the Romans and sold into slavery. There are reasons to believe that as a result of the Great Revolt of 66–73 CE, Judea lost between a third and a half of its population, considering that the total number of Jews living in their country in the first century was approximately 5 million people. To these losses must be added at least another hundred thousand victims of anti-Jewish pogroms in the Hellenistic cities of the Eastern Mediterranean, where the Jewish diaspora numbered about 3 million people. It was then that the pagan rabble, taking advantage of the Roman-Jewish war, rushed to plunder and kill Jews in their cities. For example, "in Damascus, 18,000 Jews died along with their wives and children, and in Egypt, the number of those tortured to death exceeded 60,000" (*Jewish War,* 7.6.7). In coastal Caesarea, the pagans wiped out the entire Jewish community, although it had no intention of revolting against the Romans. The most instructive example was that of Scythopolis (Beth She'an), where Jews took up arms for the Romans, against their own Jewish brothers. But this loyalty to the Romans and Hellenes did not help them. "Together with their families, they were mercilessly slaughtered. This is how they were thanked for their help" (*Jewish War,* 7.6.7).

As punishment for the revolt against them, the Romans imposed a so-called "Jewish tax" on all Jews in the empire, in the amount of half a shekel. The Jews of the empire used to pay this sum annually to the Jerusalem Temple. Now, the Romans began to take this money for the benefit of the temple of Jupiter Capitoline in Rome. Not satisfied with this, the Romans not only forbade the reconstruction of Jerusalem but also expelled all Jews from the territory adjacent to the city. All the lands around Jerusalem were confiscated from the Jews and distributed among Roman colonists. In place of Jerusalem, the Tenth Roman Legion was stationed, whose main task was garrison duty in Judea. All military and civil power was given to the Roman governor in Judea, while religious authority was represented by the Sanhedrin in Yavne. The vengeful Romans were not limited to the destruction of the Jerusalem Temple; by order of Vespasian, they also destroyed the famous Temple of Onias in Egypt, which was a copy of the First Jerusalem Temple and was built around 154 BCE by the high priest Onias IV for the Jews of Hellenistic Egypt. This was despite the fact that the Egyptian Jews remained loyal to Rome and did not take any part in the first anti-Roman revolt.

2. The Second Jewish-Roman War (115–117 CE)

The Great Revolt of 66–73 CE, which led to the destruction of Jerusalem and the Temple and the devastation of Judea, became a turning point in the relationship between Romans and Jews. From that point on, Roman pagans and monotheistic Jews became mutual enemies. The new nature of these relations sharply worsened the position of the entire Jewish diaspora in the Roman Empire. Hellenistic pagans had always disliked the fact that Jews had equal civil rights. The fact that Jews refused to honor the pagan gods of the Hellenes and participate in their religious ceremonies and festivals was always interpreted as a reason to deprive Jews of equal rights. The Jews were constantly blamed for their refusal to deify rulers and to place their statues in their temples, for their relatively closed way of life, and for observing laws (such as the Sabbath and dietary regulations) that were incomprehensible to pagans.

However, the problems in relations between Jews and the local population were not limited to religious and cultural differences. Economic competition between the Jews and the Hellens also played a significant role, and in this rivalry the former most often prevailed over the latter. Wherever Jews constituted a significant part of the population – for example, in Egypt, Cyrenaica (eastern Libya), Cyprus, and Syria – their relations with the local Hellenized inhabitants were tense. During the reign of the first imperial dynasty, the Julio-Claudians (27 BCE–68 CE), the Roman authorities generally did not allow the local population to attack Jews or infringe upon the civil rights of their communities. The only notable exception occurred during the reign of the Emperor Caligula. This Roman policy, which took into account the particular features of Jewish monotheism, gave rise to a myth among the Hellenistic population about the privileged position of Jews under the Julio-Claudian dynasty. The First Jewish Revolt in Judea became a convenient pretext for looting and killing Jews in Egypt, Syria, Cyrenaica, and Cyprus. The anti-Jewish edicts of the Flavian dynasty (69–96 CE) effectively left the Jewish communities of the empire without protection. The new Roman policy toward the Jews emboldened Hellenistic antisemites, who began to demand not only the deprivation of Jews' civil rights but also their expulsion from the Hellenistic cities. While attempts of expulsion were still suppressed by the Roman administration, attacks on Jews and their property occurred with the full connivance of the authorities. Roman military garrisons intervened in the conflicts only when the Jews themselves fought back against the local pagans. This tense confrontation between monotheistic Jews and Hellenistic pagans was typical for all Roman provinces in the Eastern Mediterranean where numerous Jewish communities lived at the time. In Egypt alone, there were at least a million Jews, and in Alexandria, the largest city of the Hellenistic world, they made up almost half the population. The ancestors of most of the Jews in Egypt, Cyrenaica, and Cyprus were forcibly resettled there from Judea by the Egyptian Ptolemies, who used them to strengthen the defense and develop the economy of their kingdom.

In 115 CE in Cyrenaica (Hellenistic Cyrene), attacks by Hellenistic pagans on Jews led to a retaliatory response: the Jews of Libya also took up arms, killed the instigators of the pogroms, and then the entire Roman garrison that supported them. This marked the beginning of a new Jewish-Roman war, often called the Second Jewish War or the Kitos War (115–117 CE). Unlike the first anti-Roman revolt, which was limited to the territory of Judea, the epicenter of the second war with Rome was the Jewish diaspora of the southeastern Mediterranean. This revolt spread to almost all the southeastern provinces of the Roman Empire

– Libya, Egypt, Cyprus – and later encompassed recently conquered Mesopotamia, as well as parts of Judea and Syria.

To suppress the Jewish diaspora revolt, Emperor Trajan (98–117 CE), who was then in power, was forced to deploy two Roman armies at once under the command of the best generals of the time. One Roman army, which fought Jewish rebels in Cyrenaica, Egypt, and Cyprus, was led by Marcius Turbo. The other army, which operated against the Jews of Mesopotamia, was commanded by Lusius Quietus, a Mauritanian (Berber) by origin. In 117 CE, both of these armies joined forces in Judea and were transferred to the command of Lusius Quietus, who for a long time besieged the last rebel stronghold – the city of Lydda (present-day Lod). The Roman armies, having suffered huge losses, retaliated by exterminating the entire Jewish population of Cyrenaica, Egypt, and Cyprus and depleting the Jewish communities and cities in Mesopotamia.

Unfortunately, unlike the First Jewish War, the history of the second anti-Roman revolt is not well known. The Second Jewish War had no Flavius Josephus who, as a participant, could have told us about it. There are only brief and not very reliable mentions of the Kitos War of 115–117 CE by several Hellenistic authors who lived centuries after these events. The second war of the Jews against the Roman Empire was written about very fragmentarily by the 3rd-century Roman-Greek historian Cassius Dio, the 4th-century church historian Eusebius of Caesarea, the 2nd-century Alexandrian historian Appian, the 5th-century Christian theologian Paul Orosius, the 5th-century bishop Synesius of Cyrene, and, finally, the 13th-century Jacobite priest and scholar Bar-Hebraeus. There are also brief mentions in the Talmud of events related to the siege of Lydda in Judea.

The revolt of 115–117 CE occurred during the Roman-Parthian War. In 114 CE, the Roman Emperor Trajan began a military campaign against Parthia. The pretext for the war with the Parthians was the removal of a Roman vassal from the Armenian throne. In his place, the Parthians installed their own candidate. However, the true reason for the war was Trajan's long-standing desire to conquer all of Mesopotamia, which was then under Parthian rule. Trajan's campaign was successful; he managed to defeat the Parthian army, capture Mesopotamia, and reach the coast of the Persian Gulf in 116 CE. It is very possible that the Jewish rebels wanted to use the Romans' preoccupation with the war against the Parthians to resist the pagans in the Hellenistic cities without major interference. However, the military operations ended too quickly, and the main forces of the Roman army were directed against the Jews.

All Hellenistic authors agree that the Jews of Cyrenaica were the first to revolt, led by a man named Lukuas. According to Eusebius of Caesarea, he was proclaimed "king." Cassius Dio calls the leader of the Libyan Jews differently – Andreas. Whether this was one person with two names or two different leaders remains unknown. Hellenistic authors accused Lukuas of "terrible" treatment of the defeated Hellenistic population (Cassius Dio, *Roman History*, 68.32; Eusebius, *Church History*, 4:2). The essence of this "terrible" treatment was that he did to the pagans the same things they had done to the Jews: he smashed the instigators of pogroms, burned arsonists, and killed murderers and robbers. He found those who had turned Jews into gladiators and made them also fight each other and with wild beasts. Lukuas destroyed temples and shrines of the pagans, just as they had previously destroyed synagogues. He exterminated the Hellenistic antisemites with the same zeal with which they had killed Jews. After defeating the Hellenes and the Roman garrisons that defended them in Cyrenaica, he rushed with his rebel army to help the Jews of Egypt.

At this time, Roman soldiers and Hellenes who had fled from Cyrenaica vented the bitterness of their defeat on the Egyptian Jews. In Alexandria, the pagan mob, with the support of the Roman garrison, attacked the Jewish quarters of the city and carried out a massacre. Then the Alexandrian Jews, following the example of their fellow tribesmen from Cyrenaica, also took up arms and fought back against the thugs. The Roman governor in Egypt, Marcus Lupus, tried to stop the advancing army of Lukuas, but after being defeated, he left Alexandria and retreated with the remnants of the Roman garrison. The Jewish rebels from Cyrenaica, entering the deserted Alexandria, did not touch the quarters of the Hellenes, but burned pagan temples and destroyed the tomb of Pompey, in retaliation for his desecration of the Jerusalem Temple and the capture of Judea in 63 BCE. Together with the Egyptian Jews, Lukuas's army quickly took control of all of Egypt, defeating the Roman garrisons in the Nile Valley. The next target of the rebels was Cyprus, which had a large Jewish community that was also subjected to attacks by Hellenistic pagans. But the Cypriot Jews, without waiting for the arrival of Lukuas's army, created their own military detachments led by a man named Artemion and forced the Hellenes to retreat. After receiving help from Lukuas, they went on the offensive: they defeated the Roman military garrisons, captured the main city of the island, Salamis, and then all of Cyprus. Thus, by 116 CE, Jewish rebels had taken control of Libya, Egypt, and Cyprus.

The second epicenter of the revolt was Mesopotamia, which Trajan's army had seized from Parthia. This cradle of the first civilizations and the ancestral home of the biblical family of the patriarch Abraham had one of the most numerous Jewish communities. As early as the end of the 8th century BCE, tens of thousands of Israelites were forcibly resettled there by Assyria after the fall of the Kingdom of Israel. This was followed by the Babylonian captivity of the Judahites in the 6th century BCE. It is possible that at the beginning of the Common Era about one million Jews lived there, no fewer than in Hellenistic Egypt. The Jews owned entire cities, such as Nisibis, Ctesiphon, Nehardea, Pumpedita, and Mehoza, and in northern Mesopotamia, there was even an independent Jewish kingdom, Adiabene. The Jewish cities and communities in Mesopotamia had very broad autonomy, were governed by their own leaders, and represented a state within a state. According to Armenian sources, the founder of Parthia, Arsaces I (247-217 BCE), was one of Abraham's descendants through his second wife, Keturah. Byzantine sources likewise claim that the ruling Arsacid dynasty originated from the Jews. Whether this was true or whether this narrative was invented to give antiquity and nobility to the ruling dynasty is unknown, but the

Arsacids, who established and ruled the Parthian Empire, granted the Jews rights and privileges that the Jewish communities of the Greco-Roman world could not even dream of.

The Romans, having seized Mesopotamia from Parthia, took away the autonomy of the Jewish communities and subjected them to taxes common to all Jews of the empire. In the eyes of the Mesopotamian Jews, the Romans were not only foreign pagan occupiers but also the destroyers of the Temple and Jerusalem, the ruiners of Judea. This circumstance became the main reason for the revolt of the Jews of Mesopotamia. Trajan did not admire the view of the Persian Gulf for long; news of the widespread Jewish revolts forced him to end the war with Parthia ahead of schedule in order to begin a new one – with the Jews. As a result of the Jewish revolt, Trajan lost almost all the territories he had conquered in Mesopotamia; even Hellenistic cities such as Edessa, Arbela (Erbil), and Seleucia broke away. Unlike Cyrenaica, Egypt, and Cyprus, the non-Jewish population of Mesopotamia supported the Jewish communities. They were also helped by the Parthians and the Jewish kingdom of Adiabene. A sick (or wounded?) Trajan decided to return to Rome urgently. All Roman forces were divided into two parts: one, under the command of Marcius Turbo, was sent to suppress the revolt in Egypt, Cyrenaica, and Cyprus, and the other, led by Lusius Quietus, remained in Mesopotamia and Syria to pacify the rebellious Jews. The entire Roman fleet was attached to Turbo's army, as it was to land on Cyprus. The second anti-Roman revolt also affected Judea itself. Jewish rebels were also active there, led by men named Julian and Pappus, but we know almost nothing about them.

Marcius Turbo's armies managed to restore Roman rule in Egypt, Cyrenaica, and Cyprus only after a whole year of intense fighting and huge losses. Turbo's Roman legions lost up to 30–40% of their personnel. The remnants of Lukuas's rebel army, pursued by the Romans, went to Judea, obviously to join up with the detachments of Julian and Pappus. Nothing is known about the further fate of Lukuas himself. Lusius Quietus's army had greater success in Mesopotamia and Syria.

The "fierce Moor," known for his brutality and ruthlessness, managed to drown the uprising in blood even before Quintus Marcius Turbo did. For this he was rewarded by the emperor Trajan: he was appointed procurator of Judea, and the army of Turbo was placed under his command. The combined Roman forces surrounded and besieged the last stronghold of the Jewish rebels in the city of Lydda (Lod). The long siege led to famine and epidemics among the city's population. The suffering and death of the besieged in Lydda are mentioned in the Talmud, and Rabbi Gamaliel II lamented them (Talmud, Ta'anit 18b; Yer. Ta'anit 66b). The Roman capture of Lydda and the execution of Julian and Pappus marked the end of the Second Jewish-Roman War of 115–117 CE.

The end of the second anti-Roman revolt coincided with the end of Emperor Trajan's reign. He was not destined to reach Rome. On the way, his health deteriorated so much that he had to stop in Cilicia (Asia Minor), where he died suddenly from an unknown cause. According to a will that was forged by his wife Plotina after the emperor's death, all power was transferred to his great-nephew Hadrian, although Trajan had much closer candidates for the throne. Such a dubious nature of the succession to the imperial throne caused Hadrian's potential rivals to suspect him of usurping power. For his part, Hadrian hastened to get rid of all potential competitors for the throne. One of them was Lusius Quietus, a successful general who commanded the main forces of the Roman army in the East. In 118 CE, the "fierce Moor" was urgently summoned to Rome, where he was immediately executed without a stated reason (Cassius Dio, *Roman History*, 69.1-2). Having become emperor, Hadrian hastened to reassure the Jews of the Roman Empire, promising them that Jerusalem and the Temple would be restored. However, as it turned out later, he did not keep his word.

The consequences of the second anti-Roman uprising were no less severe than those of the first. If during the First Jewish–Roman War nearly half of the population of Judea was killed or taken captive, then as a result of the Diaspora Revolt, the Romans destroyed all Jewish communities in Egypt, Libya, and Cyprus, and annihilated part of the Jewish population of Mesopotamia and Syria. In fact, approximately two-thirds of the Jewish diaspora perished, which is about one and a half to two million people. Hellenistic authors, such as Cassius Dio, Eusebius of Caesarea, Synesius of Cyrene, and Paul Orosius, wrote about the complete devastation and depopulation of huge territories in Cyrenaica, Egypt, and Cyprus. In Libya and Cyprus, not only the Jewish population but also the entire Hellenistic population was exterminated. The depopulation was so significant that Emperor Hadrian was forced to vigorously resettle these territories with new colonists. The destruction of the Jewish population of Egypt, Libya, and Cyprus led to a deep economic and cultural decline in these Roman provinces. Egypt ceased to supply Rome and Italy with grain for many years, its economy never managed to return to its previous level, and Alexandria forever lost its status as the main cultural center of the Hellenistic world. Jews began to appear there only in the 3rd–4th centuries, but they never again reached the numbers and power they had before this revolt.

The revolt of the Jews in Mesopotamia seriously influenced Roman policy in the East. First of all, it saved the Parthian Empire from complete defeat. Trajan was forced to stop his victorious campaign against Parthia and turn the Roman armies against the rebellious Jews. His successor, Emperor Hadrian, went even further – he abandoned all of Trajan's conquests in Mesopotamia and ceded this important strategic area to Parthia. Moreover, he also abandoned claims to Armenia in favor of the same Parthia.

As is known, the years of Trajan's reign are considered the apogee of the military power and territorial expansion of the Roman Empire. From the point of view of the possibility of resisting the Roman army, this was an extremely unfavorable time for a new revolt. What prompted the Jews to engage in a hopeless confrontation with the then-invincible Roman military machine? Probably two factors. First, the increased attacks by Hellenistic pagans with the direct support of Roman garrisons. The physical attacks of the urban mob were very often accompanied by attempts by the Hellenistic elite to restrict the civil rights of Jews. Second, the messianic radicalism brought by the Zealots and Sicarii who fled from Judea after the Great Revolt. The basis of this religious radicalism was laid by the leaders of the Zealot movement in Galilee at the beginning of our era – Judas the Galilean and the Pharisee Zadok. They claimed that a people who knew the true God could not obey pagans. "They considered the Lord God their only ruler and master" (*Antiquities of the Jews,* 18.1.6). The ideological followers of the Zealots and Sicarii took advantage of the chronic antagonism between monotheistic Jews and Hellenistic pagans to push the Jewish communities of Egypt, Libya, and Cyprus into a war with the mighty Roman Empire, which no one at that time could defeat. One can only wonder how farmers, artisans, merchants, and priests were able to fight the most powerful professional army of the ancient world for three years and inflict huge losses on it?

It is very likely that during the Second Jewish-Roman War of 115–117 CE, some of the Jews of Cyrenaica, fleeing from the Roman army, fled to the territory of the Berber tribes. They had no other way to salvation then. It was they who became the founding ancestors of the Jewish communities among the Berber tribes of North Africa. Under their influence, a number of Berber tribes converted to Judaism. Subsequently, despite forced Islamization by the Arab conquerors, the communities of Berber Jews were preserved and existed until the mid-20th century. Although there are different versions of when and under what circumstances the Jews came to the Berbers, the most likely of them is the one associated with the tragic end of Cyrenaican Jewry in 117 CE.

3. The Bar Kokhba Rebellion (132–135 CE)

Sixty years after the Great Jewish Revolt (66–73 CE) and fifteen years after the Second Jewish-Roman War (115–117 CE), a new, third anti-Roman rebellion broke out in Judea under the leadership of Bar Kokhba. The cause was Emperor Hadrian's (117–138 CE) decision to build a Hellenistic city on the site of the destroyed Jerusalem and name it Aelia Capitolina, in honor of himself and his Aelian family. On the Temple Mount, where the First and then the Second Jerusalem Temple had stood, Hadrian planned to erect a pagan shrine – a temple to Jupiter Capitolinus. These intentions of the emperor grossly violated his previous promises to the Jews upon his ascension to the throne to restore Jerusalem and the Temple. As it turned out later, Hadrian was following the path of the Seleucid king Antiochus IV Epiphanes, who tried to ban Jewish monotheism.

Like Antiochus, Hadrian usurped the imperial throne and dealt with other, more legitimate contenders for the Roman throne. This was done with the help of a fictitious adoption that was fabricated by Trajan's wife after the emperor's death (Cassius Dio, *Roman History*, 69.1-3). Similar to Antiochus, Hadrian suffered from megalomania and was a fanatical admirer of Hellenistic paganism. He also proclaimed himself a god and identified himself with both Zeus Olympius and Jupiter Capitolinus. Following the example of the mentally ill Caligula, he forced people to install his statues and worship them in all the temples of the Roman Empire. Hadrian demanded to be portrayed as a courageous Roman warrior-commander, which he never was in reality, for he had never done anything heroic or worthy of respect. However, unlike Antiochus IV Epiphanes, he had neither children nor a normal married life, although he was formally married to Trajan's great-niece. His de facto "wife" and the greatest passion of his life was the young man Antinous, who was always with Hadrian, wherever the emperor went. However, in 130 CE, while Hadrian was in Egypt, the young man drowned in the Nile. Hadrian, insane with grief, declared Antinous a god and ordered the entire population of the empire to pray not only to himself but also to the new god. At the place of Antinous's death, the emperor founded the city of Antinoopolis, where games were held every year in honor of "the god Antinous." Hadrian ordered tens of thousands of statues and busts of Antinous to be sculpted and installed in all the temples and public buildings of the Roman Empire. More images of Antinous have survived to our time than of all the famous and outstanding Romans combined. Modern museums hold no fewer than five thousand statues and busts of this ancient gay man, Hadrian's favorite "wife."

Unlike the pagans, Jews and Christians refused, even under the threat of the death penalty, to pray to the new god Antinous, which enraged the emperor. It is not surprising that Hadrian became most "famous" for his persecution of Jews and Christians who refused to worship him and Antinous as gods. Just as Antiochus IV Epiphanes had done in his time, he decided to insult the religious feelings of the Jews by building a pagan shrine on the site of the Temple of the Lord and to humiliate their dignity by turning Judean Jerusalem into pagan Aelia Capitolina. What's more, he forbade Jews from the rite of circumcision under penalty of death, equating it with castration. Hadrian also cracked down on Christians after they, following the Jews, refused to worship the cult of Antinous. It was he who subjected the Christians who later became known as the saints martyrs Faith, Hope, and Charity, and their mother Saint Sophia, to a painful execution. Hadrian was known for his vindictiveness and intolerance of anyone who refused to deify him. As Cassius Dio wrote, Hadrian, "wishing to surpass everyone in everything, nurtured hatred for those who achieved excellence in anything." One of the many examples of this was the famous architect Apollodorus of Damascus, who dared to comment on the emperor's illiterate architectural projects. Hadrian, "bearing a grudge," executed him on a fabricated pretext (*Roman History*, 69.4).

Throughout his reign, Hadrian complained about the hostility of the Roman senators, who could not forgive him for usurping the imperial throne, his excessive megalomania, and the forced deification of Antinous. When Hadrian came to power in 117 CE, the Jewish diaspora revolt had not yet been suppressed, so he was generous with promises to the Jews, trying to prevent the unrest from spreading to the provinces of Asia Minor and Europe. However, the following years proved to be exceptionally peaceful and calm. In 130 CE, when he visited Jerusalem, which was then in ruins, he decided to restore the city, but not as a Jewish one, but as a Hellenistic one, and to glorify himself and his ancestors by giving it his family name. This decision by Hadrian turned out to be fatal: it led to the Third Jewish-Roman War, the most significant of all the years of his reign.

The Bar Kokhba revolt is also little covered in history, like the Second Jewish-Roman War. This third war of the Jews against the Roman Empire also had neither its own Flavius Josephus nor chronicles like the books of the Maccabees. Only a few Hellenistic historians, who lived much later than these events, left more than scanty information about it. Cassius Dio in his "Roman History" and Eusebius of Caesarea in his "Church History" mentioned them most. Something can be gleaned from the "Historia Augusta" – a collection of biographies of Roman emperors created in the 4th century. Some memory of the Bar Kokhba revolt has also been preserved in rabbinic literature, particularly in the Talmud. However, these references are fragmentary and largely legendary in character, and they present a strongly negative view of Simon bar Kokhba. In general, despite the scarcity of sources and the extreme paucity of their information, there is no doubt that the new, third war with the Roman Empire was caused by the openly anti-Jewish decisions of the militant pagan and megalomaniac that Hadrian turned out to be. Like his ideological predecessor Antiochus IV Epiphanes, he challenged the Jewish people, trying to destroy the monotheism they had suffered for centuries to preserve and take away Jerusalem and the Temple. This is what the Roman historian Cassius Dio writes about it: "This (Hadrian's decision) caused a cruel and protracted war, for the Jews considered it unacceptable for foreigners to lord over their city and establish pagan cults there" (*Roman History*, 69.12).

The response to this challenge was a revolt in Judea. It began in the very same place where the Maccabean wars had begun, in the town of Modi'in. It was led by Simon bar Kosiba, a man of gigantic stature and enormous physical strength, who possessed the gift of an outstanding commander and leader. The well-known legal scholar of the time, Rabbi Akiva, proclaimed him the Messiah and even changed his name to Bar Kokhba ("Son of the Star"), referring to the biblical prophecy about a rising star from Jacob: "A star shall come out of Jacob, and a scepter shall rise out of Israel; it shall crush the foreheads of Moab, and break down all the sons of Sheth" (Numbers 24:17).

Bar Kokhba was able to unite the scattered detachments of Jewish rebels into a single army and inflict a number of defeats on the Roman garrison in Judea. Cassius Dio claims that the success of the revolt was due to the fact that it was prepared in secret for several years, when the Jews stocked up on weapons, "occupied advantageous points in the area and supplied them with underground passages and walls, in order to... have shelters and secretly communicate with each other underground" (*Roman History*, 69.12.3). If this was true, then the Bar Kokhba revolt, unlike the two previous anti-Roman wars, was far from spontaneous but well-prepared. The Roman governor in Judea, Quintus Tineius Rufus, tried to suppress the growing revolt with two legions but was defeated. Then he turned his wrath on the peaceful population who helped the rebels. Eusebius of Caesarea narrates this as follows: "Governor Rufus killed many thousands of men, women, and children indiscriminately, and by the law of war confiscated their lands" (*Church History*, 4.6.1). Seeing Rufus's inability to cope with the rebellious Jews, the governor of Syria, Certus Publicius Marcellus, came to his aid along with the Roman army that was then stationed on the Euphrates in case of a Parthian attack. However, Marcellus's army was also defeated by the Jewish rebels. Bar Kokhba and his warriors managed to almost completely wipe out three Roman legions: the Tenth "Fretensis," the Sixth "Ferrata," and the Twenty-Second "Deiotariana." After this victory, the Jewish rebels took possession of not only all of historical Judea but also the territories of Idumea, Galilee, the Golan, and possibly Transjordan. Only the region of Samaria remained loyal to Rome, as the Samaritans refused to join the rebellious Jews.

31. Bar-Kokhba Revolt coins.

News of the rebels' success in Judea greatly alarmed Emperor Hadrian. The Bar Kokhba revolt turned out to be the only serious war that the Romans had to fight during all the years of Hadrian's reign. The emperor summoned the best Roman general, Sextus Julius Severus, from Britain and immediately gave him 13 legions (130-140 thousand soldiers) to suppress the Bar Kokhba revolt as quickly as possible. However, despite his clear superiority in forces, Severus was for a long time unable to force the rebels into a decisive battle involving the main forces of both sides. Simon bar Kokhba skillfully avoided engagements that were unfavorable to him against an enemy superior in numbers and armament, and instead waged a guerrilla war against the Romans. Only after Severus himself began to copy Bar Kokhba's tactics did the Romans begin to have success. Unfortunately, we do not know the course of the third Jewish-Roman war, which lasted from three to four years. Perhaps Hellenistic historians wrote about it, but their works have not survived to our time. According to the Talmud, the Romans had to spend four years and endure 54 battles to conquer Judea. But the Talmud was created 200-300 years after the Bar Kokhba revolt and only briefly mentions these events. We only know the final stage of the revolt, and that too, mainly thanks to the Roman-Greek historian Cassius Dio, whose work was lucky: it was rewritten by a Byzantine monk in the 11th century.

The Roman Empire, which was at the peak of its power at that time, possessed such military might that no one in the ancient world could withstand it. The Bar Kokhba rebels were no exception. Their last stronghold was the fortress of Bethar, located southwest of Jerusalem in the Judean mountains. The Romans besieged it unsuccessfully for more than two years and were able to take it only after the besieged rebels were completely exhausted by hunger and thirst. We know from rabbinic sources that at the end of the siege of Bethar, disagreements arose among the leaders of the revolt, which led to the death of some law teachers, including Bar Kokhba's uncle, Rabbi Elazar Modai. Probably, the main reason for the strife was the desire of the law teachers to end the revolt through a compromise with the Romans. However, Bar Kokhba, like the Zealots and Sicarii in his time, rejected any option of capitulation to the Roman pagans. According to religious tradition, the fortress of Bethar was captured by the Romans on the 9th of Av (Tisha B'Av), the same day that the First (586 BCE) and Second Temples (70 CE) fell. Although the end of the revolt is considered to be 135 CE, when the Romans took possession of Bethar, the last hotbed of resistance in the Beth She'an area was suppressed only in 136 CE. Many Jewish rebels and their families fled to the Judean Desert, where they hid in caves for a long time and made forays against the Romans. The leader of the revolt, Bar Kokhba, died in battle on the last day of the defense of Bethar, and the spiritual leader of the rebels, Rabbi Akiva, along with a dozen other law teachers, was taken prisoner and subjected to a cruel and painful execution by the Romans.

However, the victory over Bar Kokhba also turned out to be a Pyrrhic one for the Romans. The Roman legions suffered such great losses that Emperor Hadrian, in a letter to the Senate, was forced to abandon the accepted formula for reporting victories: "I and my army are in good health." As for the Jews, Cassius Dio assessed their losses as a result of the Bar Kokhba revolt as follows: "50 of their fortified cities and 985 of their most important settlements were razed to the ground, 580 thousand Jews perished in battles, and the number of those who died from hunger, epidemics, and fire cannot be counted. As a result, almost all of Judea was turned into a desolate wilderness" (*Roman History,* 69.14.1-3). The human losses of Judea during the Bar Kokhba rebellion were probably no less than during the Great Revolt of 66–73 CE. However, the tragedy was not only in the terrible numbers of human casualties and the complete destruction of the entire country. The vengeful Romans began to pursue a policy of expelling the Jews from their homeland, forbidding them not only to own land but also to live in Judea. Eusebius of Caesarea, citing the now-lost work of Ariston of Pella, writes that "by Hadrian's order, from that time on, the entire Jewish people were forbidden to even set foot on their native land in the vicinity of Jerusalem; moreover, they were not even allowed to look at their native places from a distance. Thus, the city of the Jews fell into desolation; none of the old inhabitants remained, and a foreign people settled it" (*Church History,* 4.6.3-4).

The Romans, trying to finally break the resistance of the Jews, decided not only to expel them from Judea but also to make the whole world forget even the name of their homeland. By a decree of the Roman Emperor Hadrian, Judea was renamed Palestine, in honor of the Philistines – the Indo-European newcomers who had disappeared from the face of the earth several centuries before the Romans came there. The Roman authorities, under the threat of severe punishment, obliged everyone in their empire to use only the new name, and although it clearly did not correspond to the history and population of this land, it eventually took root and supplanted all previous names. Thus, ancient Canaan, which became the "land of Israel," and then Judea, was suddenly renamed Palestine. Trying to break all ties between the Jewish people and their homeland, Hadrian also renamed the Judean capital, Jerusalem, as Aelia Capitolina. The city was returned to its former name only during the reign of Emperor Constantine (306–337 CE).

Hadrian, understanding that Jewish monotheism was the source of the Jewish people's strength and vitality, forbade the observance of all the laws and rites of Judaism. Moreover, he even forbade the study of the laws of Moses and the storage of the books of the Torah. However, this draconian ban did not last even three years; it was canceled by the new Roman Emperor Antoninus Pius (138–161 CE). However, he and subsequent Roman emperors kept the ban on the settlement of Jews in Jerusalem and the surrounding areas.

Both versions of the Talmud (Babylonian and Jerusalem) portray Simon Bar Kokhba as a false messiah: a hot-tempered and irrational man who misled the Jews of Judea and drove them into a hopeless revolt against the then-invincible Roman Empire (Babylonian Talmud, Gittin 52; Jerusalem Talmud, Ta'anit 4, 5). Moreover, all rabbinic literature portrays the decision of Rabbi Akiva, the "father of the Mishnah," to recognize Bar Kokhba as the Messiah as a deeply erroneous and purely personal one, which allegedly contradicted the opinion of the majority of law teachers of that time. It is not surprising that after the defeat of the revolt, Bar Kokhba's detractors began to call him "bar Koziva" ("son of the lie"). However, this unequivocally negative view took shape many years after the Bar Kokhba revolt, when it had already become clear what disastrous consequences the third anti-Roman war had brought. But during the revolt, not only such an authority as Rabbi Akiva, but also most of the law teachers of that time, supported the idea of proclaiming Bar Kokhba the Messiah, because it helped mobilize the people and inspire them to repeat the feats of the Maccabees. And Bar Kokhba's appearance – a giant warrior – and his victories over the Romans gave reason to call him the Savior. It is noteworthy that Bar Kokhba did not consider himself the Messiah; he was not prone to messianism or mysticism in general. On the coins minted during the revolt, he called himself only the "Prince of Israel." It was not he who invented the resounding name "Son of the Star"; it was given to him by Rabbi Akiva and later taken up and popularized by the people. In letters from the period of the revolt discovered in the Judean Desert, he signed himself modestly and only with his own name: "Simon bar Kosiba, Prince of Israel."

The negative attitude toward Bar Kokhba is characteristic not only of rabbinic literature but also of the apologists of Christianity. Thus, Eusebius of Caesarea, citing Justin Martyr, reports on the "oppression" of Christians by Bar Kokhba. In his "Chronicles," he explains that the "oppression" was caused by the Christians' refusal to help Bar Kokhba in his war against the Romans. However, the Christians who suffered were actually Judeo-Christians, that is, Jews who, although they recognized Christ as the Jewish Messiah, at the same time meticulously observed all the laws of Judaism. For Bar Kokhba, they were the same Jews as all his fellow tribesmen, and he punished any of them who evaded help, regardless of which Messiah they believed in. By the way, by the admission of Eusebius of Caesarea himself, before the Bar Kokhba revolt, "the whole Christian church in Judea consisted of believing Jews, and the first fifteen bishops there were native Jews" (*Church History,* 4.5.2). In addition, the attitude of Eusebius and Justin toward Bar Kokhba could not have been objective, because both of them came from families of Hellenistic pagans who had settled in Judea. Eusebius was from Mediterranean Caesarea, and Justin was from a Roman colony near Shechem (Nablus). Both of them looked with fear and hostility at the desire of the Jews, the masters of the country, to get rid of both Roman rule and foreign colonists, which Eusebius and Justin were. However, the loyalty of Christians to Rome was never appreciated: after the persecution of the Jews, the Roman authorities cracked down on Christians with even greater force.

The most terrible consequence of the third anti-Roman revolt was the depopulation of Judea. In the entire history of the civilization of Canaan, its population had never been subjected to such total extermination and expulsion as occurred during and after the Bar Kokhba revolt. The mass deportations of the Assyrians and Babylonians paled in comparison to what the Roman Empire was capable of. The Romans, convinced that the strength of the Jews was rooted in their native land, forever forbade them to live not only in the Jerusalem area but also throughout the territory of historical Judea. The Romans confiscated land from Jewish farmers and drove their families from their native places. The surviving part of the Jewish people was forced to move either north, to Galilee and the Golan Heights, where the Romans did not prevent Jews from living, or to leave the country altogether and settle in the diaspora. The Sanhedrin moved from Yavne to the Galilean town of Usha, and the main Jewish centers became the Galilean cities of Tiberias and Tzippori (Sepphoris). In fact, it was from the middle of the 2nd century CE that the era of the scattering of the Jewish people began and the gradual transformation of Judea into something new – Palestine. Rabbinic literature of that time testifies that the spiritual leaders of the people were extremely concerned about the depopulation of the "Land of Israel" and tried to keep the Jews at least on the outskirts of their homeland or in the Hellenistic cities of Palestine. "Let a person remain in the Land of Israel, even in a city where the majority are non-Jews, rather than live outside the Land of Israel, even in a city where everyone is Jewish" (*Tosefta*, Avodah Zarah 1:3).

4. The Completion of Jewish Ethnogenesis (2nd–5th Centuries CE)

The devastating consequences of the anti-Roman revolts made it impossible for the Jewish people to continue their previous way of life, both in their homeland of Judea and in the countries of the Eastern Mediterranean. From the mid-2nd century, a devastated Judea began to rapidly lose its Jewish population and transform into Roman Palestine, which was being settled by foreigners. Similarly, the once numerous and flourishing Jewish communities of Egypt, Libya, Syria, and Cyprus were either completely destroyed or bled dry. While the surviving Jews were expelled from Judea by the Romans, they were driven out of the countries of the Eastern Mediterranean by pagan Hellenes.

Where did the remaining Jewish population go? Some moved east to Mesopotamia, which, despite Roman attempts to conquer it, remained under the control of the Parthian kingdom. Jewish communities had existed there in the land between the Tigris and Euphrates for a long time, since the Assyrian and Babylonian exiles in the 8th–6th centuries BCE. Others went northwest to Europe: Italy, Gaul, Rhineland and Spain. This marked the beginning of the historical division of the Jewish people into European and Middle Eastern (Mizrahi) Jews. Later, European Jews, in turn, split into Ashkenazic and Sephardic Jews (Ashkenazim and Sephardim).

During the Jewish-Roman wars, several hundred thousand Jews, mostly young men, were taken captive by the Romans. According to Hellenistic historians, some were sold to circuses in Roman and Hellenistic cities and died in gladiatorial combat. However, most of them, as Josephus testifies, were either ransomed by Jewish communities in Italy or were granted their freedom in exchange for becoming Roman colonists among the restless Germanic, Gallic (Celtic), Spanish, and Illyrian tribes. There, according to the Roman plan, the Jewish settlers were to civilize the barbarians and help develop the economies of these territories. Thus, tens, and perhaps hundreds, of thousands of young Jews ended up in the territory of modern-day Italy, France, Germany, Austria, and the Balkan countries. This movement into Europe, which was by no means voluntary, and which primarily involved the male population, could not help but influence the ethnogenesis of modern Jewry. The wives of the first Jewish settlers in Europe came from non-Jewish backgrounds, namely from the peoples of Italy, and the Germanic, Gallic, Spanish, and Illyrian tribes. These women had to undergo *giyur*, or conversion to Judaism. However, Judaism at that time, unlike in a later period, actively encouraged proselytism, so the acceptance of Jewish monotheism by pagans, especially women, was not difficult then. In this way, Italic, Gallic, and Germanic blood entered the veins of European Jews – what is now called Italian, French, and German blood. But when could this mixing happen, and how significant was it? The answer to the first part of the question can be found in history, and the second in genetics.

It is easiest to pinpoint the time of the most significant mixing: the period when a huge number of former Jewish captives, unable to return to their homeland, found themselves in a non-Jewish environment in Europe. This period was quite short, from the 70s of the first century to the middle of the second century CE. It includes the years of the Great Jewish revolt, the Second Jewish-Roman War, and the Bar Kokhba rebellion. Even if we assume that some of the former captives managed to remain in the Jewish communities that ransomed them, they or their fellow Jews in those communities would still have been left without Jewish wives. There was only one solution – to take local women as wives and perform the conversion ceremony. Later, Jews began to appear in Europe in another capacity: as merchants and traders, often without their families. This circumstance forced them to marry non-Jewish women and convert them to their faith. We have historical evidence that even much later, up to the end of the 5th century, women from Western European peoples often converted to Judaism. At that time, such conversions were a common and widespread phenomenon, and the church and the synagogue had not yet built impassable walls between their followers. Moreover, even the rapid Christianization of the "barbarians" did not at first prevent their close relations with the Jews, as many Germanic tribes initially adopted Christianity in an Arian form, which was friendly to Judaism. It was only in the 6th–7th centuries, after the introduction of harsh anti-Jewish laws, that the Christian church managed to put an end to the mass conversions of women to Judaism. In the Middle East and North Africa – similar phenomena occurred, but they also ceased after the forced Islamization of the local peoples in the 7th century.

Research in the field of genetics not only confirms the fact of intermixture between Jews and the peoples of Western Europe during the first four centuries of the Common Era, but also supports the historical model described above regarding the emergence of Jewish communities in Europe. Geneticists used the Y chromosome, which is passed only through the male line from father to son, and compared its characteristics in Jews and non-Jews from various European countries. It was found that Jewish men from the most diverse communities, even their sons from marriages with non-Jewish women, are genetically identical to each other and at the same time have no connection with the native population of their countries. The genetic kinship of Jewish men is found only with the Semitic population of Palestine.

On the other hand, the results of studies of mitochondrial DNA, which is passed exclusively through the female line from mother to daughter, were stunning: the female part of the Jewish population has a completely different genetic history than the male part. DNA analysis led to two discoveries at once. First, Jewish women from different countries, unlike men, are in no way related to each other, have nothing in common with the inhabitants of the Syro-Palestinian region of the Middle East, and at the same time are genetically close to the population of the European countries. Second, the DNA analysis of Jewish women showed that, being originally of pure European origin, they did not mix at all with the native population of the countries of residence afterward (*Nature Communications*, 4, Article # 2543 (2013)).

The confirmed genetic kinship of the male part of Jewish communities and their clear Middle Eastern origin refutes the claims of some historians that Jews are different peoples connected only by a common faith – Judaism – and allegedly have nothing in common with the Middle East. The latest studies in genetics have once again confirmed the direct connection of Jewish men with the Southern Levant: according to their DNA, modern Ashkenazi men are at least half direct descendants of the ancient Canaanites – the indigenous population of Palestine (*Cell*, May 2020; *Bible History Daily*, June 2020).

According to Halakha, the code of Jewish law established in the Middle Ages, Jewish identity is determined by the mother. For Orthodox Jews, a "halakhic," that is, a genuine Jew, is someone whose mother is Jewish or who has converted to Judaism through an Orthodox ceremony. The same principle applies in modern Israel. However, this was not always the case. In ancient Israel and Judea, during both the First and Second Temple periods, Jewish identity was determined by the father. Genetics confirms the correctness of this ancient Israelite tradition of determining ethnic origin by the father, not the mother. By the way, if Jewishness were to be established by the mother, as it is today, it would turn out that the absolute majority of Israelite and Judahite kings, as well as the children of the lawgiver Moses himself, were not Jews. According to Shaye J. D. Cohen, a Harvard University professor, an Orthodox rabbi, and one of the world's leading authorities on the history of Judaism, the principle of establishing origin by the mother is alien to Jewish tradition and was borrowed from the Romans (Shaye J. D. Cohen, *The Beginning of Jewishness*, 1999).

If so, when and why did Jewish spiritual leaders decide to abandon the ancient Jewish tradition of determining origin by the father and adopt a foreign law, and from their sworn enemies at that? According to Cohen, with whom many experts on the history of Judaism agree, the idea of determining Jewish identity by the mother arose around the 3rd–5th centuries CE and was caused by very serious reasons. The assimilation of Jews with women from Western European peoples did not end with the mixing of former Jewish captives but continued for the next two centuries. As a result, some Jewish women remained unmarried. Over time, another problem arose: the mass Christianization of pagans turned any conversion of local women to Judaism into a sharp conflict with the church and the authorities. To avoid dangerous clashes with local rulers and the Christian church, the Jewish spiritual leaders forbade proselytism and, in the interest of Jewish women, began to determine Jewish identity by the mother.

By the 6th–7th centuries, the fathers of the Christian church on one hand and the spiritual leaders of the Jewish people on the other had managed to put an end to the conversions of Western European women to Judaism. "Culprits" were punished with death by Christian authorities, while rabbis expelled them from Jewish communities. From that time onward, nearly insurmountable barriers arose between the Jewish people and the Christian peoples of Europe, barriers that were fully dismantled only in the twentieth century. Thus, the early Middle Ages became the last frontier in the ethnogenesis of the Jewish people. From then on, it no longer accepted anyone into its ranks, but it continued to give its sons and daughters to the peoples around it. Christian authorities in Europe, and later Muslim rulers in the Middle East and North Africa, forbade conversion to Judaism under penalty of death, but they wholeheartedly welcomed the conversion of Jews to Christianity and Islam.

If one tries to give the most accurate ethnic description of modern Ashkenazim – Jews of European origin, and they make up about 80–85% of the total Jewish population – they should be defined as a **West Semitic people of Amorite origin with a significant admixture of European blood**. But how significant is this admixture? Geneticists answer this question differently, but most of the authoritative researchers define it as ranging from one-fifth to one-third. These European genes of the Ashkenazim are closest to the genotype of the modern population of Italy, southern France (Provence), southern Germany (Bavaria), and Austria. This also applies to Sephardic Jews, but only to those who are direct descendants of the exiles from Spain and Portugal. They are also Western Semites, like the Ashkenazim, but their European admixture brings them closer to the modern population of southern France and Spain. However, the connection between the Sephardim and Spain is two-way: not only did the peoples of Iberia leave their mark on the genes of the Sephardic Jews, but the latter also greatly influenced the current population of the country. According to some genetic studies, every fifth Spaniard is an ethnic Jew. One should not forget that in 1492, when the Jews were faced with a difficult choice: either to convert to Catholicism or to leave Spain, most of them were baptized and, remaining in that country, gradually mixed with the local peoples.

The third group of modern Jewry – the "Mizrahim" (Middle Eastern and North African Jews) – also underwent some mixing with the population of the countries where they lived. Moreover, some communities of

Eastern Jews, for example, from Yemen, India, Ethiopia, and China, are clear proselytes, that is, local people who adopted Judaism.

Speaking of the ethnic "infusions" into the composition of European Jews during the early Middle Ages, one cannot fail to mention the so-called Khazar hypothesis. As is well known, it boils down to the claim that the ancestors of the Ashkenazim are allegedly not Semitic Jews from Palestine, but Turkic Khazars who adopted Judaism in the early 9th century. However, today we have such a mass of archaeological, linguistic, and, most importantly, genetic evidence that turns this hypothesis into an absurd myth. Those who, against common sense and obvious facts, continue to adhere to it are either outright anti-Semites or fraudsters from science. True, in the recent past, when we did not have enough genetic and archaeological data, the Khazar myth found supporters even among some Jews. They liked the fact that the huge Turkic empire, the Khazar Khaganate, which ruled over almost all of Eastern Europe, was ruled by Jewish kings who protected and patronized their co-religionists everywhere. The idea of the Khazar origin of the Ashkenazim deprived the Christian church of its traditional anti-Jewish arguments, including those related to the crucifixion of Christ. Arab authors also seized on this hypothesis, seeing in it a convenient pretext for denying the Jews' rights to Palestine. However, the Khazar myth remains just a myth. In reality, only the Khazar aristocracy and the royal court adopted Judaism, while almost the entire mass of the Turkic population of the khaganate remained pagans. It is possible that the small community of Crimean Karaites traces its origin to the Khazar Jews, but this version has not yet been confirmed.

EPILOGUE

The Transformation of Judea into Palestine (2nd–7th Centuries CE)

For a long time, the prevailing view in historical scholarship held that after three anti-Roman revolts, the Jewish people were quickly forced to leave their homeland under Roman pressure. It was believed that the Jewish majority in Judea virtually disappeared during the first centuries CE, and that the country became Palestine – an abandoned home deserted by its owners. However, archaeological discoveries of recent decades have significantly revised these assumptions. It has become clear that until the end of the 5th century, Jews, together with the Samaritans, constituted the numerical majority in Palestine. While the Samaritans formed an absolute majority of the population in central Palestine, the Jews, even after the Bar Kokhba revolt, continued for a long time to dominate the country's northern regions – Galilee and the Golan. Moreover, in the Golan itself, Jews remained the majority of the population for an even longer period, until the 7th century.

The early Church Fathers in Palestine confirm the predominance of Jews and Samaritans even at the end of the 4th century CE. For example, Epiphanius of Salamis, canonized in both the Orthodox and Catholic churches, testified that in the 370s, all the major settlements in Galilee were entirely Jewish. Another early Church Father, Archbishop John Chrysostom of Constantinople (347–407 CE), noted the "extraordinary multitude" of Jews in Palestine. This fact was also confirmed by another theologian and historian, Jerome (345–420 CE), who was the author of the Vulgate – the Latin translation of the Bible – and spent many years in Bethlehem. The multitude and strength of the Jewish population of 4th-century Palestine are also evidenced by a new anti-Roman revolt of the Jews in 351–352 CE. The Jewish rebels managed to seize Sepphoris (Tzippori), Tiberias, Acre, Lydda (Lod), Beit She'arim, and even Jerusalem – that is, all of northern and even part of central Palestine – even though the Samaritans did not participate in this revolt. The revolt lasted for almost two years and was with great difficulty suppressed by Constantius Gallus, co-ruler with the Roman Emperor Constantius II (337–361 CE). Jerome noted that "Gallus suppressed the Jewish uprising... Many thousands were killed, including innocent children, and their cities of Diocaesarea (Sepphoris), Tiberias, and Diospolis (Lod), as well as countless villages, were put to the torch" (*Chronicon,* A352). From all these testimonies of the early Church Fathers, it follows that although Judea was renamed Palestine, this country still remained predominantly Jewish in its population.

Despite the devastation of Judea and the enormous human losses resulting from the Bar Kokhba revolt, the surviving Jewish population managed to adapt to the new conditions and even achieve economic prosperity. Jewish Galilee became the main producer of olive oil and flax, while Judea became a center for winemaking and wool processing. Most of this produce was exported to Italy. Palestinian figs and dates from the Jordan River Valley were especially famous in Rome. The highest quality dates were from the Jericho area. Palestine was the only place in the Roman Empire where incense – balsam and myrrh – were produced. They were extracted from plants and trees in the Jordan River Valley and the Dead Sea region. Almost all the agricultural products exported to Italy were produced in Jewish settlements. And this is not a coincidence. Until the end of the 5th century CE, the vast majority of the rural population of Roman Palestine was composed of Jews and

Samaritans, while in most Palestinian cities, newcomers – Syrians and Greeks – predominated.

The economic recovery of Jewish Palestine was largely made possible by the rule of the Severan dynasty (193–235 CE), whose members had great sympathy for the Jews. The Roman Emperor Alexander Severus (222–235 CE) showed special favor to the Jews (as well as to Christians), returning to them some of the lands that had been confiscated and repealing discriminatory taxes and laws. During his reign, Jews began to return from the diaspora to Palestine and, moreover, to re-settle the Jerusalem area, where the Romans had previously forbidden them to live. The supreme religious court – the Sanhedrin – continued to function in Galilee. Its location often changed, however; from the city of Usha, it was moved to Shfaram, then to Beth She'arim, then to Tzippori, and finally to Tiberias. However, the Jewish revival in Palestine did not last long. In the following years, the Roman Empire began to be torn apart by political crises, and the imperial administration began to collapse, which sharply worsened the economic situation in Palestine. Since most Palestinian farmers were Jews, the Jewish part of the country's population suffered the most from all these crises and anarchy.

32. The Jewish clay oil lamp from Jerusalem. 4th century CE.

The situation of the Jewish and Samaritan population in Palestine changed fundamentally after the Emperor Constantine the Great (306–337 CE) made Christianity the state religion of the Roman Empire. From this time, Christianity ceased to tolerate the existence of other religions and cults. Hellenistic cults began to be banned and their temples destroyed. After the Council of Nicaea in 325 CE, persecution of any deviations from the official interpretation of Christianity also began. Judaism, unlike pagan religions, was not banned and continued to be recognized by law. However, the Roman church tried to prove to Christians that, having made a "new covenant" with the Lord, it had become the "new Israel" and the rightful heir to everything that belonged to the Jewish people; therefore, it claimed, all the spiritual heritage of the Jews and their country should pass to Christian Rome. Moreover, the Roman church initiated the issuance of anti-Jewish decrees, although Paul the Apostle had warned that the Jews' failure to accept Christ does not mean that they thereby lose their status as the chosen people of God or that the Lord's covenant with them loses its force (Rom. 11:16, 25–29).

As Christianity became a state religion, the status of Palestine also changed: from an ordinary Roman province, it became a Holy Land and a place of pilgrimage for all Christians of the empire. In turn, this forced the Roman church to carry out a forced Christianization in the homeland of Christianity. From this time, the intensive process of displacing Jews from Palestine resumed, and their place was taken by newly converted pagans from among the Greeks and Syrians. With the consent of the Romans, their new allies – Arab tribes from Arabia – came to the Negev and Transjordan. At the same time, the transformation of Christianity into the official religion of the Roman Empire was slow, with comebacks and setbacks, so the anti-Jewish edicts of the Roman church were not always enforced.

The situation changed significantly in 395 CE after the division of the Roman Empire into the Western Roman Empire and the Eastern Roman Empire. The formation of the Eastern Roman Empire (Byzantium) accelerated the forced Christianization of Palestine and worsened the situation of the Jewish and Samaritan population. If pagan Rome imposed Hellenization, Byzantium imposed Christianization. The Samaritans found themselves in the most difficult situation: their monotheism, unlike Judaism, was not recognized by the Byzantine church and was equated with paganism. Samaritan synagogues were destroyed and their religion was banned. During the 5th and 6th centuries, the Samaritans repeatedly rebelled against the religious and economic oppression of Byzantium, but they were unable to withstand the military superiority of this empire. Each time their revolts were brutally suppressed, and their cities and villages were mercilessly destroyed. As a rule, due to deep religious differences, the Jews did not support the Samaritans, and the Samaritans did not support the Jews during their revolts against Byzantium. But there were also exceptions when Jews joined the Samaritan rebels. This happened in 415 CE, when the Byzantine Emperor Theodosius II limited the civil rights of the Jews and persecuted the Samaritans. It was repeated in 529, 547, and 554–556 under Emperor Justinian I, when the anti-Jewish and anti-Samaritan policies of Byzantium reached their climax. Although the revolts of the Samaritans and Jews had no chance of victory, the Jews, as a freedom-loving people who remembered the greatness of Israel and Judea, could not but resist the yoke of foreign invaders. The very fact of these revolts testifies that even in the 5th–6th centuries, the Jewish population of Palestine was more than significant and played an important role in the life of the country. This is also indicated by another fact: despite the unfavorable living conditions for Jews in Palestine, it was in this country that the most important works for Judaism – the Mishnah and the Jerusalem Talmud – were created in the 2nd–5th centuries.

Although Judaism remained the only legal non-Christian religion, Byzantine churchmen created a vast body of anti-Jewish literature in the 5th–7th centuries that became a source of enmity and hatred towards Jews in both Byzantium and medieval Europe. These anti-Semitic works attributed all imaginable and unimaginable vices to the Jews and poisoned the minds of European peoples for many centuries. The ministers of the Byzantine church, themselves recent pagans, transferred not only a lot of pagan customs and beliefs into Christianity but also the anti-Semitism that arose from the long-standing rivalry between the Greeks and Syrians on one side and the Jews on the other. The hostility of the Byzantine clergy – the same Greeks and Syrians – towards Judaism was not limited to their persecution of Jews and Samaritans in Palestine but also significantly influenced the foreign policy of Byzantium. It was anti-Judaism that forced Emperor Justinian I to help Ethiopia in the war against the Himyarite kingdom (southern Arabia), whose rulers professed Judaism. Later, the same factor was the main cause of conflicts between Byzantium and the Khazar Khaganate, whose kings also adopted Judaism and patronized the Jews.

In the first half of the 7th century, Palestine became the object of a fierce struggle between three powers: Byzantium, Sasanian Iran, and the Arab Caliphate. In 614 CE, the Persian army very quickly captured all of Palestine. This was made possible by the active support of the local Jews, who, having suffered from the oppression of the Byzantines, met the Persians as liberators and helped them take possession of the entire country. In turn, the Persians granted the Jews a share of administrative authority over the country, including Jerusalem. Despite the short period of Persian rule (only 15 years), the Jews quickly restored their positions in Palestine and put an end to the tyranny of the Byzantine churchmen. However, in 629–630, the Byzantine Emperor Heraclius recaptured Palestine and cracked down on the Palestinian Jews for their help to the Persians. It was at this time that, due to the massacres, persecution, and oppression of the Byzantines, the majority of the Jewish population was forced to leave their homeland. But the triumph of Byzantium was short-lived. Already in 634, the army of the Arab Caliphate captured Transjordan, and four years later, it finally drove the Byzantines out of Palestine. Thus ended the Byzantine period (395–638 CE) in the history of Palestine. It was characterized by forced Christianization and persecution of the Jews and Samaritans, which in turn led to a sharp decrease in the country's population and its complete economic decline. The Byzantines, in effect, completed the work of the Romans: they displaced the Jewish people from their country. From the mid-7th century, Jews became a clear minority in their own country. Judea finally turned into Palestine, as the Romans had wanted after the Bar Kokhba revolt.

According to archaeological data, in the first half of the 7th century, Jews constituted the majority of the population in only one area of Palestine – the Golan. To date, 29 ancient synagogues and 32 Jewish settlements built in the 1st–7th centuries CE have been excavated in the Golan Heights, which is convincing evidence of a more than significant Jewish presence in this territory. Thus, unlike other areas of Palestine, the Jewish population in the Golan managed to survive both Roman and Byzantine rule and dominated the Golan until the arrival of the Arab conquerors. This was probably due to the fact that the restrictions imposed by the Romans and Byzantines on the residence of Jews in Palestine did not extend to Galilee and the Golan. The Jews left the Golan only after the invasion of Muslim Arabs, who forced the Jewish population to leave there in a hurry and en masse. Since then, the Golan has been in complete desolation and oblivion for many centuries.

The forced departure of the Jews from Palestine did not mean that this country was left without its Jewish population. From the mid-7th century, the main representative of the Jewish people in Palestine was not the Jews themselves but the Samaritans. However, during the years of Byzantine rule in this country the size of the Samaritan population decreased at least threefold and, by the time the Arabs arrived, they numbered approximately 350 thousand people. However, in central Palestine, the Samaritans still made up the majority of the population, and in the capital of this province, Caesarea, there were at least 30,000 of them. Most Samaritans lived in the rural areas of Samaria and were engaged in farming. They cultivated mainly olives and grapes, made olive oil and wine, and raised sheep. After the oppression and persecution of the Byzantines, they met the arrival of the Arabs with great benevolence. However, the new conquerors quickly disappointed the Samaritans, and already in the 8th–9th centuries, their attitude toward the Arabs changed diametrically. The Arabs imposed even greater taxes on the Samaritans and, most importantly, began to confiscate their lands and drive farmers from their own plots. The new authorities settled Muslims, newcomers from Syria and Arabia, on the Samaritans' lands. Often, the inhabitants of Samaria were subjected to predatory raids by nomadic Arab tribes. But most of all, the Samaritans suffered from forced Islamization. Refusal to accept Islam was punishable by death, or, at best, by exile. In fact, the Arab Caliphate pursued the same policy of genocide against the Samaritans as Byzantium, only even more vigorously. The result was not long in coming: by the 10th century, the number of Samaritans had sharply decreased, and they, like the Jews in their time, turned into an insignificant minority in their own country. The Samaritan population was preserved, for the most part, in Shechem, which the Arabs renamed Nablus, as well as in the rural settlements around it.

A distinctive historical feature of Palestine over the last two millennia has been its demographic instability and the periodic replacement of its population. If Asia Minor became a "graveyard of peoples," where numerous groups arrived but none departed because they were completely assimilated by others, then the Palestine of the Common Era could well be described as a "thoroughfare of nations." After the Romans, Byzantines, and Arabs squeezed almost all of its indigenous population – Jews and Samaritans – out of this country, none of the numerous newcomers and conquerors managed to take root in Palestine for a long time. The foreign Hellenized population, which was first Christianized during the Byzantine rule and then Islamized during the period of Arab dominance, for the most part fled or was massacred by the Western Europeans during the numerous Crusades. The remnants of this population, forcibly Christianized by the Crusaders, were then subjected to new massacres and new forced Islamization by the Seljuk Turks and the Egyptian Mamluks.

The four-hundred-year rule of the Ottoman Turks (1516-1917) again did not bring peace to those who still survived on the land of Palestine.

This time, all who remained in this country were destroyed not by wars, but by the greed of the Turkish rulers. The Turks imposed such taxes and levies on the local residents that twice during the 18th century alone, Palestine lost its population, which went to neighboring countries. Farmers and artisans had no reason to work, since all the income from their labor could not even cover taxes.

However, the population situation in Palestine, both in the Middle Ages and in modern times, was consistently depressing. Between the 11th and 16th centuries, the population of Palestine did not exceed 150,000–300,000 people. The first Ottoman cadastre, conducted in 1525 for tax purposes, showed that Palestine had about 300,000 inhabitants, while the data for 1554 recorded only 205,000. Centuries of Ottoman rule did not improve the demographic situation: in 1800, Palestine still had no more than 300,000 inhabitants. In fact, the country remained sparsely populated and was in deep economic decline. For comparison, in Judea in the 1st century CE, there were 15–20 times more people than in Palestine in the 19th century. By the end of World War I, when the British defeated and expelled the Turks from Palestine, this ancient country presented a sad sight: it was devastated and empty. Only a few Arabs and Jews lived in wretched towns and rare settlements.

The current Arab population of Palestine for the most part came from Syria and Arabia quite late, in the 18th-19th centuries. Many of the newcomers retained their Syrian self-identification until the 1920s and considered Palestine only as a part of Greater Syria. Later, Bedouin tribes arrived from northwestern Arabia. As for the Jewish population, the mass return of the people to their historical homeland began at the end of the 19th century and was associated with the development of the Zionist movement among the Jews of Europe. However, it would be a great mistake to assume that the Jews returned to their homeland only in the 20th century. In fact, individual groups of deeply religious Jews never left the territory of Palestine at all. And many of those who were in exile also did not lose touch with their country, periodically returning there for a while or permanently. It is noteworthy that already in the middle of the 19th century, most of the population of Jerusalem, the largest city in Ottoman Palestine, were religious Jews. Finally, we must not forget about such a group within the Jewish people as the Samaritans, who never left the borders of Palestine and have managed to preserve their identity to this day, despite massacres and persecution by the Byzantines, Arabs, Crusaders, and Turks. However, the price of their heroic survival proved to be exorbitant. From a people numbering more than a million in the 3rd–5th centuries, by the 21st century they had become an ethno-religious group of only about 800 people. However, the Samaritans are the only ones who have lived in Palestine continuously for the last two thousand years. Together with the Jews, they are the only direct descendants and heirs of the peoples of ancient Canaan. They came to the modern world under the name of "Jews" and have a history that is unmatched in the annals of mankind.

SELECTED BIBLIOGRAPHY

Aharoni, Y. Nothing Early and Nothing Late. Re-writing Israel's Conquest. *Biblical Archaeologist* 39: 55-76.

Albright W.F., *The Biblical Period from Abraham to Ezra*, 1963.

Barns G.W., *The Ashmolean Ostracon of "Sinuhe"*, London, 1952.

Bar-Yosef, O., 'Prehistoric Palestine' in: *The Oxford Encyclopedia of Archaeology in the Near East,* ed. E.M. Meyers, 4.207-12, New York: Oxford University Press, 1997.

Ben-Tor D., 'The Historical Implications of Middle Kingdom Scarabs found in Palestine bearing Private Names and Titles of Officials' in *BASOR* 294 (1994), 7-22.

Ben-Tor, A. (ed.), *The Archaeology of Ancient Israel.* New Haven, 1992.

Bietak M., *Avaris: The Capital of the Hyksos,* London, 1996.

Boling, R.G. *Judges.* New York, 1975

Bourriau J., "The Second Intermediate Period," in *The Oxford History of Ancient Egypt,* ed. Shaw I., New York: Oxford University Press, 2000, pp.185-217.

Bright J., *A History of Israel,* 4th edition, New York: Oxford University Press, 2001.

Brinkman J.A., *A Political History of Post-Kassite Babylonia, 1158-722 BC* (1968).

Campbell E.F. Jr. 'A Land Divided' in: The *Oxford History of the Biblical World,* ed. M.D. Coogan. Oxford University Press, New York, 2001.

Clayton P. A., *Chronicle of the Pharaohs. The Reign-By-Reign Record of the Rulers and Dynasties of Ancient Egypt,* New York: Thames & Hudson, 1994.

Coogan M.D. (ed.), *The Oxford History of the Biblical World,* New York, 2001.

Coogan, M. D., ed. and trans. *Stories from Ancient Canaan,* Philadelphia: Westminster, 1978.

Cross, F. M., *Canaanite Myth and Hebrew Epic: Essays in the History of the Religion of Israel,* Cambridge, Mass: Harvard University Press, 1973.

Dever W. G. "Archaeology and the Israelite 'Conquest'." *In Anchor Bible Dictionary,* ed. Freedman D.N., 3.545-58. New York: Doubleday, 1992.

Dever W. G., *Beyond the Texts. An Archaeological Portrait of Ancient Israel and Judah,* SBL Press, 2017.

Dever W.G., *Who were the early Israelites and where did they come from?* Wm. B. Eerdmans Publishing Co., Cambridge, 2003.

Dothan T., *The Philistines and Their Material Culture.* New Haven: Yale University Press, 1982.

Dothan, T., and Dothan M., *Peoples of the Sea.* New York: Macmillan, 1992.

Eichler, B. L, 'Nuzi and the Bible: A Retrospective' in: *Dumu-e-dub-ba-a: Studies in Honor of Ake W. Sjoberg,* ed. H. Behrens, D. Loding, and M. T. Roth, pp. 107-19, Philadelphia: University Museum, 1989.

Finkelstein I, Mazar A. and Schmidt B.B., *The Quest for the Historical Israel. Debating Archaeology and the History of Early Israel.* Society of Biblical Literature: Atlanta, 2007.

Finkelstein I. and Silberman N.A., *The Bible Unearthed: Archaeology's New Vision of Ancient Israel and the Origin of its Sacred Texts,* New York: Free Press, 2001.

Finkelstein, I. and Naaman, N. (editors). *From Nomadism to Monarchy: Archaeological and Historical Aspects of Early Israel.* Jerusalem, 1994.

Finkelstein, I. *The Archaeology of the Israelite Settlement.* Jerusalem: Israel Exploration Society, 1988.

Flavius Josephus, *The Antiquities of the Jews,* (Oxford World Classics), 2017

Flavius Josephus, *The Jewish War* (Oxford World Classics), 2017

Freedman D.N. and Graf D.F., eds., *Palestine in Transition,* Sheffield, 1983.

Frerichs, E. S., and Lesko L.H., eds. *Exodus: The Egyptian Evidence.* Winona Lake, Ind.: Eisenbrauns, 1997.

Friedman R.E., *Who Wrote the Bible?* New York: HarperCollins Publishers, 1997.

Gernot W., *The Hurrians,* 1989.

Gitin, S., Mazar, A. and Stern, E. *Mediterranean Peoples in Transition: Thirteenth To Early Tenth Centuries BCE.* Jerusalem, 1998.

Giveon R., *The Impact of Egypt on Canaan,* Gottingen, 1978.

Gottwald N.K., *The Tribes of Yahweh: A Sociology of the Religion of Liberated Israel 1250-1050 B.C.E.* Maryknoll, N.Y.: Orbis, 1979.

Grabbe L.L., *Ancient Israel.* New York: T & T Clark, 2007.

Greenberg M., *The Hab/piru,* New Haven, Conn., 1955.

Gurney O.R, *The Hittites,* revised edition, New York: Penguin, 1990.

Halpern, B. "Erasing History: The Minimalist Assault on Ancient Israel." *Bible Review* 11/6, 1995.

Hayes W.C., *A Papyrus of the Late Middle Kingdom in the Brooklyn Museum*, Brooklyn, 1955.

Hazel M.G., 'Israel in the Merneptah Stela', *BASOR* 296 (1994), pp. 45-61.

Helck W., *Die Beziehungen Agyptens zur Vorderasien*, Wiesbaden, 1972.

Hoffmeier, J.K. *Israel in Egypt: The Evidence for the Authentisity of the Exodus Tradition.* New York: Oxford University Press, 1997.

Isserlin B.S. J., *The Israelites.* Minneapolis: Fortress Press, 2001.

Josephus, *Against Apion*, Book 1, Section 73 (P., 1912).

Kenyon K. M., *Archaeology in the Holy Land*, 4th ed, 1985.

Killebrew, A.E., *Biblical Peoples and Ethnicity.* Atlanta: Society of Biblical Literature, 2005.

King, Philip J. *Amos, Hosea, Micah-An Archaeological Commentary.* Philadelphia: Westminster, 1988.

Klengel, H., *Syria: 3000 to 300 BC: A Handbook of Political History*, Berlin: Akademie, 1992.

Krauss R., *Das Ende der Amarna-Zeit* (Hildesheim, 1976).

Kuhne C., *Die Chronologie der internazionalen Correspondenz von El-Amarna* Neu-Kirchen-Vluyn, 1973.

Kuhrt A., *The Ancient Near East c. 3000-330 BC*, 2 vols, London: Rutledge, 1995.

Leonard, A., Jr, 'Archaeological Sources for the History of Palestine: The Late Bronze Age', *Biblical Archaeologist 52*, 1989, 4-39.

Lipinski, E. *The Arameans: Their Ancient History, Culture, Religion.* Leuven, 2000.

Lipovsky, I.P. *Israel and Judah: How Two Peoples Became One,* Boston: 2014.

Lipovsky, I.P. *Judea between Two Eras*, Boston: 2017.

Lloyd S., *The Archaeology of Mesopotamia: from the Old Stone to the Persian Conquest*, 1984.

Loretz O., *Habiru-Hebraer: Eine sozial-ling. Studie*, Berlin, 1984.

Machinist, P. "Outsiders or Insiders: The Biblical View of Emergent Israel and Its Contexts." In The Other in Jewish Thought and History: Constructions of Jewish Culture and identity, eds. L. J. Silberstein and R. L. Cohn, 35-60. New York: New York University Press, 1994.

Manassa C., *The Great Karnak Inscription of Merneptah: Grand Strategy in the 13th Century B.C.*, Yale Egyptological Studies 5, New Haven: Yale Egyptological Seminar, 2003.

Manetho, *Aegyptiaca*, frag. 42, 1.75-79.2.

Mazar A., *Archaeology of the Land of the Bible, 10,000-586 BCE,* New York: Doubleday, 1992.

McGovern P., *The Foreign Relations of the 'Hyksos'. A neutron activation study of Middle Bronze Age pottery from the Eastern Mediterranean*, Oxford, 2000.

Metzger, B.M., and Coogan M.D., eds, *The Oxford Companion to the Bible,* New York: Oxford University Press, 1993.

Miller, J. Maxwell, and John H. Hayes. *A History of Ancient Israel and Judah.* Philadelphia: Westminster, 2006.

Moran W.L., *The Amarna Letters,* Baltimore: Johns Hopkins University Press, 1992.

Murnane W., *Texts from the Amarna Period in Egypt*, Atlanta, 1995.

Na'aman N., 'Habiru and Hebrews: The Transfer of a Social Term to the Literary Sphere', *JNES* 45, No. 4 (1986), pp. 271-88.

Na'aman, N. "The 'Conquest of Canaan' in the Book of Joshua and in History." In *From Nomadism to Monarchy: Archaeological and Historical Aspects of Early Israel,* Jerusalem, 1994. ed. I. Finkelstein and N. Na'aman, 218-81. Washington, D.C.: Biblical Archaeology Society, 1994.

Nelson, R.D. *Joshua: A Commentary*. Louisville, 1997.

Nicholson, E. W. *Exodus and Sinai in History and Tradition* (Oxford: Blackwell), 1973.

Oren E., ed., *The Sea Peoples and Their World: A Reassessment.* Philadelphia: University of Pennsylvania, 2000.

Oren E.D. (ed.), *The Hyksos: New Historical and Archaeological Perspectives*, Philadelphia, 1997.

Orni, E., and Ephrat E., *Geography of Israel.* 4th ed., Jerusalem: Israel Universities Press, 1980.

Parrot A., *Abraham and His Times*, 1968.

Pitard, Wayne T. *Ancient Damascus: A Historical Study of the Syrian City-State from Earliest Times until Its Fall to the Assyrians in 732 B.C.E.* Winona Lake, Ind.: Eisenbrauns, 1987.

Postgate N., *The First Empires*, 1977.

Potts, D.T, *Mesopotamian Civilization: The Material Foundations*, Ithaca, NY: Cornell University Press, 1997.

Pritchard J.B., ed., *Ancient Near Eastern Texts Relating to the Old Testament*, Princeton: Princeton University Press, 1969.

Provan I., Long V.P., and Longman T. III, *A Biblical History of Israel*, Louisville, Kentucky: Westminster John Knox Press, 2003.

Quirke S., *The Administration of Egypt in the Late Middle Kingdom*, New Malden, 1990.

Rainey A.F., "Israel in Merenptah's Inscription and Reliefs", *IEJ* 5, pp.57-75.

Rainey, A. F. (ed.) *Egypt, Israel, Sinai: Archaeological and Historical Relationships in the Biblical Period.* Tel Aviv: Tel-Aviv University, 1987.

Redford D.B., *Egypt, Canaan and Israel in Ancient Times*, Princeton: Princeton University Press, 1993.

Roaf M., *Cultural Atlas of Mesopotamia and the Ancient Near East*, 1990.

Rogerson John, *Chronicle of the Old Testament Kings*, Thames and Hudson, 1999.

Ryholt K., *The Political Situation in Egypt during the Second Intermediate Period*, Copenhagen, 1997.

Sandars, N.K., *The Sea Peoples: Warriors of the Ancient Mediterranean 1250-1150 BC.* Rev.ed. New York: Thames and Hudson, 1985.

Sarna, N.M., *Exploring Exodus*, New York: Schocken Books, 1996.

Shanks H., ed., *Ancient Israel: From Abraham to the Roman Destruction of the Temple.* 2nd rev. ed. Washington: Biblical Archaeology Society, 1999.

Shaw Ian (ed), *The Oxford History of Ancient Egypt* (New York/Oxford), 2000.

Singer, I., 'A Concise History of Amurru', appendix in Sh. Izre'el, *Amurru Akkadian: A Linguistic Study,* 2, pp. 135-94, Harvard Semitic Studies, 41, Atlanta: Scholars Press, 1991.

Smith H.S. and Smith A., A Reconsideration of the Kamose Texts', *ZAS* 103 (1976), 48-76.

Smith M.S., *The Early History of God. Yahweh and the Other Deities in Ancient Israel.* 2nd ed. Dearborn, Michigan: Dove Booksellers, 2002.

Snell, D.C., *Life in the Ancient Near East, 3100-332 BCE,* New Haven, Conn: Yale University Press, 1997.

Stager L.E., 'Forging an Identity: The Emergence of Ancient Israel' in *The Oxford History of the Biblical World*, ed. D. Coogan. Oxford University Press: New York, 2001.

Stern Ephraim (ed.), *The New Encyclopedia of Archaeological Excavations in the Holy Land* 4 Vols. (New York: Simon and Shuster), 1993.

Stern Menahem (ed.), *Greek and Latin Authors on Jews and Judaism,* 3 Vols., Jerusalem: 1984.

Stiebing, W. H., *Out of the Desert? Archaeology and the Exodus/Conquest Narratives,* Buffalo, New York: Prometheus, 1989.

The Book of Jubilees or the Little Genesis, trans. R.H. Charles and G.H. Box, Kessinger Publishing, LLC, 2006.

Vaux R. de, *Ancient Israel: Its Life and Institutions,* 2nd ed., 1973.

Wiener M.C. and Allen J., 'Separate Lives: the Ahmose Tempest Stela and the Theban eruption', *JNES* 57/1 (1998), 1-28.

Yurco, F. J. "3,200-Year-Old Picture of Israelites Found in Egypt." *Biblical Archaeology Review* 16, no. 5 (September-October 1990): 20-38. idem, 'Merneptah's Canaanite Campaign and Israel's Origins', in *Exodus: The Egyptian Evidence,* pp. 27-55.

INDEX

N

Z

Ç

www.ingramcontent.com/pod-product-compliance
Lightning Source LLC
LaVergne TN
LVHW090545110826
845146LV00001B/32

* 9 7 9 8 2 3 4 0 5 9 4 1 3 *